This book provides a powerful new theoretical framework for understanding cross-national cultural differences. Focusing on France and America, it analyzes how the people of these two different cultures mobilize national and cross-national 'repertoires of evaluation' to make judgments about politics, economics, morals and aesthetics. The analysis draws on eight case studies by eleven French and American researchers who have worked together over a number of years to develop systematic comparisons between these countries. The topics are wide-ranging, comparing how individuals use the cultural tools at their disposal to answer questions such as: Are races equal? What constitutes sexual harassment? What is the value of contemporary art? Should journalists be neutral? How can the defence of the environment be reconciled with economic imperatives? How does private interest contribute to the public good? Moving beyond simplistic essentialist models of national character, this comparative approach offers important insights that will interest not only sociologists but also political scientists and anthropologists.

MICHÈLE LAMONT is Professor of Sociology at Princeton University. She is author of *Money, Morals, and Manners: The Culture of the French and the American Upper-Middle Class* (1992) and *The Dignity of Working Men: Morality and the Boundaries of Race, Class and Immigration* (2000). She is editor of *Cultivating Differences: Symbolic Boundaries and the Making of Inequality* (1992) (co-edited with Marcel Fournier) and *The Cultural Territories of Race: Black and White Boundaries* (1999).

LAURENT THÉVENOT is Professor at the Ecole des Hautes Etudes en Sciences Sociales, Paris, and director of the Groupe de Sociologie Politique et Morale. His previous books include *Conventions économiques* (1986), *Justesse et justice dans le travail* (1989, with Luc Boltanski), *De la justification* (1991, with Luc Boltanski), *Les objets dans l'action* (1993, with Bernard Conein and Nicolas Dodier), *Cognition et information en société* (1997, with Bernard Conein). *Sociologie pragmatique. Les régimes d'engagement* is forthcoming.

Rethinking comparative cultural sociology

Cambridge Cultural Social Studies

Series editors: JEFFREY C. ALEXANDER, *Department of Sociology,
University of California, Los Angeles, and* STEVEN SEIDMAN, *Department
of Sociology, University at Albany, State University of New York.*

VERA L. ZOLBERG AND JONI M. CHERBO (eds.), *Outsider art*
0 521 58111 7 hardback 0 521 58921 5 paperback

SCOTT BRAVMANN, *Queer fictions of the past*
0 521 59101 5 hardback   0 521 59907 5 paperback

STEVEN SEIDMAN, *Difference troubles*
0 521 59043 4 hardback   0 521 59970 9 paperback

RON EYERMAN AND ANDREW JAMISON, *Music and social movements*
0 521 62045 7 hardback 0 521 62966 7 paperback

MEYDA YEGENOGLU, *Colonial fantasies*
0 521 48233 X hardback   0 521 62658 7 paperback

LAURA DESFOR EDLES, *Symbol and ritual in the new Spain*
0 521 62140 2 hardback   0 521 62885 7 paperback

NINA ELIASOPH, *Avoiding politics*
0 521 58293 8 hardback   0 521 58759 X paperback

BERNHARD GIESEN, *Intellectuals and the German nation*
0 521 62161 5 hardback   0 521 63996 4 paperback

PHILIP SMITH (ed.), *The New American Cultural Sociology*
0 521 58415 9 hardback   0 521 58634 8 paperback

S. N. EISENSTADT, *Fundamentalism, Sectarianism and Revolution*
0 521 64184 5 hardback   0 521 64586 7 paperback

MARIAM FRASER, *Identity without selfhood*
0 521 62357 X hardback   0 521 62579 3 paperback

LUC BOLTANSKI, *Distant suffering*
0 521 57389 0 hardback   0 521 65953 1 paperback

PYOTR SZTOMPKA, *Trust*
0 521 59144 9 hardback   0 521 59850 8 paperback

SIMON J. CHARLESWORTH, *A phenomenology of working class culture*
0 521 65066 6 hardback   0 521 65479 3

ROBIN WAGNER-PACIFICI, *Theorizing the Standoff*
0 521 65244 8 hardback   0 521 65915 9 paperback

ALI MIRSEPASSI, *Intellectual Discourse and the Politics of Modernization*
0 521 65997 3 hardback   0 521 65997 3 paperback

RONALD N. JACOBS, *Race, Media and the Crisis of Civil Society*
0 521 62360 X hardback   0 521 62578 5 paperback

RON LEMBO, *Thinking through Television*
0 521 58465 5 hardback   0 521 58577 5 paperback

Rethinking comparative cultural sociology

Repertoires of evaluation in France and the United States

Edited by

Michèle Lamont and Laurent Thévenot

CAMBRIDGE
UNIVERSITY PRESS

PUBLISHED BY THE PRESS SYNDICATE OF THE UNIVERSITY OF CAMBRIDGE
The Pitt Building, Trumpington Street, Cambridge, United Kingdom

CAMBRIDGE UNIVERSITY PRESS
The Edinburgh Building, Cambridge CB2 2RU, UK http://www.cup.cam.ac.uk
40 West 20th Street, New York NY 10011-4211, USA http://www.cup.org
10 Stamford Road, Oakleigh, Melbourne 3166, Australia
Ruiz de Alarcón 13, 28014 Madrid, Spain

First published 2000

Printed in the United Kingdom at the University Press, Cambridge

Typeface Plantin 10/12   *System* QuarkXPress™ [SE]

A catalogue record for this book is available from the British Library

Library of Congress Cataloguing in Publication data

Rethinking comparative cultural sociology: repertoires of evaluation in France
and the United States / edited by Michèle Lamont and Laurent Thévenot.
    p. cm. – (Cambridge cultural social studies)
Includes bibliographical references and index.
ISBN 0 521 78263 5 (hardback) – ISBN 0 521 78794 7 (paperback)
1. Sociology – Comparative method – Case studies. 2. Evaluation – Cross-
cultural studies. 3. Evaluation – France – Case studies. 4. Evaluation –
United States – Case studies. 5. Cognition and culture – France – Case
studies. 6. Cognition and culture – United States – Case studies. I. Lamont,
Michèle, 1957– . II. Thévenot, Laurent. III. Series.
HM585.R45 2000
301′.07′23–dc21   00-462248

ISBN 0 521 78263 5 hardback
ISBN 0 521 78794 7 paperback
ISBN 2-7351-0867-8 (France only)

Contents

Part III   Political cultures and practices

Contributors

AGNÈS CAMUS-VIGUÉ wrote her PhD dissertation at the Ecole des Hautes Etudes en Sciences Sociales (Paris) on involvement in philanthropic associations. She also studied patient management in hospital emergency services. The result of this work (with Nicolas Dodier) was published in *Annales, Histoires, Sciences Sociales,* and *Communications.* She is a member of the Groupe de Sociologie Politique et Morale and a Research Fellow at the Public Library of the Georges Pompidou Center (Paris), where she studies how library users utilize and customize computerized services.

JASON DUELL received his BA in sociology from Vassar College, and his MA from Princeton University. His work has focused on the sociology of knowledge, particularly on tensions between professionalism and democracy in academia and their effect on academic discourse.

NATHALIE HEINICH is director of research at the Centre National de la Recherche Scientifique. Her work has focused on artistic professions, the reception of contemporary art and, more generally, the management of professional identities. Her books include: *The Glory of Van Gogh. An Anthropology of Admiration, Le triple jeu de l'art contemporain. Sociologie des arts plastiques, L'art contemporain exposé aux rejets. Études de cas, Ce que l'art fait à la sociologie,* and *La sociologie de Norbert Elias.*

CLAUDETTE LAFAYE is assistant professor at the Université du Littoral (Dunkerque) and member of the Groupe de Sociologie Politique et Morale. Her past work has focused on governmental decentralization and on state modernization. She also studies local politics and the local application of national public policies. She published recently *La sociologie des organisations.*

MICHÈLE LAMONT is professor of sociology at Princeton University. She has published extensively in the areas of comparative sociology, cultural sociology, inequality, sociological theory, and the sociology of knowledge. She is the author of *Money, Morals, and Manners: The Culture of the French and the American Upper-Middle Class*, and the co-editor of *Cultivating Differences: Symbolic Boundaries and the Making of Inequality*. In recent years, she has turned her attention to race and immigration. Her edited volume *The Cultural Territories of Race: Black and White Boundaries* was published in 1999 by University of Chicago Press and her book *The Dignity of Working Men: Morality and the Boundaries of Race, Class, and Citizenship* was published in 2000 by Harvard University Press and the Russell Sage foundation.

CYRIL LEMIEUX is a sociologist at the Institut National du Sport (INSEP) and member of the Groupe de Sociologie Politique et Morale. His past work has focused on the media and the ethics of journalists in contemporary France (published in *Politix. Travaux de science politique* and *French Politics and Society.*). He recently completed a book: *Mauvaise Presse. Une sociologie compréhensive du travail journalistique et de ses critiques.*

MICHAEL MOODY is assistant professor at Boston University. He recently completed a dissertation at Princeton University on interest advocacy and the debate about the public good in water conflicts in California. In addition to his work on environmental conflicts and political culture, he has also written on philanthropic giving and non-profit organizations, the theory of reciprocity and social exchange, cultural meanings of success, and civil society in suburban America.

ABIGAIL COPE SAGUY received her PhD in sociology at Princeton University and the Ecole des Hautes Etudes en Sciences Sociales (Paris) (2000) and is assistant professor at UCLA. She has conducted research on French and American feminism and on sexual attitudes in France and the United States. Her dissertation "Defining Sexual Harassment in France and the United States" will be published by the University of California Press. In this study, she explains why the French and Americans have defined sexual harassment so differently in law, the media, and firms.

JOHN SCHMALZBAUER is E. B. Williams Fellow and assistant professor of sociology at the College of the Holy Cross in Worcester, Massachusetts. He recently completed a post-doctoral fellowship at the Center for the Study of Religion and American Culture at Indiana University-Purdue University, Indianapolis. He has published in journals such as *Sociology of Religion, Poetics*, and the *Journal for the Scientific Study of Religion*, and is currently writing a book on the experiences of Catholics and evangelical Protestants in the academic and media élite.

LAURENT THÉVENOT is professor at the Ecole des Hautes Etudes en Sciences Sociales (Paris) and senior researcher at the Centre d'Etudes de l'Emploi. Currently director of the Groupe de Sociologie Politique et Morale (EHESS-CNRS), he co-authored, with Luc Boltanski, *De la justification* (English translation forthcoming). This book, which analyzes the most legitimate forms of evaluation governing political, economic, and social relationships, has been influential in new French sociology, and in institutional economics. Other publications include *Conventions économiques*, *Le travail; marchés, règles, conventions*, and *Les objets dans l'action, Cognition et information en société*. These last two co-edited books concern the sociology of action and practice, and social cognition. He is now completing a book on *Ways of Engaging the World: Rethinking Evaluation in Action*.

DANIEL WEBER is presently a PhD candidate in the Department of Sociology at Princeton University. His dissertation is a comparative study of evaluation processes in the book publishing sectors in France and the United States. His general interests revolve around the sociology of culture and organizations. Recent publications include "Cultural and Moral Boundaries in the United States: Structural Position, Geographic Location, and Lifestyle Explanations" (co-authored) in *Poetics*, and an article on French publishing in the *MacMillan Encyclopedia of Publishing*.

Acknowledgements

We acknowledge grants from the National Science Foundation, the Centre National de la Recherche Scientifique, the Center of Excellence in French Studies (Princeton University), the Institut International de Paris – La Défense, the French Ministry of the Environment, and the Maison Suger (Maison des Sciences de l'Homme, Paris) which have supported the meetings that have made possible our collective intellectual endeavor.

1 Introduction: toward a renewed comparative cultural sociology

Michèle Lamont and Laurent Thévenot

This volume's first objective is to propose a theoretical approach for comparative cultural sociology to analyze national cultural differences while avoiding the traditional essentialist pitfalls of culturalism: in particular, we develop the concept of national cultural repertoires of evaluation to point to cultural tools that are unevenly available across situations and national contexts. Our second objective is empirical: we document the extent to which different criteria of evaluation are salient in the French and American national cultural repertoires and the rules that people follow in justifying their use. These criteria have to do with market performance, the defense of the public interest, human solidarity, morality, aesthetics, and so forth.

The analysis draws on eight case studies conducted by eleven French and American researchers who have worked together over a period of four years toward developing systematic comparisons. The cases bear on issues as varied as the value of contemporary art, what constitutes sexual harassment, the legitimacy of interests in environmental conflicts, and whether racial groups are morally equal. Most are "hot" areas generating intense passion or disagreement, which we study through participant observation. Alternatively, through interviews, we push actors involved in these hot areas to make explicit the criteria of evaluation they use when they confront others with whom they disagree.[1]

The case studies were conducted either by a bi-national team of French and American researchers collaborating on all the phases of an integrated comparative research project, or by a single researcher responsible for fieldwork on each side of the Atlantic. The two collective projects focused respectively on the range of criteria used by participants in environmental conflicts in California and the South of France to define their positions and evaluate those of others (Lafaye, Moody, and Thévenot) and on the ways in which journalists (including Communists in France and the Religious Right in the United States) evaluate the legitimate boundary between personal commitments and professional roles (Lemieux and Schmalzbauer). The *solo* projects deal with how

French and American workers assess racial inequality (Lamont), how French and American activists and intellectuals appraise what constitutes sexual harassment (Saguy), how identity politics shape what is valued in literary studies in French and American academia (Duell), how publishers in Paris and New York understand the market and literary value of books (Weber), what kind of rhetoric the French and American publics use to evaluate contemporary art (Heinich), and how French and American Rotary Club members understand their voluntary activity in terms of particular professional self-interest and universal humanitarian purposes (Camus-Vigué). The presentation of these case studies is organized around three areas. The chapters presented in Part I examine evaluation as it articulates with aspects of identity, namely race, gender, and multiculturalism. Part II concerns evaluation in cultural institutions, namely in publishing, journalism, and the arts. Part III concerns politics and the public sphere. It focuses on the articulation of private and common interests in evaluation within philanthropic associations and environmental conflicts.

By making our case studies as diverse as possible, we aim to tap the full range of principles of evaluation used in each national context. Hence, each case study was chosen because it could teach us something particular about how different principles of evaluation coexist. For instance, the study of public rejection of contemporary art tells us about the relative importance social actors attach to aesthetic criteria in contrast to criteria having to do with morality, the market, or the democratic process. The publishing industry is a particularly relevant terrain to examine how social actors understand the importance of high culture in its relationship to the profit motive. Finally, environmental disputes are an appropriate site for the study of conflicting interpretations of what constitutes the public interest. By juxtaposing results from a range of cases, we are able to identify repeated taken-for-granted cultural differences across societies and to produce an understanding that is more qualitatively nuanced than is generally achieved from comparative survey research.[2]

These case studies reveal important similarities and differences in the cultural repertoires of evaluation used in France and the United States. In a nutshell, and we now greatly simplify for heuristic purpose, we show that evaluations based on market performance are much more frequent in the United States than in France, while evaluations based on civic solidarity are more salient in France. Furthermore, moral and aesthetic evaluations are often subsumed to market evaluations in the two national contexts, whereas aesthetic objects are also more often evaluated through moral standards in the United States than in France. Finally, we find that the rules of democratic life shape very differently, in the two countries, individual attempts to show that one speaks to collective interests. More details will be provided below.

While the comparative literature on France and the United States is sizable, it is not yet integrated. It underscores some of the findings that emerge from our case studies – concerning the more important role played by market criteria of evaluation in the United States than in France, for instance. One of the advantages of our research strategy is that by bringing together several integrated case studies (to the extent that this can be achieved), we can submit specific cross-national similarities and differences noted in the literature to empirically rigorous exploration across many contexts and subject areas.[3] Another advantage is to add a comparative dimension to the literature on French and American national identity.[4]

France and the United States offer especially fruitful cases for sociological comparison. Because the relationship between the public and the private; between the political, the moral, and the religious; or between the individual and the collective, are so different in the French and American contexts, a close examination of these contrasts might be theoretically profitable. Furthermore, the two countries have historically defined themselves as having privileged missions toward humanity in that, through their revolutions (Higonnet 1988), they carried values for which universality is claimed: modernity, progress, rationality, liberty, democracy, human rights, and equality (also Lacorne 1991). Yet, these competing cultural models with hegemonic pretensions are partly defined in opposition to one another, and hence make for an especially rich contrast (on this topic, see also Lacorne, Rupnik, and Toinet 1990).

The next section presents the intellectual tools mobilized in our comparative project to capture the different repertoires of evaluation used by American and French actors. We focus on the notions of symbolic boundaries and orders of justification, which are anchored in recent developments in American and French sociology. The third section discusses the potential contribution of the concept of cultural repertoire to the literature in comparative cultural sociology. The fourth section describes each chapter and its main contributions, while the fifth section provides a selected overview of key findings concerning differences between French and American national cultural repertoires. We conclude with a brief reflection on the nature of our collective comparative experiment.

The final chapter in the volume draws the implications of our findings for understanding social integration in a context where many criteria of evaluation coexist and potentially conflict. Turning toward issues having to do with the nature of the polity and the public sphere, we provide exploratory elements of analysis concerning (1) what kind of community boundaries are presumed by different types of criteria (closed or open); (2) how the polity is defined in civic terms; (3) the place of private ties in the public space and the boundary between the public and the private; (4) the political grammars used in a democratic and pluralist polity.

Tools for a new comparative sociology: boundaries and orders of justification

Our research agenda is not built *ex nihilo*. Indeed, in recent years, comparativists have produced several innovative studies that point to the institutionalization of cultural categories cross-nationally. An important current has focused attention on the international standardization of the notion of personhood through the diffusion of rights as a taken-for-granted feature of citizenship (Meyer et al. 1997; Thomas et al. 1987; Soysal 1993). Others have identified cultural variations in models of policy-making, in the legitimate role given to the market, the state, and individuals as engines of social organization, for instance (Dobbin 1994). Cultural models are also central foci in the dynamic field of comparative immigration and racial and ethnic studies (Brubaker 1992; Noiriel 1996), although the concept of "model" itself has come under serious attack (Kastoryano 1996). Finally, an important current in political science is focusing attention on the importance of ideas and culture in shaping political outcomes and on shifts in how actors understand their interests (Berman 1998; Hall 1993; Katzenstein 1996; McNamara 1998; Putnam 1993a; Ross 1997), partly as a reaction to the new hegemony of rational choice theorists. These studies all point to the importance of institutionalized cultural models and practices, and on how they converge or vary cross-nationally. However, while this work tends to emphasize macro-institutional and political levels, we are concerned more exclusively with grammars of available cultural positions that are not centered around political institutions. In order to help the reader understand the nature of our intellectual agenda, we turn to the intellectual tools that we bring together.

   In recent years, two lines of work have converged in their programmatic emphasis on the importance of analyzing the relationship between different criteria of evaluation. In the United States, researchers drawing on the Durkheimian tradition have focused on the content of symbolic boundaries defined as (1) group boundaries that demarcate the limits of groups – or outsiders from insiders – who share common values or common definitions of the sacred, of stigma, or of exclusion; and (2) cognitive boundaries organizing mental maps on the basis of symbolic distinctions.[5] Their empirical studies have centered on symbolic classifications, symbolic codes, mental maps and their relationships with group structures.[6] Within this literature, Lamont (1992, chap. 7) has shown the importance of documenting empirically and inductively the plurality of criteria of evaluation that individuals use, after critiquing Bourdieu's work for defining the content of boundaries *a priori* through the concepts of cultural capital and fields[7] (also Lamont and Lareau 1988; Hall 1992). While drawing on interviews with professionals, she shows that the relationship between criteria of evaluation varies across time and space. For instance, moral and cultural criteria of evaluation are more readily subsumed to economic criteria in the United States than they are in France, and these criteria are unequally salient across national settings. Her more recent work (Lamont 1998, 2000) centers on the relationship between moral criteria of evaluation and the relative salience of distinctions based on race, citizenship status, and class in the definition of national communities across national settings.[8]

Simultaneously in France, Boltanski and Thévenot (1987, 1991)[9] have proposed an analysis of orders of justification that people deploy to assess whether an action benefits the common good.[10] Their framework is designed to illuminate the most legitimate types of arguments, which are those agents use when debating public issues to appeal to common interest. Focusing on the different ways actors can make their claims general and legitimate, contrary to Bourdieu (1976), these authors do not regard actors' universalistic claims as hiding particular interests. Drawing both on fieldwork observations of disputes and critiques and on a reading of the classical literature in political philosophy, they distinguish a plurality of "grammars of worth." In a nutshell, these refer to the following forms of evaluation: "market" performance; "industrial" efficiency based on technical competence and long-term planning; "civic" equality and solidarity; "domestic" and traditional trustworthiness entrenched in local and personal ties; "inspiration" expressed in creativity, emotion, or religious grace; and "renown" based on public opinion and fame. They suggest that each kind of worth is a way to raise persons and things to "commonness."[11] The various worths encompass economic, political, technical as well as moral criteria of evaluation.[12] These are analyzed in the context of a broader research agenda designed to study political and moral commitments through different modes of practical engagement, and to scrutinize the place of material arrangements in such engagements.[13]

Building on these lines of work, we focus on repertoires of evaluation as they appear in France and the United States.[14] We regard them as elementary grammars that can be available across situations and that preexist individuals, although they are transformed and made salient by individuals. We are concerned with documenting how these schemas are unevenly present across national cultural repertoires. Hence, the following chapters focus specifically on (a) the content of criteria or orders of justification used to draw boundaries between the more and the less valuable; (b) whether and how different criteria compete with one another and are used in conjunction with one another. For instance, are moral boundaries less readily subordinated to aesthetic boundaries in the United States than in France? Does civic solidarity more often prevail over market performance as a principle of evaluation in France than in the United States?

There is a literature on the plurality of criteria of evaluation and how they compete with one another. This includes Max Weber's (1978) *Economy and Society*, which points to a plurality of types of legitimacy (charismatic, authoritarian, and rational legal) and a plurality of types of social relations, including market and status relations. Weber wrote about claims for legitimacy grounded in domination, and about how class and status hierarchies compete. But Weber did not clarify why some criteria of evaluation are more legitimate than others. This topic is of great interest to us. More recently, Michael Walzer (1983) described a plurality of spheres of justice, each dedicated to the distribution of a specific social good. Instead of focusing on how actors propose justifications, put them to a test, and shift from one order of justification to another, he associates each order with specific institutions and a community of shared understanding.[15] Along similar lines, in a theoretical piece, Friedland and Alford (1991) point to the relative autonomy of potentially competing institutional logics, while Elster (1995) empirically studies allocation criteria across such critical areas as college admissions, kidney transplants, employee layoffs, and legalized immigration. He focuses on contradictory criteria of justice such as need and merit (see also along these lines the comparative work of Engelstad (1997).

Note that by examining the dynamic between moral principles of evaluation and other principles, we hope to make a contribution to the sociology of morality as it is practiced in France and the United States. In France, this area has been neglected for a long time because of the profound influence of Weber, Marx and Nietzsche in sociology, which has generated moral skepticism and relativism. This has led contemporary sociologists to bracket or ignore moral issues, or to suggest that they hide "real" interests.[16] Recent philosophical debates on justice and ethics have questioned these positions and several research groups are presently working on these issues.[17] Boltanski and Thévenot have studied a range of conceptions of common good involved in practical engagements. In the United States, morality has been the object of important and sophisticated sociological writings drawing on the Durkheimian and Parsonian traditions (e.g. Bellah et al. 1985; Wuthnow 1996). The comparative perspective we supply complements this literature by showing how definitions of morality vary across populations.

This volume addresses another set of issues relating to the legitimacy of arguments within the democratic polity. The literature in political sociology has traditionally been concerned with showing how individuals "frame" their personal interests as compatible with group interest (Lukes 1974; Snow et al. 1986). We go further than this literature by analyzing the characteristic requirements of the most legitimate forms of evaluation that ground criticism of injustice and the abuse of power.[18] One privileged issue is how actors mobilize the notion of common human dignity to assess standards of evaluation. This analysis of modes of justifications draws on a pragmatist approach to the public space and can be compared with other approaches to public debates focusing on different types of rhetoric (Jasper 1992, 1997), the underlying patterns of civil society and democratic civility (Alexander 1992; Alexander and Smith 1993), or public communicative action (Habermas 1984).

Finally, we are also concerned with how actors demonstrate the situational appropriateness of their criteria of evaluation, and with "investments of forms" processes by which people and things are defined as belonging to similar classes across contexts (Thévenot 1984).[19] Unlike political and moral philosophers, we approach this issue by analyzing how people put their arguments to the test, i.e. how they find material proof that their arguments are grounded. Here we draw on the writings of Latour (1983, 1987) and Callon (1986b) on how scientists find support for their statements by aligning non-human beings with human beings in actor-networks. However, we focus on the plurality of ways human beings and other entities can "qualify" for such "alignments."[20] For instance, the treatment of persons (as customers) and things (as merchandise) that is required for market evaluation is quite different from their treatment as experts and techniques that is required for an evaluation in terms of efficiency. This plurality of ways that persons and things are arranged in congruent orders raises critical tensions.[21] Actor-network theorizing usually cannot account for conflicts between competing criteria of evaluation.[22]

By focusing on national cultural repertoires, we address the conditions under which different types of evaluation prevail and discuss their relative availability in France and the United States. This moves us toward a more structured understanding of the context in which individuals draw boundaries, allowing us to develop a more sophisticated approach to the concept of context, which often remains an unproblematized black box in contemporary sociological literature. Finally, we offer elements of explanations of differences in the salience of different types of criteria across national cultural repertoires, and refer to the structural conditions that prompt actors to draw on some aspects of repertoires rather than others (see below, note 25). However, we do not bring together in a systematic fashion all elements of explanation – although our analytical description of course includes many explanatory elements.

Repertoires and comparative cultural sociology

The United States has produced a growing literature on forms of symbolic boundaries and the relationship between different criteria of evaluation.[23] This literature points to the creation of group boundaries, for instance at the level of the creation of imagined communities (Anderson 1991; for reviews, see Berezin 1997 and Calhoun 1994) and the definition of citizenship (Brubaker 1992; Kastoryano 1997; Somers 1995; Zolberg and Long Litt Woon 1998). It is often concerned with comparative issues similar to those that are at the center of our research agenda.

Recent developments in American cultural sociology have been concerned in part with the relationship between repertoires and networks (Emirbayer 1997; Erickson 1996; Tilly 1993), and repertoires and agency, following a seminal article by Ann Swidler (1986).[24] This piece proposed an important correction to the Durkheimian/Parsonian unified "values" model by pointing to the fact that individuals use the cultural tools they have at their disposal. This practice-focused approach emphasizes not the determination of representations by group position and structure, so much as agency in the use of cultural tool-kits. It made it possible to better account for individual variations in cultural practices.[25] Moreover, the study of available cultural repertoires was seen as a necessary complement to the literature concerned with the embeddedness of identities in networks (Gould 1995; Tilly 1997), which stresses the role of interpersonal interaction in the definition of identity and pays less attention to the role of cultural institutions in diffusing cultural models.

It is in this context that we turn our attention to schemas of evaluation mobilized at the discursive or interactional level (examples also include Lichterman 1992 and Spillman 1997).[26] We identify and analyze the relative presence of such schemas across countries – what we might call national cultural or historical repertoires (Corse 1997, p. 159; Lamont 1992, p. 136). These are defined as relatively stable schemas of evaluation that are used in varying proportion across national contexts.[27] Each nation makes more readily available to its members specific sets of tools through historical and institutional channels (e.g. Griswold 1992), which means that members of different national communities are not equally likely to draw on the same cultural tools to construct and assess the world that surrounds them. Indeed, socially available meaning systems privilege the importance and symbolic weight of some distinctions over others (Griswold 1981, 1992). These unevenly available distinctions, which can also be referred to as national boundary patterns (Lamont 1995) or orders of justification (Boltanski and Thévenot 1991), are the common objects of the chapters assembled here. Again, we are concerned with their content and use in France and the United States. We are also concerned with the role they play in the delimitation of social and political communities, i.e. of group boundaries and the types of bonds that link their members.

As it is practiced today, comparative sociology has tended to focus on macro-economic, political, and institutional differences. Recent methodological debates center on the relative advantages and disadvantages of comparing a smaller or larger number of countries and of using quantitative or qualitative data (Engelstad and Mjoset 1997; Ragin 1994). As cultural sociologists and social theorists, we labor toward tipping the discussion in another direction, i.e. toward the study of national cultural repertoires which can be illuminated through comparative analysis. By using theoretical tools developed by cultural sociologists over the last ten years, we hope to move beyond the psychologism, naturalism, and essentialism that characterized much of the comparative cultural analysis of the 1960s – including studies of "modal personalities" and "national character" (e.g. Inkeles 1979).

For the purpose of our analysis, we are primarily concerned with national differences, although we refer to intra-national variation at times. However, one of the advantages of our approach is to downplay the contrast between national and intra-national differences. We take elements of repertoires to be present across geographical units such as nations or regions, but in varying proportions. Concretely, for instance, instead of simply contrasting the importance of the market or civic solidarity in France and the United States, we suggest that cultural repertoires prevailing in the United States make market references more readily available to Americans and enable them to resort to such references in a wide range of situations, whereas the French repertoires make principles of civic solidarity more salient and enable a larger number of French people to resort to them across situations, and often precisely in situations in which Americans would resort to market principles. However, this does not mean that market criteria of evaluation are absent from the French repertoires, but only that they are used in a small number of situations by a smaller number of people (Lamont 1992, chap. 3). As is often argued in the comparative literature, generalizations concerning national differences can be dangerous as they are bound to lead one to overlook variations and the specificity of structured contexts in which people use principles of evaluation. They can also lead one to confirm a view of differences as national character traits attributed to almost all the citizens of a country and expressed in an heterogeneous range of situations.[28] We believe that our approach allows us to avoid these pitfalls.[29]

Content of the volume

These various concerns are present throughout the chapters included in this volume. As mentioned above, the chapters in Part I examine evaluation as it articulates with aspects of identity, namely race (the rhetoric of racism and anti-racism), gender (conflicts surrounding the definition of sexual harassment), and other aspects of identity (in academic evaluations). Part II concerns evaluation in cultural institutions, namely in publishing (the nature of literary judgments), journalism (the issue of objectivity and personal commitment), and the arts (criteria for rejecting contemporary art). Part III concerns politics and the public sphere; more specifically, it focuses on the articulation of private and common interests in evaluation within philanthropic associations and environmental conflicts.

Part I   Identity: race, gender, and multiculturalism

In "The rhetorics of racism and anti-racism in France and the United States," Michèle Lamont draws on in-depth interviews conducted with blue-collar workers and low-status white-collar workers residing in the suburbs of Paris and New York to analyze the criteria majority groups and victims of racism in both countries use to demonstrate and explain the equality or inequality of racial groups. In the two countries, this is accomplished primarily via moral arguments. However, in the United States, blacks and whites also point to socio-economic success and to market criteria as well as to differences in intelligence. The French are more likely to point to fundamental cultural and religious differences. Furthermore, the French rhetoric of anti-racism mobilizes themes of solidarity and egalitarianism more than its American counterpart. Finally, majority groups are more likely to use universalistic arguments, drawing moral and racial boundaries simultaneously. In contrast, African Americans and North African immigrants to France more frequently resort to particularistic arguments, pointing to the superiority of their own culture.

In "Sexual harassment in France and the United States: activists and public figures defend their definitions," Abigail C. Saguy analyzes how sexual harassment is legally defined, and how activists opposing sexual harassment and public intellectuals who have taken positions on the issue conceptualize it. She finds that the American respondents are more likely than the French to talk about group-based discrimination and to use market and professional logic to denounce sexual harassment. Similarly, American law condemns sexual harassment because it constitutes a form of employment discrimination that limits equal access to the labor market and that harms a specific group. In contrast, the French respondents are more likely than Americans to conceptualize sexual harassment as a form of interpersonal violence than as group-based discrimination in employment. Likewise, French law condemns sexual harassment as a form of interpersonal sexual violence. This approach emphasizes the abuse of "official authority" without explicitly recognizing how sexual harassment is enabled by and perpetuates gender inequality. Finally, Saguy shows that French feminists draw on American, European, and Canadian cultural and material resources in defending their definition of sexual harassment, while those who oppose this idea do so by denouncing perceived American cultural imperialism and insisting on the specificity of French culture.

In "Assessing the literary: intellectual boundaries in French and American literary studies," Jason Duell draws on interviews conducted with French and American literature professors to show that they use very different standards to define what constitutes good work. In the United States, the focus is increasingly put on non-traditional subject matters, and critical approaches are often politically charged and/or related to group identity (gender, race, etc.). Standards for good work, and the institutional stability of the discipline in general, are described as in flux both by those opposed to and those in favor of these developments. In contrast, French literary scholars describe their field as being in a period of return to traditional forms of scholarship, and report much lower levels of contention and change in their discipline. These cross-national differences are explained by the status of literary intellectuals, differences in broader national repertoires for group representation, and the differing "disciplinary ecologies" in the two countries. The reasons for (and future prospects of) the influential practice of importing French theory into American literary studies is also examined in light of these factors.

Part II   Cultural institutions: the publishing industry, journalism, and the arts

In "Culture or commerce: literary judgment among French and American book publishers," Daniel Weber analyzes how the transformation of the publishing industry in the two countries is affecting the ways professionals make judgments about the quality of books, authors, and literary genres. In France, even commercial publishers who are oriented toward a popular audience use a grammar of evaluation which refers to the collective conventions that maintain a vertical division between what might be called "sacred" literature and "profane" entertainment. American publishers divide the book world into such categories as "high brow" and "low brow", or "trash" and "quality." But most interviewees, whether employed by literary or commercial houses, classify books in a very utilitarian fashion, i.e. on the basis of whether they are part of a particular editorial strategy, correspond to a social or intellectual trend, or (most commonly) fit a specific category used by book marketing specialists.

In "Involvement and detachment among French and American journalists: to be or not to be a 'real' professional," Cyril Lemieux and John Schmalzbauer look at how journalists on both sides of the Atlantic talk about professional norms of objectivity, fairness, and balance. Drawing on interviews with twenty-four journalists from across the political spectrum, this chapter shows that French and American reporters make use of different modes of evaluation to justify the inclusion or exclusion of personal political opinions from professional life. At the same time, Lemieux and Schmalzbauer challenge the widespread assumption that American journalists are more committed to the ideal of professional detachment than their more "ideological" European counterparts. They argue that journalistic professionalism is best conceptualized as a complex set of rules governing the boundary between the public and the private domains.

In "From the rejection of contemporary art to culture war: Paris, New York and back," Nathalie Heinich explores hostile reactions to visual arts from the public, focusing on moral and aesthetic rejections. She finds that issues of artistic authenticity are more present in France, particularly in establishing the boundary between art and non-art. In the United States, conflicts are articulated around free speech and the defense of moral values. Hence, conflicts about contemporary art raise political issues that are of relevance not only to the artistic realm, but to American society at large.

Part III   Politics and the public sphere: interests, community and the common good

In "Community and civic culture: the Rotary Club in France and the United States," Agnès Camus-Vigué analyzes the importation to France of an American association. Drawing on participant observation and interviews with Rotary Clubs in Normandy and Vermont, she shows that the relationships between common and private interests, or between solidarity, philanthropy and business interests, are construed differently in the two countries. In the United States, the combination is made possible by the construction of a polity based on a local community of citizens. By contrast, in France, the civic dimension of the locality has been defined in opposition to the personal bonds that sustain a local community. In this context, the business groups that are associated with the Rotary Club are construed as being unable to carry solidaristic civic actions, because business interests are understood to be incompatible with the general interest, both on political and moral grounds.

The last case study draws on a comparative survey of two environmental conflicts in France and the United States conducted by Laurent Thévenot, Michael Moody and Claudette Lafaye. This is presented in two chapters that are intended to be read together. Chapter 9, "Forms of valuing nature: arguments and modes of justification in French and American environmental disputes," starts with a general introduction to environmental disputes in the two countries and outlines the case studies, one French and one American, that provide the empirical data for the analysis presented in Chapters 9 and 10. It then goes on to compare how actors in the two conflicts justify certain actions as valuable and legitimate, while questioning the validity of other logics of justification. In the United States, actors often draw support for their position in environmental conflicts by appealing to public opinion, to the legitimacy of the market logic, and to the equal rights of all citizens to have access to natural resources. There is also tension between those who promote efficacy ("the wise use of natural resources") and those who defend "wilderness," the latter group arguing that their claim is more powerful because it is grounded in a pre-human world. In France, such deep ecological arguments are not found, and are replaced by claims pointing to the defense of a "domesticated" nature and the protection of a historical landscape to which residents are attached. Emotional attachment to the landscape is used to criticize arguments having to do with market competition or technical efficacy.

The case studies presented in Chapter 9 are analyzed further in the next chapter, "Comparing models of strategy, interests, and the public good in French and American environmental disputes." Chapter 10 suggests that the traditional opposition between an American political culture that centers on individual interest and a French political culture where the state would defend the common good is too simple. "Special interests" are commonly denounced in both countries. However, while in the United States, the legitimacy of specific positions as aiming for the public good is more often defined in terms of a "coalition of interests"; in France substantive models of the public good that exclude all particular interests are more frequently mobilized. Moreover, when used in the United States, arguments about the public good are frequently made on the basis of a strategic division of rhetorical work between associations dealing with different types of logic (profit maximization, public opinion, ecology). In contrast, French *collectifs* or *comités locaux* make claims that are defined in terms of the common good of a community.

The relative salience of some criteria of evaluation and how they are brought together

In this section, we describe the key findings of our collective endeavor by discussing the relative salience of specific criteria of evaluation across cases, how criteria combine, and which criteria tend to predominate when they are combined. We also point to the frequency with which different criteria of evaluation are used and how they are combined within the two national cultural repertoires. This section draws on information that is presented elsewhere in this book.

One of the unsurprising findings of our collective project is that market-based arguments are more often used in the United States than in France. This is evident in the rhetoric of racism and anti-racism studied by Lamont. Drawing on interviews, she demonstrates that American racists and non-racists alike often draw on market performance to show that racial groups are unequal or equal. The centrality of market arguments is also evident in other chapters. For instance, when Saguy interviews French and American feminists to document their attitudes toward sexual harassment, she finds that American feminists are more likely to denounce it because it affects women's equal access to the labor market. In fact, in all of the case studies we conducted, arguments pointing to actors' relationship with the market (as producers or consumers) were used more often by Americans than by the French.

Another finding concerns the importance of civic criteria of evaluation in the two countries. Civic criteria evaluate action on the basis of whether it is designed to reduce inequality in the name of human solidarity.[30] This criterion is more often used in the French than in the American context. For instance, in the study of the French and American environmental conflicts conducted by Thévenot, Moody, and Lafaye, the French readily engage in large-scale public demonstrations to ask for policies that would reduce inequality (in this case they denounce the lobby of long-distance transportation corporations who are pushing for the construction of a highway that will destroy the quality of life of powerless local residents).

Similarly, in their interviews with French and American journalists, Lemieux and Schmalzbauer find that French journalists on the Left define civic solidarity in terms of social solidarity and stress the importance of working toward the reduction of inequality more than their American counterparts. The relative salience of this criterion of evaluation is sustained in French society and in Europe more generally by the Left, as well as by a Catholic tradition, which has traditionally promoted moral obligation toward the oppressed and the marginal (particularly the homeless and the unemployed.)[31]

This comparative preponderance of market and civic types of arguments in the two countries is reflected in their relationships when they are combined in France and the United States. Indeed, unsurprisingly, market arguments more often triumph over civic solidarity in the United States than in France. It is notably the case in the discourse elaborated by American as compared to French activists involved in environmental disputes: Americans citizens involved in the conflict put more importance on market arguments concerning the price of deregulated electricity than on universal access to public utility (which presumes civic solidarity). Similarly, Camus-Vigué's study of French and American chapters of the Rotary Club shows that philanthropic gestures typical of American members of this club, when made by French businessmen, were rapidly denounced by their recipients as economically motivated, and hence illegitimate in part because not generated by genuine civic solidarity.

The same trend appears across our case studies bearing on evaluation based on aesthetic or cultural value: the latter are more often assessed on the basis of market performance in the United States than in France. As shown by Daniel Weber in his study of the publishing industry in Paris and New York, American publishers more frequently refer to market performance to evaluate literary work than do their French counterparts. Similarly, in Heinich's comparative study of forms of denunciation of contemporary art, French artists are less likely than their American counterparts to judge the value of art by the demand for it. Hence, high culture more readily functions as a basis for distinction in France (Bourdieu 1984; Lamont 1992).

Finally, our case studies, and particularly Heinich's study, reveal that cultural excellence is more frequently evaluated through moral lenses in the United States than in France. For instance, Heinich finds that rejection of contemporary art is more often legitimized by a defense of traditional morality in the United States than in France – the Mapplethorpe case is illustrative of this. Especially moral is the Helms Amendment which, since 1989, has subordinated public financial assistance for the arts to moral criteria.[32] An amoral aesthetic (or one that is anti-moral, cf.

Boltanski 1993) is not part of the cultural repertoires available to Americans when they want to protect art objects from moral or political judgment, with the consequence that aesthetic criteria of evaluation are more frequently subordinated to moral ones than is the case in France.[33]

A comparative experiment

We conclude this introduction with a short reflection on our interactions as a group and their impact on our intellectual project.[34] On the one hand, the bi-national research subgroups worked in a highly coordinated fashion and in a sustained dialogue on their joint projects. On the other hand, all the participants met as a whole on several occasions for a few days, with the support of grants from the National Science Foundation and the Centre National de Recherche Scientifique. The purposes of these joint meetings were (1) to discuss each of the projects as they were being conducted; (2) to identify common theoretical questions and common findings concerning how evaluation is performed across national contexts; (3) to use the "other" national group of researchers as a testing ground or sounding board for interpretations and analyses. Through this joint process, a common vocabulary and set of intellectual practices emerged and were used to write each of the chapters with the hope of producing an intellectually integrated volume. Hence, the project is better described as a collective construction than as the aggregation of individual chapters, precisely because these meetings formed an integral part of the research process. *A posteriori*, we might even think of each study as a collective breaching experiment where taken-for-granted meanings were made salient by intense discussion. By asking one another questions, we were forced to foreground and make concrete and explicit individual and collective/national assumptions.

Two examples will help the reader understand the nature of our collective endeavor. At our last meeting, acting as a native informant, Michael Moody, a Midwesterner, explained to the French colleagues his understanding of the articulation between individual sovereignty and standards of interpersonal interaction. He made the point that in his view, narcissism, as manifested in the act of monopolizing a discussion, is incompatible with democratic culture and with "being considerate," a virtue that he claimed is cardinal in middle class American society. This led to a broader exchange contrasting the taken-for-granted codes of interpersonal interaction which result from the meanings given to individualism in French and American society. At that same meeting, it transpired that all the French collaborators believed that cultural patrimony can be of universal value, i.e. be of significance for all human beings (for instance, *patrimoine de l'humanité* as it is defined by UNESCO). In contrast, all the American collaborators believed that patrimony tends to be national (or associated with Western high culture) and questioned whether it can truly reflect a universal value.

These examples are telling not because of their anecdotal relevance, but because they point to the true originality of our collective research endeavor, which forced reflection on our respective cultural assumptions. It required "talking things through" in a kind of therapeutic process. Abstract differences became very concrete as researchers deeply committed to them (as, for instance, "progressive" Americans opposing narrow and archaic French definitions of sexual harassment or as "enlightened" French people critical of a merciless market logic) attempted to make their colleagues understand the inner logic of their thinking. Interestingly enough, this aspect of our collaboration had not been anticipated and turned our collective meetings into a true laboratory. By reflecting on the social and intellectual conditions of our work, we attempted to use these sessions to increase our intellectual leverage for capturing national repertoires of evaluation. Indeed, we viewed our justifications and claims in these sessions as templates of positions available in national repertoires. Simultaneously, we remained wary of the pitfalls of culturalism (in terms of the naturalization of differences) and made a systematic effort to search for basic schemas that are behind emotional commitment. Hence, our repeated interactions played a crucial role in shaping our collective intellectual output.

Notes

We gratefully acknowledge the contributions of colleagues who took the time to react to this introduction: Jeffrey Alexander, Thomas Bénatouïl, Luc Boltanski, Frank Dobbin, Fredrick Engelstadt, Eric Fassin, James M. Jasper, Riva Kastoryano, Denis Lacorne, Paul Lichterman, Peter Meyers, and Renaud Seligman. Among the contributors to the volume, Cyril Lemieux, Michael Moody, and Abigail Saguy, also provided us with detailed feedback.

1 The privileged use of these data-gathering techniques leads us to collect snapshots of reality instead of information on process or historical change. This leaves room for future studies on how cultural repertoires vary across contexts (other than national) and over time. While we often focus on the situationality of judgment, we also consider the role played in judgments by historical, material, and organizational arrangements.

2 Within our methodological choices, what is gained in precision is lost in generalizability.

3 It includes on immigration Benson 1996, Body-Gendrot 1995, Body-Gendrot and Schain 1992, Hein 1993a, Horowitz 1992, and Weil 1991; on poverty, Silver 1993 and Wacquant 1994; on race and racism, Fassin 1997b; Hein 1993b; Jackson with Kirby, Barnes and Shepard 1992; and Weir 1995; on gender, Fassin 1993 and Saguy forthcoming [a]; on the state and politics, Dalton 1988, Dobbin 1994, Jasper 1990, Klaus 1993, and Esping-Anderson 1990; on culture, Lamont 1992; on class, Hamilton 1967 and 1972, and Crawford 1989 and Zussman 1985; on intellectuals, Clark 1979 and Lamont 1987b, and Mathy 1995. There is also of course a large comparative survey literature that includes France and the United States among other cases. See, for instance, Inglehart 1990; Langlois with Caplow, Mendras, and Glatzer 1994, and Stoetzel 1983. Finally, there are studies on France and on the United States that take the other country as implicit comparative reference points. These include Kastoryano 1996, Lacorne 1997, and Lipset 1977.

4 On French national identity, see in particular Kuisel 1993; Noiriel 1996; Nora 1984 and 1986; Rodgers 1991; Sahlins 1989; and Weber 1976.

5 Durkheim (1965, chaps. 6 and 7) discusses the articulation between collective representations and group membership. This conceptualization posits a direct correspondence between group structures and cognitive structures as group boundaries are defined by the sharing of mental maps. Traces of this seminal work are found in key contemporary cultural theorists including Mary Douglas (1966), Howard Becker (1963), and Erving Goffman (1963).

6 This literature includes (but is not limited to) Alexander 1992; Cerulo 1995; DiMaggio 1987; Lamont 1992; Wagner-Pacifici and Schwartz 1991; Wuthnow 1987; Zelizer 1994; Zerubavel 1991; for a review, see Swidler and Arditi 1994. Especially of interest is the interaction between classification and inequality, as illustrated by the essays presented in Lamont and Fournier 1992. See in particular Collins 1992, Hall 1992, and Epstein 1992 on gender; Beisel 1992 and Gusfield 1992 on morality; and DiMaggio 1992, Halle 1992, and Peterson and Simkus 1992 on arts and musical tastes. For a discussion of the influence of Durkheimian sociology on cultural sociology, see Lamont and Fournier 1992; and Alexander (ed.) 1988.

7 While in *Distinction* (1984), Bourdieu predefines familiarity with high culture (i.e. cultural boundaries) and the maximization of social position (i.e. socio-economic boundaries) as the stakes of social life, his theory of fields posits that individuals attempt to maximize their social position based on the stake most valued in the field (e.g. Bourdieu 1976). Although stakes vary across fields, the requirement to improve one's social position is posited in the very concept of "field."

8 She has also analyzed the salience of criteria of evaluation across academic disciplines and in academic definitions of excellence. See in particular Tsay, Abbott and Lamont (under review) and Lamont, Kaufman, and Moody (forthcoming).

9 To be published in English by Harvard University Press.

10 This research program also drew initially on the cognitive sociology of Durkheim-Mauss, with a series of experiments on social and statistical classifications that shed light on the operations and techniques through which human beings are "made similar" (Boltanski and Thévenot 1983; Boltanski

1987; Desrosières and Thévenot 1988; Desrosières 1993; Thévenot 1990b). The process of categorization was studied both in history and practice and includes: (a) an historical genesis of socio-occupational classifications showing the links with the French state and labor laws; (b) empirical surveys focusing on the cognitive operation that are required for effective construction of equivalence between persons, and that are supported by occupational titles, coders' practices and spokespersons of professions making claims based on different criteria of equivalence.

11 For instance, the efficiency worth of an engineer, of a technique or method, make them more "collective" than unskilled persons or practices, as suggested by Weber's (1978) analysis of rationalization. Similarly a celebrity embodies more collectiveness than a "nobody" because he/she potentially facilitates the coordination of other actors' actions if they share a common recognition of this fame. Thus this framework analyzes a wide range of forms of collectiveness, beyond the classical notion of "social group."

12 For a short presentation of the research agenda and of its background, see Thévenot 1995c, Boltanski and Thévenot 1999. Available English-language discussions of the framework are Dodier 1993a; Dosse 1998; Wagner 1994a, 1999. Bénatouïl 1999a and 1999b compares the framework to Latour's and Callon's actor-network theory and contrasts it with Bourdieu's social theory. Finally, for a discussion of the influence of the framework on institutional economics and so-called "economics of conventions", see *Revue économique*, 1989; in English, see Storper and Salais 1997 and, for a review of this literature, see Wilkinson 1997.

13 This larger research agenda discusses the actors' competencies to shift among a plurality of regimes of action and engagement that do not always encompass a reference to the common good. It is notably the case for the regime of love as *agapè* (Boltanski 1990), the regime governing planned agency and the functional treatment of the environment (Thévenot 1990b, 1995b), and the regime shaped by familiar acquaintance with a customized human and material environment (Thévenot 1994, 1996c). This agenda of "*sociologie pragmatique*" (Thévenot 1998, forthcoming) converges on some points with that offered by American pragmatism (Joas 1993), while opening the investigation to a broader range of pragmatic regimes and building on advances in the sociology and phenomenology of practice.

14 While some of us are skeptical toward the post-modern stance according to which cultural orientations are essentially contextual (Beck, Giddens, and Lash 1994), as explained below, we share an interest in assessing the relative availability of ideas or regimes of action across settings (Lamont 1995; Thévenot 1990b).

15 See Paul Ricœur's (1995) comparison between Walzer (1983) and Boltanski and Thévenot (1991).

16 For a remarkable analysis of the flaws of this position, including Weberien examination of "values," see Manent 1994, chap. 2.

17 These include the Groupe de Sociologie de l'Ethique (CNRS) which was founded in 1978 by Isambert, became the Centre de Recherche Sens, Ethique, Société and is presently directed by Pharo (1996), and the Groupe de Sociologie Politique et Morale (EHESS-CNRS) which was founded by

Boltanski in 1984 and is presently directed by Thévenot. For recent special issues of journals having a non-academic audience, see the issues of *Magazine Littéraire*, "Les nouvelles morales. Ethique et philosophie" (1998), and of *Sciences Humaines*, "Les valeurs en question" (1998).

18 This analysis might also be fruitfully compared to the identification of principles governing a theory of justice (for a parallel with Rawls's second principle, see Thévenot 1992b, 1996a).

19 Statistical categories, job evaluation scales, standards of competence or customary practices build equivalences among human beings. Also, norms of measurements, standards or conventional properties make things similar. On the "cognitive mastery over society" and the "conventionalization from above" which characterizes organized modernity, see Wagner 1994c.

20 On the relations between this "qualifying" process in everyday evaluations and legal processes, with concrete illustrations drawn from the present comparative project, see Thévenot 2000b.

21 The articulation between modes of evaluation and material arrangements [*dispositifs*] turns orders of worth into a useful tool for analyzing: organizational dynamics, modes of coordination of actions and conflicts surrounding them (Boltanski and Thévenot 1989, Eymard-Duvernay 1986, 1989; Thévenot 1986, 1989); labor laws and workplace practices (Chateauraynaud 1989, 1991; Dodier 1989, 1993b); banking (Wissler 1989a, 1989b); public services and local government (Lafaye 1989, 1990; Corcuff 1993; Camus, Corcuff, and Lafaye 1993); education (Derouet 1992; Normand 1999); health care (Dodier 1993a, Dodier and Camus 1997); arts (Heinich 1991, 1993a); associations (Camus 1991, Marchal 1992).

22 For an exception and a distinction of "modes of ordering" within an actor-network perspective, see Law 1994.

23 While some have taken on the task of documenting the flexible content of moral boundaries (e.g. Beisel 1997; Gusfield 1992; and Rieder 1985), others have focused on the content of cultural and aesthetic boundaries (Olivier 1997; Halle 1993), and on how different types of boundaries or principles of evaluation are brought together: moral and aesthetic/cultural boundaries (Beisel 1993; Blau 1996); moral and economic boundaries (Illouz 1997); moral and gender/sexual boundaries (Epstein 1992; Gamson 1997; Lichterman forthcoming; Quadagno and Fobes 1995); moral and racial boundaries (Bryson 1999; Halle 1984; Lamont 1997); moral and class/professional boundaries (Waller 1999; Schmalzbauer 1996); and cultural and class boundaries (Bryson 1996; DiMaggio 1987; Peterson and Simkus 1992; Zolberg 1992).

24 "The concept of repertoire is also used by students of social movements interested in "repertoires of contention." See in particular Tarrow 1995 and Tilly 1997. On the use of this concept in a historical context, see also Tarrow 1993.

25 Swidler's contribution was criticized for focusing on the supply side of ideas and downplaying the factors that push individuals to select certain tools rather than others (Lamont 1992, chap. 5; Berger 1995). Instead, it was proposed that to understand factors affecting the probability that actors use some boundaries rather than others, it is necessary to consider national cultural traditions, the relative influence of various institutions of cultural diffusion (reli-

gious organization, mass media, educational systems, etc.), and structural features of societies. The relationship between models of evaluation (or symbolic boundaries) and broader cultural and structural features of societies are explored in a multi-dimensional causal model sketched in Lamont 1992.

26 On the concept of schemas and other devices that social psychologists have developed to capture the generalizability of information and knowledge across contexts, see DiMaggio 1997.

27 They are also defined as "cultural environment(s) and the material contained therein . . . the socially constructed, readily available cultural materials of a society – the archetypes, the myths, the epigrams and adages, the morals, the means-end chains, the evaluation criteria, the categorization schemas, all of the materials of shared 'tool-kits'" (Corse 1997, p. 156).

28 We greatly benefited from the comments of Thomas Bénatouïl on these points.

29 American symbolic anthropologists are now questioning the notion that the world is made up of societies with different cultures (Gupta and Ferguson 1997). Our work is complementary to this line of work, as we also understand the apparent boundedness of cultures as something made rather than found (ibid. p. 20). However, we are not concerned with the process of making space into places, i.e. the process of formation of meaning associated with location, which is the object of the literature on national identity, for instance.

30 This specific definition of "civic" is chosen for heuristic purpose from a large pool of definitions inherited from the French and American traditions of political theory.

31 Civic solidarity is also present in our American case studies. For instance, the chapter by Lemieux and Schmalzbauer on French and American journalists shows that American Left-wing journalists consider journalism as a form of "social criticism" and describe themselves as advocates of the working class, the "marginalized," and the "voiceless," whom they define as victims of economic and political oppression. However, across our various case studies we find evidence that civic solidarity is less present in the United States than in France. For instance, while altruism is prevalent in the United States (Wuthnow 1991), it tends to be framed not in terms of an obligation to sustain human solidarity by reducing inequality, but in terms of philanthropic giving most often based on individualistic or religious beliefs (see also the chapter by Camus-Vigué that compares the role of altruism in French and American chapters of the Rotary Club; on this general point, see also Lamont 2000. Wuthnow (1991) and Ostrower (1996) provide detailed analyses of the individualistic rationales developed by ordinary and wealthy citizens for giving or engaging in institutionalized philanthropic activities; the evidence they present also suggests that the discourse on civic solidarity is marginal among available American representations of the meaning of giving. Note that Americans are considerably less willing to give welfare benefits to unemployed able-bodied adults than to children and the handicapped (Cook 1979). The interest raised by Putnam's (1993b) argument – that American democracy is imperiled by the decline of civic associations and indicates the increasing marginality of "social trust" – also points to the relative marginality of civic solidarity (as we narrowly define it) in the American context.

32 Nathalie Heinich argues that the forms of rejection are far more public in the United States (scandals, trials, petitions, demonstrations) and rely on the legal, political and constitutional resources available to the citizen.

33 This argument is also made in Lamont 1992, chap. 4.

34 The group includes six American and five French participants. It is diverse in terms of level of academic experience: While the project was in progress, it comprised two senior faculty members, one senior researcher, one junior faculty member, one junior researcher working in the non-profit sector, and six graduate students. Finally, three of the participants have intimate knowledge of both French and American societies because they have lived in the two countries for several years.

Part I

Race, gender and multiculturalism

2 The rhetorics of racism and anti-racism in France and the United States

Michèle Lamont

This chapter analyzes the rhetorics of racism and anti-racism used in France and the United States to demonstrate, dispute, and explain the inferiority of North African immigrants and African Americans, respectively.[1] I draw on in-depth interviews conducted with seventy-five randomly sampled white and black workers living in the New York suburbs and with seventy-five white and North African workers living in the Paris suburbs to reconstruct the mental maps and symbolic boundaries through which these individuals define "us" and "them," simultaneously identifying the most salient principles of classification and identification that are operating behind these definitions, including race and class.[2] These interviews do not concern racism proper, but the types of people the men I talked to say they feel superior and inferior to, and the types of people they describe as "their sort of folks" and "the sorts of folks they don't like much." In other words, I analyze the rhetorics of racism and anti-racism by focusing directly on how people define their own identity and the identity of their community, or the boundaries through which they distinguish between people like themselves with whom they identify, and others.[3]

In-depth interviews with French and American professionals and managers revealed that they rarely mention race when they describe people they like and dislike (Lamont 1992, chap. 3). However, among workers, this category is very often salient. An example is provided by a firefighter who lives in Rahway, New Jersey. When asked what kind of people he feels superior to (without any reference to race), he answers, "As far as race goes in our fire department, there is one guy who is an American Indian that is considered a minority. The other one is one black fellow but he don't work with us . . . In the service the blacks stay together and the whites stay together . . . in Rahway, the blacks have their own American Legion." Several French and American workers draw boundaries by pointing at differences between whites and others, but stress that they are not racist and refuse to put one group above the other. In many cases, however, racial hierarchies are implicitly or explicitly constructed.

This chapter focuses on the types of evidence that interviewees provide when, in their assessment of the worth of others, they attempt to demonstrate the equality or inequality of racial groups.[4] I have inductively identified the main types of evidence mobilized and they fall into the following categories: moral, biological/physical, psychological, social, religious, political, market, and human nature-oriented. Like the other contributors to this volume, I am concerned with comparing repertoires of arguments and evidences mobilized by respondents and what they tell us about structured cultural differences between two societies.[5] For heuristic purpose, I contrast racist and anti-racist rhetorics as two opposite ends of a spectrum and do not focus on intermediate positions nor on anti-racist arguments used to bolster racist positions. Following Apostles et al. (1983), Kluegel and Bobo (1993), and others, I also consider how groups explain racial differences.[6] I identify which arguments and types of evidence are present and absent in France and the United States. At times, I discuss the relative importance of these types of evidence, focusing only on the most salient differences and similarities. In the discussion, I provide elements of explanation for national differences. Although the study is based on a relatively small sample (again, N = 75 for each of the two societies under consideration), it is my hope that it taps the whole range of arguments used in the two national contexts.

I show that in both countries, racist and anti-racist rhetorics are framed in universalistic terms: the men I talked to generally use universal criteria that can be applied to all human beings to evaluate other groups and themselves, whether these criteria have to do with human nature, biology, or morality.[7] In doing so, they establish an equivalence between individuals whom they believe belong to the same universe of reference and can be incorporated in the same community, as children of God, humans, moral beings, people with similar needs, etc. In other words, they use broad principles of inclusion, which they take to transcend individual groups or ascribed characteristics.[8] Sometimes, they also use criteria that can be applied to all human beings (such as intelligence), but point to inter-individual differences in ranking with respect to these criteria. In both cases, after explaining what these universal criteria consist of, racist interviewees often describe the "other" as not measuring up to them and hence establish their superiority. African Americans and North Africans more readily use particularistic strategies to refute and/or explain racist arguments by using a standard of comparison that explicitly privileges their own group (familiarity with Islam, for instance); whites also use this strategy, but less explicitly as they take their own culture to have universal value.

Among the universalistic standards these men use, moral standards occupy a particularly important place in both countries, moral and racial boundaries being drawn simultaneously. We also find important national differences: American racists and anti-racists alike appeal to market mechanisms, and more specifically to socio-economic success, to establish the equivalence of races, a strategy not used by the French. American racists are also slightly more prone to point at biological differences in explaining racial inequality than the French, who never use biological explanations but more readily refer to their political culture to justify racism than Americans do. The French anti-racist rhetoric also draws on solidaristic and egalitarian themes that are part of the socialist and republican traditions and are absent from the American anti-racist rhetoric.

It should be noted that theories of racism that have emerged in the last twenty years have all been concerned with new forms of racism that are clearly moral in emphasis. These are contrasted with old-fashioned racism prevalent under Jim Crow segregation, which was based on the inherent biological inferiority of blacks. Most notably, theorists of "symbolic racism" (Sears 1988) and "modern racism" (McConahay 1986) argue that white Americans value individualism, self-reliance, work ethic, obedience and discipline, and that their racism derives from their belief that blacks violate these values. Proponents of the theories of "new racism" (Barker 1981) and "differential racism" (Taguieff 1988) suggest that in the last twenty years, racists have come to justify their racism not by biological determinism, but by their right to defend the distinctiveness of their culture, stressing the legitimacy of wanting to "live with your own kind" and of maintaining cultural distance between groups. Finally, the notion of "laissez-faire racism" proposed by Bobo (1995) and Bobo and Smith (1998) points to a new pattern of belief which "involves . . . acceptance of negative stereotypes of African Americans, a denial of discrimination as a current societal problem, and attribution of primary responsibility for blacks' disadvantage to blacks themselves" (pp. 20–1). For these authors, laissez-faire racism is part of the racial subtext of ongoing political debates about American welfare, crime reform, and racial discrimination. While these theories all zoom on the importance of whites' beliefs concerning the moral *qua* cultural failings of blacks to explain racism, they posit such beliefs instead of documenting them. My work, which shares the cultural focus of these theories, complements them by documenting empirically whites' perceptions of blacks through in-depth interviews.

In France, Taguieff (1986, 1988) has provided a very sophisticated analysis of the critiques of racism produced in recent years by social scientists, intellectuals, politicians and activists. However, as argued by de Rudder (1995), no one has documented the rhetoric of anti-racism produced by the French, or by the prime victims of French racism, North

African immigrants. Similarly, while social scientists have paid consider-able attention to the rhetoric of racism produced by the Front National (e.g. Schain 1987; Taguieff 1989, 1991), that used by lay people has gone largely unstudied (but for a few exceptions such as Wievorka 1992). Finally, while some have noted the prevalence of cultural arguments over biological arguments in the French rhetoric of racism (e.g. Balibar and Wallerstein 1991, chap. 1; Silverman 1992), researchers have yet to conduct a detailed and empirically grounded analysis of the range of types of arguments used in the French cultural repertoires.

In the United States, we find a large literature on the struggle against racism as manifested in the abolitionist and the civil rights movements (Aptheker 1992; McAdam 1988; McPherson 1975). Similarly, there exists a social psychological literature on whites' and blacks' accounts of racial inequality that is relevant to the study of the rhetoric of anti-racism (Sniderman 1985). However, again, no one has systematically examined the relative importance of various themes in the rhetoric of anti-racism as it is elaborated by lay people. This also holds for the rhetoric of racism: Feagin and Vera (1995), Wellman (1993), and others analyze aspects of American racism, arguing for instance that it stresses specific elements, such as individual rights and equal opportunity (Goldberg 1993; Omi and Winant 1986).[9] However, as in the French literature, researchers have yet to provide a systematic and empirically grounded analysis of arguments and of their relative saliency.[10] Focusing on thematic saliency is important for capturing how the cultural logic of racism functions across national cultural repertoires.[11] A more exhaustive analysis of these patterns is available in Lamont forthcoming.

The study draws on 150 two-hour long interviews with male workers who have a high-school degree but not a college degree, and who have been working full-time and steadily for at least five years.[12] The sample includes thirty African American blue-collar workers and thirty North African immigrant blue-collar workers.[13] It also includes a French group and a Euro-American group that each encompasses thirty blue-collar workers and fifteen low-status white-collar workers (see Tables 2.1 and 2.2).[14]

Respondents were randomly selected from phone books of twelve working-class towns located in the New York suburbs (such as Elizabeth, Rahway, and Linden) and in the Paris suburbs (such as Ivry, Nanterre, and Aubervilliers).[15] This random selection and the relatively large number of respondents are aimed not at building a representative sample, but at tapping a wide range of perspectives within a community of workers, thereby going beyond the unavoidable limitations of site-specific research.[16] Finally, if I am comparing French and American racism aimed

Table 2.1. *Occupation and age of male blue-collar and manual workers (Paris and New York suburbs)*

French	Age	Euro-Americans	Age
house painter	30	printer	31
automobile painter	39	mechanic	40
mason	45	ironworker	43
carpenter	47	construction worker	38
automobile technician	35	security system installer	51
locksmith	39	plumbing inspector	35
boiler maker	32	plumber	32
electrical technician	42	heating system specialist	59
electronics operative	35	electrician	31
heater repairman	30	stage technician	34
warehouse keeper	31	warehouse worker	30
electrical appraiser	46	warehouse worker	35
railway technician	30	electrician	34
subway conductor	30	train conductor	39
garbage recycling technician	38	pipe fitter	58
tire technician	54	petroleum co. foreman	45
steam engine operative	35	tin factory foreman	46
radar technician	31	automobile assembly line worker	45
shop foreman, lamp factory	41	foreman, cosmetics plants	45
railway technician	37	truck driver	34
railway technician	35	truck driver	44
bellman	32	tool and die maker	49
phone technician	40	postal service sorter	45
cable technician	36	firefighter	50
pastry maker	30	firefighter	33
policeman	35	policeman	34
aircraft technician	36	policeman	54
pastry chef	31	warehouse worker	63
butcher	55	letter carrier	48
cook	42	letter carrier	39
Average age	*37*		*41*

		Minority workers	
North Africans	Age	African Americans	Age
painter	57	painter	46
mechanic	37	car inspector	49
mason	59	equipment operator	62
painter	42	machinist	46
operative, car factory	46	union rep., car factory	53
goldplating craftsman	50	health inspector	38
plumber	45	plumber	32
skilled worker, car factory	52	assistant cable splicer	36

Table 2.1. (*cont.*)

North Africans	Age	African Americans	Age
electrician	34	phone technician	25
warehouse keeper, petroleum co.	55	maintenance worker	32
warehouse keeper	50	warehouse keeper	53
laborer, construction industry	53	letter carrier	57
yard worker, railways	41	newspaper worker	33
bus driver	33	truck driver	35
meat delivery man	60	recycling plant worker	31
operative, car factory	50	operative, chemical co.	30
warehouse keeper	33	chemical operator	53
skilled worker, air conditioner	50	X-ray worker	33
roofer	51	foreman, bindery	59
screwcutter	49	worker, health industry	27
truck driver	44	shear operator	31
phonebooth cleaner	47	fumigation technician	55
packer, textile industry	34	sorter, mailing co.	26
handler, textile industry	34	phone technician	44
metalworker, car factory	56	paper quality inspector	31
hotel handyman	47	security supervisor	36
operative, telemechanics	54	photo technician	45
worker, pharmaceutical industry	37	operative, textile company	59
laborer, road construction	48	park maintenance worker	44
dressmaker	42	hospital orderly	61
Average age	*45*		*42*

at North African immigrants and African Americans respectively, and the anti-racism of African Americans and that of North African immigrants, it is because these latter groups are the prime victims of racism in the United States and France.[17]

The discussion begins with the United States. After considering American white racism and anti-racism, I analyze how African Americans explain and rebut racism. The second part of the paper considers French racism and anti-racism, as well as its North African responses.[18] For now, let us note that the racist rhetoric is more widely spread in the United States than in France: 60 percent and 63 percent of the Euro-American white- and blue-collar workers made explicitly racists statements of the types described below (i.e. respectively 8 and 18 individuals) in contrast to 20 percent and 50 percent of their French counterparts (respectively 3 and 15 interviewees).[19] Conversely, the anti-racist rhetoric is less widely spread in the United States than in France: while respectively 20 percent and 13 percent of Euro-American white- and blue-collar respondents

Table 2.2. *Occupation and age of Caucasian white-collar workers (Paris and New York suburbs)*

French sample		American sample	
bank clerk	34	bank clerk	45
bank clerk	40	receiving clerk	53
bank clerk	44	civil servant	54
civil servant	42	civil servant	52
draftsman	39	draftsman	38
electronics technician	31	electronics technician	38
postal window clerk	30	postal clerk	35
train ticket salesman	33	hotel industry salesman	30
wood salesman	40	paper goods salesman	32
phone salesman	41	bank supplies salesman	60
charcuterie salesman	51	insurance salesman	52
bank clerk	39	clerical worker	53
aircraft technician	36	broadcast technician	47
photographer	35	audio-technician	29
draftsman	44	electronics technician	28
Total average age	*39*		*43*

make anti-racist statements of the types described below (respectively 6 and 5 respondents), it is the case for 73 percent and 23 percent of the French white- and blue-collar workers (respectively 10 and 7 individuals).[20]

RACISM AND ANTI-RACISM IN THE UNITED STATES

White American racism

In the repertory of arguments that white Americans use to justify their racism, moral arguments are most prominent. It is on the basis of work ethic, ambition, and honesty that white people distinguish between "good" and "bad" blacks, and the arguments they present are often an extension of the moral criteria they use to evaluate people in general, which in their views give legitimacy to their racism. In other words, when asked what kinds of people they like and dislike, the white workers I talked to often distinguished between people who work hard, live by the rules, and provide for their family and those who don't, and they then went on to evaluate blacks along these dimensions, drawing moral and racial boundaries simultaneously.[21]

A large number of interviewees view blacks as lazy or as profiteers who have undue advantages at work. In the words of a draftsman, "blacks have less of a work ethic than anybody else." A young storage worker illustrates how his own conception of self as ambitious is enmeshed in his negative view of blacks when he says:

They're happy they've got a job where they make a couple of bucks and they can go out and drink or do whatever they want to do. Like the guys I work with. They're happy working in the warehouse and to them they'll do it the rest of their lives. I don't even want to drive the trucks. Hopefully, like in 10 or 15 years, I won't have to work. Hopefully, my family town house will make more money . . . Maybe I'll get my own truck. They don't wanna move up . . . Like when 5 pm comes, everybody punches out and goes home and I'm saying "What else do you need done? The jacks have to be plugged in. Do you need anything else?"

Similarly, a hard-working electronics technician describes African Americans thus:

Blacks have a tendency to . . . try to get off doing less, the least as possible that as long as they still maintain being able to keep the job, where whites will put in that extra oomph. I know this is a generality and it does not go for all, it goes for a portion. It's this whole unemployment and welfare gig. A lot of the blacks on welfare have no desire to get off it. Why should they? It's free money. I can't stand to see my hard-earned money going to pay for someone who wants to sit on his ass all day long and get free money. You hear it on TV all the time: "We don't have to do this because we were slaves 400 years ago. You owe it to us." I don't owe you shit, period. I had nothing to do with that and I'm not going to pay for it.

White interviewees also identify moral differences between whites and blacks in the area of family values, and many believe that the two groups live worlds apart. Crucial here is the breakdown of the black family. A pipe fitter, a former gang member who grew up in Newark, says: "You know I could have ended up stealing cars and stuff too if I wanted. I was brought up better than that . . . I think they have less family values. If you don't have a family, how can you have family values?" For a policeman who works in Elizabeth, NJ, among blacks, "there's no sense of family . . . I come across kids that have no conception of reality, no respect for life, no respect for property, no respect for themselves."

In explaining perceived racial differences, the men I talked to draw on a mix of biological, historical, psychological, and cultural arguments: some suggest that laziness is part of the "nature" of black people or is linked to a culture that is deeply ingrained and rooted in history and is passed on from one generation to the next in an almost unalterable manner. Speaking of the breakdown of the black family, a warehouse worker says:

But you can't [change it] because it's the generation, I think . . . It's a system that's gone on for centuries that has eroded maybe some of their morals, and their respect for what's going on. I think some find it easier to have a loud mouth and cry for a handout rather than try to go out and get their piece of the American dream . . . They just lack the education. You can't make them learn.

It is this conflation of biological, historical, psychological, and cultural explanations that, for many, justifies having little hope for the improvement of the situation of African Americans.

In this context, it should be noted that one of the distinctive features of the American rhetoric of racism is the place given to intelligence/learning ability *qua* genetics in white accounts of differences between whites and blacks. Lower intelligence, measured by learning ability, is at times used to explain the lesser educational success of blacks. A warehouse worker speaking of blacks says, "I don't think they have the knowledge which is from grade school where you learn. White people pick up much faster." For another warehouse worker, blacks also lack practical intelligence, as exemplified by people like Michael Jackson who make millions and are unable to save. "Ten years down the road they have nothing, nothing . . . They don't know how to save. That goes back to the days of Joe Louis. The white man is intelligent, he invests immediately. They live day to day. Everybody knows that. Big cars, jewelry. Hooray for today, the hell with tomorrow . . . They love money, they love money . . . The faster they get it, the faster they spend it."

Finally several justify their racism not by referring to the distinctive characteristics of blacks, but by their view that "preferring and protecting your own kind" is a universal "natural" tendency. This belief is expressed by a worker who says that he thinks he is racist because "I have a tendency to trust my own kind. I relate to them better. If I was in a position to help others, I would probably help my own kind before I would help someone of another race." We will see that this belief is shared by a number of black interviewees, who also use it to argue that racism is part of a universal human nature.

Whether focusing on differences attributed to biology, history, psychology, and culture or on racism as a universal disposition, these "white racists" appeal to what they perceive to be universal criteria of evaluation that transcend particular groups to demonstrate the inferiority of blacks. This allows them to be racist while feeling that they are themselves good moral people at the core.

White American anti-racism

White interviewees who oppose racism use the same type of moral arguments as are used by racist interviewees. However, unlike racist interviewees, they are often reluctant to universalize moral traits to all members of a racial group (such universalization being typical of social categorization processes involved in stereotyping; see Hamilton and Trolier 1986). Instead, they argue that good and bad people are found in all races. It is notably the case of a truck driver who says:

> If you treat me nice, and you and I get along, great. If you treat me bad, then I try to decide on my own how people are and how I'm going to deal with people, and it does not matter if you are black or white, or pink, or purple, or yellow, or green. If you're a miserable SOB, you're just a miserable SOB, no matter what color you are.

These anti-racist interviewees are more likely to engage in a discussion of the universality of human failings across races than racist interviewees are.[22] They use a universe of reference or an implicit definition of community that includes all human beings without color restriction, hence presenting themselves as universalistic.

Others describe market mechanisms as the ultimate arbitrator of the value of people, arguing that earning capacity makes people equal. For instance, a petroleum company foreman says:

> No matter who you are at Exxon, you're making pretty good money, so it's not like you've got a disadvantaged person. Their kids are going to good schools. They're eating, they're taking vacations because of Exxon. You don't see the division or whatever, so Exxon kind of eliminated that because of the salary structure . . . With black people, you talk sports, you talk school, you're all in the same boat. It isn't 'What's it like to have a new car?' You know, you talk to the guy, and you went on vacation, and he went on vacation.

This statement presumes that the market is a legitimate and efficient arbitrator of worth. As such, it posits a distinctly liberal stance and contrasts with a socio-democratic model that views the market as producing inequalities that need to be remedied by the state (Esping-Anderson 1990). This statement also presumes a community of citizens in which membership is based on work and self-reliance.[23] As such, in contrast to biological arguments, it is distinctively universalist, because it is potentially available to all. In this case, one's ability to "succeed" is taken to be an objective (i.e. racially unbiased) criteria of evaluation – hence the fact that market arguments can be used to support racist and anti-racist positions.

Like "white racists," these anti-racist interviewees make important distinctions based on socio-economic success and work ethic. However, they use these universalistic criteria to demonstrate diversity among whites and blacks and the value of blacks they know. References to the market as a creator of equivalence are also made by African Americans to demonstrate the possibility of equality.

African-American responses

I now turn to how blacks explain, rebut, and cope with racism. Rebutting first: Both biological and religious arguments are used by blacks to demonstrate equivalence across races – biological arguments were only used by racists in reference to intelligence, and religious arguments were absent from the discourse of white "racists" and "anti-racists" alike. African American men I talked to refer to the fact that we all spend nine months in our mother's womb and that we all have ten fingers to demonstrate biological/physical universalism. As a park maintenance worker puts it: "If I cut myself and you cut yourself, red blood is going to run out." They oppose the theory of evolutionism because they believe it suggests that blacks are genetically closer to apes than whites, and therefore inferior. Others demonstrate racial equivalence by stressing that we are all children of God. Drawing on the theme of equal creation often alluded to by Martin Luther King (Condit and Lacaites 1993, p. 192), a plumber firmly wishes that "people would realize that we have one creator, and not many creators, and as there are many different colors of birds, and trees, and fishes, and everything that cross this globe." Mixing biological and religious arguments, a photographer critiques both the Afro-centric view that the Bible is an instrument of domination of the white man, and the theory of evolution, by saying:

We're all equal. Some people say this guy gave you the Bible to keep you cool over here. That's when you start going down to the zoo to see your family. We all come out one way, whether you want to believe it or not. Whether you came from Poland, or Scotland, or China. It all started one way: family of men; we are all one. We might not look like it, our noses might be little, or our skin tones [are different], and all that other stuff, but we are all the same.[24]

In a move similar to that of white racists who focus on the universality of human failings, other black men demonstrate the equivalence between races by stressing that we all have similar basic universal needs and values. A worker in the textile industry says that both groups "want a decent paying job, a few credit cards, a car that's decent and a nice place to live. I think people in a certain age, I mean a certain income bracket, their thinking is just about equal or the same."

The black men I talked to also rebut racism by demonstrating equality based on group membership criteria such as nationality: several argue that "we are all Americans" and equal as such. Again, like the white anti-racists quoted above, others believe that earning capacity gives access to equality and social citizenship. In the words of a chemical worker: "I'm accepted [at work] and I work with really white people. I think when you get into the money scheme, it doesn't really matter [what color you are], 'cause then the money makes it equal." He adds "I'm overcoming [the limits put on me because of my race] because I am achieving the same thing [as my co-workers] money-wise. If I was poor and on welfare, they would just call me another nigger on the street. I may not be as equal as them, but they know it's not too much below. If they buy a house, I could buy a house too." It is this reasoning about income that leads him to say that class is a greater divider than race in American society. Finally, still others point to their competence to establish that they are equal to their white co-workers. A worker in a recycling plan puts it simply:

> Basically it comes down to, once you prove yourself that you're just as good as them that you can do anything they do just as well as them, and you carry yourself with that weight, then people respect you. You come there and do what you're supposed to do, and you don't get caught into any controversy, they kinda back away from you. I'm kind of quiet, I just go there, I don't miss a day on the job, I do what I gotta do, and I'm one of the best throughout the whole plant at what I do.

Demonstrating that competence or income can act as equalizers implies that these are general criteria that transcend ascribed characteristics and should be given more weight than skin color in assessing the value of people. Therefore, although these criteria are particularistic, in the sense that they are more characteristic of some cultures than others (i.e. more frequent as one moves up on the social ladder), they are, in principle, available to all, independently of their skin color. As principles of equalization, competence and income make available individual strategies for coping with racism.

Providing evidence of the greater morality of blacks as compared to whites is another familiar strategy used to rebut racism. Indeed, the men I talked to often believe blacks to be superior to whites because "Black people are sensitive toward human needs because we are concerned humans, whereas the white people that I have met in my life seem detached from the human thing" (a machinist). A little more than third of them made statements indicating that they believe blacks to be superior to whites. A third indicated that whites have significant flaws and a third did not discuss these issues.

The spiritual realm is one area where workers find evidence of the moral superiority of blacks over whites. A worker in a car factory describes the situation thus: "White people, they go to church too, but their worship, mostly, is different than blacks. I don't think they get the same feeling, the same results. We go to Church and we feel the Holy Ghost." The moral superiority of blacks is also grounded in the fact that they have weaker domineering tendencies than whites. For instance, Larry Smith, talking about blacks, says: "We didn't create the bombs, we didn't play with gunpowder, we didn't do this . . . The interest of white America was always to build and be better and be competitive, and in doing that, that's more reading and sitting and studying and being more manipulative, and more deceiving, and more, you know . . . whereas we weren't." Finally, the greater strength and moral character of blacks is also proven by pointing at their ability to handle hardship. In a particularistic move, Larry, a recycling worker, links physical resilience, the experience of slavery, and having special godly protection to demonstrate the superiority of blacks over other races:

I guess one way to describe and bring it out to you is, if blacks wouldn't be the superior race, I don't think we'd be living now . . . If there wasn't a God, black people shouldn't exist in this country. Throughout the slavery, the way the black women was raped, the way black people was hung and killed by animals and dogs, and stuff like that . . . The white race, they tried to destroy the Jewish race. They destroyed the Indians, they don't exist anymore, very rarely do you see some. The black race was under the same situation, but it was worser for the black race than for them races. And you look at the population of the black race now . . . Somebody above had to look out for them. The black race is the only race you can marry with a thousand nationalities, have a kid, that kid is going to come out black, you know when you mix that blood. There's a lot of different things that make me wonder why is the black race superior.

Finally, like the white men I talked to, black interviewees explain the prevalence of racism in white America by arguing that it is a universal trait deeply ingrained in human nature, and explainable by a universal need to create a pecking order across groups. The notion that racism is a universal tendency reinforces a zero-sum view of race relations according to which one group always attempts to assert its dominance.

While we saw that white "racists" and "anti-racists" draw on moral themes to justify or condemn racism, focusing on work ethic or family values, or on the moral failings inherent in human nature, blacks also draw on moral themes in rebutting racism, stressing the greater morality of blacks in spirituality and other areas, and the domineering tendencies of whites. Therefore, like white racists, they do draw moral and racial boundaries simultaneously and they believe racism is a universal trait. Furthermore, like whites, they define the market as the arbitrator of the value of races. However, they are more prone to use religious, and to some extent, biological evidence to demonstrate the equivalence between races than whites are. Finally, they more readily use explicitly particularistic criteria to demonstrate the superiority of their own group as is the case when Larry affirms the superiority of blacks because of their physical resilience linked to their unique experience of domination.

THE RHETORIC OF RACISM AND ANTI-RACISM IN FRANCE

French racism

Like Americans, French interviewees justify their racism by (1) drawing racial and moral boundaries simultaneously, based on perceived group differences in work ethic, responsibility, and self-sufficiency; and (2) arguing that racism is a universal human trait. However, unlike Americans, the rhetoric that French interviewees use to justify their racism includes: (1) a critique that the French state privileges immigrants instead of applying republican principles; (2) a broader critique of the national civic culture; (3) a more exclusive focus on fundamental cultural and religious – as opposed to biological, historical or psychological – differences between the French and the Muslims.

We also find important contrasts in the rhetoric of anti-racism in both countries. In France, this rhetoric puts greater emphasis on the principle of egalitarianism. Influenced in part by the socialist and republican traditions, it also stresses solidarity. Furthermore, unlike American interviewees, French interviewees do not stress the role of socio-economic success and market mechanisms in demonstrating equivalence between self and others. Their account of cultural differences and racial tensions is also more environmental and less individualistic, pointing at how the living conditions of North African immigrants explains their deviance and fosters animosity between groups.

Moral boundaries against immigrants are drawn by pointing at their laziness and the fact that they live at the expense of French workers. For instance, echoing the electronics specialist quoted in the first section, a heater repairman expresses his strong dislike of parasites, and goes on to describe North African immigrants as typically falling into this category. He says that he hates

people who don't take their responsibilities. When you look at your pay stub and you see how much you make and you see everything that is taken way . . . And it isn't the *Gaulois* who benefits from it. Families with fourteen children, I have seen very few of them among the French. Two or three children maybe but, we have to work hard to support these people. They are parasites. I know them and they don't work.

This theme comes up time and time again during the course of the interviews. An aircraft technician, for instance, says:

What I don't like about foreigners is that they don't work and they want everything. They want an apartment even if they don't work. They want social security, it's for them. Two North Africans work with me, and they work hard to do what they have to do. I respect them like I would a Frenchman because they are people who are working. They are not going around stealing radios.

Denouncing how North African immigrants take advantage of the welfare state raises the issue of the decline of universalism in the relationship between individuals and the state: one of the keys to French political culture inherited from the French Revolution is the notion that the state treats equally all its members independently of birth, class, race, or religion.[25] Defending this principle, several of the men I talked to denounce the fact that the French state does not apply the law equally to all. For instance, an electrician complained that a policeman he knows tolerates vandalism by North Africans because his higher-ups want to avoid making waves with immigrant communities. Hence, immigrants are viewed as being illegitimately given a privileged status, implicitly bringing about a violation of republican principles, and of workers' own status.

Other aspects of the French racist rhetoric also concern political culture. Ever since the French Revolution, France has portrayed itself as the country of freedom and human rights, and it has given asylum to individuals who were persecuted politically elsewhere. French interviewees are growing increasingly critical of this policy for which, they argue, they are paying a heavy price. A pastry maker explained that he is exasperated because "you feel that you give [immigrants] a home: this is a place for people who are persecuted. So we take them in and they reject us. You feel that they would like us to leave, they would like to have our place." An electronic chip maker complained that France "will become the country of everyone, and it is our children who will suffer the consequence." It is in this context that many follow Jean-Marie Le Pen's call to send immigrants back home and to redefine France's international role. The universal principles of equality and freedom are to be upheld, but within the French territory and not at the cost of the French nation.[26]

Many stress the ways in which North African culture is fundamentally incompatible with that of the French. Here, religion is particularly salient in a way that it was not among American racists.[27] An electrician describes the situation thus:

They don't have the same religion. They say that they want peace but they like to fight and they are the first ones to commit murder, so there is something that is not working. I used to know Poles in the northern regions. There were a lot of Polish people who worked in the mines. They were also Catholic and they were able to become integrated. If you come from a foreign land, you shut your mouth and you learn the habits and customs of people. [Muslims] are the ones who want to come here and impose their customs to us. You go to their country and they cut your hand for stealing, and here they come, steal, and keep their hand. This is impossible: everyone mixes up and we will all turn metisso.

Others produce more general critiques of Muslim societies that point at differences in the treatment of human rights and the value attributed to human life (an argument with universalistic intent). A railway technician also stresses the role of religion in maintaining these differences when he says:

We have to be honest, the problem is that they don't have the same education, the same values as we do. We have a general Christian education, most of the French do not believe in God but they all have a Christian education that regulates our relationships. But in the Muslim world, the Koran doesn't have the same values at all. They send children to get killed in the minefields of Iraq. But in France, if you kill children, it is really a major drama. And women have no place in the Muslim world.

These interviewees do not account for differences by a mix of biology, history, and psychology as Americans do. They clearly privilege specifically cultural/religious factors. An electrician, for instance, states:

I am talking about the Muslims because you can see Arab customs and they don't have the same culture as we do. The parents have worked, because they came to France to work. It is fine to have them come here, but they have to learn our customs, the advantages and inconveniences of the country, everything. If they want to be in France, they have to be like the French. If I go to work in another country, I will do what they do, I don't drink alcohol. But here in France they don't care . . . It should be the same rule for all.

Because the sources of problems are perceived to be specifically cultural, these interviewees insist on the importance of cultural assimilation.

A number of influential authors have stressed the importance of cultural membership and of the republican ideals for the definition of community in France and for French debates about racism (Brubaker 1992; Noiriel 1992; Silverman 1991). In this context, biological explanations of differences are much more alien than they are in the American context. Similarly, few interviewees appeal to psychological or individual explanations of racial inequality. The French are primarily concerned with the clash between French and Islamic cultures, and in their eyes the solution is either the assimilation or the departure of immigrants.

French anti-racism

Many Frenchmen oppose racism in the name of egalitarianism, which they uphold as a principle. They argue that all should be treated equally "whether they are Buddhist or Catholic." This egalitarianism is also expressed through a few denunciations of sexism or ageism. A draftsman, for instance, says: "Wherever I go, the secretaries I see are always pretty and young. I ask myself where are the old ones now? It is a form of racism."

There is not only the racism of color." Paradoxically, none of the American anti-racists defended egalitarianism as a general principle, although it is a founding principle of American liberal republicanism.[28]

Egalitarianism translates into a support for human solidarity that was also rarely voiced in the American context.[29] An electronic chip maker, for instance, says: "Concerning race, I don't think that there are superior and inferior races. I think we are all equal. But I would like us to help poor countries, to help Africans, but not let them come here. This is not the solution. I think that it is normal that we pay income tax to help them, but help them in their country, not here." This solidaristic discourse has to be situated in the French political context, where the welfare state remains relatively strong and where the republican and socialist tradition strengthens solidarity across classes as well as egalitarianism. The influence of these traditions is also perceptible in the French anti-racist rhetoric in that some respondents view racism as an extension of hierarchical thinking that suggests that wearing a tie makes someone a better human being. For instance, a railway technician says that racism is a disposition that he does not like because "it is the lack of respect for the other, and the person who is racist against black people, Arab people, can also be racist against the butcher or the sweeper, against anyone." A car technician says that he is very sensitive to the misery of others. He defines racism as "the dark side of human nature" that inevitably leads to oppression.

Whereas the French do not use income, or the market, as arbitrator of the value of people the way American anti-racists do, some justify their acceptance of North Africans on the basis of work ethic and refer to the fact that good and bad people are found in all races. A locksmith, for instance, says of *Maghrebins*: "they are people who work and who are serious. These are people that I like and have respect for. There are white kids who are into delinquency, who steal, who attack old ladies, and who break things. And for me, whether they are black or yellow or red, it is the same thing . . ." Finally, this locksmith sociologizes differences when he says "These people often are unskilled and unemployed. They don't have money. They are depressed and end up taking drugs." By providing an environmental explanation for cultural differences, these workers denaturalize racial differences and provide a powerful counter-argument to racism. These environmental explanations are generally absent from the discourse of American anti-racists.[30]

North African responses

The most prevalent strategy for rebutting French racism used by North African respondents is to provide evidence of high personal moral character. They also blame other North Africans for French racism. Such individualized strategies are rarely found among African Americans.[31] These differences could be explained by the fact that as immigrants in France, North African workers often do not belong to strong communities and have no claim to social citizenship; also, they are frequently atomized, as many leave their family in their country of origin.

The importance of being "serious" and of following a straight path was greatly emphasized by most interviewees. In the view of an electrician, "someone who is serious is someone who choose his friends carefully, who doesn't drink. I have never smoked, never drank, and it has help me a lot because I have never had problems, have always worked. I have never had problems finding work. I make a good impression, I never do bad things to anyone. This is seriousness, this is my own model." A mechanic says that in order to avoid racism, it is important to revert to immortal rules of morality:

It is important to follow the rule of respect. At home or at other people's place, this rule of respect allows you to have good relationship with people. Whether you are Algerian or French has nothing to do with this, because people will judge you based on your behavior . . . We find this rule everywhere, independently of time and space. It is not because you are old or because it is the year 2000 that this rule does not apply. No, this is an immutable rule.

Conversely, while providing evidence of their own high moral character, a few North African men I talked to explained French racism by blaming North Africans, a strategy that is absent among African Americans. For instance, an electrician explains that

no one is racist except if they have a reason. It is us who provoke racism. This is true: I am an Arab and if I see an Arab breaking into a place and assaulting someone, it is I who becomes racist toward this Arab. It is not normal: racism is supposed to be between different races. Normally I should be racist toward someone who is not from my country or my race, but often I am racist toward Arabs when I see them do this.

While some of these men also view racism as a universal tendency, they at times explain racism as an idiosyncratic personal trait, stressing that some people are born good, others are born bad, there is nothing one can do about it, and there is no reason to get upset at racist people. Others attribute racism to social factors such as class position, again an explanation absent in the United States. A meat delivery man argues that racism is most prevalent

among the young people who have never walked outside of their home, who are spoiled by their father and mother, who came to the world all dressed up . . .

they're rich from the beginning. You can't tell them anything. The ones who started small, who scratched themselves, have fallen down, who have done all the professions to make a living, they are not racist because they have been all over the world.

Furthermore, like African Americans, North Africans promote universalism as a response to racism, stressing that all should be treated the same irrespective of religion, color, or ethnicity; they justify this universalism by demonstrating equality on the basis of a shared kinship with God or a common physiology. Echoing African Americans, a warehouse worker says: "Look at my fingers, they are not the same: some are small, some are large . . . There are some people who are rich and others who are poor." Others also argue that we all have similar needs and values as human beings.

Like blacks, North Africans also rebut French racism by affirming the moral superiority of their own tradition and values over that of the French (it is the case for a third of them). Interviewees perceive their own culture as more humane, therefore richer, than French culture. This is a recurrent theme that is best illustrated by a controller in the automobile industry. Speaking about French people who take the risk of penetrating his milieu, he says that "They appreciate this kind of human warmth that does not exist among them, it is bizarre. Human warmth is what gives us a taste for life, what helps us avoid being sad. It makes you forget when you hurt, when you are hungry, when you are cold." The correlate of the lack of human warmth in French society is the greater isolation of the French. A packer in the textile industry describes the disadvantages of France with reference to the fact that a woman disappeared in his building. He says: "I had never seen her, never, and I have lived there for five or six years. In my country, [my neighbors] would know my grandfather, my great-grandfather. Here, it is not the same, and this has a lot of value. We don't run as much, we see life more. Life is longer, the days are longer too."

In North Africa, the greater density of the community translates into more altruism toward the needy. A skilled worker who specializes in air conditioning explains that "Here in France, if you have nothing to eat, you will cross your hand, stay with your wife at the table, look at one another, talk, discuss, watch TV. In Algeria, if we have nothing, it is not shameful. If we have nothing in the house, my wife or I, we will go to someone and say 'Give me this,' and he will give it to me." This man also explains that in France, "Old people are badly treated and their children don't come to see them. In contrast, in our country, we live in the milieu, the old people stay with their children. We have to help them, live with them, and this is human warmth. Although the parents are old, they don't feel alone. They are there among their children and grandchildren." A very large number of interviewees describe the custom of placing parents in nursing homes as what they dislike most about French society. Furthermore, North African immigrants believe that their familial culture is superior to the French. A packer in the textile industry says: "Here, we often hear that a father has slept with his daughter. This is a catastrophe for us. Our parents, they don't know. If someone tells them there is a father who slept with his daughter, they become sick, they go crazy. This is how I react when I hear that a father slept with his daughter. I see this as an enormous earthquake." In a particularistic move, some explicitly link these cultural differences with Islam, suggesting that Christians cannot be as moral as Muslims.

Discussion

The goal of this paper was to analyze how workers in France and the United States demonstrate or rebut the notion of racial inequality. More specifically, I focused on the evidences they provide to establish the equality or absence thereof, between whites and African Americans in the United States, and whites and North African immigrants in France. Simultaneously, I analyze the criteria they use to incorporate the other into their own group, or to establish social membership. Hence, I illuminate how the cultural logic of racism functions across two societies.

At the end of the twentieth century, racism cannot find a justification in itself. Hence the importance of exploring the full range of evidence used to demonstrate or rebut the inferiority of the other. "Common nationality," "children of God," "same needs," "all human beings," "as successful:" these are all principles of equivalence used by respondents to demonstrate that people belong to a same category as a matter of principle. They are also ways of drawing boundaries between "us" and "them," and again, of using particular kinds of evidence to create closure and to incorporate people into a single community.

The rhetorics of racism and anti-racism are shaped by the broader moral worldview of respondents. North Africans and African Americans more explicitly describe their own culture as morally superior to that of majority groups. In contrast, in the two majority groups, racism is expressed largely through a moral critique of the values of racial minorities, particularly concerning self-reliance, individualism, and family values. In this, the men I interviewed resemble participants in national surveys, at least in the United States.[32] The use of universal criteria of evaluation combined with a negative assessment of minority groups in reference to these criteria allows white respondents to be racist without perceiving themselves as bigots.[33] Indeed, in both countries, racist respondents do not discuss the superiority of their own culture explicitly: it suffices for them to evaluate everyone using their own criteria, which they perceive as neutral and which are *de facto* dominant. This suggests that, contrary to the liberal myth, the use of universalistic arguments is as conducive to exclusion as is the use of particularistic arguments.

This moral/cultural argument resembles in some respects familiar arguments offered over the last twenty years by social scientists concerned with the place of morality and culture in new forms of racism. Indeed, theories of symbolic racism (Sears 1988), modern racism (McConahay 1986), new racism (Barker 1981), differentialist racism (Taguieff 1988), and laissez-faire racism (Bobo and Smith 1998) all point to the ways in which the majority excludes or discriminates against minorities in the name of moral *qua* racial differences. However, whereas these various theories have tended to predefine which moral traits majority groups reject, again, the present chapter documents empirically the types of cultural cues on the basis of which moral boundaries are drawn.

Major differences exist in the cultural tools that French and Americans have at their disposal for demonstrating and rebutting racial inequality in their countries. Most importantly, in the United States, interviewees more often explain racial differences with reference to biology, history, and psychology, and use market-related arguments.[34] In contrast, these arguments are very rarely used by French workers I talked to,[35] who more exclusively refer to specifically cultural and religious explanations in accounting for racial inequality. They also have more structural explanations than Americans do and at times ground their racism in political culture and their anti-racism in egalitarian and solidaristic principles. However, "racists" in both countries believe racism is a universal trait, justifying their commitment to limiting the improvement of minority groups.[36]

Turning to the two minority groups, data suggest that African Americans and North Africans use similar types of strategies to cope with racism: they oppose solidarity and human warmth on the one hand to egotism and individualism on the other. They put the former above the latter and describe themselves as warmer and more solidaristic than majority groups, drawing moral and racial boundaries simultaneously. Both groups ground their superiority in their distinctive historical experience, religious or cultural identity, as Muslims or former slaves, using distinctively particularistic arguments. Both groups also evoke biological arguments to demonstrate similarity among all human beings, suggesting that we all have the same needs and values. However, African Americans argue for equality on the basis of competence and income, whereas North Africans do not. The latter are slightly more likely to use individual strategies to demonstrate equality than African Americans, providing evidence that they, personally, are good people.

These differences are intriguing at a time when the National Front is maintaining its popularity in France (gaining approximately 15 percent of the national vote) and when racial politics continue to shape most major political debates in the United States, including welfare and crime reform. More research is needed to compare the content (and frequency) of the racist rhetorics present in the public sphere in the two countries with that of the men I interviewed.

Some of the cross-national differences described above – in particular, the relative preponderance of cultural arguments in France in contrast to biological, market, and other types of arguments in the United States – could be explained in part by the structure of our comparison, which focuses on the one hand on Muslim immigrants to France who are clearly culturally differentiated from the majority, religiously and otherwise; and on the other hand, on native (African) Americans, who in principle should share a common culture with the white majority. This asymmetry in the populations under consideration cannot fully account for our findings. Indeed, based on an analysis of indicators such as ethnic intermarriage and transmission of the language of origin, Tribalat (1992) shows that North African immigrants are not remarkably less well integrated into French society than are other immigrant groups. Furthermore, in the United States, data on divergence in linguistic patterns across racial groups point to the fact that the culture of African Americans is increasingly differentiated from that of Euro-Americans (Glazer 1996). Hence, North African immigrants and African Americans might be more similar in their degree of cultural differentiation from the majority population of France and the United States than one might expect *a priori*. However, to explore this issue further, data at national level on the degree of cultural differentiation between majority and minority groups in the two countries are needed.

National differences in the relative salience of various types of arguments can be accounted for by elements of cultural repertoires available in the two countries. If in France, cultural explanations of racial differences are relatively more prevalent than in the United States, it is in part because the diffusion of a French *qua* universal culture among immigrants and within the population of former colonies has historically been a central component of France's national identity defined through its civilizing mission[37] – this is particularly important given that the colonial legacy reinforced views of Muslims as inherently morally flawed and culturally backward.[38] Furthermore, whereas European immigrants who came to France in previous eras were assimilated relatively easily into the working class, in part because of the integrative role of institutions such as the Communist Party, the army, and the schools (Noiriel 1992), contemporary Left-wing and Right-wing politicians share the conviction that North African immigrants are nearly un-assimilable (Schain 1996, p. 14). Finally, whereas the French republican model is not supportive of expressions of ethnic and racial identity in the public sphere, but confines them to the private sphere,[39] in the United States, the political tradition is based on a pluralist interest-group model that encourages both assimilation and the expression of identity politics in the public sphere. In the 1990s, French politicians are vigorously reaffirming the republican model; they cite American-style ethnic or civil rights politics as leading to social balkanization and as threatening French national identity in the context of cultural globalization (Hollifield 1994)

Along the same lines, national differences in the use of market arguments in demonstrating racial inequality and equality can be explained by how such arguments speak to central themes in the political and civic culture of each country. As suggested by Esping-Anderson (1990), Dobbin (1994), and others, in France the market is not viewed as a legitimate mechanism of distribution of resources and positions as it is in the United States; instead, it is construed as producing inequality and its pernicious effects are perceived as correctable through state intervention. To quote Wievorka (1996a, p. 9), liberalism is understood as "incompatible with the maintenance of a 'French exception' which is expressed in particular in the French public conception of public service and therefore of collective solidarity."

Finally, if biological arguments have often been downplayed in the French context as compared with the American context, it is in part because evolutionist and geneticist ideas, including the view that races are clearly distinct entities, are associated in France with a notion of progress promoted by the American neo-liberal model of society (Wievorka 1996b). This model is rejected because it is incompatible with the republican model. Furthermore, it presents itself as the ultimate model of social organization and posits the market as a legitimate mechanism of distribution of resources. In contrast, as documented by Bobo, Kluegel, and Smith (1996), a number of historical forces have sustained the notion of the biological inferiority of African Americans during the Jim Crow era, which notion is now considerably weakened but still survives as suggested by the remarkable popularity of Herrnstein and Murray's *The Bell Curve* (1994). Smith (1993, p. 553) also points out that racialist scientific writings gained considerable popularity during as late a period as the 1920s, suggesting that "Americans favored scientific accounts of biological differences to explain their hierarchies because these accounts comported [an] Enlightenment attachment to rationalism." Racist readings of the Bible were also "immensely important," feeding the notion that Americans are chosen people especially favored by God. Hence, egalitarian inclusiveness did not become the norm until the 1960s, and to this day, elaborate theories of racial and gender hierarchy remain embodied "in laws governing naturalization, immigration, deportation, voting rights, electoral institutions, judicial procedures, and economic rights" (Smith 1993, p. 559).

This paper should be read as an empirically systematic effort to contribute to our understanding of national differences in the rules of inclusion and exclusion. It aims at enriching our grasp of the articulation between racism and national cultural repertoires. Much remains to be done, and I hope elsewhere to be able to explore in greater details this relationship in its full complexity.

Notes

Earlier versions of this paper were presented at the Conference on "Culture and Hatred in France," at Dartmouth College; the Princeton-Rutgers Conference on the Sociology of Culture; the Department of Sociology, Cornell University; the Department of Sociology, City University of New York-Graduate Center; the Department of Sociology and Anthropology, Tel Aviv University; the Institute for French Studies, New York University; the Program on Culture and Society, University of California at San Diego; the annual meetings of the American Sociological Association, New York, August 1996; and the 1996/7 Visiting Scholars' seminar, Russell Sage Foundation. I gratefully acknowledge the support that this research received, namely fellowships from the German Marshall Fund of the United States, the Russell Sage Foundation, and the John Simon Guggenheim Memorial Foundation, and a grant from the National Science Foundation (SES 92–13363). I also wish to thank Joe Feagin, Jennifer Hochschild, Eva Illouz, Riva Kastoryano, Annette Lareau, Herman Lebovics, Gérard Noiriel, Martin Schain, and Howard Winant for their helpful comments, and Cheryl Seleski for her editorial assistance. I also thank the members of the Princeton-Paris Project on Evaluative Models for their many insightful comments. Finally, for its hospitality I thank the School of Social Science of the Institute for Advanced Study, where this paper was revised.

1 For the purpose of this paper, I borrow from Aptheker (1992) in defining anti-racism as a rhetoric aimed at disproving racial inferiority. Drawing on Goldberg (1993, p. 98), I define racism as a rhetoric aimed at promoting exclusion based on racial membership and produced by a dominant group against a dominated group. While sociologists such as Van den Berghe (1978), Winant (1994), and others have called for or written comparative studies that explore historically specific forms of racism, Bowser (1995) makes a case for the study of racism and anti-racism from a comparative perspective.

2 The opposition between "us" and "them" is a central feature of racism (Blumer 1958; Guillaumin 1972; Memmi 1965) and of inter-group relations (Barth 1969; Moscovici 1984; Tajfel and Turner 1985; Turner 1987).

3 Following Sniderman, I take these descriptions of categories of individuals to be revealing of broader social and political attitudes. Sniderman (1985, p. 16) points out that "The average citizen, though he (or she) may know little about politics, knows whom he likes, and still more important perhaps, whom he dislikes. This can be a sufficient basis for figuring out a consistent policy stance." In his view, this is particularly true of racial attitudes and of race-targeted policies.

4 This focus on the use of evidence in rhetoric is borrowed in part from Latour (1983), Boltanski and Thévenot (1991), and from discourse analysts studying how disputes and conflicts shape argumentation (Billig 1987).

5 Aristotle defined rhetoric as the art of discovering available means of persuasion in a given case. Accordingly, I use the word "rhetoric" to describe *established rules* of how to vouch for certain claims or the *conventional and widely shared mental maps* that people mobilize to demonstrate an idea. Ultimately, this type of endeavor would aim at documenting alternative systems of thought that organize discourse and guide the formulation of new arguments. It would also aim at establishing a "storehouse of codified ways of thinking, seeing, and communicating that may be tested for goodness-of-fit to the matter at hand" (Simons 1990, p. 11).

6 Using a national sample, Kluegel and Bobo (1993) contrast individualist and structuralist accounts of the black/white gap in socio-economic status: individualist accounts attribute the inferiority of blacks to character, culture, and genes, whereas structuralist accounts blame the "system," focusing on racism or institutional arrangements. Similarly, drawing on in-depth interviews conducted with white Bay Area residents in 1975, Apostles et al. (1983) identify various modes of explanation of racial differences, differentiating between individual and environmental explanations. These authors identify six modes of explanation that focus on various causes or sources of racial differences and inequalities: supernatural (cause = God); genetic (cause = laws of nature); individualist (cause = free will); radical (cause = white oppressors); environmental (cause = social factors); and cultural (cause = cultural dissimilarity, which the authors view as a form of genetic or environmental explanation: ibid. chap. 2). Whereas the interviews conducted by Apostles et al. explicitly and systematically probed respondents on the causes of racial differences, I examine explanations that emerged spontaneously from my interviewees' descriptions of the types of people they like and dislike. On explanations of racial inequality, see also Sniderman 1985.

7 The term "universalism" is used differently in sociology, in the French literature on racism, in anthropology, and in philosophy. The functionalist literature
in sociology compares cultural orientations cross-nationally along a number of
dimensions including "universalism/particularism." A universalistic orientation consists in believing that "all people shall be treated according to the same
criteria (e.g. equality before the law)," while a particularistic orientation is
predicated upon the belief that "individuals shall be treated differently according to their personal qualities or their particular membership in a class or
group" (Lipset 1979, p. 209). In the French literature on racism, universalism
is opposed not to particularism, but to differentialism. For instance, Taguieff
(1988, p. 164) opposes a universalistic racism (that posits that *we* are the
humanity) and a differentialist racism (that posits that *we* are the best). The
anthropological literature opposes a universalism that posits an absolute and
shared human essence – which includes the liberal notions of freedom and
equality – to a relativism that affirms the diversity of cultural identities. Finally,
the philosophical literature juxtaposes a universalism defined through shared
moral orientations or Platonic ideals (the good, the right, the just) and communitarianism, which stresses moral norms that emerge from the collective life
of groups (e.g. Rasmussen 1990). In this paper, drawing in part on Walzer's
(1994) notion of thick and thin morality, I contrast universalism, defined as the
application of abstract general standards to all, to particularism, defined as the
use of standards that are specific to certain groups.

8 Boltanski and Thévenot (1991) are concerned with constraints prevailing in
situations of disputation pertaining to justice. More specifically, they analyze
situations where individuals want to show that their actions serve the common
good. They posit that to achieve this, individuals refer to principles of justice
that are shared by a community of people; this requires first defining the community by demonstrating similarities or equivalence between individuals that
ground their common identity (Thévenot 1992, p. 228; Dosse 1995, p. 190).
These authors are more concerned than I am with the rules that must be followed to establish similarities or equivalence in different types of realms of
justice (what they call "*cités*"; ibid. p. 236; for a summary, see Wagner 1994b).
However, like these authors, I stress that establishing equivalence requires
demonstrating that units share characteristics that include them in larger categories, as is the case when my respondents argue that whites and blacks are
equal because they have the same human needs or physiological features.

9 From a historical perspective, see also the classic studies of Fredrickson
(1971) and Jordan (1968).

10 Despite the absence of systematic efforts, scholars have long been concerned
with the topic. For instance, the American philosopher Goldberg (1993, p.
39) stresses the central role played by moral distinctions in processes of racial
exclusion, arguing that cultural arguments are more salient than biological
arguments about racialization under modernity. In the British literature on
racism, Small (1994, p. 98) suggests that working-class men promote racialized ideologies revolving around sex and sports, but he does not examine
empirically whether these themes are more salient than others in working-
class discourses. Finally, Balibar (1991) also suggests that biological racism
has been historically strong in Anglo-Saxon countries "where they continue

the tradition of social Darwinism and eugenics while directly coinciding at points with the political objectives of an aggressive neo-liberalism." Essed's (1991) study of perceptions of racism among Dutch and American women is exceptional in its use of a delimited corpus of interviews to document the framework within which racist experiences are interpreted, which framework concerns in part (although marginally) the mobilization of biological and cultural evidence.

11 On the notion of national cultural repertoire, see Lamont 1995.

12 This study is part of a larger research project that compares upper-middle-class and working-class men in France and the United States. The working-class interviews are paired with interviews I conducted with upper-middle-class men – I interviewed men only, because they exercise most control in the workplace. The bulk of the interviews concerns how respondents draw boundaries between the people they like and those they dislike, whom they feel inferior and superior to, and whom they feel similar to and different from. Respondents were encouraged to answer these questions with reference to people in general, and to specific individuals they know, at work and elsewhere. Discussions of racism generally emerged while exploring these issues. In the rare cases where race was not salient, I probed respondents at the very end of the interview on whether they perceived similarities and differences between *whites* and *blacks* in the American case, and North Africans and the French in the French case. I adopt this indirect approach because interviewees often present facework and downplay racial prejudice when explicitly questioned on racism. I acknowledge that they may produce several types of discourse on racism adapted to various audiences (close kin and friends, co-workers, outsiders, a white North American female like me, and so forth). Each of these discourses can be tapped for what it tells us about the social representations that respondents have of the other and of themselves. None of these discourses exhausts the reality of racism, yet each enriches our understanding of it.

13 North African interviewees identified themselves as North African, Algerian, Moroccan, Tunisian, or as Kabyle or Berber originating from Morocco, Tunisia, or Algeria. Similarly, African American interviewees include only individuals who identified themselves as such. All North African respondents are legal immigrants and all but a few have been in France for more than twenty years. None has taken French citizenship although several have children who are French or who plan to claim French citizenship when they turn 21. North Africans immigrants make up 8 percent of the French population (Arnaud 1986, p. 16).

14 None of the French respondents described themselves as immigrants, and all non-black American respondents were Caucasian and born in the United States. All respondents are between 25 and 65 years of age.

15 In most cases, respondents were first sent a letter that described the project and asked for their participation. These letters were followed by a phone call to screen potential participants for the various criteria described above. I would then conduct the interview with qualified respondents in their home or at a location of their choice. All interviews were recorded with the respondent's permission.

16 By using in-depth interviews instead of ethnographic observation, I sacrifice depth to breadth. Furthermore, while interviews cannot tap racism "in action," they can tap broader cultural frameworks that are transportable from one context of action to another.

17 Racist statements against immigrants were comparatively rare in interviews I conducted with Americans. Indeed, *blacks* were more often the object of racist comments. This resonates with Smith's (1990) analysis of images associated with various ethnic and racial groups in the United States. He shows (p. 11) that *blacks* are consistently rated as further from whites than members of other minority groups that include large numbers of immigrants. The mean score of *blacks* on a scale of group difference from *whites* is -6.29 compared to -5.70 for Hispanic Americans, -2.65 for Asian Americans, -2.32 for Southern *whites*, and +0.75 for Jews. On the relative importance of racism targeted at North Africans as compared to that targeted at other groups in France, see Jackson et al. (1992, pp. 252–3).

18 It is worth explicitly stressing that this paper does not aim to: (1) determine whether, how, and how often specific respondents simultaneously upheld racist and anti-racist positions; (2) analyze the effect of racist rhetorics on racial inequality; (3) explore variations in racial boundary work across sub-categories of workers (e.g. between French workers who are former Communist militants and French workers who are not); (4) explore the connections between the racism and anti-racism of lay people and that formulated by political parties such as the French National Front; (5) compare the rhetoric used by racists against African Americans and North African immigrants and used against other people of color or other immigrant groups; and (6) examine whether the same types of arguments are used to rebut racism aimed at different racial and ethnic groups.

19 Some of these "white racists" combined racist and anti-racist arguments in the course of the interviews. They were classified as "white racists" because their arguments about racial equality stressed racial differences rather than similarities (in line with our working definitions of racism and anti-racism presented in note 1).

20 More Americans have neutral positions or do not discuss racial inequality. It is the case for 20 percent of the American white-collar workers and 30 percent of the American blue-collar workers, compared to respectively 6 percent and 26 percent of their French counterparts.

21 Lamont (forthcoming) provides a detailed discussion of moral boundaries and of their relationship with racial boundaries (chap. 3).

22 Frankenberg (1993) would not consider this type of anti-racism – which she calls race or color-evasiveness – truly anti-racist: it supports assimilation and white culture by downplaying differences, hence "preserving the power structure inherent in essential racism" (p. 147). She suggests that affirming racial diversity is the only truly anti-racist stance possible. Her research, which draws on in-depth interviews with thirty Bay Area white women, contrasts three types of discourse about racial differences: essentialist racism which stresses biological inequality; color-evasiveness which promotes assimilation and downplays cultural and biological differences; and race-cognizance (or multiculturalism) which affirms the cultural autonomy of people of color and

recognizes that race makes a difference in people's life. Frankenberg argues that while these three types of discourse coexist in contemporary America, color-evasiveness predominates. Her typology is not detailed enough to describe the various types of anti-racist arguments that emerge from my data. Furthermore, this typology attaches much importance to race-cognizance, a stance absent from my interviews.

23 Wellman (1993, chap. 6) remarks that several of his respondents also view the market as an equalizer: home ownership, for instance, makes people equal. However, he also notes that the market makes people responsible for their lower position in a hierarchical system (p. 57); that it valorizes the achievements of individuals who have a certain level of socio-economic success (p. 168); and that it reinforces faith in the American dream and the notion that what people have done with their life should be a prime criterion of evaluation.

24 This is what Miles (1989, chap. 1) refers to as a lineage account of racial inequality, which stresses common descent. He suggests that this account gained in popularity between the sixteenth and the nineteenth century, after which it was superseded by scientific racism that views human species as divided into permanent and discrete groups. Scientific racism had an important role in shaping modern lay discourse on racial *qua* biological inequality.

25 Republicanism prohibits the affirmation of particularistic identities (having to do with religion, ethnicity, gender, and so forth) in the public sphere by not recognizing their legitimacy as bases for claim-making. It presumes that the assimilation of minority groups is compatible with universal interest, i.e. the interest of the majority (on this issue, see Noiriel 1992, chap. 3; for an analysis of the ways in which state intervention reinforces multiculturalism in practice, see Schain 1996). It should be noted that France was slow to pass anti-discrimination laws toward immigrants and ethnic minorities because, according to Freeman (1979, p. 156), French decision-makers believed that all citizens were equally protected by French law because they perceived French society as *de facto* embodying republican principles. Furthermore, Hollifield (1994) notes as an egalitarian and universalistic right-based regime, republicanism extends to immigrants the social, civil, and human rights (but not the political rights) available to citizens. Although, as several analysts have argued, this republican model is now in crisis, it still largely prevails.

26 One could also say that these principles are questioned when they are applied beyond the national borders.

27 Many authors have commented on the fact that French racism construes Islam as a major obstacle to assimilation and that it poses a concrete threat to French society. According to Wihtol de Wenden (1991), since the beginning of the 1980s, North African immigrants have played an important symbolic role in discourses on the loss of French identity and the fear of national invasion. Indeed, "immigration is visualized as inevitable, inexorable, and irrevocably destructive, synonymous with the abdication of the West" (p. 107).

28 Smith (1993) points out that the American liberal democratic tradition, as described in Tocqueville's *Democracy in America* (1980 [1835]), stresses the absence of one type of ascriptive hierarchy in American society – that based on monarchical and aristocratic lineage – and this absence makes the United

States appear egalitarian in comparison with Europe. He argues that American political culture is also shaped by other political traditions, such as racism, nativism, and patriarchy, which justify that until recently, ascriptive hierarchies, such as that based on race and gender, have remained a mainstay of American society.

29 It is telling that in the United States, the main policies developed to deal with racial inequality are affirmative action policies aimed at creating equal opportunity, whereas in France the government has promoted a policy of social solidarity to fight exclusion. White Americans defend egalitarianism by supporting the creation of equal opportunity programs aimed at creating equal conditions of competition, as opposed to equal outcomes. Hence, Fischer et al. (1996) show that American welfare and redistributive policy choices are less oriented toward social solidarity than the welfare programs of a number of European countries. For Taylor (1992, p. 51), equal dignity, non-differentiation of roles, or the sharing of universal capacities are the very basis of the republican conception that grounds French society and, contrary to liberalism, this conception negates natural and social differences and promotes universal solidarity against individualism. On this point, see also Nicolet 1992. For a comparison of the relationship between the state and the common interest in France and the United States, see Rangeon 1986.

30 However, note that the findings of Apostles et al. (1983) differ from mine: 53 percent of their respondents adopted an explanation of racial inequality that is structural in nature (42 percent adopted environmental explanations, while 11 percent adopted a radical explanation). In contrast, only 19 percent adopted an individualist explanation. Again, their 1975 survey is based on a random sample of Bay Area residents.

31 For a more detailed analysis of North African rebuttals of French racism, see Lamont forthcoming.

32 Using the 1990 General Social Survey, Smith (1990, p. 90) shows that *blacks* are perceived by whites and members of other ethnic groups as most different from whites in their ability to be self-supporting (the difference between their rating on this dimension and that of whites is -2.08; this compares with a differential rating of -1.60 for wealth, -1.24 for work ethic, -1.00 for violence, and -0.93 for intelligence. Along the same lines, 21 percent of non-*blacks* who participated in a 1993 national survey agreed that African American men enjoyed living on welfare (National Conference 1994, p. 72). Finally, 69 percent of *whites* surveyed in a 1972 national study explained *blacks'* continued disproportionate poverty by the fact that they don't try hard enough and 52 percent explained it by the fact that black culture is dysfunctional (Sniderman 1985, p. 30).

33 Feagin and Vera (1995), Sears (1988), Wellman (1993), and others also point that Americans who articulate their critique of *blacks* around the defense of American values, such as individualism, can view themselves as non-racist moral people because they do not construe *blacks* as inherently inferior.

34 Biological arguments are also popular among American participants in national surveys: 31 percent of the participants in a 1972 national survey explained the disproportionate poverty of *blacks* by racially determined genetic defects (Sniderman 1985). Hochschild (1995, p. 113) also cites data

showing that 12 percent of whites agree that African Americans have less native intelligence than other groups.

35 Rex (1979, p. 100) argues that skin color has not traditionally been a strong social marker in France, in part because it is not a reliable indicator of colonial status. Furthermore, color discrimination was inconsistent with the republican model which downplays biological differences between races. However, Silverman (1992) notes that since the 1970s, France has experienced a turn toward a more racialized view of immigration, which he perceives to be part of a broader process of racialization of national boundaries opposing Europeans to non-Europeans throughout the continent. Indeed, in the fall of 1996, Le Pen made an important declaration on the "*inégalité des races*" that was vehemently denounced by the Right and the Left.

36 Other types of evidence are absent from both the rhetoric of racism and anti-racism deployed in both countries: most respondents view the sources of racism in its victim and not in the characteristics of its perpetrator. Furthermore, they do not refer to legal arguments to demonstrate racial equality. This absence is surprising because France as much as the United States has a strong tradition of grounding equality in legal rights.

37 In the words of Lebovics (1996, p. 31), during the colonial era, the French came to equate French culture with civilization, and to promote the idea that "the colonial people of Greater France were, or could be, French." For Freeman (1979, p. 32), this view was based on "a firm commitment to the universality of the French culture and language and to its infinite adaptability to circumstances." On this topic, see also Mauco (1977, pp. 203–14). However, the assimilation of immigrants into the American nation is also central to American national identity.

38 Contemporary accounts of the moral character of North African immigrants are shaped by accounts from soldiers, missionaries, and other agents of colonization (Rex 1979). Horne, in his authoritative study of the Algerian war (1977, p. 54), suggests that the dominant stereotype of the North African male among the French colonials was that he "was incorrigibly, idle, and incompetent; he only understood force; he was an innate criminal and an instinctive rapist."

39 See note 25 above.

3 Sexual harassment in France and the United States: activists and public figures defend their definitions

Abigail Cope Saguy

A saleswoman is continually badgered by her superior. He tells her that she has a "nice ass" and that he would like to see her naked. He asks her out frequently, despite her continual rejections. He touches her when they talk. At first, he would touch her shoulder or her waist, but today, he runs his hand down her thigh. When she pushes him away, he says: "Loosen up. Are you some kind of prude?"

Is this sexual harassment? Why or why not? Various answers are typically offered to this question. One might claim that it is sexual harassment because it is degrading and makes the woman feel threatened. Alternatively, one could note the negative impact the behavior has on this employee's work and point out that she is targeted because she is a woman, which is discriminatory. On the other hand, one might respond that such conduct is not sexual harassment but only normal flirtation. One might even argue that the woman could deflect such behavior if she chose to, and if she does not, she probably welcomes it. One could conclude that the behavior does not constitute sexual harassment since the woman's supervisor has not dismissed, demoted, or otherwise penalized her in any "tangible" way. While one could focus on the supervisor's intent, one could alternatively prioritize the woman's perceptions.

Each of these responses reveals different conceptualizations of sexual harassment as a social harm and legal wrong. Using the concept of national cultural repertoires of evaluation, developed in this volume, I will explain why certain types of justifications are more common in the United States than in France and vice versa. I will show how, in the United States, the heavy reliance on market logic and industrial logic (i.e. arguments about professionalism and productivity) (Boltanski and Thévenot 1991), and ("minority") group-based conceptions of inequality shape definitions of sexual harassment. Alternatively, I will demonstrate how French definitions of sexual harassment are shaped by political and legal concepts of individual rights, violence, and abuse of power. Finally, I will discuss how members of one French feminist association, intent on expanding sexual harassment law, draw on American,

European, and Canadian cultural and material resources in defining sexual harassment, while those opposing such an expansion do so in part by denouncing perceived American cultural imperialism and insisting on the specificity of French culture.

I use the term "gender" to refer to the social implications of being a man or a woman (see, for example, West and Zimmerman 1987). Expressions like "take it like a man" imply that men should be tough, while a "woman's touch" assumes that women are innately more sensitive. Gender theorists show how gender varies over time and space, and how the politicization of certain issues can challenge ingrained assumptions of gender. The term "marital rape," coined in the 1970s, for instance, dramatically redefined a practice that until then was legitimized by a legal system that only recognized stranger rape. Men were assumed to have unqualified sexual access to their wives. Women were expected to be always sexually available to their husbands. To speak of "marital rape" was to develop a competing theme of female autonomy and sexual desire (see Brownmiller 1975, pp. 380–1).

Likewise, formulating sexual harassment as a social harm and legal wrong subverts older concepts of gender and sexuality. It sends a message to men that they can no longer treat women as sexual objects but have to respect their autonomy. It challenges the assumption that men have sexual access to all women who do not explicitly object. Women are told that putting up with their bosses' or colleague's unwelcome advances is not "part of the job." Considering the stakes involved – sexual, political, and economic power – it is not surprising that sexual harassment incites such heated political debate. The intense passion and disagreement surrounding sexual harassment forces people to make explicit otherwise taken-for-granted views regarding not only gender but also politics, work, law, and the public/private divide. For these reasons, differences in how sexual harassment is conceptualized in France and the United States provide a "strategic research site" for exploring the theoretical questions posed in this volume (Merton 1987).

Methodology

This chapter is part of a larger study of the different ways sexual harassment is conceptualized in France and the United States. The study draws on a wide range of data. To understand legal differences in how sexual harassment has been defined in the two countries, the study examines the major French and American sexual harassment legal texts, including statutes and jurisprudence (Saguy 1998). To compare media depictions of sexual harassment in the countries, 590 randomly sampled articles from the French and American press were examined, using a complex coding scheme and statistical analysis (Saguy 1999a).[1] The articles span from the mid 1970s, when the term is first coined, until December 31, 1998. During the summer of 1997, a series of short telephone interviews with representatives of twenty-three French branches of large multinational corporations were conducted. Finally, between the summers of 1995 and 1998, over sixty interviews with French and American feminist activists, public figures, lawyers, human resource personnel, and union activists were conducted (Saguy 1999b, forthcoming). In this chapter, I focus primarily on legal definitions and on the interviews with the public figures and feminist activists, although I do occasionally refer to the other data to support my arguments.

I conducted the bulk of the interviews with the activists and public figures during the summer and fall of 1995. At that time, sexual harassment was a relatively new issue. The term "sexual harassment" or *harcèlement sexuel* only had meaning in some feminist and legal circles from the mid 1970s and mid 1980s, in the United States and France, respectively. In 1986, the Supreme Court first ruled that "sexual harassment" was a violation of Title VII of the Civil Rights Act of 1964.[2] Yet, it was not until 1991, when Supreme Court judge nominee, Clarence Thomas, was accused of sexual harassment by his former hierarchical subordinate Anita Hill, prompting extensive Senate hearings, that the American mass media began to report heavily on this topic (Saguy 1999a). While there were only nine articles published in *The New York Times, Time* and *Newsweek* in 1989 and only 48 in 1990, there were 198 published in these publications in 1991 and no less than 107 per year thereafter (Saguy 1999a). French Legislative debates over sexual harassment in 1991 and 1992 provoked public debate of this issue that went beyond the feminist associations that had pioneered in this area.[3] At seven articles published in the leading newspaper *(Le Monde)* and two leading news magazines *(L'Express, Le Nouvel Observateur),* French media coverage of sexual harassment *in France* peaked in 1992 and leveled at between one to six per year thereafter.[4]

I regard the respondents as cultural entrepreneurs. Unlike the general population, of which they are *not* representative, each of the women interviewed has been actively engaged in shaping the public meaning of sexual harassment. The women I call "activists" are involved members of one of two national associations – the *Association Européenne Contre les Violences Faites aux Femmes au Travail* (AVFT – European Association Against Violence towards Women at Work), in France, and *9to5: National Association of Working Women* (9to5), in the United States.[5] These include but are not limited to: lobbying, raising public awareness through tracts and publications, support for victims through legal advice and emotional support, and research on sexual harassment and other forms of gender discrimination or violence towards women. As these activists try to create and develop conceptualizations of sexual harassment, they are forced to confront cultural and material constraints and draw on social resources. In so doing, they both reveal such constraints and resources, and suggest how they can be changed.

In order to cover a wider spectrum of positions, I also interviewed six "public figures," who I expected would understand sexual harassment differently. Each is considered an "expert" by the media on issues of gender and sexuality in general, or sexual harassment in particular, yet approaches these issues differently from one another. Like the activists, these "public figures," many of whom are or have also been activists, have been engaged in a public contest over the meaning of sexual harassment.[6] The arguments they deploy are therefore interesting, not because they are representative of the general population, which they are not, but because they are innovative. The three American public figures are theorist, lawyer, and law professor Catharine MacKinnon; social critic and professor of humanities Camille Paglia; and lawyer, syndicated columnist, radio commentator, and national spokesperson for the conservative movement Phyllis Schlafly. The three French public figures are intellectual and activist Marie-Victoire Louis; writer, social critic, and professor of philosophy Elisabeth Badinter; and former Secretary of Women's Rights and author Françoise Giroud.

Elisabeth Badinter is a well-known intellectual, closely affiliated with the French Socialist Party, who studies male-female social relations in France, and is often interviewed by the mass media on subjects concerning gender (Badinter 1986, p. 1992). In addition to having served as Secretary of Women's Rights from 1974 to 1976 under the Centre-Right President Giscard d'Estaing, Françoise Giroud is a nationally renowned writer and editor, has published abundantly on the topic of gender and sexuality, and is often cited in the mass media (Giroud and Lévy 1993). Marie-Victoire Louis is a self-identified radical feminist, scholar and activist who represents a vocal challenge to the French establishment. In 1985, she co-founded the AVFT, which led the campaign for a sexual harassment law, and she was serving as president of this association in 1995 when the interview was conducted. In *Le droit de cuissage* (1994), she explored the French history of sexual violence towards women.

Catharine MacKinnon is known worldwide for her pioneering and influential legal writings, especially on sexual harassment – the term she is most responsible for promoting – and pornography. Her 1979 book, *Sexual Harassment of Working Women*, now provides the basis for sexual harassment law in the United States. Camille Paglia and Phyllis Schlafly are among the most vocal critics of this legal interpretation, its political and social implications, and what they perceive to be "American feminism."[7] Camille Paglia has received enormous media attention for her provocative theories of gender and sexuality and her virulent criticism of "mainstream American feminism" (Paglia 1991, 1992). Since the 1970s, Phyllis Schlafly has been a more traditional opponent of "American feminism," arguing that the women's movement undermines "traditional values" of the family and female domesticity. She is a highly visible spokesperson for the conservative movement and the Christian Right.[8]

In addition to these six public figures I interviewed twelve activists – six in each country.[9] The sample size is directly constrained by the small number of core French activists – all of whom I interviewed – at the AVFT during the two years in which I conducted the interviews.[10] The AVFT is based in Paris, though its activists receive calls from and meet with people outside Paris.[11] Four of the AVFT members interviewed were paid employees and two were volunteers at the time of the interview. I initially interviewed both 9to5 hot-line volunteers in the New York-New Jersey-Connecticut-Pennsylvania area, since there were no paid employees in this region, and one former 9to5 volunteer who, at the time of the interview, was providing independent counseling for a fee. I then expanded my sample to include three of the five "most important activists" among paid 9to5 employees in the nation, according to several leaders at the national headquarters.

The interviews were semi-structured, which means that I tried to cover several topics but allowed each interviewee to introduce themes that she considered relevant. The interviews lasted between 35 minutes and three and a half hours, averaging about one hour and a half. I began each interview by asking: "How do you define sexual harassment?" I then asked the respondent if she considered the legal definition appropriate or whether she took issue with it. We explored any reservation the respondent had with national sexual harassment law, including proscribed remedies. In the interviews with the activists, I asked them about their job and the types of cases they encounter. I asked them to discuss their most difficult cases, especially those that seemed to defy the qualification "sexual harassment." This question revealed contradictions in legal and social definitions of sexual harassment.

In interviews with both activists and public figures, I also presented respondents with a series of vignettes, which describe behavior that might be labeled sexual harassment (see Appendix). The vignettes were used to see how the respondents reacted to specific situations, rather than abstract categories. The first paragraph of this article describes one of the vignettes. After reading the story, I asked the respondent the same question I asked of you, the reader, in the introduction: Is this sexual harassment? Why or why not? The vignettes prompted respondents to offer a variety of arguments, like the ones I suggest in my discussion of this vignette in the introduction. In this chapter, I analyze and compare the range of arguments offered by the four groups of respondents in response to these same vignettes to identify cross-national differences and how they play out differently depending on people's political orientation.

Feminist research, legal theory, and recorded cases provided the inspiration for my vignettes.[12] By systematically varying the hypothetical people's motives, gender, hierarchical position, sexual orientation, relationships with each other, the vignettes reveal the respondents' criteria of evaluation. For instance, the story above, about the saleswoman who is badgered by her superior, explores whether respondents consider the incident "sexual harassment," even though sexual cooperation is not made a requirement of continued employment or advancement. This issue is interesting because of one of the main differences between French and American sexual harassment law. According to French law, sexual harassment involves someone in power, using his position of authority to demand sexual relations from a subordinate.[13] American law, on the other hand, has a category called "hostile environment" that refers precisely to situations in which sexual attention, from a boss or colleague, is so severe or pervasive that it negatively alters the employee's "conditions of work." Through the vignette above, I examine whether the French respondents follow the spirit of their national law by refusing to label the behavior "sexual harassment" since there is no clear threat or coercion involved. Alternatively, I see whether they interpret coercion more broadly to include this kind of persistent sexual attention. I examine whether American respondents consider the behavior in this vignette to be "hostile environment" sexual harassment. Alternatively, I see if they take issue with the law or think the behavior is not sufficiently "severe or pervasive" (legal terms) to qualify. In most cases, I am interested in exploring the ways in which the national differences between French and American legal definitions of sexual harassment affect or are similar to differences found in conceptions of sexual harassment between the two national groups of interviewees.

Sexual harassment between hierarchical peers is addressed by American but not French law. To see whether respondents consider hierarchical authority a prerequisite of sexual harassment, I describe a variation of the vignette above, in which the saleswoman is continually pestered, not by her supervisor, but by a fellow salesman.

French law defines sexual harassment as an abuse of hierarchical power. In this theoretical model, the gender of the supervisor and employee is irrelevant. American law, however, defines sexual harassment as gender discrimination. American feminist legal theorists have argued that sexual harassment is the quintessential form of sex discrimination, because when men harass women – the overwhelming majority of cases – they enact and perpetuate sexism and gender inequality (MacKinnon 1979). Courts have reasoned that sexual harassment of a woman by a man is sex discrimination on the grounds that the woman is targeted because she is a woman. Had she been a man, they have argued, she would not have been victimized. Using parallel logic, the courts have also declared sexual harassment of a man by a woman to be sex discrimination. American sexual harassment jurisprudence is less clear about a person who sexually harasses members of the same sex or members of both sexes.[14] To explore the issue of gender, I included variations in which a female supervisor harasses a saleswoman, a female supervisor harasses a salesman, a female saleswoman harasses a salesman, a male supervisor pesters a salesman, and a male supervisor torments both men and women under his command.

In the course of each interview, I described nine basic vignettes and several variations of each one. At the phase of data analysis, using full interview transcripts, I systematically compared how each respondent evaluated each vignette and justified her position.

The Paris-Princeton meetings, organized by the editors of this volume, shaped the analysis presented here. During these discussions, the French researchers often challenged me to rethink my categories of analysis. This "breaching experiment," as Lamont and Thévenot aptly refer to it in the introduction, sometimes revealed an American bias in my own political and cultural analysis. These confrontations were intellectually and emotionally trying, but they served to hone the analysis in the paper. Marie-Victoire Louis also offered particularly challenging remarks to several drafts of this paper, which forced to me to analyze cultural assumptions that I had taken so much for granted that they seemed irrefutable. Though often painful, this type of intellectual labor is a prerequisite of work that aims to compare different national cultures on their own terms.[15]

In what follows, I draw on the interviews and legal history to discuss some of the major national differences in evaluation that emerge. I focus on themes that are developed elsewhere in this volume: the heavy reliance on market logic and arguments about professionalism, and ("minority") group-based concepts of inequality in the United States and models of political "universalism" in France. In the two sections that follow, I address first the American and then the French case. For each nation, I describe the state of sexual harassment law and analyze some of its main cultural assumptions. I then explore the extent to which respondents reinforce, challenge, or transform these basic assumptions of legal definitions. In the final section, I show how "globalization," or contact with foreign nations and international institutions, can both mitigate and deepen national specificity.

The United States: market, industrial logic, and group-based inequality

In the last chapter, Lamont shows how, compared to the French, American anti-racists appeal more to market mechanisms and especially socio-economic success to refute racism. As a black chemical worker explains, "money makes people equal." Lamont argues that Americans are more likely to regard economic success as providing a key for social acceptance. In contrast, in France, the market is generally not viewed as a legitimate mechanism of distribution of resources and positions. Instead, it is construed as producing inequality, which the state is then expected to remedy through intervention (Dobbin 1994; Esping-Anderson 1990).

This national difference informs French and American views of sexual harassment, including those expressed in formal law.[16] Let us first turn to the American case, where arguments about the market, professionalism, and ("minority") group-based inequality is crucial in defining why sexual harassment is unacceptable. While Americans have several bodies of law at their disposal for protesting sexual harassment in the workplace, the bulk of jurisprudence is based on Title VII of the Civil Rights Act of 1964.[17] This statute makes it illegal employment practice for employers of fifteen or more employees to "fail or refuse to hire or discharge any individual or otherwise discriminate against any individual with respect to his compensation, terms, conditions, or privileges of employment because of such individual's race, color, religion, sex, or national origin."[18] This statute exists to check discrimination that threatens the ideal nature of the market as open and impartial.

It was not until ten years after the passage of Title VII that lawyers first began using it in cases of sexual harassment. In the first cases, women complained that they were fired or compelled to resign after refusing their boss's sexual advances.[19] The courts initially rejected the argument that such behavior constituted sex discrimination. Instead, by calling it "personal," they argued that it did not fall under the jurisdiction of Title VII.

In taking issue with these rulings, feminist legal theorists and other academics argued that this kind of behavior is anything but personal. Rather, they contended that sexual harassment is a form of sex discrimination in employment that should be prohibited by law (Farley 1978; Ginsberg and

Koreski 1977; MacKinnon1979; McGee 1976; *Michigan Law Review* 1978; *Minnesota Law Review* 1979; *NYU Law Review* 1976; Seymour 1979; Taub 1976; Vermeulen 1981). For instance, in her 1979 book, *Sexual Harassment of Working Women*, Catharine MacKinnon (1979, p. 7) argued that sexual harassment is sex discrimination because it disadvantages women in employment, especially through occupational segregation. According to her analysis, sexual harassment at work uses women's employment positions to coerce them sexually, while using their sexual position to coerce them economically. MacKinnon thus drew on and altered what was, at the time, a relatively new legal and cultural category of sex discrimination, but which has become a particularly salient element of an American cultural "tool-kit" (Swidler 1986).

Largely in response to such legal research, in the late 1970s, courts progressively began ruling that sexual harassment was a violation of Title VII.[20] In 1980, relying on work by feminists like MacKinnon and Nadine Taub, the Equal Employment Opportunity Commission (EEOC) – the federal agency responsible for enforcing Title VII – drafted sexual harassment guidelines for the courts (Oppenheimer 1995, p. 115). These guidelines defined sexual harassment as:

Unwelcome sexual advances, requests for sexual favors, and other verbal or physical conduct of sexual nature . . . when:

(1) Submission to such conduct is made either explicitly or implicitly a term or condition of the individual's employment.

(2) Submission to or rejection of such conduct by an individual is used as the basis for employment decisions affecting such individual.

(3) Such conduct has the purpose or effect of unreasonably interfering with an individual's work performance or creating an intimidating, hostile, or offensive working environment (CFR 1604.11(a))

The Supreme Court embraced these guidelines in its first sexual harassment ruling, *Meritor Savings Bank v. Vinson*.[21] In this decision, the court institutionalized in law the two-prong definition created by MacKinnon (1979) and affirmed by the EEOC. In "quid pro quo" sexual harassment, a boss uses official authority to coerce an employee into having sexual relations. In "hostile environment" sexual harassment, no clear ultimatum is offered. Rather, sexual innuendo – by a boss or a peer – is so "severe or pervasive" that it "unreasonably interferes with an individual's work performance." In both cases, *employers* can be sued under Title VII for sexual harassment occurring at their place of work.

By making Title VII the privileged legal avenue for addressing sexual harassment, feminist scholars, lawyers, and judges emphasized: (1) the employment consequences of sexual harassment, and (2) gender inequality.[22] MacKinnon argued that "work is critical to women's survival and independence" and that the government has greater obligation to protect women's rights at work than elsewhere: "Legally, women are not arguably entitled, for example to a marriage free of sexual harassment any more than to one free of rape, nor are women legally guaranteed the freedom to walk down the street or into a court of law without sexual innuendo. *In employment, the government promises more*" (MacKinnon 1979, p. 7, emphasis added). The public status of sexual harassment was thus established by squarely positioning it within the workplace.[23]

Advocates of Title VII sexual harassment law further disputed the idea that sexual harassment is "personal" by showing how it is "based on sex." For instance, MacKinnon (1979, p. 173) argued that sexual harassment is not "merely a parade of interconnected consequences with the potential for discrete repetition by other individuals." Rather, it is a *group-defined injury*, suffered by individuals (usually women) because of their sex.[24] She favored the use of Title VII for addressing sexual harassment (rather than tort law, which applies to harm between individuals) because it clearly conveys the *group injury aspect* of sexual harassment. The focus on group-based employment discrimination is also institutionalized in the structure of the association 9to5. According to an undated letter by 9to5 to its members, "the workplace issues most often raised by hot-line callers include" (in order): Family and Medical Leave law, sexual harassment, gender discrimination, pregnancy discrimination, work and family, computer health and safety, racial discrimination, and pay equity.

I am not arguing that American legal traditions – even Title VII – uniformly or entirely promote a model of group rights. On the contrary, as any first-year law student knows, the dominant legal tradition in the United States is liberal individualism. However, by recognizing that individuals are persecuted or discriminated against because they belong to particular groups, which are officially recognized by institutions like the census, the law does – if inadvertently and impartially – acknowledge group rights (Ehrenreich 1990; Minow 1990, 1997; Scott 1996). Moreover, the United States has institutionalized traditions of categorizing people by group – especially "race" and ethnic – affiliation. For centuries, African Americans were denied basic human and civil rights because of their "race." Today, affirmative action programs use the category of "race" to redistribute power and resources. In "identity politics" racial, gender, religious, and other identities provide a basis for political mobilization (Appiah 1994; Austin 1992; Steinberg 1981). Time and again, the American's women's movement has drawn on arguments about racism to develop claims about sexism (Evans 1989).[25]

The following excerpt, from an interview with an American activist, reveals a common emphasis on both the labor market and on group-based discrimination in the United States. In the course of the interview, I read the first vignette, in which "an employer asks a female job applicant during their interview to spend the weekend with him in San Francisco. He tells her that he will make up his mind about the job after the weekend." I further clarified that the employer is "thinking of a romantic weekend in which they'd be sharing a hotel room." This respondent explains why she considers this to be sexual harassment: though not yet an employee, she is "being looked at as an employee . . . I'd say because she's coming on a job interview to be an employee, at that point, she's covered. And if he wants it to be an intimate rendezvous, and basically says that, then that would be harassment to me." When I ask why, the respondent replies: "Because that's [made] a condition of her employment." When probed about why it is wrong to make sex a condition of someone's employment, the activist laughs and says: "Well I thought that was one of our basic rights, freedom from gender discrimination."

While the American activists rely heavily on market rationale and arguments about group-based discrimination, they also discuss competing themes of non-material losses and personal dignity. For instance, in response to a variation of the vignette described in the introduction, in which a saleswoman is pestered by a colleague, one New Jersey activist says: "Her whole career is threatened. She can't work in that environment. It's a hostile environment. I don't care who's doing it to her. If it's the janitor . . . It's a hostile environment. The impact will be the same. She'll go home and she'll be the same way with her husband, her children, she'll not feel good about herself. You can't work like that." This respondent thus stresses both the threat this behavior poses for the woman's continued employment and the strain it creates in her personal and family life.

Many of the American activists use arguments about professionalism and productivity to condemn sexual innuendo in the workplace that falls short of sexual harassment. For instance, when probed about the risk that over-zealous employers might stamp out playful, harmless, fun flirtation in the workplace, one respondent explains: "Why do people have to . . .? Really they don't have to have everyday seduction and flirtation in the workplace . . . Has it been proven that that helps productivity?"[26] Likewise, Catharine MacKinnon says in her interview: "Somebody ought to get worried about the fact that no work is getting done. And the workplace is not a place for sexual recruitment exclusively. Now people are supposed to be getting things done." These arguments echo those made by human resource departments across the United States that refer to the "bottom line" to ban a range of behavior, like consensual dating or sexist jokes, that fall short of sexual harassment, as legally defined (Saguy 1999b; Weiss 1998).

Of course, American feminists are not concerned about sexual harassment only because of its effects on industrial productivity. In a discussion with Catharine MacKinnon about the way I use the above citation in an earlier draft of this chapter, she points out that even if it were proven that sexual harassment improves productivity, she would still oppose it. Indeed, a common goal among people who call themselves feminists is gender equality not industrial efficiency. Such use of industrial logic by many American respondents is evidence that arguments about professionalism and productivity are particularly effective in legitimizing particular positions in the American context.

The American respondents use analyses based on market logic, industrial logic, or group-based discrimination strategically to strengthen their positions. However, they are not constrained by these arguments. Rather, in the interviews, they often disregard them when they do not provide a resource for condemning a given behavior. For instance, in one variation of the first vignette, I present the following scenario: "A boss is interviewing several men and women for positions as sales representatives. He lets each of them know that if they want the job, they will have to have sexual relations with him." Because the boss harasses both men and women, it is difficult to claim that his behavior is discriminatory, a necessary condition under Title VII.[27]

Notwithstanding, all of the American respondents label this conduct sexual harassment. As one respondent says: "It doesn't matter if he'll sleep with anyone. To insist on that as an aspect of your employment is sexual harassment." Another concurs: "It's sexual harassment for all of them." According to another: "As far as I understand, it's still the unwanted, offensive, usually repeated behavior of a sexual nature." In other words, while respondents are quick to use anti-discrimination arguments when useful, they disregard the discrimination component of sexual harassment when it would limit protection of employees. All of the respondents believe that this vignette illustrates a case of sexual harassment, which suggests that, even in the United States, sexual harassment is only partly conceptualized as a form of gender discrimination.[28] In the interviews, respondents draw on more popular concepts of right and wrong, coercion, abuse, and power that seem to go beyond the definition of sexual harassment as discrimination.[29]

In other instances, respondents use the logic of discrimination and the market to extend legal definitions. The most striking example of this is the frequent condemnation of discrimination against homosexuals. In one of the vignettes, I describe a woman who taunts a young gay man about his sexual preference. Five of the six American activists say that this type of behavior should be considered sexual harassment. The sixth prefers to label it "discrimination on the basis of sexual orientation." All extend the status of protected group to homosexuals, even though sexual orientation is not protected under Title VII or any other federal discrimination law.[30] As one activist explains: "That is sexual harassment. She's discriminating against him. She's calling him a fag. She's saying that he's like one of the girls. She's calling him derogatory names because of his sexual orientation."

Similarly, opponents of strong sexual harassment law also appeal to market principles, but in the name of a free market and individualism. As Schlafly says: "I just don't think we should have a government inspector at every water cooler to catch some man who's a slob." She draws on fiscally conservative politics that commend laissez-faire market models, suggesting that a free labor market is capable of dealing with sexual harassment because people who are mistreated can "get another job." In response to my query about those who might have trouble finding another job, she says that "no one has a right to a job." Such arguments are produced by the (fiscally) conservative movement in the United States, which has no equivalent in France, where the market is expected to be more restricted by social considerations (see Toinet, Kempf, and Lacorne 1989). Such reasoning draws on another popular conception of the public/private divide in the United States, in which the labor market is considered "private" and therefore beyond the scope of state intervention. For years, however, the American government has regulated the labor market out of concern for both employees and employers. In France, of course, state intervention in the market enjoys even greater public support.[31]

Paglia echoes Schlafly's arguments about free market economics and owner's prerogatives, affirming that she "believes in private property." She likens small businesses to fiefdoms and says that a small owner should be free to hire whom he chose and even to have a "harem of women that he wants to sleep with." She qualifies this statement, however, by saying that middle managers are accountable to public interests and should not "sexualize their job." To do so would be "unprofessional." Paglia explains that while a family firm is "private" and should be free from government intervention, large firms "have evolved economically into public institutions," so that outside intervention is appropriate there. Shocking as Paglia's statement about business fiefdoms may appear, her personal demarcation of the public and private, in which smaller enterprises ("the mom and pop companies") are "private" but larger ones are public, echo American political traditions. For instance, as is reviewed above, Title VII, the federal statute on which sexual harassment jurisprudence is founded, only applies to businesses with more than fifteen employees.[32] Smaller business are less accountable to federal control.

American activists do not talk about the rights of small business owners in such terms. However, they do develop the idea that one should be "professional" at work. This means being productive and maintaining social distance with co-workers. As one American activist says: "As a professional, I think about going to work and getting my work done, and having a relationship with a colleague as a professional relationship. But to even go over that line into a real personal relationship, I think that can be dangerous and not wise."[33]

The French respondents do not talk about the importance of productivity or professional relations. As we shall see, the French speak less about group-based discrimination than individual harm and abuse of power.

The French focus on dignity of persons and abuse of power

French sexual harassment law emerges from a different legal and social context than American sexual harassment law. During a far-reaching reform of the French Penal Code, in 1990/91, French lawmakers added a specific sexual harassment statute to Book II of the new Penal Code, which addresses crimes and misdemeanors (*délits*) against people (as opposed to property). Within Book II of the new Penal Code, the sexual harassment statute is included under Title II, entitled "Affronts to Persons" (*Des atteintes à la personne humaine*) (Serusclat 1992, p. 6; for a legislative history of this bill, see Cromer 1992; Cromer and Louis 1992).

The law that was ultimately approved defines sexual harassment as "the act of harassing another by using orders, threats, or constraint, with the goal of obtaining sexual favors, by someone abusing the authority conferred by his position."[34] In other words, this statute only recognizes that which American jurisprudence calls "quid pro quo" sexual harassment, or situations of sexual coercion, when employers, bosses, clients, or other people with power abuse their "official authority" to try to force employees to grant them or a third party "sexual favors." Moreover, rather than focus on the victim's perception of the behavior as "unwelcome," French law defines sexual harassment from the perspective of the perpetrator, who acts to receive "sexual favors." However, unlike American law, French law also protects potential whistle-blowers.

In France, there is a long tradition of critiquing the arbitrary use of power. Thirty-five years ago, sociologist Michel Crozier argued that many French often conceive authority to be universal, absolute, and unrestrained (Crozier 1964, p. 220). In her more recent book, Lamont (1992, p. 49) finds that this general attitude persists. French workers are more likely than their American counterparts to believe that managers exercise power for their own benefit, while American workers are more likely to say that they use such power for the collective good or for the good of the company. French activists, intellectuals, and journalists have anchored their critique of "sexual harassment" in another term that clearly evokes abuse of power: *le droit de cuissage*. This is the title of Marie-Victoire Louis's (1994) book, mentioned above. Moreover, over one third of my sample of articles on sexual harassment published in the *Nouvel Observateur* (N = 24) explicitly refer to *le droit de cuissage*. This term, also known as *le droit de seigneur* or the First Night, refers to a feudal tradition in which the Lord had a right to sleep with his serf's bride on their wedding night.[35] In the nineteenth century, the term *"droit de cuissage"* was used to refer to overseers who, because of the enormous power they had over female factory workers, engaged in (often consensual and frequently coerced) sexual relations with them, a practice that was condemned by several strikes and demonstrations (Louis 1994). This term was "reinvented" in the late 1980s to raise consciousness about what was then beginning to be called "sexual harassment."[36]

French criminal law categorizes sexual harassment as sexual violence, ranking it fourth in severity, after rape, sexual assault, and exhibitionism. "Sexual harassment" refers specifically to the *psychological* coercion that people in positions of authority can exert to obtain sexual relations from people under their control. It is differentiated from sexual assault and rape, in which physical force or touching is involved, although one can bring several of these charges at once. French law thus groups sexual harassment with other forms of sexual coercion or violence, rather than with other forms of employment discrimination. Obviously, in the United States, people who are physically abused at work or elsewhere can also appeal to criminal laws against sexual assault and rape although they then face stricter standards of evidence and cannot collect monetary compensation.[37] Under Title VII, however, assault and rape are very egregious forms of sexual harassment, condemned because they constitute employment discrimination.

As political scientist Erik Bleich (1998) shows in his study of anti-racist policy in France and England, France has primarily addressed discrimination in general in the penal rather than civil code. Moreover, if we consider inflammatory statements to be a form of verbal violence, we would conclude that the French focus on violence is not limited to sexual harassment law. For, as Bleich also demonstrates, French politicians and activists have concentrated their energies on "expressive racism," or inflammatory statements or written expressions made against individuals or groups because of their ethnicity rather than, like their English counterparts, "access racism," or discrimination in employment, housing and goods and services,

The violence paradigm is not unique to French law. The focus on violence is also institutionalized in the European Association against *Violence towards Women at Work* (AVFT), which was founded in 1985 to combat "violence towards women at work," including sexual harassment. According to an article presenting the association in an anthology edited by the AVFT:

> The deliberately broad title of our association and the use of the term "violence" can without a doubt be explained by the diversity of demands that we receive and of the situations that confront us: sexual blackmail in employment, battery, rape, psychological pressures, sexually vulgar environments, use of pornography, discrimination, sexual harassment – all situations that generally end in a wrongful discharge. (Cromer 1990)

Note that this small passage mentions both discrimination and the employment consequences of this "violence at work." Yet, it does not subsume all forms of sexual violence – including rape and assault – under the term "sexual harassment," nor in turn does it subsume sexual harassment under the term "gender discrimination." Rather, the AVFT establishes violence as the primary category and lists sexual harassment and discrimination as forms of violence against women. This declaration, published before the French sexual harassment laws were passed, is therefore quite consistent with French law in its categorization of sexual harassment. Yet, it uses the term "violence" to target a wider range of behavior, including discrimination, sexist and sexually offensive language, and pornography.

Similarly, the French activists are more likely to discuss sexual harassment as an act of violence than as an impediment to equal opportunity in employment. Yet, they use the concept of violence more broadly than does French law. One French activist explains why she thinks sexual harassment among colleagues is wrong by saying: "For me, that's an act of violence. To be constantly behind someone harassing them, that's a kind of violence." Another says that she considers pornography an *agression sexuelle* or sexual assault.

Moreover, like their American counterparts, the French activists often mix several rationales in their arguments about sexual harassment. In the following citation, a French activist explains why sexual harassment is wrong:

Sexual harassment is a denial of [women's] right to work, but what [harassers] try to do more profoundly is to dominate [women] by denying their word. In fact, we find that women often say no, maybe implicitly initially and then very explicitly, but the [harassers] do not hear the "no." Refusing to hear what another says is like saying: "you don't exist." So it's really destruction. "You don't exist and I destroy your intimacy, your personality, the psychological and physical barriers that you have constructed." I think that, for many women, this has a certain resonance in a patriarchal society that continually tries to oppress them with violence.

This woman skillfully weaves arguments about employment opportunity, psychological harm, violence, and systematic oppression of women into a few sentences.

After passage of the penal code law, in 1992, a complementary statute in the labor law was passed with the support of the Secretary of Women's Rights, Véronique Neiertz. This statute (*Art. L. 122–46*), which allows employees who have been fired or demoted to demand back pay and unemployment benefits, states:

No employee can be penalized or dismissed for having submitted or refused to submit to acts of harassment of an employer, his agent, or any person who, abusing the authority conferred by their position, gave orders, made threats, imposed constraints, or exercised pressure of any nature on this employee, in the goal of obtaining sexual favors for his own benefit or for the benefit of a third party.
No employee can be penalized or dismissed for having witnessed or recounted the acts defined in the preceding paragraph.
All contradictory provisions or actions are void of legal standing [*nul de plein droit*].[38]

Addressing specifically the employment consequences of sexual harassment, this statute is close in spirit to American sexual harassment law. However, even this statute differs from Title VII sexual harassment jurisprudence in an important way: it is not framed as a form of discrimination. Like the criminal statute, there is no reference to discrimination in *article L. 122–46* of the Labor Law.[39]

That the discrimination component of sexual harassment was largely abandoned during legislative debates is not surprising given the context of discrimination law in France. Unlike the United States or Great Britain, where discrimination is addressed in civil law, French employment discrimination laws are inscribed in *penal* law. On one hand, using criminal law – which carries the possibility of prison sentences – to punish discrimination sends an important message about the seriousness of this problem. On the other, French discrimination law is rarely invoked in court, according to the AVFT activists and the ten French lawyers I have interviewed (see also Bleich 1998; Banton 1994). In 1991, for example, British civil procedures led to 1,471 cases of employment-related racial discrimination, whereas employment-related convictions for racial discrimination in France, totaled four (Banton 1994: 485, cited in Bleich 1998, p. 8).[40] This stems largely from higher standards of proof demanded under French discrimination law.[41] Unlike American and British law, where one can protest against "indirect discrimination" – for instance, using statistics to demonstrate discriminatory *impact* on a group – under French law, one must demonstrate discriminatory *intent*.[42] Without a legal tradition of indirect discrimination and differential impact, French social actors have little cognitive and legal basis in which to ground claims about discriminatory environments.

There is also less of a political and cultural basis in France for categorizing people according to racial, ethnic, or religious affiliation.[43] By separating the church and state, the Third Republic hoped to confine customs and beliefs to the "private sphere," meaning both that the state should not segregate citizens according to these criteria and that citizens should not "politicize" these differences (Noiriel 1992, p. 109).[44] Consequently, and in accordance with republican principles, France's census does not gather information about race, ethnicity, or religion, which subsequently makes it difficult to measure racial discrimination. Of course, the state practice (or lack thereof) is self-reinforcing. Without an objective measure of racial inequality, it is difficult to make this a political rallying point. While racial categorization in the United States can serve to reify "races" and reinforce racism, the lack of statistics in France on racial disparity can obscure discrimination and racism.[45] In the United States, the politicization and theorization of racism has provided a basis for denouncing other forms of group-based discrimination. In France, opponents of the politicization of group identity can and do appeal to long political traditions of an assimilating model of nationhood (Brubaker 1992; Scott 1997).[46]

As was mentioned, French law defines discrimination purely in terms of employment decisions, unlike American law, which condemns behavior that creates a discriminatory environment, especially when sexual innuendo is also involved.[47] French law does not, for instance, categorize as illegal discrimination the behavior of a boss, described in a vignette, who insults his female – and only his female – employees, calling them incompetent and slow. Yet, half of the AVFT members call this behavior "discrimination," while the other half call it "sexist." Those who label it "discrimination" admit that it would be difficult to maintain such a position before the law but think that it should nonetheless be pursued legally. Those who call it "sexist" adopt a gender inequality analysis but do not consider it compatible with French law.[48]

Elisabeth Badinter and Françoise Giroud, on the other hand, resist categorizing this type of gender-based hostility. They each condemn "quid pro quo sexual" harassment because it involves coercion of individuals by people in positions of authority. While they recognize that women are more often harassed than men, they do not understand the harassment as customarily legitimized by sexism or as a form of employment discrimination. Rather, they stress the abuse of hierarchical power involved. For instance, when I ask Françoise Giroud how she defines sexual harassment, she says: "It's generally an attitude of supervisors [*petits chefs*] in offices, in factories, who think they can do anything because the employees are without defense . . . There are even [laughter] cases of sexual harassment of men by women. There was one last year, I don't know if you saw that, who was absolutely persecuted by a woman. Still, that's very rare." While emphasizing the formal power of the boss and institutional vulnerability of the employee, Giroud does not analyze the power men have over women by virtue of being men.[49] Giroud does not discuss situations in which, for example, female managers and professionals are sexually harassed by colleagues who perceive them as a threat and use sexuality to "put them in their place."

For Françoise Giroud and Elisabeth Badinter, sexual harassment is necessarily sexual. They resist seeing sexual harassment as an instance of gender discrimination. In response to a vignette describing a boss who insults his female but not male employees, calling them "incompetent and slow," Françoise Giroud says: "That's just someone with a bad character. You can't condemn him for sexual harassment." When I then ask if this person could be condemned for anything, Giroud replies: "I don't think so. That's the case of lots of supervisors [*petits chefs*]. The hierarchy needs to be changed. That's something else!" I try to make the insults more specifically discriminatory (e.g. "dumb broad!"). Giroud repeats that it is not sexual harassment and finally says that it could be considered an insult and that he could be "condemned for insults." I point out that there is a French law against racist insults and ask if there should not also be a law against sexist insults.[50] Giroud replies: "I don't believe there is a need to be specific. It should be recognized simply as an insult . . . because it's an insult regardless of whether or not it is sexist. An insult should be condemned." After much prodding, Giroud agrees that the behavior should be tempered, but refuses to group it with either sexual harassment or gender discrimination.[51]

Similarly, Elisabeth Badinter resists the idea that certain supervisors are verbally abusive to female employees because of their gender, making this vignette particularly frustrating for her: "Listen, this is one of the most unbelievable cases [*cas de figure*] because why would he hire her then? Knowing that she's a girl and he can't stand women? I don't know. I can't answer." Badinter thus takes issue with a point that French and

American gender scholars have been making. Based on empirical studies, several scholars have argued that many women workers are targeted for abusive behavior precisely because their colleagues and/or supervisors resent working with women (e.g. AVFT 1990; Cockburn 1991; Cromer 1995; Epstein 1992; Kanter 1977; Schultz 1998; Williams 1995).

Bridging gaps and erecting symbolic boundaries

In the previous two sections, I discussed the United States and France independently of one another. The reality of sexual harassment law and social conceptions, however, is not so neatly divided along national boundaries. In this section, I examine how AVFT activists draw on cultural and material resources from outside France to promote their definition of sexual harassment. I also point to the "boundary work" (Lamont 1992) produced by lawmakers and public figures – including Françoise Giroud and Elisabeth Badinter – against foreign nations to oppose the position advocated by the AVFT.

AVFT members often speak about their ties to feminist intellectuals and activists across the globe, with whom they share written texts, oral presentations, and personal ties. Through national, international, or foreign conferences and workshops, organized by the United Nations, universities, or various associations, AVFT activists frequently participate in international feminist dialogues that shape their perspectives. This is suggested by the following quotes, where activists describe ideas which they explicitly attribute to such international influences: "[the primacy of the woman's viewpoint] is a position defended by American feminists." "As the Canadian women say, 'For guys, it's clear . . . A woman is there to be pretty, made up, in a short skirt, even fondled.' . . . It's because she's a woman that she is treated like that. So if that's not discrimination, I don't know what is!"

One of the activists, who is trained as a jurist, is particularly skillful in drawing on American, Canadian, and European legal concepts and French legal categories. For instance, in response to the vignette described in the introduction, she says:

If we took out the physical touching and only kept the language, one could consider that this creates a sexist environment. It's the type of environmental harassment that would not at this moment be pursued by the law narrowly conceived [in France]. But, in my opinion, that could change because, you have to be logical . . . I don't see what [the victim] can think besides: "If I don't smile, if I don't laugh when he says these stupid things, I could be fired at the next downsizing." One must be realistic. In my opinion, there is constraint. And . . . if she says yes, he won't say no. So, implicitly his remarks aim at obtaining sexual favors."

This respondent's use of the term "environmental harassment" resembles the utilization of the category "hostile environment" sexual harassment in American law. However, because French law does not recognize hostile environment sexual harassment, this respondent expands explicit components of French law – "constraint" and "sexual favors" – so they can accommodate the behavior in the vignette. Largely due to the influence the AVFT has had on the courts via their influence on plaintiff lawyers, jurisprudence has evolved in this direction (Minet and Saramito 1997).

Marie-Victoire Louis explains that before beginning her book on the history of the *droit de seigneur* in France, she read American and Canadian work that "saved [her] years of reflection." Other AVFT members also mention having read research in women's studies by American, Canadian, and English authors. The first AVFT conference on sexual harassment and the anthology that grew out of it includes work by a range of French and international scholars, including, for instance, Catharine MacKinnon (AVFT 1990). Since its inception, the AVFT has collaborated with many American activists, students, and scholars. Members of the AVFT strategically use recommendations, studies, and theory generated by international bodies like the European Union, and foreign nations like the U.S. and Canada to gain leverage in national debates over sexual harassment.[52] As Marie-Victoire Louis explains:

We leaned sociologically and intellectually on the United States and on Europe . . . The [European] Council's decisions and recommendations allowed us to push the [French] legislation. It was an extraordinary tool . . . [Our use of it] was strategic. The association got its first concrete financial support from [the European Community] . . . So Europe allowed us to live financially and we could draw on those different declarations . . . and sexual harassment surveys [to argue our case].

The Council of the European Community issued its first directive on sex equality at work in 1976 (76/207/CEE). In 1987, the EC published the Rubinstein report on sexual harassment (Rubinstein 1987). By framing sexual harassment as a form of sex discrimination, the EC justifies intervening under the equality clause in the Treaty of Rome. In 1991, the European Union issued a specific, non-binding recommendation concerning sexual harassment that states:

The member states are recommended to take measures to promote consciousness that all behavior of sexual connotation and all other behavior based on sex that affects the dignity of men and women at work, whether such behavior is committed by hierarchical superiors or colleagues, is unacceptable if:

(a)   this behavior is inappropriate [*intempestif*], abusive, and hurtful for the person who is its object;

(b)   the fact that a person refuses or accepts such behavior from an employer or
      a worker (including a hierarchical superior or a colleague) is used explicitly
      or implicitly as the basis for a decision affecting the rights of that person in
      matters of professional training, employment, maintaining employment,
      promotion, salary or any other decision relative to employment,

      and/or

(c)   such behavior creates a climate of intimidation, hostility or humiliation for
      the person who is its object and that this behavior can, in certain circum-
      stances, be contrary to the principle of equality of treatment in terms of
      articles 3, 4, and 5 of the directive 76/207/CEE [on gender equality at
      work].[53]

The similarities between these recommendations and the EEOC guidelines are striking. Note in particular, that they both stress the victim's perspective by describing the behavior as "unwelcome," in the American
case, and as "inappropriate, abusive, and hurtful," in the European case.
The two texts recognize both behavior that has tangible employment
repercussions and that which simply creates a hostile or intimidating
environment. Both acknowledge that employees can be harassed by their
colleagues as well as by their hierarchical superiors. Like the United
States, the European Community justifies the recommendation on sexual
harassment by stressing the link to sex discrimination. However, the EC
recommendations also justify the intervention as a protection of
"dignity," a theme not present in the American legal debates.

The AVFT used the European recommendations to argue for the
necessity of a sexual harassment law in France.[54] In June 1990, the AVFT
drew on the European recommendations, among other resources, to draft
a proposal for the penal code, which defined sexual harassment as:

Any act or behavior towards a person that is sexual, based on sex or sexual orientation and has the aim or affect of compromising that person's right to dignity,
equality in employment, and to working conditions that are respectful of that
person's dignity, their moral or physical integrity, their right to receive ordinary
services offered to the public in full equality.

This act or behavior can notably take the form of: pressure [*pressions*], insults,
remarks, jokes based on sex, touching, battery [*coup*], assault, sexual exhibitionism, pornography, unwelcome implicit or explicit sexual solicitations, threats, or
sexual blackmail.

Note that this bill defines sexual harassment more broadly than American
law. Like American law, it includes a range of sexual innuendo and gender
harassment. It goes beyond American law by condemning discrimination
on the basis of sexual orientation. While stressing people's rights to
employment opportunity, it also stresses their rights to dignity, moral and
physical integrity, and services.

As we know, the law that was eventually passed is narrower than the AVFT guidelines. The AVFT promptly pointed out what they perceived to be shortcomings in the bill, namely its limited provisions for employer liability and its refusal to recognize either peer harassment or hostile environment sexual harassment.[55] In an article, three members of the AVFT write:

Touching, sexist language and insults, pornography, etc. – whose function is not to obtain sexual relations with a specific person, but most of the time is a product of *sexist behavior* and has the goal of humiliating the harassed person, is not accounted for. Yet, such repeated sexual and sexist behavior can gravely affect the person's health, upset their work and professional relations and usually lead her to resign. (Benneytout, Cromer, and Louis 1992, p. 3)

They point to several negative effects of hostile environment sexual harassment, including in employment and health. These authors further point out that this definition contradicts the European Community Recommendation (No. 92/131/CEE). Yet, as we will see, while the AVFT urges that France look to Europe, the United States, and Canada for legal and cultural models, other more influential social actors argue that such foreign influence should be resisted.

Recently, there has been both much speculation and important social scientific research about the effects of "globalization," or the perceived increasingly international nature of, for instance, economic markets, politics, and/or culture (see Boli and Thomas 1997; Meyer 1994; Meyer et al. 1991; Strang and Meyer 1994). Boli and Thomas, for instance, identify the principles of universalism, individualism, voluntaristic authority, rational progress, and world citizenship as central elements of world culture. According to these authors, work on international change in the status and role of women shows that world cultural models now make state action on behalf of women virtually obligatory, as states learn that they have an interest in placating transnational and domestic women's groups committed to equality (Berkovitch 1994; cited in Boli and Thomas 1997, p. 186). This work is insufficient in at least two intimately connected respects. First, because it examines "globalization" at an extremely macro level, it does not adequately theorize the ways in which local women's groups use international law, institutions, and rhetoric in concrete struggles. Second, this body of literature does not explore the multiple ways in which other local social actors oppose "international models" on the grounds that they do not account for the "specificity" of "national culture." Both of these tendencies have had an important role in French debates over sexual harassment.

For example, based on a content analysis of press articles (N = 133) in the leading French newspaper and news magazines, half of the French articles about sexual harassment focus on sexual harassment in the

United States rather than in France (Saguy 1999a). The French press thus portrays sexual harassment as an American issue, of little concern at home. French articles about the United States are significantly more likely than French reporting about France to present sexual harassment as a moral issue, to suggest that women routinely use their sexuality to "sleep up" the corporate ladder, or to present sexual harassment plaintiffs as gold-diggers. When reporting on the United States, the French press is also more likely to portray sexual harassment regulation as an invasion of privacy. By documenting such "American excesses," these articles serve as a warning to French readers that sexual harassment law should be approached with caution. They transfer concern about the *harm* of sexual harassment to anxiety over sexual harassment *law* and they make a domestic problem a question of national identity.[56]

Such concern shaped debates in the National Assembly. Opponents of the first sexual harassment bills argued that sexual harassment bills *à l'américaine* would disrupt gender relationships and threaten everyday seduction (Serusclat 1992, p. 32). Eventually, Yvette Roudy and Véronique Neiertz, the lawmakers who proposed the criminal and labor sexual harassment laws, respectively, played off such fears. They each presented revised bills that defined sexual harassment narrowly – as abuse of official authority to obtain sexual relations – and argued that these modest proposals would respect the "specificity of French culture." In legislative debates, these bills were portrayed as modest, "avoid[ing] the excesses of North American legislation" that lead "to the repression of libertine discussion [*propos grivois*], *gauloiseries* [literally meaning "typical of the French", also called the Gauls, but referring to lewd discussion], or simple light jokes or comments having to do with sexual relations" (Assemblée Nationale 1992, p. 28). Yvette Roudy explained why she compromised in order to pass the bill at all:

When I proposed it to the Socialist group, the first reaction was: "You aren't going to prohibit flirting. We aren't in the United States." I explained to them. Sexual harassment in the corporation, abuse of power, exploitation. If there wasn't a hierarchical dimension, the group would not have accepted it, fearing that it would be penalizing flirtation. (*Libération*, April 30, 1992)

In other words, Roudy strategically emphasized the most taken-for-granted ideas about inequality in France – hierarchical power – rather than developing new, more controversial themes of sexism and discrimination. Likewise, when presenting her proposal of a sexual harassment labor law, Véronique Neiertz disarmed her adversaries by contrasting the "reasonable" character of the French initiative with American "excesses" and by limiting the content of the project to address only sexual harassment of an employee by her or his boss (Jenson and Sineau 1995, p. 287).

Such public representations were used by most of the French activists, public figures, lawyers, human resource personnel and union activists I interviewed. Respondents often ask me if the rumors in France about American workplaces and universities are true. "Is it true," they typically ask, "that men won't enter an elevator alone with a woman out of fear that she would then accuse him of sexual harassment?" "Is it true that professors always leave their door open to protect themselves from accusations of sexual harassment?"

Indeed, the two public figures who have been among the most vocal skeptics of sexual harassment law are neither Right wing nor opponents of women's rights. On the contrary, Françoise Giroud is politically in the center and a former Secretary of Women's Rights. Elisabeth Badinter is a prominent intellectual, a self-identified and press-identified "feminist," and closely affiliated with the French Socialist Party. This can partly be explained by media practices that aim to maximize the element of surprise in reporting; it is particularly "newsworthy" when a prominent feminist criticizes a feminist law. However, the disagreement over sexual harassment between women like Elisabeth Badinter and Françoise Giroud, on one hand, and Marie-Victoire Louis, on the other, is symptomatic of a more general division among people who call themselves "feminists" about "republicanism." For instance, Louis was among the prominent feminists who recently championed a constitutional amendment that would impose gender parity in the National Assembly, while other feminists, like Badinter, opposed it on the grounds that it violated "republican principles of universality" (see *Projets féministes* 1996; Scott 1997).

In France, Françoise Giroud and Elisabeth Badinter praise the French sexual harassment law for its exclusive focus on abuse of power and criticize the broader reach of American regulation. In defending the French law, Giroud and Badinter draw symbolic boundaries against Americans and, more specifically, against American feminists. They present American society as seized by gender warfare and France as a place of harmonious relations between the sexes. Françoise Giroud explains: "Two big centuries ago, the French invented a way of speaking amongst each other, of loving each other – I'm talking about men and women – and of making conversation, of having relationships that are a lot softer and sweeter than American relationships. There is no comparison. And that's felt in the whole history of these last years." In this context, Giroud and Badinter argue that French women can negotiate most situations well on their own.[57]

Likewise, Elisabeth Badinter describes American society as typified by asexual and distant social relations: "Do you see what kind of ideal [of relationships between men and women] shines through your examples?

The comrade. Do you see what that means in French? It's a bit like the model in Nordic society. In Sweden, it's like that. I find it terrifying, just terrifying!" Badinter juxtaposes this image with that of the French workplace, which she describes as a place of pleasant flirtation and playful seduction. She argues that this atmosphere should be preserved: "You know it's at work that people meet their lovers, their mistresses, who sometimes become their wives or husbands and sometimes don't . . . So if you start saying: 'Oh, but a gaze a bit insistent or a reflection of bad taste is harassment,' that's going to rule out the possibility that couples will form, that people will date, court, have flings [*aventures*]. It'll all be over."

There are people in the United States who also criticize sexual harassment policies as threats to "sexual freedom." However, in France, such arguments are often framed in opposition to the United States (e.g. Badinter 1991). Some French journalists and intellectuals contrast alleged French respect for *vie privée* (a personal sphere outside state control) to American disregard for this principle, manifested in articles about politicians' sex lives and in "over-zealous" sexual harassment laws. Yet this "French character" is contested by other French social actors, like members of the AVFT who criticize the "narrowness" of French sexual harassment law and the uneven protection of privacy among the powerful (men) and powerless (women). One French study of Mitterrand's presidency, for instance, describes how the French press has targeted female French politicians' physical appearance and sexual behavior (Jenson and Sineau 1995, p. 334). Likewise, French scholars have denounced the fact that courts rarely respect rape victims' privacy, but rather, scrutinize their sexual past for signs that they welcomed the assault (Mossuz-Lavau 1991).[58] Activists at the AVFT express similar concerns about the privacy of sexual harassment plaintiffs.

In the interview and in a recent article, Marie-Victoire Louis regards negative caricatures of American feminists as a means to disqualify and intimidate French feminists (Louis 1999; see also Ezekiel 1995). Other AVFT activists and many of the French plaintiff lawyers I interviewed concur that myths about "American excesses" are often used to discredit their work. The need to dissociate themselves from such negative images reinforces national differences in approaches to sexual harassment. One young AVFT activist explains how such a social climate leads her to avoid the term "sexual harassment" altogether when describing her work. Instead, she speaks of sexual violence:

I prefer to talk about violence to women at work . . . Because of this trend [that consists of saying that] women make up things, women invent things, the movie *Disclosure*, Demi Moore . . . – you can't imagine the damage that [movie] did to mentalities – ["sexual harassment"] is a totally discredited term. When people ask me what I do, I don't mention sexual harassment. I'm sure they would burst out laughing: "Oh but women make up stories, oh but sexual harassment, it's like in the United States. It's anything goes. It's all about making money in court cases." No, I say that I work on violence towards women at work.

Conclusion

This study set out to explore how different national cultural repertoires shape representations of sexual harassment in France and the United States, in both formal law and among activists and public figures. I found that rhetoric about the market, ("minority") group-based concepts of inequality, productivity, and professionalism are more common in the United States, while arguments about interpersonal violence and abuse of power are more prevalent in France. These findings are consistent with those of the other chapters in this book and point to the robust nature of these particular elements in respective French and American cultural "tool-kits" (Swidler 1986).

This chapter, however, also reveals that national cultural repertoires are neither stable nor universally agreed upon. For instance, in the United States, while Phyllis Schlafly and Camille Paglia stress the importance of a free labor market in their criticisms of "over-zealous" sexual harassment regulation, Catharine MacKinnon and 9to5 activists argue that some constraints must be imposed on the market to achieve gender equality. Likewise, French sexual harassment law uses the concept of violence to condemn only a boss's imposition of his sexual desires on one of his subordinates, but the AVFT activists define "sexual violence" more broadly to include, for example, pornography. In France, Elisabeth Badinter and Françoise Giroud argue that "French" cultural and political traditions, characterized by harmonious gender relations and respect for privacy, are inconsistent with "American" concepts of sexual harassment. Yet, members of the AVFT denounce as dangerous ideological rhetoric, such arguments about the nature of "French" political and cultural traditions. They dispute that "American" definitions of sexual harassment are inherently American or in any way incompatible with the pursuit of gender equality in France.

Sociologists of culture need not only to document cultural repertoires, but also to explore how different elements are contested or reinforced at particular historical moments. For instance, this study suggests that arguments about national specificity intensify when the principles for which they stand are increasingly challenged (see also Ezekiel 1995; Scott 1995; Louis 1999). Stated differently, "globalization," or "American imperialism" (see Bourdieu and Wacquant 1998), does not erase local social actors, who interpret, translate and dispute symbolic meaning (see Fantasia 1995; Frenkel, Shenhav, and Herzog 1996; Guillén 1994, forthcoming; Fourcade-Gourinchas 1999). Unless serious attention is paid to historical change or contradictions across different national institutions and groups, cross-national studies run the risk of essentialism.[59]

In this chapter, the law was examined as one important site of symbolic meaning. As a social code, the law has particular sway because it is backed by authority and ultimately force. Nonetheless, it is still a human-made code. This chapter examined briefly how various social actors, such as activists, politicians, lawyers, and judges, draw on cultural and material resources in struggles over legal definitions of sexual harassment. It found that, once institutionalized, legal definitions of sexual harassment are highly influential. Yet, social actors, including many of the respondents, often dispute, expand upon, or reinterpret legal definitions when making judgments about particular types of behavior. Social actors also challenge legal definitions more directly through proposed amendments to statutes and/or in court cases that aim to change jurisprudence.[60]

Previous work has documented how social actors draw on cultural repertoires to make arguments (e.g. Lamont 1992). However, as this study of struggles over the particular issue of sexual harassment has shown, through such disputes, social actors can redefine the initial terms of the debate. For instance, contests over sexual harassment have challenged prevailing conceptions of gender, discrimination, sexuality, power, violence, law, the market, and the workplace, to name just a few. Social meaning is thus created and recreated in political struggles that are increasingly transcending national borders.

APPENDIX

VIGNETTES (WITHOUT THE VARIATIONS OF GENDER, HIERARCHICAL POSITION, ETC.)

1. During a job interview for a position as sales representative, the boss invites the applicant to spend the weekend with him in San Francisco. He says he'll give his answer after the weekend.
2. A saleswoman complains that her boss calls her by her first name, often undresses her with his eyes, compliments her body, has asked her if she ever cheated on her husband, suggests they go out on a date, puts his hands on her buttocks.
3. The boss has been dating one of his subordinates. She is entirely consenting. But the other employees complain that the boss's mistress has privileges. They decide that they are penalized because they are not sleeping with the boss. They say this is a form of sexual harassment.

4. Pornographic posters are hanging behind the desk of an executive. One of his colleagues complains that she feels very uncomfortable every time she walks into his office. However, no other employee has ever complained.
5. Chris is known as a joker. Among other subjects, he often jokes about "dumb blondes," bad women drivers, or "bimbos." Despite these jokes, he claims to love women. He says they are closer to nature, more tender, give life. . . . He sometimes says, in the tone of a joke, things like, "It's up to the women to save the firm." Most of his colleagues laugh at his jokes but Sue finds them unbearable. She says that even his supposed compliments are generalizations that confine women to very limited roles and considers this a form of sexual harassment. She expresses her point of view but is not taken seriously because she is considered a "feminist."
6. A woman has been dating her boss. The relationship was completely consensual but now the woman wants to break up. She lets him know, but he does not want to end the relationship. He calls her several times a day on the phone, sends her letters, stops her in the hallway to discuss his suffering. She says that she can't work under these circumstances and complains that she is being sexually harassed.
7. A woman complains that her boss calls her "stupid," "incompetent," "slow." He doesn't make any sexual propositions, but she says that he does not have this attitude with male employees.
8. A female boss of a firm dates one of her employees. The relationship is completely consensual. However, when the female boss decides she wants to break up with him, her male subordinate refuses to accept her decision. He calls her incessantly on the phone. He sends her letters and flowers. He stops her in the hall to discuss his sorrow. She claims that not only is he not doing his work and preventing others from doing theirs, but that his behavior is disturbing and frightening. She says that he is sexually harassing her.
9. A male boss of a firm dates one of his female employees. He breaks up with her to go out with another female employee in the same firm. The ex-lover is hurt and insults the new lover. She makes allusions to the other's sexual contact with the boss, humiliating her in front of their colleagues all the time: "You slut, whore, you know he's only interested in one thing" . . . "You'd do anything to get ahead, wouldn't you?"

Notes

Earlier versions of this chapter were presented at the Graduate Women's Studies Colloquium (Princeton University), the Council of European Studies Conference, the Eastern Sociological Association, and the Princeton-Rutgers Conference on the Sociology of Culture. This research is supported by funding from the department of sociology at Princeton University, several grants from the Center of Excellence in French Studies (Princeton University), a pre-dissertation fellowship from the Council for European Studies (Columbia University), and a Woodrow Wilson fellowship. I wish to thank the women interviewed for the time they generously gave me for the interviews. I am also grateful for the wonderful job that Jennifer Boittin and Anne Fonteneau did transcribing the bulk of the interviews. I greatly benefited from the commentary of several scholars on earlier drafts of this chapter, including Erik Bleich, Mia Cahill, Paul DiMaggio, Judith Ezekiel, Eric Fassin, Marion Fourcade-Gourinchas, Michal Frenkel, Erin Kelly, Nathalie Heinich, Michèle Lamont, Catherine Le Magueresse, Marie-Victoire Louis, Catharine MacKinnon, Serge Moscovici, Geneviève Paicheler, Joan Scott, Charles W. Smith, Laurent Thévenot, and Viviana Zelizer. I alone, however, am responsible for the limitations and errors that remain.

1 I surveyed two of the leading French and American newspapers, *Le Monde* and *The New York Times*, and the most widely circulated news magazines in each country, *L'Express*, *Le Nouvel Observateur (Nouvel Obs)*, *Time*, and *Newsweek*.

2 *Meritor Savings Bank v. Vinson*, 106 SCt 2399, 40 EPD Par. 36,159 (US 1986). The *Meritor* ruling left for future High Court decisions the chore of defining many aspects of the infraction. In *Harris v. Forklift Systems, Inc.* (114 S. Ct. 367 at 370, 126 L. Ed. 2d 295, 1993), the court ruled that "Title VII comes into play before the harassing leads to a nervous breakdown." While the court concluded that there is no precise test to measure a hostile environment, it did offer guidelines. It said that the plaintiff must establish two facts. First, she or he should demonstrate that the conduct objectively creates a hostile or offensive environment, so that a "reasonable person" (a legal term referring to a theoretical person of average sensibilities) would find it hostile. Second, the plaintiff should show that she or he personally found the behavior abusive. The Supreme Court shed light on two major issues in 1998. In *Burlington Industries v. Ellerth* (No. 97–569, Supreme Court of the United States, 1998 US Lexis 4217) and *Faragher v. City of Boca Raton* (No. 97–282, Supreme Court of the United States, 1998 US Lexis 4216), the High Court clarified rules of employer liability. In *Oncale v. Sundowner Offshore Services, Inc.*, (No. 96–568, Supreme Court of the United States, 118 S. Ct. 998, 1998 US Lexis 1599), the High Court ruled for the first time that sexual harassment among members of the same sex is an infraction of Title VII. Nonetheless, sexual harassment law remains ambiguous and polemical in 1999. In the aftermath of the Lewinsky scandal, sexual harassment law is particularly contested, as several American social critics blame it for Clinton's impeachment and Senate trial. See, for instance, the *New York Times* Op-Ed piece by Richard Dooling (1998).

3 *Art. 222–33 du nouveau Code Pénal; La loi no. 92–1179 du 2 novembre 1992 relative à l'abus d'autorité en matière sexuelle dans les relations de travail.*

4 French press coverage of high profile cases of sexual harassment in the United States, however, increased over time. In 1998, in the publications cited above, there were four articles published on sexual harassment in France and twenty-eight articles about sexual harassment in the United States (overwhelmingly related to one of the concurrent Presidential scandals).

5 Not only are 9to5 and the AVFT not representative of American and French society at large, but they are not representative of American and French women's movements either. 9to5 does not officially call itself a "feminist" association and none of the 9to5 activists I interviewed used this label either. In contrast, the AVFT does identify itself as a feminist association, as do many of the members. However, some of the AVFT members I interviewed said they had not considered themselves "feminist" before joining the association and/or were not yet full-fledged feminists. In that sense, the 9to5 and AVFT activists are similar to each other. The AVFT's official line is that both pornography and prostitution should be prohibited, a position that is highly contested among French "feminist" groups.

6 I did not use gender as a criterion in my selection of respondents. The fact that the people who speak out on sexual harassment are women is testimony to how sexual harassment is perceived as a women's issue in both countries.

7 I have intentionally avoided using the label "feminist" (except in quotes or as "self-defined feminist") to describe the respondents, since this label is itself highly contested. For instance, Camille Paglia calls herself a feminist, but her work is labeled "anti-feminist" in many feminist circles (Dimen 1993; Wolf 1992). Catharine MacKinnon calls herself a "radical feminist" while others label her a "prohibitionist" feminist". Elisabeth Badinter considers herself a feminist but this status is disputed in some French "feminist" circles. Disputes over the label "feminist," "radical feminist," etc., and the way they are articulated differently in France and the United States, is itself a topic ripe for investigation. I thank Eric Fassin for bringing this to my attention.

8 Obviously, the women I interviewed do not come in perfectly comparable pairs. I consider Catharine MacKinnon and Marie-Victoire Louis to be most analogous in their analysis of sexual harassment, although they, of course, differ on several points. Moreover, both MacKinnon and Louis wrote pioneering books on this topic and fought for laws that would provide legal recourse to victims of sexual harassment. Both also lead a life of activism and scholarship, MacKinnon in Law and Louis in Social Science. Finally, both women are self-defined feminists.
    The violent criticisms Camille Paglia has launched at "American feminists" are the closest I found to the anti-American feminist discourse used by Elisabeth Badinter, Françoise Giroud, and others (e.g. Ozouf 1995; for a critique, see Ezekiel 1995; Scott 1995). Both Badinter *and Paglia* identify themselves with feminism and the Left. Yet, other American self-defined feminists call Paglia's politics "anti-feminist" (Dimen 1993; Wolf 1992) and other French women who call themselves feminist question Badinter's feminism (in personal discussions or reactions to earlier versions of this paper).
    I interviewed Phyllis Schlafly because of her prominent position within a movement that has had considerable sway over gender issues in the United States. I chose not to interview a comparable figure from the French Right because I could find no one from this movement who had made any public statement on sexual harassment, and my criterion of selection was participation in a public debate.

9 This does not include one AVFT activist – Marie-Victoire Louis – who is counted as part of the public figure sample.

10 Core AVFT activists are defined as those who meet with and advise victims of sexual harassment who appeal to the association.

11 To better assist those who reside outside the capital, the AVFT has tried to develop networks with lawyers, *Inspection du Travail* agencies, and local unions. Their success has been uneven across different regions.

12 Laurent Thévenot encouraged me to use ambiguous vignettes as a way of leading the respondents to articulate judgments and clarify their criteria of evaluation.

13 For the sake of simplicity, when speaking of sexual harassment in general, I use the masculine pronoun to refer to the aggressor and the feminine pronoun to refer to the person who is harassed, since this is the situation in the overwhelming majority of cases. I use the term "harasser" to refer to the aggressor and "victim" to refer to the person who is harassed.

14 In 1998, the Supreme Court ruled that same-sex sexual harassment is actionable under Title VII if the plaintiff can demonstrate that he (or she) is harassed because of his (or her) sex in *Oncale v. Sundowner Offshore Services, Inc.* (No. 96–568, Supreme Court of the United States, 118 S. Ct. 998,1998 US Lexis 1599); 140 L. Ed. 2d 201, 66 US L.W. 4172, 76 Fair Empl. Prac. Cas. (BNA) 221; 72 Empl. Prac. Dec. (CCH) P45,175, 98 Cal. Daily Op. Service 1511; 98 Daily Journal DAR 2100; 11 Fla. Law W. Fed. S 365. Demonstrating this, however, is often difficult (cf. Franke 1997).

15 The importance of such work needs to be explicitly theorized in the sociological methodology literature. As in a "breaching experiment," this work, in which one challenges one's categories of analysis and assumptions, is *necessarily* painful. If it is not painful, the work has not been done. Thanks to Laurent Thévenot for insisting that I analyze this part of the methodology.

16 For a more complete comparative account of French and American sexual harassment law, see Saguy 1999a.

17 42 USC §§ *2000e* to 2000e-17 (1988 & Supp. II 1990), amended by 42 USC §§ *2000e* to 2000e-16 (Supp. III 1991). Employees can also sue for sexual harassment under state tort law, contract law, worker's compensation or unemployment compensation statutes. In certain cases, charges of sexual assault or rape can be brought against the harasser. Sexual harassment in education is covered under Title IX of the Education Amendments Acts of 1972, which makes it illegal to discriminate according to sex in educational institutions that receive federal money. In a lower court ruling, a landlord was even convicted of sexual harassment under Title VIII of the Fair Housing Act (*New York Times* 1983).

18 Plaintiffs can often get around the 15 employee requirement by using state laws on sexual harassment or tort law. For a thoughtful history of how "sex" is added to the Civil Rights Act of 1964, see Bird 1997. Bird convincingly disputes the myth that the sex discrimination provision was a big "Congressional joke," used as a ploy to sink the entire bill with a controversial measure. Rather, Bird argues that feminists played an important role in advancing the amendment. They, and their supporters, strategically used the civil rights movement to advance women's rights. Even before the civil rights movement, in the abolitionist movement, racial oppression provided a point of entry into politics for a diverse group of American women, as ideas about the rights of

African Americans were used to conceptualize women's rights in new ways (Evans 1989).

19 *Barnes v. Train*, 13 FEP 123 (D.D.C. 1974); *Corne v. Bausch & Lomb Inc.*, 390 F. Supp. 161, (D. Ariz. 1975); *Miller v. Bank of America*, 418 F. Supp. 233 (N.D. Cal. 1976); and *Tomkins v. Public Service Electric and Gas Co.*, 422 F. Supp. 533 (D.N.J. 1977).

20 *Williams v. Saxbe*, 413 F. Supp. 654 (D.D.C. 1976). *Barnes v. Costle*, 561 F.2d 983 (D.C. Cir. 1977); *Garber v. Saxon Business Products*, 552 F.2d 1032 (4th Cir. 1977); and *Tomkins v. Public Service Electric and Gas Co.*, 568 F.2d 1044 (3rd Cir. 1977).

21 *Meritor Savings Bank v. Vinson*, 477 U.S. 57(US 1986).

22 Ironically, according to an influential article by law professor Vicki Schultz (1998), American courts are progressively decoupling sexual harassment from gender discrimination. This leads to a situation, documented by Schultz, in which women who have suffered severe forms of workplace hostility, verbal abuse, physical violence, or ostracism, directed at them by their male colleagues or supervisors because of their sex, have little success using Title VII.

23 There is an inherent danger in this claim. Making sexual harassment subject to government intervention chiefly because it occurs in a "public sphere" (the workplace), reinforces cultural understandings of the public/private divide, in which the family and other "private spheres" are to be free of state intervention. As feminists have pointed out, this legitimizes men's unfettered control over (and often abuse of) their wives and children.

24 This critique of the public/private divide could fruitfully be extended to condemn violence towards women that has no economic consequences and occurs in more "private" spaces, like the home. Indeed, this is the strategy behind the Violence Against Women Act (Violence Against Women Act of 1994, Pub. L. No. 103–322, 108 Stat. 1902, codified as amended in scattered sections of 8, 18, 42 USC (1995)).

25 As Marie-Victoire Louis has pointed out in reaction to an earlier version of this paper, this is also true of French women's movements, some of whom proposed an anti-sexist law (that would prohibit gender hate speech and sexist representations of women) on the model of the anti-racist law. However, the analogy between racism and sexism has had less force in France – largely, I would argue, because France has not known America's painful history of racial oppression, nor the ensuing powerful civil rights movements and extensive anti-discrimination policy.

26 Rather than a positive phenomenon for women, Vicki Shultz (1998) has argued that such regulation of workplace sexuality is an unfortunate and dangerous result of American jurisprudence's focus on sexuality rather than on economic and political inequality between the sexes.

27 This was reaffirmed by the High Court in *Oncale v. Sundowner Offshore Services, Inc.* (561 U.S., 118 S. Ct. 998 (1998)).

28 Rather than simply bracket the discrimination requirement of Title VII in the case of the bisexual harasser, Catharine MacKinnon tries to demonstrate how such a person might fall under the law. She explains that a situation in which a

person sexually harasses both men and women in a way that is entirely indiscriminate regarding gender is not actionable under Title VII because such behavior is not discriminatory. However, she argues that, in real life, sexual behavior is rarely if ever indiscriminate by gender. Men are pursued because they are men and women because they are women; gender always shapes the form sexuality takes. In other words, in any incident of sexual harassment, elements of gender discrimination can be found, even when a person harasses people of both sexes, because he will still harass men and women differently. This is a difficult issue for judges as well as lay people to conceptualize. For a thoughtful discussion of how Title VII could be recast to better accommodate the phenomenon of same-sex harassment, see Franke 1997.

29 If we were to interpret these findings in light of Vicki Shultz's (1998) work, we would arrive at the more pessimistic conclusion that the discrimination component of sexual harassment has been replaced by an exclusive focus on sexuality. Yet, when presented with a vignette in which a (male) boss calls his female but not male employees "stupid, slow, and incompetent" without using any sexual innuendo, over half say that he is creating a hostile environment under Title VII. While only one calls this behavior "sexual harassment," the others label it "gender discrimination."

30 Discrimination on the basis of sexual orientation is prohibited by several state laws and institutional guidelines, although not under sexual harassment regulation.

31 This said, free market or *libéralisme du marché* arguments are gaining influence in France. Thanks to Marie-Victoire Louis for reminding me of this.

32 Yet many states have their own sexual harassment statutes that also cover businesses with fewer than fifteen employees. France also has laws that only apply to businesses of a certain size, such as those that require a Committee of Hygiene and Security. Future research should explore more systematically and in greater depth the connection between such limitations and popular conceptions of the public/private divide.

33 Again, this line of reasoning can be dangerous if it leads to a double standard in which abusive behavior is condemned at work but not in more "private" spheres like the family.

34 *Art. 222–33 du nouveau Code Pénal.* This statute defines the penalty as "[a maximum of] one year of imprisonment and [a maximum] fine of [$20,000]." In 1997, this statute was amended to say: "The act of harassing another by using orders, threats, constraint, *or serious pressure...*" The National Assembly initially proposed that the statute refer to "pressure of any nature," like the labor law statute (Assemblée Nationale 1997, p. 27). Twice the more conservative Senate rejected the amendment, arguing that the term "pressure of any nature" was too vague (Jolibois 1998, p. 33; *Journal Officiel de la République Française* 1998, pp. 1369–70). Finally, in a joint meeting between the Senate and National Assembly, Parliament approved the inclusion of "serious pressure" as a compromise (Bredin and Jolibois 1998). In actuality, to date, no one has been sentenced to jail for sexual harassment alone, under this law. Several convicted harassers have received suspended sentences. When harassers have been sentenced to jail, they have been convicted not only of sexual harassment but also of

the legally more serious crime of *agression sexuelle*, which involves physical sexual attacks. In many of these cases, the judge was aware that the victim had been raped but could not prove that charge, according to AVFT activists who were involved in such cases. Even then, jail terms for sexual assault are no more than a few months, which is less than typical sentences for theft. Unlike the American system, the French legal system allows the aggrieved party to *porter partie civile*, or demand compensatory damages during a criminal trial. However, compensatory damages are smaller in civil law countries like France than in common law countries like the United States. In France, they are less substantial when human dignity is at stake than when property is on the line. In the case of sexual harassment, most awards have been no more than a few thousand dollars.

35 Whether *le droit de cuissage* actually existed or was a "myth" is contested (Boureau 1995).

36 As Eric Fassin has pointed out to me in a personal conversation, the practice of *droit de cuissage* has much in common with sexual violence under American slavery. Yet, I have found little trace of this linkage among American activists, intellectuals, or journalists. I intend to explore this question further in future work. I expect, however, that this is a product of America's painful history of slavery and current racial inequality, which is still largely taboo. It is also consistent with a critique made by African American feminists: in Americans' minds, "black" means "black man" and women are assumed to be white women (Collins 1990; Crenshaw 1989; Frankenburg 1994; Hull, Scott, and Smith 1982; Wallace 1990). By extension, few Americans think to extend the experience of black women under slavery to sexual harassment of women in general. Yet, Clarence Thomas did use the image of a "high tech lynching" to denounce Anita Hill's accusations that he, an African American man, sexually harassed her, an African American woman (see Fassin 1991).

37 In the United States, defendants must be proven guilty "beyond a reasonable doubt" in criminal court, while plaintiffs in civil cases need only demonstrate a "preponderance of evidence" (that the defendant is more likely than not to be guilty). Many Americans saw this principle in action in the O. J. Simpson murder trials. O. J. Simpson was acquitted for the murder of his wife Nicole Brown Simpson and her friend Ron Goldman in criminal court but pronounced guilty for the same crime and made to pay monetary damages to the families of the deceased, in civil court. In France, it is not necessarily harder to convict someone of criminal charges than of civil ones, according to the activists and lawyers I interviewed. In fact, criminal charges can often be *easier* to bring than civil ones under the inquisitorial system of French law, since state prosecutors have far-reaching powers of discovery (the resources and power to subpoena people and documents). Moreover, in France, unlike the United States, one can request compensatory damages during a criminal trial through the procedure called *porter partie civile*.

38 *La loi no. 92–1179 du 2 novembre 1992 relative à l'abus d'autorité en matière sexuelle dans les relations de travail*. Few statutes in the French labor code include a *"nul de plein droit"* clause, making this law relatively strong (Le Magueresse 1998).

39 The only surviving link in French law between sexual harassment and discrimination is found in a relatively unknown and unused statute (*article L.*

123–1) of the Labor Law. This statute states that employment decisions should not account for whether the employee submitted to or refused to submit to demands for sexual relations from someone with "official authority" over her or him. This law is included in the chapter on professional equality. The inclusion of sexual harassment under sex discrimination in this statute is analyzed as an "opportunistic text" (Roy-Loustaunau 1995, p. 3). In conjunction with another labor statute (*article L. 152–1–1*) the Inspector of Work has the prerogative to investigate all infractions of *article L. 123–1* and to impose criminal penalties. Because the Inspector usually forgoes the penalties for employers who demonstrate goodwill by trying to rectify the problem, this law serves primarily as an arm of dissuasion (Roy-Loustaunau 1995, p. 3). Some argue that revisions in the new version of the criminal code (after 1994), make concrete application of these criminal penalties impossible (Dekeuwer-Defossez 1993, p. 139). Since 1999, however, the AVFT has been pushing their lawyers to refer to this text, in the hope of thereby developing a jurisprudence of employer liability for sexual harassment (interview with Catherine Le Magueresse, current President of the AVFT, March 18, 1999). If the AVFT succeeds in developing a jurisprudence based on this statute, it could have important implications for employees, employers, and the general conceptualization of sexual harassment in France.

40 However, as Bleich (1998) notes, these figures are not perfectly comparable since not all British cases result in convictions, and since the number of French convictions is higher than officially enumerated, given that, as Costa-Lascoux (1994, p. 376, quoted in Bleich 1998) notes, the statistics only contain the primary offense for which the guilty party is convicted. Nevertheless, the cross-national differences in cases brought to court and convictions obtained remains substantial.

41 Contrary to what American observers would assume, the use of penal law instead of civil law does not automatically toughen standards of proof in France. As explained above (note 37), the inquisitorial legal system of France can even make criminal charges *easier* to bring than civil ones because of state prosecutors' far-reaching powers of discovery that provide vast resources and power to subpoena people and documents.

42 "Indirect discrimination" refers to practices that do not explicitly discriminate on the basis of race, sex, or other criteria but have a "disparate impact" on a particular group. In the United States, the precedent for indirect employment discrimination was established by *Griggs v. Duke Power Co.*, 401 US 424 (1971), in which the High Court ruled that the use of a pre-employment test having discriminatory impact violates Title VII, despite the absence of discriminatory intent. American courts extended this landmark decision on racial discrimination to gender discrimination, for instance, by declaring height and weight requirements that prevent women from being hired for certain male-dominated professions a violation of Title VII.

43 On the other, France has a long history of politicizing work-based group identities in its social policies, social theory, labor law, unions, and occupational-group representations, such as *socioprofessionnels*, within the *Commissariat au Plan* committees (Boltanski 1987; Desrosières and Thévenot 1988).

44 Scott (1996) demonstrates that this political model presents a paradox for feminists, who simultaneously argue that women should be permitted to participate in government because they are like men and yet, by demanding rights for women, affirm the specificity of women as a group.

45 In other words, as Minow (1990) has argued, inequality is reproduced whether it is noticed or ignored.

46 Arguments about "French universalism" intensify when competing models gain support, as was demonstrated in the recent social movements for *Parité* (gender parity in the National Assembly) and PACS (homosexual marriage) (Fassin 1998; Scott 1997).

47 But see Vicki Schultz (1998) on the difficulty plaintiffs face in situations of hostile environment gender discrimination that does not involve sexual innuendo.

48 While the definitive French legal texts do not analyze sexual harassment in terms of sex discrimination, such arguments are nonetheless present in the legal debates. Notably, Senator Frank Serusclat's report to the Senate 1992 includes a sophisticated analysis of gender inequality in France (Serusclat 1992).

49 Her description of the *"petits chefs"* echoes the *droit de cuissage* of the nineteenth century (Louis 1994). Political scientists Jane Jenson and Mariette Sineau find that this type of analysis dominates French press coverage of sexual harassment (Jenson and Sineau 1995, p. 288).

50 The AVFT supports the passage of an "anti-sexist" bill – like the one proposed by Yvette Roudy but killed in Parliament – that would condemn sexist statements just as the anti-racist law condemns racist ones (see Jenson and Sineau 1995).

51 Law professor Vicki Schultz (1998) convincingly argues that while sexual harassment is increasingly penalized in the United States, plaintiffs have little success in cases of non-sexual forms of gender harassment. In France, the legal basis for denouncing non-sexual forms of gender harassment as such is even weaker, although French labor law provides employees with greater job security in general.

52 According to the current president of the AVFT, Catherine Le Magueresse, in a personal discussion on June 6, 1999, the AVFT and the lawyers it works with have not yet used the policies from the United Nations, but intend to do this in the future. As Le Magueresse pointed out, "laws are only useful if activists and lawyers use them."

53 Unofficial translation.

54 I am focusing here specifically on the AVFT. I provide a fuller account of the legal history of French sexual harassment law in Saguy 1998.

55 As mentioned above, the employer can theoretically be held liable under a penal law in the labor code. Although this statute has not yet been used against employers, in 1999, the AVFT planned to begin to use it in this way.

56 "Narratives within the narratives," or how French and American social actors construct national difference, is one of the most fascinating aspects of any Franco-American cultural comparison (see Baudrillard 1986; Faure and Bishop 1992; Kuisel 1993; Fassin 1993, 1997a, 1997b). I only scratch the surface of this important topic here. There are multiple forms of French anti-

Americanism, each with a slightly different rationale (see Ezekiel 1995; Scott 1995; Lacorne, Rupnik, and Toinet 1990). Even French feminists who borrow heavily from the United States are also extremely critical of aspects of American society, as Marie-Victoire Louis pointed out to me in response to an earlier draft of this chapter. She, for instance, is particularly critical of America's unfettered capitalism (*capitalisme sauvage*) and American politics in the Middle East. In analyzing French anti-Americanism, one should keep in mind that many French leaders feel that they are in a defensive position in relation to the United States – a lone superpower and an aggressive exporter of cultural images and objects. To much of the French élite (the popular classes embrace American cultural models more readily), American "cultural imperialism" is understandably perceived as a menace to French specificity (Lacorne, Rupnik, and Toinet 1990). This puts some French people on the defensive, leading them to caricature both American and French society, so that MacDonalds and Battle of the Sexes become symbolic of the United States while camembert and flirtation epitomize France.

57 Mona Ozouf (1995) went furthest in developing this argument. For a critique, see Ezekiel 1995; Scott 1995.

58 It is only recently prohibited for defendants in rape (and by extension sexual harassment) cases to use as evidence the sexual past of the plaintiff to demonstrate that she welcomed the assault (Violence Against Women Act of 1994, Pub. L. No. 103–322, 108 Stat. 1902, codified as amended in scattered sections of 8, 18, 42 USC (1995)).

59 I thank Eric Fassin and Joan Scott for pushing me on this point.

60 The AVFT held a conference on June 4, 1999 to discuss amending French sexual harassment law. The proposed amendment would define sexual harassment from the perspective of the victim, would include "hostile environment" sexual harassment, and would remove hierarchical authority as a necessary component.

4 Assessing the literary: intellectual boundaries in French and American literary studies

Jason Duell

Has American literary criticism "gone French"? Affirmative answers to this question have become commonplace. Many literature professors in America credit French scholars such as Michel Foucault, Roland Barthes, Jacques Derrida, Louis Althusser, Jacques Lacan, and Julia Kristeva with having revitalized their field after the long post-war reign of New Criticism.[1] Citations of these thinkers have steadily increased in American journals of literary criticism since the late 1960s,[2] and a large number of the leading literary scholars in America have drawn heavily upon them in their own work.[3] It is difficult to think of a major critical paradigm in American literary studies today – be it deconstruction, psychoanalysis, Marxism, gender and race studies, New Historicism, or post-colonialism – in which the work of French theorists does not figure prominently.

Given the vast influence that many American literary professors attribute to French theory – a vision shared by many of their critics (e.g. Hughes 1989; Paglia 1991; Kimball 1990), who deplore such influence[4] – one might expect to see a great deal of intellectual commonality today between academic literary studies in France and the United States. Yet here a puzzle presents itself: if American literary critics have indeed "gone French," they seem to have done so in a manner quite different from the French themselves. Interviews I conducted for this study with twenty literature professors in both countries show significant cross-national differences in their prevailing conceptions of what "literary studies" are and ought to be.[5] Literature professors in the United States, for example, consider a much wider range of material to be appropriate for literary studies than do their French counterparts. The two groups also differ in the types of criteria they perceive as legitimate for determining "good work." And French and American literature professors exhibit very different amounts of professional consensus over these boundaries and evaluatory criteria, with the French showing much more agreement over the basic goals and definition of literary studies. Finally, the two groups forward opposing narratives of how their discipline has evolved intellectually in the past generation, and of where they think it is headed in the future.

94

Why, despite the apparently massive influence of the French upon American literary scholars, do literary studies show such marked variance between the two countries? I offer three explanations for these cross-national differences. First, the more diffuse and contentious sense of national cultural identity of the United States and the greater legitimacy there of claims based on ascribed group characteristics has weakened the traditional boundaries of the Anglo-American literary "canon," and promoted the use of "representation" as a criterion for scholarship, whereas the opposite is the case in France. Second, national differences in the ability of humanist intellectuals to influence public debate drive the presence of "political" criteria in the American literary studies and their relative absence in France. Third, differences in the national consensus over the status of high culture and differences in the "disciplinary ecology" in both countries have influenced the professional strategy of literary studies, with French literary scholars choosing to maintain their traditional intellectual niche, while American literary scholars are increasingly moving into intellectual terrain traditionally the province of the social sciences and philosophy.

Finally, I examine the paradoxical "Frenchness" of contemporary American literary studies – why certain French scholars have become so influential, despite their waning or non-existent influence in literary studies in France itself. I propose that these French thinkers have provided an "alternative canon" for American literary scholars, allowing them to maintain their professional distinctiveness (and legitimacy) as they enter fields in which their work might otherwise be indistinguishable from social science or philosophy. I conclude, however, that for reasons of both supply and demand, the further importation of French theory is unlikely to play a significant role in American literary studies in the future.

Literary studies in the United States

[I]t took more years than anyone could possibly have imagined for the earth to move in the world of American literary and cultural studies. What Jacques Derrida calls "white mythology" has held uncommon sway for centuries in the male hands of those who believe themselves to be completely responsible for both the sun's light and the legacy of the Enlightenment. Toni Morrison stunningly captures the entailments of this control in *Playing in the Dark*, where she notes that any "others" in the American literary and cultural enterprise were, until quite recently, considered dark or in the dark, the exclusive property of, and instrument for, white males who were living in the light – or who thought that they were.

It is precisely a new sense of a full, diversifying, and ever-proliferating household on earth that has brought us to the sign "multiculturalism." The sign has unfolded in the same critical and intellectual space that has witnessed the coming to fullness of such denominations as black studies, women's studies, Chicano and Chicana studies, gay and lesbian studies, Native American studies, and Asian American studies. Here, we might say – in these denominations – is the earth's plenty. And there can be no doubt that the old order has changed, yielding paradigmatically to the new. (Baker 1993, p. 5)

The above quote captures a number of themes that permeate much of American literary scholarship today: the conflation of "literary" and "cultural" study; the belief that traditional literary scholarship has been politically oppressive, especially to women and minority groups; the citation of French theorists to help expose the false Enlightenment rationalism by which that oppression was justified; and the conviction that a cluster of "critical" (or, often, "postmodern") scholarly approaches based around categories of race, ethnicity, gender, and sexual orientation has arisen to replace the older theories and set the situation right. And while the author states these ideas with a degree of force and conviction that is probably greater than that which would be used by the majority of literature professors in America today, the fact that he was the president of the Modern Language Association when he wrote them (and that his comments were published in a journal distributed to every member of that organization) seems enough to merit concluding that his perspective on literary studies is not entirely out of the mainstream. And indeed, all of the literature professors interviewed for this study in America agreed that there have been major changes in the discipline in the last twenty-five years, and that the academic study of literature has become more imbued with theory, more concerned with politics (especially issues of race, class, gender, and sexual orientation), and less tightly focused upon a traditional "canon" of "great" literary works. Most also noted that the discipline has witnessed more intellectual conflict in this period, or at least that such conflict has acquired more explicitly political overtones than was the case previously.

Throughout most of the post-war period until the late 1960s, American literary studies were dominated by the New Criticism, which provided a number of clear standards for work in the discipline. First, it drew a fairly clear line between "literature" and "non-literature"; literary works were characterized by their richer, more ambiguous language. Second, it emphasized the formalist study of the internal workings of literary texts, without reference to their social context; indeed, New Critical doctrines such as the "heresy of paraphrase" and the "intentional fallacy" (Wimsatt and Beardsley 1954) militated against any attempts to summarize or explain the meaning of literary works via factors external to the text, even including authors' stated intentions about their own work.

Aggressively challenged by a host of theoretical movements, such as deconstruction, feminism, African American studies, Marxism, and psychoanalysis, the New Criticism began to decline in the late 1960s, and had essentially disappeared by the late 1970s. American literary studies have since seen an explosion of new paradigms – New Historicism, postcolonialism, queer theory, and Cultural Studies, to name some of the most prominent – and this new theoretical landscape has resulted in major shifts in the scholarly boundaries of the discipline that had held during the reign of New Criticism.

One of these shifts is that literary studies in America have become more political in their focus. Many of the most prominent paradigms in the discipline are explicitly political, and often base their legitimacy upon the notion that they represent perspectives which have traditionally been excluded from literary studies for political reasons. The intellectual climate appears to be sufficiently permeated by politicization that even those scholars who have no particular wish to be "political" often cannot help but see many of their everyday activities through a political prism (or, as many in the profession might put it, a "hermeneutic of suspicion"[6]). For instance, when asked if he considered his work to be a political activity in any way, an Ivy League professor (who specializes in drama) noted:

I don't think of it that way while I'm doing it . . . [But] just by the choice of the people whose work I consider most important in contemporary theater, I'm engaged in a political action. And when I make up the syllabus for the contemporary drama course, those are the people I'm teaching, and from some people's point of view this would look less like a syllabus than, you know, like a political correctness canon or something, so, yeah [my work is political].

While this particular professor showed ambivalence about treating his work as political ("I don't think of it that way while I'm doing it"), some other literature professors fully embrace the idea of literary criticism as a politically engaged practice. One interviewed professor (a former tenured literature professor at an Ivy League university) responded to the question "Do you see your work as political?" by stating: "The only reason why I do what I do is for political reasons – I couldn't see any reason for doing it otherwise." In the course of a discussion of the criteria for good scholarly work, it further became evident that the professor viewed political concerns as inevitably extending to matters such as evaluating job candidates:

I like work to have a goal. That's something I would look for in someone's work – that they have a clear sense of purpose.

Does it matter what kind of purpose they have?

To my mind, it would have to be – it would have to be a political stake, that was relevant.

Would you have a problem with hiring someone whose politics you found repugnant?

Oh yeah – I wouldn't hire him. No way. I mean, I have to work with these people. [laughs]

To be sure, there are many literature professors in America who disapprove of the highly politicized atmosphere in contemporary literary studies, or who at least feel that its political aspects are being overblown and/or overextended into inappropriate areas. The majority of professors interviewed, for instance, felt that one could and ought to draw a line between a scholar's politics and the quality of his or her work, and that the former should be excluded as a criterion in hiring. But these professors often expressed the concern that in practice, this separation does not happen, and that instead the two aspects are conflated; for instance, one professor at a noted public research university complained that job candidates often get evaluated on their skill in a kind of political theater, in which they compete to appear ever more "radical," and in which a savvy performance gains one vital recognition as the "smart" candidate:

What counts as a better reading is actually a reading that does what the paradigm is supposed to do even better than the paradigm. So usually people correct Said by showing that he's not "Saidish" enough; he could be even more post-colonial – or Eve Sedgwick could be even more queer . . . And then you show that you're even more queer than Eve Sedgwick. You never get points by saying that Eve Sedgwick is too queer, Edward Said is too post-colonial . . . It's just this constant outflanking. It's "how do I take a position just to the Left of everybody else?" So you find somebody who's already on the Left, and then you find some reason why *part* of their position might possibly lead to fascism [laughs], there's *still* some lingering degree of oppression, and then you get rid of that . . . It just becomes a kind of dance. It's very predictable.

Besides causing what they perceive as an unwarranted intrusion of political concerns into the evaluation of scholarship, politicization is also seen by some literary scholars as beginning to exact a heavy toll on the discipline in the form of decreased public legitimacy for the profession, and also in a frequent breakdown of collegial relations, to the point where many departments witness open feuding and bureaucratic breakdown:

The problem has been that it's become much more difficult to defend what people are doing in the academy because it looks rather shallowly adversarial in a way that possibly it didn't before – in the fifties and sixties . . . It's put everybody in a very uncomfortable position, and it's produced a lot of stridency, I think, and I think the stridency results in increasingly simplistic political paradigms. So I think things are not in a great way right now . . . Departments just *collapse* because they get so factionalized, and everybody's so suspicious of everyone else's motives – rightly so, probably! [laughs] – and it's made for a bad situation. It hasn't shaken out, in other words, terribly well – it's been about ten or fifteen years since all this has been going on.

Another major shift that has occurred in American literary studies is in the area of subject matter and methodology; the New Critical criterion of close and fairly atheoretical readings of a narrow canon of aesthetically defined literary texts no longer holds. Scholars from various minority groups have challenged the boundaries of the traditional canon, by examining and problematizing the historical process of its selection,[7] by promoting the inclusion of certain minority authors in the canon, and, increasingly, by demanding separate canons for various minority groups.[8] Scholars from paradigms such as New Historicism, post-colonialism, and Cultural Studies have often left literature behind entirely and moved into historical and social scientific terrains, to the point where their range of subject matter is virtually anything that can be read as a "text," or that can be considered "cultural." Along with this vast broadening in subject matter has come a proliferation of methodologies and paradigms. Literary scholars today borrow freely from other disciplines such as psychology, history, sociology, anthropology, philosophy, semiotics, and linguistics, to the point where many scholars feel there is no common denominator for defining a "literary" method.

The result of these changes is that the scholarly terrain and the array of methods perceived as legitimate for literary study is remarkably broad, and goes well beyond any traditional definition of "literature" and "literary studies"; as the editor of the *Publication of the Modern Language Association* recently put it in an editorial column: "[I]sn't *literature* today, for some readers at least, capacious enough to include any text that can be studied from a historical or sociological perspective?" (Stanton 1994, p. 359).

All of the interviewed scholars noted this expansion of literary studies' intellectual domain. But they split sharply on its desirability. Some lauded the development as a positive development for the field, while others felt that literary scholarship is extending itself into areas in which it has little methodological competence, thus producing bad work. As a member of the latter group put it:

The problem is that not everything is culture. But it's being treated like it is. So that humanities professors – English professors particularly – treat the building across the street as a text. And, you know, it's also the building across the street, but we don't have any way to talk about it in those terms, and the thing about Cultural Studies is that is does that – it grinds everything down to text, and then does semiotic interpretation of it. And I think the usefulness of that is really questionable . . . It works for literature because it *is* text, but it doesn't really work for everything else very well, and it becomes this very obvious and self-serving way of analysis.

Where are literary studies headed in the United States? For some scholars, the seeming lack of any scholarly boundaries in the discipline is causing it to lose any coherence or definition, and they fear the discipline is in danger of disintegrating. For instance, in a 1993 report to the American Council of Learned Societies (ACLS) on the state of American literary studies, Barbara K. Lewalski – a professor of literature at Harvard, and the 1993 MLA delegate to the ACLS – noted the proliferation of subject matter and methods as the primary problem facing the profession:

As I see it, the chief intellectual issues facing our discipline arise from one central fact: the enormous expansion of what may be said to constitute literary studies. Postmodern theory and the recent emphasis on cultural studies combine to make all kinds of texts and discourses (verbal and even non-verbal) proper subject matter for us, overwhelming received notions of a core, or canon, or common theoretical ground, or common methodology for our discipline. There is, as well, a new attention to literary texts and traditions hitherto ignored or marginalized . . . We might add to these factors the permeability of disciplinary boundaries . . . In the contemporary critical milieu, the distinction between background and foreground, literary and subliterary, is blurred or obliterated . . .
At the root of the problem is the lack of consensus about what the discipline of literary studies really is: if it is not a shared body of knowledge, not an agreed-on canon of texts, and not a common methodology, then what is it? . . . These questions afford a genuine basis for anxiety, and they have no ready and easy solution . . . (Lewalski 1993, pp. 92–4)

While several of the literature professors interviewed dismissed such talk of a crisis in their profession, a majority had concerns about the potential "break-up" of literature as a discipline. Most of these professors were troubled by the possibility of this development, but not all of them. One professor at a major public university was actively pleased by the prospect of literary studies breaking down into some sort of "post-disciplinary" form, as he already saw literature departments (along with most other humanities departments) as obsolete institutional artifacts with no intellectual reason for existence:

If English departments start kind of proliferating into Cultural Studies, women's studies, gay and lesbian studies, etc., and all this other stuff is interdisciplinary by definition – and even to some extent anti-disciplinary, in the sense that it was founded more to react against what was going on – then who knows what will happen to them . . . I think that's actually a great development, from my point of view, because I think disciplinary authority is pretty fraudulent . . . The problem is that you still have this shell left called the "department" or the "discipline," and everybody still operates frantically within the shell because that's the way you have a career – but nothing intellectually conforms to what the shell is supposed to stand for.

Similarly, the chair of an Ivy League literature department observed that literary studies may well eventually be replaced by "media studies," in which literature could be overshadowed by studies of film and television; while he noted that this development was not something he himself was pushing for, he stated that he would have no problem with it if it came to pass.

Literary studies in France

Twenty-five years ago in literary studies many people appeared who wanted to introduce new disciplines into the field – structuralism, psychoanalysis, Marxism, things like that. At the time, there was an extreme intensity about literary study – when one did literature when I was a student, around 1968, one had the impression that literary studies could be a really very important terrain: that one wasn't doing just literature, that it concerned the entire symbolic order; that it was eminently political, even if one didn't directly do politics; that language was fundamental, that language was the symbolic key to institutions, etc. In a lot of this work – there wasn't a disappearance of literature exactly, but it was nonetheless a bit phased out . . . So, there was both the sense that these were important stakes, and at the same time a certain dissatisfaction that literature was being a bit obscured, or that it was serving just as a pretext.
We're certainly in a totally different phase now.

This sentiment – that literary studies in France were in a state of political and intellectual ferment in the years surrounding 1968, but that there has since been a shift to a qualitatively new stage in the discipline's history – is from an interview with a prominent literary scholar at a CNRS research institute in Paris. It has been chosen for its conciseness, but could be replaced by many others, for the fact is that every single literary scholar interviewed for this study, when asked "how have literary studies in France changed in the last twenty-five years?", expressed a similar sentiment, and drew a similarly strong boundary between literary studies "then" and "now."

The first characteristic cited as proof of this difference was inevitably the observation that the heated debates which existed in the discipline in France in the late 1960s and the 1970s between advocates of traditional literary history and those of newer, "modernist" positions (such as Marxism, psychoanalysis, and structuralism) have diminished to the point where they are generally considered "ancient history."[9] In contrast to the turbulent situation many American literary scholars considered their discipline to be in, French literature professors invariably described literary studies in France as in a period of relative calm. As one professor put it:

The great wars of the epoch – where there had been a kind of war between the modernist positions and those of the old Sorbonne – all that's gone. It hasn't completely disappeared, but it's pretty much gone. You can still find a few professors at Paris IV [i.e. the Sorbonne] who continue the war from twenty-five years ago, and who say things like "Barthes was an impostor" and that "all those types are dangerous," but it's become a bit rare, eh? [smiles]

You could say instead that there's been a phenomenon of assimilation, of absorption . . . I have the impression that by all evidence there has been a lowering of the intensity of debate over literature in France today . . . There's not at all the passion that there was twenty-five years ago.

As the mention of "assimilation" and "absorption" suggests, this period of calm has not been precipitated by the victory of one side or another within the discipline. Unlike in America, where the New Criticism and the older model of literary history have essentially been vanquished, and conflict remains among the victorious paradigms, in France the older and newer methods of scholarship both remain, and seem to be co-existing relatively peacefully. Many professors described the discipline as being in a state of "eclecticism," in which varied methods often mix in the work of individual scholars to the point where it has become difficult (and pointless) to try to label their scholarship as belonging to one tradition or the other.

But if French literary studies are indeed now "eclectic," it is an eclecticism that operates within much clearer and narrower boundaries than those found in the United States. In the process of entering the mainstream of French literary studies, modernist scholars appear to have shed most of their original interdisciplinary and political ambitions, and have instead increasingly adopted the traditional criteria of the discipline.

This trend can be most clearly seen in the range of subject matter covered by French literary scholars today. Whereas pioneering modernists like Barthes (1957) once implicitly challenged the notion of a literary "canon" as the appropriate boundary of scholarship by producing works on subjects as various as travel guides, television wrestling shows, and laundry detergent advertising, attempts to recast French literary studies into something analogous to the Cultural Studies model seen in the United States today appear to have been fairly weak and short-lived. Interviewed professors described the move into the analysis of non-literary objects like film and mass culture as a brief trend in the early 1970s, which acquired little inertia and quickly fizzled out, at least in university departments. There appears to be little or no push for such studies today, and few literary scholars in France today deviate, at least in their professional work, from the study of traditional literature.[10]

Beyond choices of subject matter, an increasing consensus also appears to be emerging in French literary studies about the appropriate relation between theory and literature, and this too is a change from initial modernist positions. Just as current standards discourage literary scholars from drifting into social science in their choice of topics, so do they increasingly discourage styles of work which adopt an overly social-scientific tone and discuss literary works only to validate social, psychological, or other theories. The threat that literature is being "obscured" by theory thus seems to have waned. Few purely theoretical works are being written by French literary scholars today, and most professors now appear to believe that attempts to fit literary works into overarching social or psychological theories are a thing of the past. As a CNRS researcher explained:

Literature used to be a pretext for bringing in an exterior discourse – Marxist literary studies, for example. I think now that's finished; their points have been made. It's true that there are still psychoanalytic studies, but I think that it's understood now that it's been turned around, and that it can be interesting for literature to interrogate psychoanalysis, but not the other way around. So all that kind of research is I think a bit out of fashion, or is no longer productive.

In contrast to a transdisciplinary or post-disciplinary identification, many literary scholars feel that despite the methodological eclecticism of literary studies in France today, the discipline is not merely the branch of *les sciences humaines* that deals with literature as its object; in contrast, several scholars drew the distinction that while other disciplines might draw upon literature as "evidence" in social or historical analysis, the mark of the literature scholar is to use social and historical analysis (among other methods) to "enrich the meaning" of the literary text.

Finally, the highly political overtones that accompanied modernist literary scholarship at its inception appear to have largely disappeared in France today. Whereas one's intellectual alignment in the 1960s and 1970s usually predicted one's politics, and many modernists challenged the legitimacy of the older scholarship by accusing it of reflecting conservative and/or oppressive political values, today the equation of paradigms with politics has broken down. The salience of political issues generally seems to have subsided in literary studies; while most of the professors interviewed were willing to grant that literary scholarship inevitably contains some political assumptions and overtones (two professors categorically denied even this, and insisted that their work had nothing at all to do with politics), they typically did not feel that the literary profession was in any meaningful sense an arena for political debate or engagement. Only two of the interviewees embraced a description of their work as a "political activity," and if another professor is to be believed, the proportion of such politicized scholars in the profession is declining: when asked if he felt that many literature professors see their research and teaching as political activities, he replied:

I don't know. Of course, there are a certain number of instructors – who tend to be a bit older than me [the interviewee was in his mid-forties] – who still have the idea that it's very political. I don't have the impression of encountering that among younger scholars. In any case, it's not big. It exists at the level of the individual, of course, but I don't think that today it's something with much resonance.

Another indication of the subsiding of political concerns in French literary studies today is that political concerns seem to have diminished dramatically as a factor in the job market. While a number of professors noted that literature departments had until recently tended to align themselves as a whole towards either radical or traditional scholarship, and had only hired like-minded professors, they all noted a general sea-change in the profession away from hiring practices based on such litmus tests, and towards more meritocratic criteria. As one professor put it:

It seems to me that conflicts [over hiring] are based more on the quality of work. That's to say – to put it really very roughly – one used to say "he's on our side," or "he's not on our side," and today one would say instead "his work is good" or "his work isn't good." It's "good" or "not good."

Similarly, a professor at a department at one of the newer Parisian universities (i.e. created in the late 1960s or early 1970s) told me that while he felt that the initial deliberate establishment of his department as a home for "radical" scholarship was "necessary at the time," he now feels that the separation of perspectives is the worst thing for the discipline intellectually, and that departments should no longer impose intellectual or political litmus tests upon candidates for jobs.

Where are literary studies in France headed in the future? Most of the professors interviewed declined to speculate, but many noted that the current trend seems to be towards work of a more traditional style. Several scholars mentioned that much of the current scholarship in the field resembles the "old literary history" with only slight modifications, and that a large number of the new books in French literature today consist of fairly atheoretical scholarly works, such as definitive scholarly editions of individual writers' works. As one professor with modernist leanings put it:

There's a tremendous amount of work which has a more traditional allure. There's a return to more in-depth works, more critical editions, more scholarly editions, more than there are works of polemics or essayism. I think that's the tendency. I'm not a good example, but this is [pulls off his shelf and displays a volume from a recently published definitive scholarly edition of a minor eighteenth-century author]. This isn't at all what would have been done twenty years ago.

This should not be taken to mean that "modernist" scholarship is on the wane, although it does seem to lack the vitality of the traditionalist revival, and although certain "modernist" paradigms – most notably Marxism – do seem to be disappearing. But it does seem to indicate that there are few signs at present that literary studies in France will head soon towards anything approaching the direction of the discipline in America. If anything, they appear to be moving in the opposite way.

Explaining the variance

Why have French and American literary studies developed in such different directions in recent years? Without wishing to discount the effects of individual agency or other important contingent factors, there appear to be a number of sociological variables, both at the national and academic levels of social organization, which may account for much of the observed variance between the French and American cases. I will focus here upon three sets of factors whose cross-national differences seem particularly salient in this regard: (1) the differing amount of racial, ethnic, and cultural diversity in each country, and the differing ways in which these kinds of diversity are institutionally recognized and mediated; (2) the differing social position in each country of humanist intellectuals; and (3) the different "disciplinary ecology" in which literary studies are positioned in each country.

Multiculturalism

From its initial transformation in the late 1960s to the present, American literary studies have shown more concern over issues related to ethnic, racial, or other minority or "marginalized" groups than has been the case in the discipline in France. This concern has been manifested both in the conflicts over the traditional canon for literary studies, and in the appearance of scholarly paradigms based upon inserting categories like gender, race, and sexual preference into the analysis of texts. In contrast, French literary studies have witnessed neither of these movements. Why has this difference existed, and what have been its consequences for literary studies in the two countries?

One reason for the difference may be simply that the United States is a more ethnically and racially diverse society than France. Given this greater diversity – and the fact that certain groups, most notably African Americans, have not assimilated along the ideals of the "melting pot" – and given the fact that this diversity is increasingly represented in an academic system that was previously fairly culturally homogeneous along

WASP[11] (and largely masculine) lines, it is perhaps unsurprising that literary scholarship in America is more attentive to issues of diversity.

While this simple reflection model (more diversity leads to more attention to diversity) makes a certain amount of intuitive sense, and may account for some of the variance between literary studies in France and America, it also presents certain problems. For while France is certainly less culturally diverse than the United States, it is by no means lacking in groups which might plausibly have challenged the French canon in a manner similar to the challenges in the United States. Why, for instance, has the French literary canon not seen significant challenges from women, or from French citizens of African descent whose Francophone literary traditions are scarcely visible in French literature departments?[12] Women are certainly not a smaller percentage of the population in France than in the United States, and while Francophone blacks are a smaller group proportionally than African Americans, they are not a smaller percentage of the population than are some of the other groups in America (Native Americans or Asian Americans, for instance) which have successfully mobilized around charges of their group's exclusion from literary study.

Accounting for these issues requires moving beyond a simple reflection model to an examination of the differing ways in which social categories like ethnicity, race, and gender are treated in France and the United States in various contexts of claim-making and justification. As Paul Starr (1992) has noted, all bureaucratic institutions must choose from the potentially infinite array of possible social classifications a limited set which will be treated as legitimate for use in institutional classification and decision-making; in the ideal-typical democratic-liberal state, for instance, the use of many ascribed and/or group characteristics (such as religion, race, or gender) in the evaluation, rewarding, and sanctioning of individuals is legally forbidden (one cannot employ such a category to discriminate for or against someone in an employment decision, for instance). But as Starr also notes, liberal democracies often deviate from this model in specific situations; in the United States, for instance, while the legal system forbids discrimination against individuals on the basis of such "suspect classifications," it has permitted the use of these same classifications in certain programs, such as affirmative action, which seek to remedy previous discrimination based on those categories. There thus exists what Starr calls a "classificatory tension," in which the use of these suspect categories is simultaneously forbidden and permitted, depending on context and purpose, and in which many predominantly "liberal" American institutions veer at times into a "corporatist" model of governance whose principle is the mediation between officially recognized groups rather than the liberal principle of mediation between "suspect classification"-free individuals.

The presence of this sort of classificatory tension is evident in the American university system, where "suspect classifications" have been embodied not only in the presence of affirmative action hiring and admissions for various minorities, but also in the creation of separate programs, institutes and/or departments centered around minority concerns. First established for Afro-American and women's studies, these programs have proliferated as more groups have organized and come forward as marginalized identities demanding representation within a university system which they feel has ignored or suppressed them and their concerns. As we have seen, such movements also exist within literary studies, in the form of claims by these same groups that they merit separate canons, courses, and/or theoretical perspectives.

While French society certainly has its share of corporatist tendencies (such as in the sphere of industrial and labor relations), French universities are much freer of this sort of corporatist mediation than are their American counterparts. One reason for this seems to be that the use of "suspect classifications" in France is largely confined to work and class-based categories (or what Laurent Thévenot calls "industrial" orders of worth: see Desrosières and Thévenot 1988; Boltanski and Thévenot 1991). "Suspect" classifications based on ethnic, gender, and racial categories are much more uniformly forbidden in institutional decision-making than in the United States. Also, the very open admission policies of French universities and the relative lack of an institutional "pecking order" among them means that there has been little concern over whether disadvantaged groups are being excluded from admissions or being shunted off into lesser schools.[13] There are no affirmative action-style policies in place for disadvantaged groups in French higher education, and French universities also lack their American counterparts' long and continuing history of preferential treatment for alumni offspring and athletes. In this relatively meritocratic and universalistic environment, American-style ethnic, gender, race, or other "group studies" movements are not perceived as legitimate: when French literature professors were asked why such movements do not exist in France, for example, the most frequent response was that they are *impensable* (unthinkable) within the context of French "universalism" and "republicanism."

The fact that scholarly groupings based upon ethnic, racial, and other group status do exist in American literature departments and do not in French ones explains some of the differences observed between them along the dimensions of subject matter, politicization, and intellectual conflict. In the area of subject matter, the challenges such groups have made to the traditional canon in America have obviously broadened the range of subject material for the discipline, at the very least by adding more literary works by minority authors. It may have also contributed to the move in American literary studies towards the study of mass culture and other "non-literary" (in the classical sense) texts; since many marginalized groups have historically participated less in the production of "high literature" than in other cultural forms, many literary scholars (e.g. Baker 1992) from these groups have focused at least part of their efforts on other cultural products of their groups, such as slave narratives or rap music. Finally, since these scholars are often interested in how their group has been marginalized or oppressed in society in general, and not just in the sphere of literature, they have often pushed into Cultural Studies terrain, textually analyzing non-written social phenomena like movies and television or public debates to reveal racist, patriarchal, or homophobic images and discourses.

It is also likely that the presence of these scholarly groupings has contributed to the more politicized and contentious atmosphere in American literary studies. Most basically, these scholarly movements have usually relied upon charges of discrimination as the foundation for their legitimacy, and typically are predicated upon actively combating what is seen as the continuation of such discrimination in society and/or the profession. Even when talk of discrimination is replaced by the notion of "representing multicultural diversity," certain corporatist dynamics which often lead to politicization remain inescapable. For "multiculturalism" by definition (or if perhaps not by all possible definitions, then certainly by the definitions most often used in practice) involves a form of corporatist mediation, as it implies a number of different cultures or groups which merit representation. Not only does this framework invite conflict over how much representation (i.e. resources, space in the curriculum, etc.) each group will receive, but it also inevitably involves the contentious issue of which groups merit recognition in the first place. Realistically, only a limited number of groupings can be granted official institutional recognition, and this fact has created the necessity for mobilization around group identities that are broad enough to achieve the critical mass sufficient for recognition. Afro-American and women's studies clearly long ago reached this critical mass and are well represented institutionally, while movements around other identities, such as Latino studies, gay studies, Native American studies, and Asian American studies, are still struggling (with varying degrees of success) for similar levels of institutional recognition. These broad identity labels often include considerable diversity within them (such as differences between American and Caribbean blacks), which can give rise to internal conflicts, and this problem is especially acute in cases where groups fall under several labels at once, yet feel insufficiently represented within any of them. Feminist studies, for instance, have witnessed a great deal of internal division and conflict over whether they have marginalized the perspectives and interests of women of color or lesbians.

Finally, but certainly not least in significance, besides these conflictual dynamics internal to multiculturalism, the corporatist form that multiculturalism has taken in American academia is itself a highly controversial issue (both within academia and the public at large), with many scholars (and a very large number of politicians and public critics) strongly disapproving of what they see as the "balkanization" of academia (Schlesinger 1992). Some of these scholars and critics are themselves members of the marginalized groups, and their dissent from the multicultural consensus (often on the ground that the identity politics and corporatism typical of multiculturalism produce a damaging "victim mentality" among minorities, and/or only serve to further underscore group differences, thus impeding integration) has been the cause of some of the most heated polemics and political recriminations in literary studies in recent years.[14]

The position of humanist intellectuals

While the national differences in how issues of race, gender, and other marginalized categories are handled clearly account for much of the difference between French and American literary studies in recent years, there are other significant national differences which seem likely also to have been factors. Among these are the differing legitimacy and position of humanist intellectuals (particularly those of a Leftist or "progressive" stripe) in each country, and the differing way that intellectual life relates to academic work.[15]

French humanist intellectuals have long been noted for their exceptionally prominent place in their nation's public and political discourse. While the amount of this influence has declined since the days when Sartre and other intellectuals championed the opposition to France's war in Algeria, and led protest marches in 1968, French intellectuals and their ideas remain quite visible in the public sphere, especially within the press but also on certain television shows like the popular *Bouillon de culture* (formerly *Apostrophes*). In contrast to their French counterparts, American humanist intellectuals – particularly those on the Left – have traditionally had a much less prominent and legitimate position in American public life. The notion that artists, writers, and humanist academics have by grace of their intellectual positions the right to have influence on public issues is much less widely accepted by Americans than by

the French, and many observers have commented on the general suspicion of the American public towards intellectuals (e.g. Hofstadter 1943;
Ross 1989). And while certain conservative humanist intellectuals have
succeeded in achieving a fair amount of public attention in recent years
(often thanks in large part to their connections with certain major newspapers, a number of well-funded conservative institutes, and the
Republican Party), intellectuals on the Left and/or from minority groups
commonly feel that they have been shut out of the media, out of the
narrow spectrum of the two-party system, and thus out of any significant
presence in public life.[16]

The peripheral position of progressive humanist American intellectuals may account for a good deal of the politicization of American literature departments. Given their perceived lack of access to the major organs
of public debate, many of these intellectuals have decided to utilize the
academy as a sort of "headquarters of last resort" for radical political
change and expression. During the course of one interview, for instance, a
professor described his vision of the mission of his department in precisely such terms:

What we're trying to do here is to create a program where people who think of
themselves as intellectual activists can train themselves. It's a very distinct category – it's people who come to the academy to do the kind of work that they can't
do outside of the academy – but the academy is not necessarily the only location
for that work . . . It has a lot do to with the lack of journalistic organs that are available in the independent public sphere. Since officially the Left does not exist in
America, at least in terms of mainstream media definitions, there are very few Left
intellectuals, academic or otherwise, who really have access . . . The structure of
the academy gives you openings to speak in certain areas, it gives you access to
certain forms of media that you wouldn't have otherwise – and if you don't speak,
surely someone else will, whose politics you may not agree with. So, I say "seize
the day" under those circumstances.

While the number of professors who view their academic positions with
this degree of political calculation is almost undoubtedly a minority
within American literature departments (and academia generally), they
have been numerous enough to spawn a backlash from conservative (and
some liberal) critics in the media and politicians, who have seized upon
the presence of these "tenured radicals" (and often on related phenomena like multiculturalism) as proof that American higher education is in
the thrall of "political correctness." These charges of "PC" (as it has
become commonly referred to) received enormous amounts of coverage
in the national press in the early 1990s,[17] have been the subject of many
books (e.g. Kimball 1990; D'Souza 1991), and remain a staple in many
conservative publications. Responding to these attacks, politically

engaged literary scholars have charged that their subject matter is inherently and unavoidably political, and that their conservative critics are hypocrites who want not to depoliticize academia, but rather to align it with conservative politics and values (Graff 1992).

The overall effect of these public conflicts has undoubtedly been to highlight the political dimension of literary studies in America, and to create an atmosphere where many scholars feel caught between polarized camps of conservatives and radicals. As one professor lamented, literary studies has "become fodder for the culture wars":

The culture wars have clearly replaced anti-Communism as a sort of national political hot button thing . . . So that's created this kind of siege mentality, which then produces even more aggressive scholarship and posturing. I just think it's a very unpleasant situation for people when they get caught in the middle of it.

Since it is not very easy to take a neutral position in these disputes, it is not surprising that, as we have seen, many literary scholars who would probably not describe their work as "political" in different circumstances feel compelled to do so in the current atmosphere of literary studies: political prisms have become difficult to avoid.

French literary studies (and French academia generally) have avoided anything resembling the "political correctness" debate in America. In large part this may be because there are no significant groups who have both the incentive and the means to start such a debate. In the absence of multicultural movements, there is no struggle over minority group representation in the academic profession. Those literary scholars who wish to take public intellectual stands on political issues tend to do so outside the profession in the general public intellectual sphere; an academic career is thus typically for *engagé* intellectuals more of a stepping stone and resource base for their public activities rather than their principal field of engagement.[18]

Also, none of the political parties in France seems to be very interested in making an issue of the political orientation of university professors. Unlike in America, where attacks on "political correctness" and multiculturalism often seem to fit into a broader conservative populist rhetoric against "liberal élites," who are accused of fomenting "the welfare state," cultural decline, and unpopular affirmative action programs, none of these issues has much resonance in mainstream French politics, and the one political party that has made a major issue of protecting a French "way of life" – Jean-Marie Le Pen's National Front – has seen the threat to French culture as emanating mainly from immigration, and not from any vision of countercultural élites in academia or the media preying upon traditional values.[19]

The professional ecology

One final set of factors that may account for some of the differences between French and American literary studies – particularly their different conceptions of appropriate subject matter – concerns the different possibilities that the "disciplinary ecology" in each country has offered for the expansion of literary studies' intellectual terrain, and the incentives that the discipline in each country has had for such expansion.

One of the more fruitful ways of looking at professions, as Andrew Abbott's work (1988) has documented, is by seeing them as existing within a larger professional "system" or "ecology," within which both nascent and existing professions must compete with each other for recognized and exclusive expertise over different "niches" of specialized services. Professions are thus seen as engaged in a process of "turf wars," in which – much as in Paul Starr's discussion of corporatism – conflict often centers as much upon the definition and delimitation of the various "niches" as upon which profession will have dominion over each of them. The result of these definitional struggles is often a situation where a single broad service area (care of the mentally ill, for instance) is traversed by a number of different professional niches (psychiatrists, psychologists, social workers, counselors), sometimes in an orderly and stratified manner, and sometimes in a more hodgepodge, overlapping, and/or conflictual way.

In the academic context, the various professional disciplines have historically competed with one another for dominion over intellectual terrain, and the same sort of overlapping jurisdiction over broad categories exists (economic phenomena, to take one example, are the terrain of an entire discipline – economics – but are also studied in other disciplines in fields such as political economy, economic sociology, economic history, anthropology, public policy programs, and occasionally psychology, each of which studies different aspects of economic phenomena and/or utilizes different theoretical paradigms and methodologies, and/or simply overlap). The same sort of rise, fall and contestation of specific niches is also present, with the occasional new discipline emerging (computer science, for instance), certain once quite central disciplines seeing their niches wane in importance (classics), and some disciplines making moves into others' terrain, either because their traditional niche is on the decline (for instance, anthropology's increasing move towards the ethnographic study of "modern" societies – traditionally sociology's preserve – because of the dwindling number of already often overstudied "premodern" societies), or out of imperialistic ambitions (such as in the efforts of rational choice theorists to "economize" the study of many social and political phenomena outside the traditional terrain of economics).

Using this perspective to look at literary studies, it seems that in many ways the heightened attention to "theory" and the recent expansion of subject matter in American literary studies are the result of professional dynamics similar to those in these last two examples of anthropology and rational choice theory. Motivated either by concerns about literary studies' waning professional fortunes, and/or by a desire to spread the insights of literary analysis to the terrains of other disciplines, American literary scholars have in recent years shown a pronounced tendency to move into subject areas that overlap with the professional domains of other disciplines.

Literature departments in America witnessed a pronounced decline in undergraduate enrollments in the 1970s,[20] and much of the move towards more interdisciplinary and theoretical work in literary studies seems to have been influenced by literature professors' concern to reverse this decline. For instance, in an influential 1981 book on literary theory, Jonathan Culler (a professor of literature at Cornell, and one of the more widely read disseminators and interpreters of French post-structuralist theory) advocated more attention to mass culture and interdisciplinary theory in literature departments precisely for the reason that such a method would attract more students:

> In most universities the traditional English courses organized according to periods have suffered a decline in enrollments . . . The problem is structural, involving the marginal situation of literature within the students' cultures . . . Confronted with students for whom literature is simply one aspect of their culture, and an aspect with which they are relatively unfamiliar, teachers need to be able to discuss literature in relation to more familiar cultural products and in its relations to other ways of writing about the human experience, such as philosophy, psychology, sociology, anthropology, and history. (Culler 1981, pp. 212–13)

Furthermore, Culler also advocated that English departments begin to pick up intellectual niches that were being left behind or neglected by other disciplines, particularly the "humanistic" tradition: towards the end of his book he offered

> [w]hat may seem a peculiar suggestion – to have English departments go "outside the field" to teach what other departments neglect . . . This is especially important, it seems to me, in universities where philosophy departments fail to teach traditional philosophy and psychology departments reject psychoanalysis, producing a situation in which the central texts of the humanist tradition – Plato, Descartes, Hegel, Nietzsche, Freud – are neglected, unless they are taught in literature courses. (Culler 1981, p. 221)

Finally, Culler put forward the idea that literary studies could use literary theory to shore up its professional legitimacy *vis-à-vis* other academic disciplines. In a manner similar to the way in which economistic paradigms like rational choice theory have recently gained professional ground by redefining many social and political issues as "economic," literary studies could deconstruct the theories and methods of many other disciplines to show how they relied upon "literary" images and conventions, thus raising the relative professional status of literature departments:

> [W]e can think about literature in relation to other types of discourses by focusing on a theoretical topic, such as narrative or theory of tropes, that will enable us to see the importance and pervasiveness of structures that we traditionally regard as "literary" and thus to justify the importance that we think literary study ought to have. (Culler 1981, p. 217)

In the years since Culler voiced these suggestions, American literary studies have moved along many of the directions he proposed.[21] Scholarship studying literature from interdisciplinary perspectives has proliferated, as has work relating literature to other cultural forms. The approach of analyzing social science discourse to reveal its implicit "narratives" and "rhetorics" has caught on quite widely, and has precipitated major discussions and autocritiques in a number of disciplines; while this has not wholly been the result of the efforts of literary theorists, their work often figures prominently in these discussions (e.g. Brown 1987; Clifford and Marcus 1986; Hunter 1990; McClosky 1985). Literary theory, particularly through deconstruction, has kept a window open to continental philosophy and the humanist tradition, and while some have complained that this has led to a situation where undergraduate English majors tend to "discuss the logocentrism of the philosophical tradition without having read a single classic of philosophy" (Lamont 1987b, p. 593), it does seem to have made English departments attractive to many students.[22]

The most dramatic attempt at securing a new "niche" for literary studies, however – and the one which appears to have both the most momentum at present, and the most potential ramifications for the future of the discipline and the disciplinary ecology in general – is the contemporary push to redefine the professional subject matter of literature departments from "literature" to "culture" (or "discourse," or "text"). As we have seen, this is the program of many American literary scholars today. Their effort to secure "culture" as the province for literary study seeks in essence to legitimate the movement of many literary scholars onto intellectual terrains traditionally the province of history and the social sciences.

Some of these scholars see this project in a way analogous to literary studies' appropriation of Continental philosophy and the humanist tradition; they believe that the social sciences and history have neglected the study of cultural phenomena to the point of abdication, and that literature

departments can profit by picking up the abandoned niche; as Russell
Berman (a professor of literature at Stanford) recently put it in *Profession*:

Despite some recent developments, the study of culture is still marginal in history
departments, and culture is barely a factor at all in the quantitative social sciences.
So the interdisciplinarity that devolves from the replacement of literature (narrowly defined) by culture (broadly defined) has the advantage of revitalizing the
language and literature model by using an innovative pedagogy that examines a
culture through a range of objects, including but not restricted to canonic literature. (Berman 1995, p. 91)

For many of these scholars, however, "culture" is defined more broadly,
and is not just a question of subject matter but also one of politics and
methodology. They perceive their model of Cultural Studies as opposing
interpretive, textual, and/or "postmodern" methods to what they see as
the positivist and technocratic orientation of the quantitative social sciences.[23] From these scholars' perspective, a "critical" and culturally
focused literary studies discipline has as its legitimate terrain the entire
range of social phenomena, and is often seen as existing in a contested
relation to the mainstream social sciences, which are viewed as reflecting
a number of intellectually and politically regressive and outmoded "modernist" assumptions about objective knowledge, value-neutrality, and/or
human nature. Many of the more Cultural Studies-inclined professors
interviewed, for instance, expressed a generalized skepticism about quantitative work and positivistic rhetoric in the social science disciplines,[24]
and one explicitly described his work as entering onto social science
terrain in order to combat such tendencies:

Most of what I do I see as being more in social science terrain rather than the
humanities nowadays.

What's the difference?

Once you move into social science terrain, the local battles are a little different.
You tend to be at loggerheads with quantitative paradigms. And you can see from
department to department how there's a war going on, very clearly.

Do you see yourself as warring against quantitative paradigms?

Oh, yeah, I would be part of that. I'm part of that crusade, to save what we can.
[laughs] In a way it's the frontline between humanistic values and natural science
values.

For a variety of reasons, then – to react to a threatening drop-off in enrollments and prestige, to grasp perceived opportunities to seize intellectual
turf that is seen as "up for grabs," and to further methodological and
political agendas – American literary scholars have sought to expand their
discipline's professional intellectual niche.

In contrast, French literary studies have witnessed little of this kind of activity, and remain focused fairly narrowly upon the traditional terrain of canonical literature. Part of the reason for this may be that such efforts would be difficult and seen as out of place for literary studies within the French disciplinary ecology. With regard to the appropriation of other disciplines' abandoned professional terrain, there are few niches – at least of the sort which American literary studies have seized upon – for literary studies to pick up within the French disciplinary ecology. Psychology departments in France still teach Freud and Lacan, and French philosophers retain interest in both the history of philosophy and the Continental philosophical tradition. Many of the philosophically oriented social theorists often imported and appropriated by American literature departments (such as Michel Foucault, Jean Baudrillard, and Gilles Deleuze) are also the products (and the province) of French philosophy departments.

Attempts by literary scholars to appropriate the sphere of cultural phenomena from the social sciences, or to mount a humanistic challenge against them, would also seem implausible in the French context. While (often American-influenced) quantitative work and paradigms do exist in the French social sciences, they are fairly marginal. The mainstream of French social science has a long tradition of being "critical," interpretive, and attentive to culture; indeed, many of the thinkers often cited by Cultural Studies scholars in the United States (Pierre Bourdieu, for instance) are French social scientists. Generally, there seems to be more common ground and much less of a sense of intellectual separateness between the social sciences and the humanities in France than there is in the United States; French professors in both the humanities and the social sciences report less sense of intellectual foreignness or "otherness" across the social science/humanities divide than do their American counterparts, and many reject the distinction entirely in favor of a composite conception of *les sciences humaines* (the human sciences).[25] Given the situation in French social science, then, any attempt by French literary scholars to turn their discipline into a sort of refuge for a "shadow," humanist social science would seem superfluous; the social sciences in France already are largely humanist.

But by themselves, these greater obstacles to the discipline's expansion do not seem sufficient to fully explain why French literary studies has remained so canonical in focus. Some subject niches – popular fiction, for instance, and perhaps some other parts of mass culture – could certainly be within the professional domain of literature departments in France if literature professors wished to incorporate them. But by and large, they have shown little interest in making such an appropriation, and are content to remain focused on canonical literature. Why the lack of interest?

Partly, this seems to do with some of the national differences in literary studies already described earlier. The lack of any strong multicultural movement among French literary scholars, for instance, takes away a group that in the American context has had a whole set of incentives to push the borders of traditional subject matter, and the absence in France of American-style displaced political intellectuals would seem to have a similar negative effect.

It also seems likely that French literary scholars have had less reason to feel anxious about the prestige or institutional security of canonical literary study than have their American counterparts, and so have had less incentive to try to move into other areas of scholarship. Institutionally, literature departments in France have had little reason to fear being "downsized." Funding for academic departments is seldom tied to changes in undergraduate enrollments (which in any case seem to have been steadily rising for literature departments)[26] and funding for universities generally in France comes directly from a central government which is much less likely than American state and national governments to view funding for literary scholarship as an expendable luxury item in yearly budgets. In an era in which Francophone culture is often seen as under siege from "Hollywood" and other Anglophone influences, there is considerable and broad public support in French society for measures to protect and preserve the national culture. Besides the well-known instances of the French government's protection of the French film industry against American competition, and the Académie Française's efforts to resist the Anglicization of the French language, this cultural nationalism is manifested generally in the presence of state support for projects and institutions related to *patrimoine* (patrimony, or national heritage). The preservation and dissemination of classic French literature in the nation's universities fits directly into this goal of preserving *patrimoine*, and while literature departments are hardly lavishly funded, none of the scholars interviewed felt that there was any danger of their support being significantly cut. As one of the CNRS literary scholars put it:

Our society, despite its hypermodernism, is obsessed with patrimony. The word that is the most saleable today is the word "patrimony." If one wants to obtain money for a project for no matter what, one doesn't speak the language of "breakthroughs", et cetera; one must only say the word "patrimony," and the money rains down. This is a society which is at the moment completely patrimonial, and it's evident that there's nothing more patrimonial than literature as a cultural treasure. It has an obvious patrimonial aspect.

Beyond assured state support, it appears that canonical literature remains a cultural status item of more general and widespread importance in France than in the United States. Attempts to transpose Pierre

Bourdieu's (1984) model of how "cultural capital" plays a key role in social stratification and reproduction from its initial context of French society to American society seem to have demonstrated that cultural capital has a less significant role in American society than in France; Americans are less likely to value being "cultured" than are the French.[27] Furthermore, the very definition of cultural capital is more problematic in the United States; while the French seem to have a fairly homogeneous understanding of what sort of knowledge and culture make one a "cultured" person, Americans seem to share much less common ground on this issue, and the value of having a familiarity with the national canon of "high literature" is much less self-evident for many Americans than it is for a solid majority of the French. This greater social significance and appreciation of canonical literature in France may constitute a final reason why French literary studies have kept their canonical focus; with their object of study retaining a strong and generalized social prestige, French literary scholars may feel no need to move into other subject areas in order to maintain their discipline's "relevance" or intellectual profile.

Conclusion: the paradox of French influence?

In conclusion, let us return to the puzzle posed at the beginning of this essay: if French theorists have been so influential upon American literary scholars, why are literary studies so different in the two countries? Since most of this paper has already been devoted to explaining these differences, it is perhaps best at this point to reverse the terms of this apparent paradox: why have American literary scholars devoted so much energy to importing French scholarship, given that literary studies in the two countries are so "out of step" intellectually?

The paradoxical aspects of this importation largely disappear when one examines the specific French thinkers that American literary theorists have imported, for these thinkers are themselves largely "out of step" with contemporary French literary criticism. First and foremost, virtually all of these French thinkers are (or were) members of the more radical preceding generation of French intellectuals, against which the current generation of French literary scholars draw sharp intellectual boundaries. Furthermore, many, such as Lacan, Foucault, Derrida, and Althusser, were (or, in Derrida's case, are) not literary scholars, but rather hailed from other disciplines. Some, such as Barthes, were literary scholars, but never held regular academic appointments. Of the pantheon of French theorists imported to the United States in recent years, only Julia Kristeva holds a regular university appointment in a literature department in France. Of course, the fact that most of these thinkers have not held literature chairs does not mean that they have not been influential in French literary studies: many of them have been, particularly Barthes and Foucault. But their influence seems to have coincided largely with the atmosphere of radical politics that permeated France in the years following 1968, and with the relative waning of anti-statist and anti-capitalist sentiments in France since that time, their intellectual influence in French literary studies has declined.

By contrast, the "hermeneutics of suspicion" that form the common intellectual denominator of most of the French theories imported to the United States have proven more resiliently resonant with an American audience of literary scholars who remain more concerned with issues of power and domination than do their French counterparts.[28] While the focus of their concerns is obviously somewhat different, with more attention paid by Americans to issues of gender, race, and sexual preference, the French theorists who have become the most popular among American literary scholars are those whose theoretical apparatuses have proven sufficiently flexible to fit these issues. Michel Foucault's dissections of the intertwining of "discourse" and power, Derrida's deconstruction of hierarchical concepts of "difference," and Lacan's notion of the "other" are all capable of being transposed onto issues of race, gender, and sexuality, and have been by American literary scholars.

One would not, however, want to attribute the importation and influence of French theory solely to its elective affinity to the contemporary sociopolitical concerns of American literary theorists. In a number of articles, Michèle Lamont (1987b; Lamont and Witten 1988) has offered some other explanations for the popularity of Jacques Derrida and other French thinkers in American literary studies: their initial championing by professors at certain leading universities; the fact that "French theory" has been perceived as sophisticated, and has thus been used as a form of "cultural capital" within the academic literary field; and the fact that the applicability of deconstruction (and other French theories) to a wide variety of literary products has offered literature departments a way of creating a degree of intellectual community across the divisions of periodization.

This study suggests another cause related to Lamont's point about theoretical unification. Beyond internally unifying literary studies across periodizations, the importation of French theories has also strengthened American literary studies in its struggles with external disciplines over intellectual terrain. In particular, the importation of French theory has given literature scholars a "canon" of theories and theorists that is in effect social-scientific, yet which differs from the set of canonical theories and texts in the American social sciences themselves. It has thus aided those American literary scholars who seek to turn the discipline into a competing variant of the social science disciplines, helping to maintain the distinctiveness of their work from mainstream social science and thereby legitimating the discplines' coexistence in traditionally social-scientific terrain.

To the extent that a set of French theorists have played such a key role in the founding of contemporary American literary and cultural studies, their influence has been undeniable. But is this influence likely to continue? I would suggest that this is unlikely, for reasons of both supply and demand. On the supply side, there seem to be few "undiscovered" French theorists from the generation of Derrida and Foucault who have not already been imported by American literary theorists, and as we have seen, the contemporary generation of French literary scholars is not producing similar work. On the demand side, I would posit that American literary scholars no longer need an external theoretical canon on which to base their work. There are now enough "homegrown" canonical theorists and texts in American literary studies to form a basis for new scholarship, and a dissertation in literature in America today can just as easily build upon the work of American theorists such as Said, Sedgwick, or Butler as it can on Derrida or Lacan. Indeed, to the extent that American theorists have taken French theory in directions different from those of the French themselves, further importation of French theory might prove unwelcome and jarring. I would posit that the situation of American literary studies today is in some ways like that of sociology just after the rise of Parsonian structural functionalism: in that situation, too, a set of European theorists was used as the basis and legitimation for a new and sharply different style of scholarship, but with a tenor and an emphasis that made the field soon diverge from developments on the Continent, after which the direct influence of European scholars on their American counterparts dropped off sharply.

This study has confined itself to the examination of literary studies, and while this discipline has been among those most influenced by French theory, performing a satisfying analysis of the importation of French theories to American academia in general would require a broader focus than is provided here. The less successful (but still quite influential) attempts to bring French theories into disciplines such as anthropology, sociology, history, and political science would need to be accounted for, and this is beyond the scope of what can be accomplished here. It is hoped, however, that by providing an analysis of the differing state of literary studies in France and the United States, this paper has gone some distance towards examining the social factors affecting academic disciplines in France and the United States, and shed some light upon their often complicated international relations.

Notes

1 Frank Lentricchia, a literature professor at Duke University, has compared his generation's discovery of Derrida to an "awakening" from a "dogmatic slumber" (Lentricchia 1980, p. 159). It is worth noting that Lentricchia's opinion on the benefits of French theory has since changed dramatically.

2 Figures compiled by Michèle Lamont and Marsha Witten show a steady increase in articles on French thinkers in American academic journals of literary studies. Between the periods 1970–1977 and 1980–1987, for instance, there was an increase of 52 percent in articles on Foucault (44 vs. 67), an increase of 32 percent in articles on Barthes (94 vs. 124), and an increase of 390 percent in articles on Lacan (21 vs. 82). Figures for articles on Jacques Derrida show a similar trend, with an increase from 60 in 1970–1977 to 147 in 1980–1984 (Lamont 1987b). My thanks to Michèle Lamont for making these figures (some unpublished in the form presented here) available to me. For expanded discussion and numbers on the diffusion of French thinkers into a variety of disciplines in the United States, see Lamont and Witten 1988.

3 Such scholars would include, for instance, Edward Said, J. Hillis Miller, Gayatri Spivak, Eve Sedgwick, Fredric Jameson, Judith Butler, Henry Louis Gates, Jr., Houston Baker, Barbara Johnson, Barbara Herrnstein Smith.

4 Critics of recent trends in American literary scholarship tend to see it as in thrall to trendy French theories. For instance, Robert Hughes (1989) laments American academic literary critics' infatuation with "the lake of jargon whose waters (bottled for export to the United States) well up between Nanterre and the Sorbonne and to whose marshy verge the bleating flocks of poststructuralists go each night to drink." Camille Paglia daydreams a scenario where "Aretha Franklin ... shouting 'Think!' blasts Lacan, Derrida, and Foucault like dishrags against the wall, then leads thousands of freed academic white slaves in a victory parade down the Champs-Elysées" (*The New York Times Book Review*, May 5, 1991). Similar sentiments can be found in Kimball (1990).

5 Interviews were split evenly between each country (ten in France, ten in the United States), and took place in Paris and the New York area in the summer of 1995. Interviewees were chosen via snowball sampling: an initial list was derived from surveying approximately half a dozen professors familiar with the discipline in either country, and interviewees were then asked to provide further names. The criteria for inclusion given to respondents was that they try to compile a list that both included "prominent" scholars, and that represented the diversity of intellectual perspectives within their discipline. The institutional affiliations of interviewees in France included the Universities of Paris III and IV (the Sorbonne), VII, and VIII; the Ecole des Hautes Etudes en Sciences Sociales; the Maison des Sciences de l'Homme; and the Collège de France. In the United States, they included Columbia University; the City University of New York Graduate Center; New York University; Rutgers University; Princeton University; and Yale University. The decision was made to interview professors of French literature in France, and of English literature in America, rather than professors of the same literature (French or English) in both countries, on the assumption that scholars of the national literature of their respective countries would form more structurally homologous groups

than would scholars of a single literature that was foreign in one of the two contexts. All interviews were done under signed agreement that interviewee comments would be anonymous in attribution, so that participants could speak with a maximum of candor.

6 The phrase "hermeneutic of suspicion" derives from philosopher Paul Ricœur's (1970) work on Freud and Marx, and has come to refer generally in the humanities to any intellectual methodology which, given a truth claim, immediately seeks to problematize it by uncovering the power interests driving such claims.

7 Books and articles on the process of canon formation and/or the social influences on the reception of various authors have become a popular scholarly subject among American literary scholars. See, for instance, Tompkins 1985; Spender 1986; Crawford 1992; and Guillory 1993.

8 These demands are being made on behalf of more groups than ever, with the initial movements for the acceptance of Afro-American literature and women's literature as legitimate and professionally recognized categories being matched by calls for Hispanic, Asian American, Native American, and gay literatures as well. Attempts to formulate canons for these groups have been made via the publication of anthologies, and it is also increasingly common to see university literature courses based around these categories.

9 I use the term "modernist" as it is the term which is used by French scholars themselves. In the United States, however, many of the same intellectual positions (such as those of Foucault, Lacan, Barthes, etc.) are typically referred to as "postmodern," and the term "modernist" instead is used to refer to older forms of scholarship (or to current scholarship perceived to be operating under antiquated assumptions), typically in a derogatory way. The fact that "postmodernism" – perhaps the most (de)central referent in American literary studies in the last fifteen years or so – is a term with little or no meaning for French literary scholars is itself suggestive of wide cross-national intellectual differences in the discipline.

10 Two of the scholars I interviewed did do work that is non-canonical in focus (one on journalism in the nineteenth century, and the other on a range of symbolic phenomena in the Middle Ages), but both were connected with interdisciplinary CNRS research institutes. Both labeled themselves as "impure" literary scholars, however, and noted that they have little contact with the mainstream of their discipline.

11 WASP is an acronym for "White Anglo-Saxon Protestant," though it is generally used more to refer to the white, well-educated and established élite in the United States, rather than being strictly applied to Protestants of English origin.

12 While individual feminist literature scholars are present in France, none of the French scholars interviewed noted any feminist challenge to the canon analogous to that in the United States. None of the scholars in the sample worked on Francophone literature, and the one scholar who mentioned Francophone literature in an interview did so only to note its absence; he stated that Italian literary scholars have actually done more work in the area than French scholars themselves.

13 The great exception to the general lack of hierarchy among higher educational

institutions in France is of course the small number of élite Grandes Ecoles, and there has been some recent concern about the demographic make-up of the students at these institutions, whose graduates comprise a quite disproportionate percentage of France's élite. At a recent talk at Princeton, for instance, a professor from the Ecole Normale Supérieure presented statistics showing that the composition of the student body has increasingly been dominated by the upper classes. So far, however, admission to the Grandes Ecoles remains entirely based upon competitive examinations, and the schools are seen by many as the epitome of French educational meritocracy.

14 The loud objections many minority literary scholars have directed towards dissidents like Shelby Steele, Camille Paglia, and Katie Roiphe have been matched in polemical force perhaps only by those directed at Republican appointees to the National Endowment for the Humanities such as William Bennett and Lynne Cheney.

15 The term "intellectuals" is notoriously vague, and I should make clear here that I am using "humanist intellectuals" to refer to artists, writers, philosophers, and critics, etc., who wish to intervene in public debates, and not to political figures, policy experts, or professional journalists.

16 A list of humanist intellectuals in America today who are both publicly prominent and conservative could include, for instance, William Bennett, George Will, William F. Buckley, and Irving Kristol, to name a few. For documentation of the rise of public conservative intellectuals, and its connection with the broader rise to power of conservatism in America in recent decades, see Blumenthal 1988. It should be noted that the sense of media isolation among intellectuals from minority groups in America may be diminishing with the increasing rise to public prominence of a group of black intellectuals such as Cornel West, Henry Louis Gates, Jr., and Bell Hooks, among others (Anderson 1994).

17 The phrase "political correctness" first appeared in the press in a *New York Times* article by Richard Bernstein (1990). At its height the controversy over PC received a cover study in *Newsweek* (1990), a major feature article in *Time* (Henry 1991), stories in *USA Today* (e.g. Grabmeier 1992) and similarly high-profile coverage in most other major journalistic publications.

18 Priscilla Parkhurst Clark notes that public intellectuals in France today tend to use university appointments as "a springboard to general intellectual life and to a broad, heterogenous public" (Clark 1987, p. 197).

19 Of course, if French academia were witnessing affirmative action programs for scholars of Algerian and African descent, and/or if attacks were being made on the French canon in the name of a Francophone or Franco-Arab multiculturalism, this situation might be quite different – which perhaps underscores the role these types of phenomena may have had in the United States in making literary studies the subject of political controversy.

20 The number of bachelor's degrees awarded in English literature in the United States declined from 64,342 in the 1970/71 academic year to 32,254 in 1980/81 – a drop of 50 percent. This number has gradually recovered strength since the mid to late 1980s, with 56,133 degrees reported in 1992/3, the latest year for which statistics are available at the time of this writing (National Center of Education Statistics 1995, Table 243).

21 It should be made clear that I am not trying to claim that these ideas originated with Culler, or to place any specific measure on the effects of his advocacy; rather, I cite him to show that concerns such as his were evident in American literary studies at least as far back as the early 1980s.

22 The noted American philosopher Richard Rorty has suggested that literary theory in the United States today fills an important role for intellectually minded students that philosophy used to fill in America, and still does in France and other European countries:

> I think that in . . . America philosophy has already been displaced by literary criticism in its principal cultural function – as a source for youth's self-description of its own difference from the past . . . This is roughly because of the Kantian and anti-historicist tenor of Anglo-Saxon philosophy. The cultural function of teachers of philosophy in countries where Hegel was not forgotten is quite different and closer to the position of literary critics in America. (Rorty 1980, p. 168)

23 In the case of certain literary scholars associated with "Science Studies," this suspicion about positivist methodology also extends to the natural sciences, and has produced much controversy, such as in the recent "Sokal Affair," in which New York University physicist Alan Sokal submitted to *Social Text* (a prominent Cultural Studies journal) a paper which contained many erroneous statements about physics but was written in a "postmodern" style. The paper was published, and Sokal's subsequent revelation that it was a hoax attracted a great deal of media attention. See Alan Sokal 1996a and b; Scott 1996; Berkowitz 1996; and Begley and Rogers 1996.

24 A representative quote: "I'm generally skeptical of positivistic claims, outside of the hard sciences . . . I think that human stuff doesn't quantify terribly well, and I further have doubts about the people who do it [laughs], in terms of their infallibility. I'm skeptical of the general face that quantitative work, positivistic work, presents in the social sciences."

25 In related research I have also interviewed twenty political scientists in France and the United States. When asked about scholarship across their side of the social science/humanities divide, American political scientists and literary scholars were much more likely to report feelings such as a lack of intellectual familiarity or a sense of strong intellectual difference, and more often expressed the sense that they lacked the competence to evaluate such work as good or bad (frequently with explanations such as "I don't understand what the rules are in those disciplines"). French scholars, by contrast, were much less likely to report such feelings of difference, and tended to be quite confident in their ability to evaluate all but the most technical or specialized work across the breadth of *les sciences humaines*.

26 Eric Fassin, personal correspondence.

27 For an empirical and theoretical examination of how Bourdieu's model fares when applied to the United States context, see Lamont 1992.

28 Michèle Lamont and Marsha Witten, noting the often significant intellectual differences between the theorists imported to United States humanities departments, conclude that they "converge substantively only to the extent that [most] of them study the process by which culture . . . contributes to the reproduction of power relations" (Lamont and Witten 1988, p. 19).

Part II

The cultural sphere: publishing, journalism, and the arts

5   Culture or commerce? Symbolic boundaries in French and American book publishing

Daniel Weber

Book publishing is a particularly fertile ground for the comparative study of how people construct and use classification schemes in their evaluation processes. The main activities of book publishing revolve around a core set of decisions which are firmly rooted in underlying assessments of worth about what to publish and why. Moreover, the sector as a whole and its inhabitants are the focus of debates over the status of books in an age of multimedia, global information technologies, industry consolidation, and shifting cultural hierarchies among large segments of the reading public. Publishing professionals are presently confronted with unprecedented opportunities and threats, their positions and role-expectations are changing, and their daily tasks and responsibilities are in flux. The contemporary transformation of book publishing creates an unstable terrain of new conflicts and compromises which are inextricably bound to the edification and defense of symbolic territories and boundaries.

This study examines the book publishing communities in France and the United States in order to understand how publishers evaluate and classify the realm of literature and ideas. In general, I will identify the criteria used to construct *symbolic boundaries*, that is, the lines publishers sketch when they categorize literary and intellectual work. A primary focus of the research is on the rhetorical language used to define "worthy" and "less worthy" books, authors, genres, and contemporary cultural tendencies. A secondary goal is to clarify the criteria mobilized by publishers to characterize professional peers and perceived readers of different kinds of books. I draw on sixty in-depth interviews conducted with book editors and publishers in Paris and New York to determine the symbolic boundaries through which the interviewees assign value and meaning to the world of books and their professional lives.

The book publishing industries in France and the United States share numerous common traits and they are presently experiencing many similar changes. At the same time, however, we observe striking divergences in market structures and organizational practices which correspond to different conceptions of "book culture" and of the roles and missions of publishing professionals. A central aim of this study, therefore, is to *explain differences* in the rhetorics used to pronounce and justify viewpoints about salient themes in the book domain through a comparative analysis of variation in the organization of publishing and in national cultural frameworks.

I will show, for instance, that American publishers do not make systematic references to cultural hierarchies as the French do. They tend to classify books in a more utilitarian manner, with particular emphasis on whether or not books are in line with specific editorial objectives and successful bookselling categories. American interviewees see the audience and book retailers as the main forces behind the construction of new genres and classifications. By contrast, French interviewees appeal more to literary and intellectual heritage and how a new book, author, or genre relates to that tradition, either continuing it or deliberately breaking with it.

The book publishing sectors in both France and the United States include a wide spectrum of houses and imprints which vary not only in size but also in degree of literary or scholarly versus commercial and mass market orientations. The present study takes this reality into account in the sampling of interviewees to correct for possibly inflated national differences. Nevertheless, despite many forms of symmetry, I will demonstrate that French interviewees, whether they work more toward the commercial or the cultural end of the spectrum, are frequently uncomfortable with what they perceive as an inherent contradiction between "popular" and "noble" books. For example, they often justify a desire to launch a bestseller as a means of subsidizing a more difficult or experimental work. American interviewees, by contrast, regardless of their publishing background, see a greater congruity between sales results and a good book. For instance, they are more appreciative of a viable marketing strategy and the efforts of sales personnel in assuring the success of a new publication. The appeal to the market is a salient and taken-for-granted element in the American definition of cultural value.

We will also explore the theme of cultural domination and subordination in an increasingly global literary marketplace. Like movies, television programs, videos, and music recordings, the United States is a major supplier of books to the world. In particular, American bestsellers in the adult fiction category tend to be highly successful in many countries, including France. The sale of French translation rights, on the other hand, is much smaller in value and its worldwide share has declined significantly. Contemporary French works of fiction are especially weak in the American market. The unequal exchange of literature is a source of anxiety among many French publishers, namely those working in literary houses. They voice fears of standardization and a threat to diversity and originality in the supply of books. American publishers, by contrast, are confident about what they see as growing diversity within the United States market due to efforts to cultivate ethnic, gender, and sexual orientation genres.

In this study, I try to make sense of such opposing sets of criteria mobilized by interviewees to construct symbolic boundaries through an analysis of the context of book publishing in France and the United States. First, organizational structures and practices exhibit sharp contrasts which are often related to differences in the way that the sectors have developed in the two countries. Differences in the structure of the book market and in collective conventions about publishing generate dissimilar incentives and constraints which influence classification schemes. Secondly, the specificities of national cultural frameworks, including perceptions of the place of books and literature in society, provide unique repertoires from which French and American publishers draw criteria to build, maintain, and shift symbolic boundaries.

Theoretical background

In recent years, sociologists have examined processes of evaluation as submerged in social relations. They point out that the interests and actions of any one actor are constrained or enabled by the structural relations among actors (Granovetter 1985). These works suggest that evaluations are embedded in concrete social ties such as those found in networks, organizations, or fields (DiMaggio 1982). The strength of these analyses is that they can account for variations in how decision-makers evaluate, classify, choose, and justify their actions by controlling for differences in the objective conditions of specific contexts. Moreover, the theoretical constructs and predictive hypotheses of these approaches are particularly adapted to the realities of cultural industries such as book publishing which operate within interpersonal networks or what Peterson (1979) calls "specialized milieux of symbolic production."

Similarly, much of the recent work on organizations emphasizes that evaluation processes are shaped by "institutions," that is, routinely reproduced, taken-for-granted social practices and shared conventions (Powell and DiMaggio 1991).[1] Such analyses help us to understand how classifications and judgments are related to collective conventions that define what is legitimate and feasible. Furthermore, these assumptions and concepts are especially relevant for the present study, which takes a cross-national comparative perspective. After all, organizations such as publishing houses are themselves woven into a larger cultural fabric that varies from country to country.[2]

In sum, the new directions in the study of evaluation processes mark a radical departure from past efforts, especially those that rely on rational choice models. In particular, these approaches make two powerful assertions which are relevant to the present project: first, such processes are shaped by an overarching order of meaning that designates the criteria for legitimacy, appropriateness, and worth; and secondly, this order of meaning is itself influenced by and enacted within specific national and historical contexts.

But how does one identify this order of meaning empirically? This study applies the framework developed by Michèle Lamont for analyzing the structures of thought or "mental maps" through which people classify and evaluate objects, events, and other people (Lamont 1992). In particular, we use the analytical tool of "symbolic boundaries" to illuminate the way in which French and American publishers define their profession and role in the world of books, literature, and ideas.[3]

The context: book publishing in France and the United States

Book publishing is a highly complex industry with multiple orientations and editorial strategies. In fact, most sociologists in both France and the United States who analyze book publishing as an organizational field stress its dual nature.[4] In general, we can place publishing houses along a continuum ranging from more "literary" or "scholarly" orientations to more "commercial" ones. As we move from literary to commercial publishing, we observe a greater emphasis on the following: a broad audience, the current frontlist, bestsellers, subsidiary rights, competitive bids, television talk-shows, book marketing specialists, and sales forecasts. On the other hand, as one moves from commercial to literary publishing, greater importance is assigned to a narrow audience, intellectual networks, backlist potential and development, and book reviews in key periodicals. A primary hypothesis of the present study is that variation in these book publishing parameters foster different motivations and expectations which influence the way publishers and editors make judgments about books, the reading public, their professional peers, and even their own self-identity and worth.

On both sides of the Atlantic, we find similar patterns and tendencies at work within the organizational field of book publishing. In addition, however, the structure and composition of French and American book publishing exhibit several significant differences.[5] A few of these differences have deep historical roots and are linked to collective representations about the position of the publishing enterprise within the world of books and its mission as a cultural gate-keeper.

Literary publishing is extremely concentrated in France, with a large portion of sales attributed to only a handful of distinguished Parisian houses located within the same neighborhood, such as Gallimard, Grasset, Le Seuil, Flammarion, and Albin Michel (Greffe, Pleiger, and Rouet 1990; *Livres Hebdo*, December 1997). By contrast, literary and scholarly publishing is more diffuse in the United States because of relatively greater geographical dispersion and the vitality of university presses (*Livres Hebdo*, January 1998; Parsons 1989). At the more commercial end of the spectrum, French publishing is no less concentrated. The trade book sector is dominated by the towering presence of two multimedia giants: Hachette and Havas.[6] These two groups, moreover, control the distribution channels that funnel over half of all books to retailers and readers. American commercial publishing has experienced consolidation through numerous mergers and acquisitions over the past two decades, but so far there has been little forward integration into distribution.

The retail side of the market is quite different in the two countries. In the United States, book clubs, chainstores, and now superstores are concentrated in the hands of a few owners. Centralized buying is a key feature of the American book market, which gives the chain retailer considerable leverage in negotiating orders and discounts from publishers. In France, the "single price law" established by Jack Lang has effectively discouraged discounting practices and the development of powerful retail chains (Maruani 1992; Piault 1995). Independent booksellers still account for a significant portion of total sales in France compared with the 14 percent in the United States (Bouvaist 1991; *Publishers Weekly*, May 1997).[7]

The professional organization of the publishing industry also reveals significant differences between the two countries. American trade book publishing is dominated by literary agents who play an increasingly important role. There are very few agents in France, where publishers and editors are in closer contact with authors with whom they discuss directly book projects and contractual matters. In the United States, particularly in the fast-moving sector of commercial trade publishing, agents have come to assume many of the rights and responsibilities once reserved for publishers and editors.[8]

In sum, we find considerable sources of variation in the organizational field of book publishing both within and across national contexts. A central hypothesis of this study is that in both France and the United States, contrasting orientations to the book market produce different incentives and constraints which shape the way editors and publishers make judgments about books, genres, readers, peers, and professional self-identity. Furthermore, this study also argues that the specific criteria mobilized to make these judgments and draw symbolic boundaries vary even more so according to the cultural backgrounds of the two countries.[9]

Data and methods

The author conducted in-depth interviews with thirty French and thirty American book publishers and editors in order to identify the criteria they used to evaluate the publishing world and their role in it. Six informants familiar with the French and American publishing sectors helped to classify houses according to their book market orientation; i.e. more commercial trade or more literary and scholarly.[10] The study focuses on the job categories most directly responsible for editorial decisions, namely, editors and publishing directors.[11]

The data were collected through confidential semi-structured interviews at the publishing house. Most of the French and American interviews were recorded. Several interviewers, however, asked not to be recorded, but allowed note-taking. All interviews covered the same general topics, though not always in the same order: descriptions of daily activities, working with colleagues, new book selections, evaluation of genres and authors, perceptions of different types of book readers, opinions about publishers and where the sector is heading.

During the interviews we discussed a variety of topics related to book publishing, literature, and readership trends. Interviews varied in terms of time, the emphasis on certain topics, the sequence of themes covered, the number of interruptions, and the general atmosphere of the interview situation. All interviews, however, probed two critical themes: (1) criteria for classifying books, authors, and genres; and (2) evaluations of readers and professional peers. These two broad themes yield the richest information on cross-national differences and, at least in the French case, highlight the sharp contrasts between literary and commercial publishing.

Criteria for classifying books, authors, and genres

One finding is that French editors tend to perceive a literary world in which books, authors, and genres are rank-ordered by prestige. The primary classification scheme appears to be vertical.[12] The interviewees frequently refer to the distinctions between what they label "noble" and "popular" works, or between "*littérature de création*" and "*littérature de vente*" ("original, creative literature" and "commercial works"). It is striking that this hierarchical order of value is used by most French editors in the sample, whether they work in literary or commercial publishing. What differs is the evaluation and judgment of that order. For example, I interviewed an energetic but slightly tense woman who is an editor of romantic fiction.

I realize that these books I edit are not noble and sometimes I feel a bit ashamed about that. However, by doing this work, I feel I can reach out to housewives who might otherwise watch television. Besides even romantic fiction has its own little scale of values . . . some authors really know how to create a moving story that stimulates dreams and fantasy . . . these are the ones I select for publication . . . others just apply cheap formulae and turn out unimaginative books merely to make money.

She recognizes a vertical order of aesthetic worth and draws a boundary between "noble" works and the type of work she edits. We also note a tinge of inner conflict surrounding her occasional feeling of shame associated with her job. She justifies her career, however, by making the claim that providing women with romantic fiction keeps them from watching too much television – a cultural practice that, in her mind, lies even lower in the hierarchy of worth. Furthermore, she even applies the essential principle of hierarchical classification to her own genre, once again as a justification for what she does. Although she cannot claim that her authors' books are "noble," she can draw the line between the terms "creative" and "merely to make money." In sum, her feelings of inferiority and superiority, her sense of inner contradiction, as well as her definitions of literary merit, are all aligned with a strict vision of cultural hierarchies.

Not all French interviewees working in commercial publishing feel the same degree of tension as this woman. Most of them, however, say they are often looked down upon by intellectuals, journalists, and more literary publishing peers, and they still seem to envision a book world fixed along a vertical axis. For example, I interviewed another successful editor of trade fiction in France.

Here in France people criticize us [the publishing house] for being so successful . . . they have this knee-jerk reaction that "popular" means tasteless. They claim that our novels are all the same. They cannot see that this literature has its traditions and qualities . . . that each story has subtle variations in form and content, that it speaks of the human condition, that it is thought-provoking and is not mere entertainment.

She is defensive about what she thinks is the widespread belief in France that popular genres are inferior. But then she proceeds to elevate the status of such popular fiction by emphasizing its traditions and qualities, mobilizing the criteria normally applied to "high" literature. By doing so, she can distinguish such works from what she describes disparagingly as "mere entertainment." Although she is a commercial publisher and proud of it, her grammar of evaluation belongs to the same collective conventions that maintain a vertical division between what might be called "sacred" literature and "profane" entertainment.

The same cultural totem pole is to be found among editors at the more literary and eminent publishing houses of the sixth *arrondissement*, the district considered to be the heart and soul of traditional Parisian publishing. The most common observation is that these editors seem to be deeply disturbed by what they see as the collapse of cultural hierarchies. They speak repeatedly about a crisis in book publishing for which they blame commercialization, bestsellers, American imports, television, the decline of ideological debate, compact discs, and sometimes themselves. I spoke to one editor in a small house with a distinguished backlist.

Publishing is not what it used to be . . . literary creation used to drive the business and now it is the other way around. Walk into a bookstore in Saint-Germain today and you will find celebrity biographies sitting next to an NRF. Booksellers and buyers no longer recognize the difference.

This repondent expresses a reverent nostalgia for a lost age when there were less fluid boundaries between élite works, such as those published by the venerable NRF (Nouvelle Revue Française) imprint, and popular works about celebrities. He implicitly views hierarchy as the natural order of the cultural world, and is revolted by what he sees as the disintegration of that symbolic order.[13] What is particularly nuanced is that he restricts his lamentations to his own little sphere of sixth *arrondissement* publishing. For instance, he refers critically to bookstores and imprints at the heart of the Parisian literary world instead of condemning more obvious but more distant entities such as the *FNAC* chainstore, book clubs, supermarkets that sell books, and the large commercial publishing houses. What bothers him most is the crumbling walls between the noble and the popular within his own familiar territory.

The American publishers with whom I spoke also evoke symbolic boundaries in their discussion of books, genres, and authors. They do not, however, refer as explicitly as the French to cultural hierarchies. A few admit that the book world can be divided into such categories as "high brow" and "low brow," or "trash" and "quality." But these labels and metaphors are usually limited to passing remarks. Most interviewees classify books in a very utilitarian fashion, i.e. whether they match a particular editorial strategy, correspond to a social or intellectual trend, or most commonly, fit a typical bookselling category.[14] Moreover, there are no discernible differences between literary and commercial houses in this respect, at least within the present sample. I spoke to one young woman who is editor for health books at a large commercial house in New York.

Putting a label on a book is the most important thing I can do for it as an editor. It really helps the sales reps and booksellers have a clear idea of where the book belongs in the store. A poorly classified book can be a disaster. I recently published a book on food for well-being that entered all the chainstores in the cooking section and not the health and well-being section. It flopped. I also had problems with an author who proposed a project on "morning sickness" . . . When I saw the final manuscript I saw that she had expanded it into a full-blown anthropological study on the experience of morning sickness in different cultures. It was a fine bit of scholarly research but I was really angry and told her that readers in my market segment wanted to know how to avoid puking, not about the myths and taboos of the Yoruba.

She begins with the straightforward remark about the commercial value of finding the right label for a new book. The main concern is not whether a new release can occupy a position in a hierarchy, but simply that it can be placed in a clear position in what is probably the most important classification system in American publishing – that of the chain bookstore. Her fears as an editor have nothing to do with whether a book is noble or popular; her nightmare experience is about sales representatives who mistakenly tell retailers to place the book in the wrong section of the store. All sections are treated as equal, but some books are more appropriate for certain sections than for others. This same view is confirmed in the reference to the "morning sickness" case, albeit from a different angle. In this particular instance, the interviewee recognizes the scholarly merit of the manuscript, but she justifies her anger and disappointment by pointing her finger at the lack of fit with her target readers.

The relative absence of explicit cultural hierarchies is evident even in the more scholarly and literary houses. One telling example is from a prominent university press. I spoke with the editor-in-chief about what is worthwhile publishing these days at a university press. In contrast to the person we just met in the trade house, her classification system was guided more by academic disciplines, or at least academic trends, and less by bookstore sections (although she admits the latter is becoming more important).

We have cut back on the drier social science monographs in favor of cultural studies. The latter is much more exciting and relevant. We are also trying to build collections in the areas of feminist studies, gay-lesbian-bisexual studies, and ethnic studies. We want to break from the old academic disciplines. These [the new collections] reach a broader public and if we don't act fast enough in this direction our competitors will take the lead . . . and our competitors are increasingly cash-rich trade houses capable of putting a lot of money behind a title and an author.

She mobilizes the opposition between "dry" and "exciting" or "relevant" to justify a new editorial strategy. The label "dry" does not mean more or less noble; and "exciting" does not mean more or less popular. Even the aim to meet the needs of a broader public is not evoked as a slide down the cultural ladder; it is considered to be a taken-for-granted course of action in an age when university presses and trade houses often compete in the same market. Furthermore, her desire to break away from the established academic disciplines is an increasingly common feature of American intellectual publications at a time when trends such as "multiculturalism" and "cultural studies" have become popular commodities. It also reflects the emergence of a new system of classification which is coming to dominate this end of the marketplace for ideas, at least in the United States.[15]

American publishers perceive considerable differentiation among genres and subgenres but they usually do not assign a value of one over another. How are genre categories created and sustained? This key question is at the heart of a conversation with an acquisitions editor in a large New York trade house.

Authors and critics do not create and sustain genres, but readers do. I do everything I can to take the American pulse and track the latest social trends. That's really important. For example, we are putting out several new titles about religion and spirituality. I don't know if the wave will last, but the category is booming right now. But if I position the book as religion in the old denominational sense, it won't work so well. What's going on in America today is that people are thirsty for a spiritual dimension in their everyday lives which often has little to do with going to church or belonging to a religion. We did not understand this at first, and we classified our books as religion and that's where they ended up in the bookstores and the book club lists. Now we promote them as "lifestyle" books which moves them with the current toward expanding human potentials and that sort of thing. It's no better or no worse than a religion book, it's just much better adapted to the needs of today's readers.

He claims that the audience is the driving force behind the construction of genres and categories; in other words, it is the market which establishes the symbolic order of worth and value.[16] Later on in the interview he explained to me that he monitors social trends by reading *Time*, other magazines, watching popular movies, and simply observing his friends. He repeatedly insists that understanding the audience is critical to his job as an acquisitions editor. In his discussion of popular books on religion, he points out the importance of correct classification, that is, finding the label that is in resonance with the prevailing mood. He does not disdain old-style religious books, he merely feels they are not adapted to his particular editorial strategy, which seeks to be at the cutting edge of the widest reading public possible. Like the earlier American interviewee, he emphasizes the importance of bookseller categories in defining his choice of label. Finally, his last statement reveals that he does not make evaluations according to hierarchical criteria, at least not in this case. Nor does he revert to aesthetic or moral references. A book that adapts to the market is legitimate in its own right.

Evaluation of readers and publishing peers

A key finding of this research is that the perceived worthiness of a book is often bound to judgments about its intended readers. In other words, the criteria used to discriminate between "worthy" and "less worthy" readers is implicit in the way publishers and editors classify books, authors, and genres. They share the propensity to construct images of the book-reading public which at times plays a major role in their modes of evaluation and judgment.

Publishers and editors working in more literary or scholarly houses concentrate on the selection and diffusion of works that usually appeal to smaller, and sometimes specialized, audiences. Both the American and French interviewees who work in such houses claim to feel a certain proximity to their audience, with whom they see themselves as sharing similar interests, tastes, and sensibilities. On the other hand, editors with greater commercial inclinations convey the sense that they view their audience from a distance and in a more impersonal fashion. They employ a vocabulary and rhetoric that suggest a vision of book readers as consumers, defined in terms of needs and preferences, and not the presence or absence of literary taste or requisite knowledge. For example, one publisher of romantic novels in Paris said:

Though I do not feel close to these women, I do my best to understand them and their changing outlook. I also imagine that the French romantic novel reader is more sophisticated than her American counterpart. When we translate American works we have to get rid of the disgusting gold-colored embossed titles and silly cover scenes. We also rearrange the narrative to make it more palatable for the French reader. For example, we alter the sex scenes . . . American readers seem to go for a very mechanical rendition of lovemaking, such as "he touched me here and that made me . . . " French readers expect more sensuality . . . and in the end, we deliver a superior product.

She sees her readers from a distance and maintains a boundary between her self-identity and them. But then she raises the status of her readers when discussing American imports and what they reflect about the garishness and naiveté of their readers. In this particular case, she refers to American readers to define the superiority of the "improved" French product destined for a more sophisticated reading public. Through a comparison with an "outside" group of readers, she reconceptualizes the status of French readers in the same manner that Joseph Gusfield (1963) shows how social drinkers are elevated in status when compared with drinking drivers. We also see in this example that the shift in emphasis from one social category to another (different groups of readers) acts to redefine the boundaries between legitimate and illegitimate literature in a way reminiscent of Nicola Beisel's (1997) study of Anthony Comstock and his crusade against pornography. The only difference is that the publisher of romantic novels engages in such "boundary shifting" along a dimension that is more cultural or aesthetic than moral.

Publishers frequently judge their peers as well as genres, authors, and readers. Such evaluations often reflect simmering tensions within the publishing milieu arising from different and contradictory approaches to the book market. These strains are considerably more salient and alive in the French setting than the American one. For instance, one French interviewee who is an editor in a distinguished scholarly publishing house lamented:

I did not go into this job for the money, because I knew the pay was poor and the hours long. But I thought my life would be culturally rich. However, with the staff reductions and the mountains of administrative tasks, I have little time for authors and editorial work. My job is rotten. This is why when I meet editors at houses like Laffont or Hachette [houses with a more commercial orientation], I avoid them, their simplistic self-assurance revolts me. Is this where Parisian publishing is heading?

On the other hand, an editor in a well-known commercial house sketched a very different portrait of Parisian publishing. He told me:

Some editors are really pretentious, especially those in the sixth *arrondissement*. They are mostly just failed writers and they do not realize that we are only technicians, mercenaries of literary culture, nothing more.

These opposing viewpoints and strong emotional language are common in the present sample of French publishing professionals. The diverging perspectives stem, in part, from deep differences in the construction of professional self-identity. At least in this sample, French literary editors tend to identify with a traditional publishing role which emphasizes the qualities of a rich cultural background and artistic originality. They believe they play a critical role as the defenders of aesthetic and intellectual ideals in an age of cultural massification and the commodification of literature and ideas. Conversely, commercial editors and publishers tend to demystify the profession by contending that editors can learn a few basic techniques to become competent.

These findings confirm other studies on conflicts between subgroups of professionals in the French cultural industries. For example, Dominique Mehl (1993) discovers a sharp divide between French television producers and directors in how they define legitimate culture and in how they view their moral mission. Similarly, Dominique Pasquier and Sabine Chalvon-Demersay (1993) demonstrate that these differences among television professionals can be traced to the emergence of private stations and increased commercialization which alter the internal status hierarchy within the industry. And indeed, most experts on the French publishing sector agree that the recent waves of mergers and acquisitions have lowered the professional status of the traditional type of publisher and editor. As one French editor from a prestigious medium-sized house which had been recently purchased by a multimedia giant remarked to me:

I no longer have the autonomy I used to enjoy. Now I must listen to the sales and marketing people, consider their opinions first . . . they used to listen to me. This change is really hurting the quality of books we publish since these people do not know anything about literature.

Not only are such sharply opposing viewpoints in line with the division between literary and commercial houses in France, they occur increasingly within the same house and even among editors working on the same collections. The reason is that commercial houses are starting to hire token "intellectual" editors to boost their symbolic capital, and literary houses are hiring editors with commercial skills to boost sales. For example, one interviewee in a very serious scholarly publishing house said:

The editorial staff here live in another era. They think they can continue to publish dense and specialized monographs . . . university professors and students no longer buy these things, they have them photocopied. Other houses are producing similar works but more adapted to a wider public. In the past five years sales are in a free fall . . . and they do not seem to care or try to understand why I make marketing plans.

I gathered from his tiny, grim attic office that what he said was true. He obviously had no influence in that house. Such frustrations are common in France where, at least in the more traditional houses, business-minded editors are sometimes scorned and neglected. These same people, however, may feel quite at home in a commercial trade house. One of these publishers told me point blank:

I am an opportunist. I take advantage of events and release books as fast as possible. Our sales and profits have grown while my "friends" in other houses are all complaining about the book crisis, the end of literature, and other illusions. It's my task to provide the French with as many new books as possible. Other publishers, especially those who are only produced and read on the Left Bank, are responsible for the crisis; they do not know that the rest of France is thirsty for books.

Such colliding viewpoints are not quite so visible in the United States. I did not hear in the interviews many nasty remarks about literary editors who are outmoded or commercial publishers who are rapacious. The American publishers and editors in the sample tended to be appreciative of marketing and sales personnel, claiming that their input is usually sound and beneficial. One publishing director in a New York trade house said:

You may hear some comments like "sales people are philistines" or "editors are babies," but the two groups usually get along. I have heard that in certain houses there are periodic tensions, but certainly here we get along fine. In fact, we have weekly meetings including the marketing director, the national sales director, and the editorial staff. Acquisitions and marketing matters are discussed together in the open.

Several American editors explained to me that it was normal to have such good relationships. All editors in the American sample recognize the value of a good salesperson in such a large country where competition to win a slot in a chainstore or book club is fierce. The same seems to apply to public relations people who make the prized contacts with radio and television talk-shows. In France, on the other hand, I was told that editors sometimes go themselves to the important Parisian bookstores to present new books. Many editors and publishers are personal friends with authors, literary critics, journalists, and other media professionals. The tight-knit world of Parisian publishing endows the editor with a broader and more fluid role. Finally, this study shows that there is greater mobility in American publishing. In the sample of American interviews, it is clear that people circulate more frequently among publishing houses and job categories. By contrast, most of the French interviewees indicated that they had been in the same house and similar job position for many years.

Summary of the key findings

Symbolic boundaries are patterned in a more hierarchical fashion in France and in a more horizontal way in the United States. Both French commercial trade and literary publishers see a cultural world in which books, authors, and genres are rank-ordered by prestige. They may be for or against this cultural hierarchy, but they all refer to it when defining literary value. French editors, moreover, make numerous references to the great pillars of French and world literature and thought, both past and present. They tend to describe how a new author or genre fits into that tradition, either as a signal of continuity or revolt. The appeal to heritage is a common strategy in their modes of evaluation and judgment. American publishers, on the other hand, tend to envision a cultural world that is organized according to a horizontal differentiation of more or less equal value. New books, authors, and genres are evaluated for reasons other than their links to the past or an established literary heritage or a path-breaking avant-garde. American publishers allow for diverse sources of legitimation, such as connections with contemporary debates in the mass media, trends in popular culture, and promising new book categories (e.g. cultural studies, feminist works, ethnic and gay studies, and even conservative perspectives about politics and society).[17]

Moral dilemmas surrounding the sensitive topic of the cultural leveling effects of recent publishing industry trends resonate with greater force in France. The majority of French editors and publishers in the sample use strong language to defend their positions with respect to this perennial debate. Those who support the idea that cultural hierarchies ought to be maintained claim that the recent wave of commercialization curtails editorial autonomy, thereby ultimately threatening quality, variety, experimentation, and critical thought. Those who support a greater diffusion of books through mass marketing techniques assert that it benefits public welfare and actually enhances diversity because it takes into consideration different taste segments of the reading population. Although American publishers sometimes make similar justifications, the intensity is far weaker. These matters do not appear to be framed as overtly moral issues.[18]

Finally, in contrast to American publishers who operate in a vast and diversified domestic market and export to the rest of the world, French publishers express a deep concern about massive importations and translations. There is considerable discussion about the demise of French literature and the dwindling prestige of the French language.[19] Such a prevailing sense of loss is found equally among literary and commercial publishers yet is posed in a different way. Literary publishers emphasize the waning of the French canon as well as the stifling of avant-garde experimentation. Commercial publishers stress the declining sales of their French collections, especially in the more popular genres of detective stories, mysteries, romance, and science fiction. From all the interviews, one has an acute sense that such lamentations over the troubles in French publishing are inextricably bound up with an increasingly fragmented vision of French cultural identity.

Contextualizing differences

The origins and evolution of book publishing are very different in the two countries. The early appearance of publishing in France coincided with the consolidation of a central monarchy. Cultural authority remained firmly in the hands of a relatively small, homogeneous élite. The system of extreme social inequality laid the foundations for a sharp division between "noble" and "popular" literature. The printing and distribution of books evolved rapidly into two separate circuits. Moreover, state regulation of cultural affairs and book production was prominent in France both before and after the Revolution (Darnton and Roche 1989). By contrast, the book trade in colonial America was highly decentralized and catered to a relatively broad and heterogeneous reading public. The early democratization of reading and authorship helped to limit the cultural authority of the urban patricians. The state rarely intervened in the publishing sector which from the outset operated according to market forces (Tebbel 1975).

The development of book publishing into a mature industry during the nineteenth century also differed significantly between the two countries. In the United States there was less of a sense than in France of a common literary heritage because of the nation's youth, its cultural subordination to English literature, and the pre-eminence of newspapers and magazines over books. In contrast to France, most nineteenth-century American publishers were active in many markets and manifested more eclectic tastes in their choices of books for publication. American publishers also adopted advertising techniques and mass distribution methods on a wide scale before their French counterparts. In France, the collision between encroaching commercialization and the entrenched literary values inherited from the *ancien régime* set in motion a pecular dialectic which was to shape the symbolic battles in the publishing sector down to the present. As early as the 1830s, an emerging group of artists, writers, and publishers resurrected the aristocratic distinction between aesthetic worth and commercial value (Clark 1987). In other words, the spread of market forces in the sphere of cultural production triggered a vociferous backlash among those who cried out for aesthetic purity unspoiled by money. According to Bourdieu (1992), these particular historical conditions gave rise to a highly contentious field of literary production, in which market and artistic sources of value and legitimacy are opposed.

The observation that cultural hierarchies tend to be more solid in France than the United States confirms the numerous research findings that show how high-status culture plays a central role in contemporary French society. Cultural capital is essential to maintain social class distinctions (Bourdieu 1984); to recruit political élites (Suleiman, 1979); and to succeed in the educational system (Bourdieu and Passeron, 1977). By contrast, the United States can be described as a more "loosely bounded" society in which a shared understanding of cultural hierarchies is relatively weak and classification systems are more fluid and permeable (Merelman 1984). Moreover, regional, ethnic, and racial subcultures are more independent from the cultural mainstream (Lamont, 1987a); and high-status culture plays only a minor role in defining the symbolic contours of social classes (Lamont, 1992).

Many of the differences in the social significance of cultural capital, particularly literary culture, are reinforced and perpetuated by political and educational institutions. Unlike the United States, where cultural production and legitimation are left largely to the winds of the market, France has a long tradition of influential national cultural policies (Cummings and Katz, 1987). American artistic and literary patronage was in the past, and still today tends to be, private or non-profit and decentralized (Zolberg 1992). In a similar vein, the French mass educational system has been a major centripetal force in forging a relatively cohesive national culture, particularly since the Third Republic (Prost 1968). One outcome of centralized education is a higher degree of consensus of what is deemed to be legitimate literature and ideas. The American educational system is decentralized and varied. This heterogeneity produces less consensus about what constitutes literary culture (DiMaggio 1982).

All these historical and institutional differences surrounding the birth and maturation of the book publishing trade act to shape and constrain the views and vocabularies of this study's sample of publishers and editors. Although such differences may appear far removed from the daily concerns of the publishing enterprise, they serve as a background frame of reference which colors the mental lenses though which publishers and editors perceive and describe the world of books, literature, and ideas.

Conclusion

Professionals in the publishing business occupy a key position midway between literary production and the public reception of books. Their definitions of editorial and commercial priorities play a pivotal role in the development and diffusion of knowledge, literary taste, and reading entertainment. This study shows that publishers rely on their own mental maps which help to organize the seemingly inchoate galaxy of books, authors, and genres into more or less demarcated constellations of meaning and value. These mental maps provide a basis for drawing symbolic boundaries between worthy and less worthy literary works and ideas. It is through this active process of defining and redefining these subtle distinctions that publishing decision-makers are able to impose an order of value on the complex and shifting literary marketplace.

The present study makes a contribution to the understanding of how evaluations and judgments about objects and people in the world of book publishing take shape within a specific national historical context. Furthermore, it points to the necessity to conduct comparative research to obtain a more complete picture of the way in which symbolic boundaries are an active ingredient in the process of cultural production.

But these are also the limits of the study. At present, it would be imprudent to make claims about the possible consequences of such cross-cultural variation. Future research would have to verify to what extent evaluations expressed in an interview translate into concrete publishing decisions. Specifically, more work is required in two areas: participant observation in publishing houses to reveal how symbolic boundaries are activated in a natural setting; and an analysis of the types of books published by the editors and publishers interviewed and observed. These extensions of the research design ought to provide the additional evidence needed to confirm or invalidate the impact of the way decision-makers draw symbolic boundaries on the actual production of literary culture.

Notes

1 A few of the basic propositions of this approach state that individual and collective beliefs and practices are implanted in the very foundation of organizations (Scott 1987; Zucher 1987); organizations and their environments are highly interdependent (Jepperson and Meyer 1991); legitimacy is established through reference to institutional world-views or scripts (Fligstein 1990; Friedland and Alford 1991); and that strategies for organizational change are shaped by cognitively available alternatives (Clemens 1993).

2 For example, several recent studies in the field of comparative industrial policy demonstrate that different national states often design divergent policies to cope with ostensibly similar issues because of variation in conceptions of how markets work (Dobbin 1994; Dyson 1983; Hamilton and Biggart 1988; Steimo, Thelen, and Longstreth 1992).

3 Much of the work is inspired by Durkheim's assertion that symbolic classification systems are grounded in social community (Durkheim 1965 [1912]). For example, Mary Douglas argues that the boundary between the "pure" and the "impure" is defined contextually; and that the classification of the material world is linked to the categorization of the social world (Douglas and Isherwood 1979). Other studies focus more on strategy and conflict in the construction of symbolic boundaries. Beisel (1992) shows how moral crusaders in nineteenth-century America sought to gain influence by constantly redefining the boundaries between "proper" literature and "obscenity." Similarly, Gusfield's (1963) study of the Temperance Movement highlights the way in which prohibitive moral boundaries around drinking serve to dramatize the status gains and losses of competing social groups. DiMaggio

(1982) explains how the nineteenth-century Boston élite created the non-profit organization to build a barrier between "high" and "popular" art forms.

4 The most relevant works are those of Bourdieu (1983, 1992); Coser, Kadushin, and Powell 1982; Escarpit 1965; and Powell 1985. These authors emphasize the sharp differences between commercial and literary orientations in the book publishing sector which they consider to be salient traits of cultural industries in general. In particular, Bourdieu's concept of the "field" of literary production as a symbolic battle-ground of conflict between culture and commerce is especially characteristic of this approach. The empirical reality of the publishing field is more variegated and it is better to conceptualize such differences in terms of a continuum than a simple duality.

5 The sizes of the national book markets are different but are not proportional to population. In 1997 France produced 29,000 new titles, new editions, and re-editions compared to 55,000 in the United States. The figures for other major book markets are: Great Britain 100,000; Germany 71,000; Spain 50,000 (*Livres Hebdo*, January 1998, p. 4).

6 Havas (formally CEP Communications and Groupe de la Cité) holds a 28 percent market share compared to 17 percent for Hachette. The seven largest publishing houses account for 60 percent of French book sales *(Livres Hebdo*, December 1997).

7 The most recent tendencies in France, however, point toward the rapid development of book sales in supermarkets, book clubs, and the FNAC (a powerful chain specializing in "cultural goods" such as books, CDs, and multimedia). Nevertheless, one does not find the ubiquitous presence of the large chains common in the United States. The market share for the four major American bookstore chains (Barnes & Noble, Borders Group [which also includes Walden], Crown, and Book-A-Million) is greater than 50 percent (*Publishers' Weekly*, November 24, 1997, p. 10).

8 The literary agent first emerged in Great Britain in the nineteenth century and rapidly became a central figure in the American publishing world during the last century. In the contemporary American book market the agent plays a key role in connecting authors and editors, negotiating contracts, and even in proposing titles and marketing strategies.

9 The idea is that people use culture as a "tool-kit" from which they draw symbolic criteria and motifs in order to make sense of their surroundings and strategically defend or further their interests (Swidler 1986). Moreover, the work of Lamont (1992, 1995; and forthcoming) demonstrates that French and Americans are faced with different "national cultural repertoires" and therefore utilize dissimilar rhetorical criteria to define the symbolic boundaries between "worthy" and "less worthy" individuals and social groups.

10 The classification provided a basic sampling frame from which to select interviewees whose names are obtained from the *Literary Marketplace* and *Publishers' Weekly* in the United States; and *Guide de L'Edition Française* and *Livres Hebdo* in France.

11 The job category of "*éditeur*" in France is much broader than "editor" in the American context. The French interviewees for the most part hold the title of

"*directeur littéraire*" or "*directeur de collection*" and their assistants, which correspond to the American "editorial director" and "assistant editor", respectively.

12 The anthropologist Barry Schwartz (1981) in a meta-analysis of past studies on symbolic classifications systems draws a distinction between "vertical" and "horizontal" classifications. The former refers to hierarchies of superior and inferior qualities whereas the latter refers to a differentiation of functions within the same level of perceived value or worth. In the present study we discover that French editors tend to construct more vertical boundaries, whereas American editors maintain a more horizontal vision of the realm of literature and ideas. The frequent allusions to the "noble" and the "popular" in the French case also echos the most salient pattern of distinctions revealed by Pierre Bourdieu (1984).

13 We see here an example of the fluidity of symbolic boundaries. The division between the "pure" and the "impure" can shift over time or from one context to another in a manner similar to the observations of Mary Douglas (1966) and Eviatar Zerubavel (1991).

14 The organizational setting of the American book publishing industry fosters a more pragmatic approach to classification schemes. In particular, the greater division of labor in publishing houses and the central role of detailed categories in the large chain bookstores encourage editors to focus on specific editorial and sales strategies.

15 Jason Duell's analysis of literary studies in France and the United States shows that new classifications arising from the development of post-modernists approaches based around categories of race, ethnicity, gender, and sexual orientation are shifting intellectual boundaries within the discipline in the United States but not in France (Duell, in this volume).

16 The "market order of worth" is based on exchange and the matching of supply and demand, which in the case of publishing implies adapting an editorial offer to current readership desires and unmet needs. For more on "orders of worth," see Boltanski and Thévenot 1991.

17 The role of the market and "tie-ins" with media and cinema are perceived to be important even for classics among American editors. In a recent published interview, the editorial director of Penguin Classics emphasized the positive effect of movies on the sales of certain works: "*The English Patient* did for Herodotus and *The Postman* did for Pablo Neruda what Oprah does for current novels" (*Publishers' Weekly*, November 1997).

18 American editors are more relaxed about the potentially conflicting goals of commerce and culture. By contrast, French literary editors have difficulties accepting the coexistence of these orientations, which reminds one of the annual debates among French intellectuals and journalists about literary prizes (Heinich 1993b). Furthermore, American publishing professionals use a rhetoric that emphasizes the affinity between the market and the public good similar to the way Rotary Club members legitimize their roles within American communitites (Camus-Vigué, in this volume).

19 The sale of French translation rights is stagnant despite state subsidies. The purchase of rights for foreign books, particularly Anglo-American ones, is very high and includes not only the bestsellers such as Michael Creighton,

Tom Clancy, Stephen King, and Danielle Steele, but also more literary
authors such as Paul Auster, Toni Morrison, and Raymond Carver.
Moreover, French publishers complain that the American readers and publishing gate-keepers show little interest in contemporary French literature,
especially for the young generation of authors such as Agnès Desarthes,
Vincent Ravalac, Marie Darrieussecq, Christophe Honoré and many others
(*Livres Hebdo*, January 1998)

6 Involvement and detachment among French and American journalists: to be or not to be a "real" professional

Cyril Lemieux and John Schmalzbauer

> French people want to read journalists that take a stand. Why? In con-
> trast, Americans only want to learn factual information from their news-
> paper. They believe that opinions expressed by the journalist on this
> information are not even worth reading. Their democratic culture leads
> them to believe that they know what is going on as much, if not better,
> than journalists do. But the French also define themselves as having a
> democratic culture. Where does the difference come from?
>
> Max Weber, Talk presented at first meeting of German Sociology (1910)

A writer for the French newspaper *Libération* declares flatly, "My opinion,
my personal opinion, is my private business," drawing a firm boundary
between politics and journalism. Across the Atlantic, an editor at *Fortune
Magazine* voices a strikingly similar sentiment, explaining that the media
"need to be free of any kind of partisan or religious or parochial kinds of
concerns." In different ways, both journalists are articulating rules for
professional life.

What does it mean to be a professional journalist? How do notions of
journalistic professionalism differ across national contexts? This study is
an exploration of how twenty-four French and American journalists from
across the political spectrum talk about what it means to be a professional.

It is commonplace for media sociologists to contrast American journalism's emphasis on objectivity with European journalism's greater openness to the opinions of the reporter. This comparison is usually centered
around the distinction between facts and values. While Americans are
said to make a fetish of empirical "facts," Europeans are more willing to
allow for the intrusion of the reporter's own "values" into the story. While
Americans are said to carefully separate news from opinion, Europeans
are more comfortable with a mixture of both. While American journalists
are often described as obsessively committed to the equal treatment of
both sides of a debate (referred to as "balance"), Europeans are portrayed
as more partisan, more overtly ideological, and more politically engaged
(Gans 1979; Padioleau 1985; Pedelty 1995).

We believe the conventional juxtaposition of "objectivity" oriented Americans and "ideological" Europeans is overly simplistic. Instead of asking whether or not reporters use words like "objectivity" or "balance" to describe their work, we examine the broader question of how French and American reporters talk about the boundary between the *public* world of professional journalism and the *private* world of their personal lives.[1] In doing so, we describe the ways in which journalists both *involve* themselves in the public sphere, as well as the ways they *detach* themselves from their private political and moral convictions.[2] American sociologists have conceptualized the public/private divide as both a civic public sphere (influenced by Habermas 1991) distinguishable from private life, and more basically as a distinction between that which is "kept hidden, sheltered, or withdrawn from others" and that which is revealed (Weintraub 1997, p. 7; Goffman 1963). In a similar way, a number of French sociologists have paid special attention to the constraints that frame discourse and actions in public situations (Boltanski and Thévenot 1991; Cardon, Heurtin, and Lemieux 1995).[3]

This emphasis on the differentiation of social spheres can also be found in at least one comparison of European and American news media. In a largely theoretical and historical piece, Alexander (1981, p. 25) compared the extent to which French and American journalism were institutionally differentiated from other "ideological, political, or class groupings," arguing that the profession of French journalism was more closely tied to class and party (i.e. less differentiated) than its American counterpart. Our work builds on Alexander's comparative approach by analyzing the distinctions French and American journalists make between the public and the private spheres.

At the same time, our interviews with twenty-four reporters in both countries document greater convergence between French and American definitions of journalistic professionalism than Alexander would have predicted. More specifically, we found that mainstream journalists in France were just as likely as their American counterparts to differentiate their private lives (friendships, political opinions, moral convictions) from their public roles as reporters. Likewise, both French and American mainstream journalists tended to view the reporter as an impartial moderator of the public debate, rather than an advocate of a particular political movement or perspective. Many scholars argue that the globalization (Ferguson 1992; Robertson 1992), *mondialisation*, and Americanization of the professions has led to the reduction of national differences in the discourse and representations of journalists in France and America (McMane 1992; Ramonet 1999). While we must be careful not to overgeneralize from such a limited sample, our interviews provide some preliminary support for this conclusion.

In addition to comparing the ways mainstream journalists in both countries define what it means to be a professional, our study provides a rare look at how French and American journalists on the Left and the Right differ from their mainstream colleagues. Too often media sociologists have made broad generalizations about differences between Europeans and Americans, neglecting to examine the *internal* differences within the press corps of each.[4] In doing so, they have assumed that definitions of journalistic professionalism do not vary across the political spectrum.

This study compares the way French and American journalists in the mainstream press (what we have chosen to call "centrist journalists") and those on the Right or the Left ("non-centrist journalists") talk about the boundary between the public and the private spheres. While documenting a partial convergence between the ways French and American *centrist* journalists define what it means to be a professional, we find that *non-centrist* journalists in both France and the United States (at publications such as *L'Humanité*, *National Hebdo*, *The Progressive*, *In These Times*, and the *Weekly Standard*) are more likely to challenge mainstream journalism's emphasis on professional detachment.[5] Unlike their centrist colleagues, Left- and Right-wing journalists in both countries reject the separation of political activism and journalism (and the public and the private), arguing that reporters must be involved in the public sphere.

The sample and the interviews

In the United States twelve interviews were conducted with print journalists in New York, Washington, and Indianapolis, while in France twelve interviews were conducted in Paris, Nantes, and Bordeaux. The sample is evenly divided between "centrist" and "non-centrist" journalists. Our sample of centrist journalists consists of reporters from such publications as *Le Monde*, the *New York Times*, *Libération*, and the *Washington Post*.

Our sample of non-centrist journalists is more heterogeneous, reflecting important differences in the diffusion of Right- and Left-wing journalism in France and the United States. While our French non-centrist interviewees come from large circulation publications identified with the National Front and the Communist Party (and other political movements), our non-centrist American journalists work as opinion columnists for mainstream newspapers such as the *Los Angeles Times* syndicate and the *Indianapolis News*,[6] and for opinion magazines (such as *The Progressive* and the *Weekly Standard*). These differences in our French and American samples reflect the fact that there is simply no mass circulation equivalent of the French Left- or Right-wing press in the United States.[7]

While Left- and Right-wing opinion magazines such as the *Weekly Standard* and *The Progressive* have attracted sizable circulations (between 30,000 and 75,000 readers), they are not nearly as widely read (in proportion to the total US population) or as radical as their French counterparts *L'Humanité*, *National Hebdo*, and *Regards* (Plenel 1990; Jack 1997; Day 1994; Kurtz 1996).

The interviews themselves were approximately 45 minutes to 1 hour in length and focused on how journalists saw the relationship between their private moral and political commitments and the public world of professional journalism. Journalists were probed on the role of political convictions in their writing, the importance of detachment, and the place of the emotions in their work. The interviews moved from general questions about what respondents found meaningful and important about their work to more specific questions about the tensions between involvement and detachment.

The remainder of this study compares the ways French and American journalists talked about what it means to be a professional. We turn first to examination of centrist journalists' notions of professionalism in both countries, followed by an account of the ways non-centrist journalists have challenged these professional norms.

Separating roles: the public/private boundary among French and American centrist journalists

Because centrist journalists control the most widely read newspapers and magazines in France and the United States, they have the power to define the dominant vision of journalistic professionalism in both countries. As *de facto* members of the political establishment (the press is referred to as the "fourth estate" in the US), they also play a key role in the cultural construction of the public sphere. This section of the chapter looks at how centrist journalists talk about the boundary between the public and the private spheres, engaging in both detachment and involvement. It concludes with a comparative/historical overview of mainstream journalism in both countries.

Honesty versus objectivity: detachment work on both sides of the Atlantic

In sharp contrast to their counterparts on the Left and the Right, our centrist respondents articulated a clear boundary between journalism and partisan politics, and between public and private life. Believing that reporters should detach themselves from their own political convictions, journalists in both countries emphasized the need to give equal treatment to the range of ideological perspectives that exist in political debates. In addition, French and American journalists argued that reporters should maintain a clear separation between their personal lives and their relationships with sources.

   Responsibility and honesty   For the most part, our French centrist interviewees made a strong distinction between the role of the "journalist" and that of the "politician," arguing that a reporter should never behave like an "activist" in public. "My opinion, my personal opinion, is my private business," explained Jean Guisnel of *Libération*. In this view, a reporter is said to have behaved like a "true professional" if he has refrained from both praising those whom he agrees with and from displaying aggression towards those with whom he disagrees.

   As part of this effort to distance themselves from the world of politics, respondents emphasized the importance of separating their personal friendships from their professional careers. Suspicious of the "trap of friendship," centrist journalists said they worried about getting caught in a web of obligations and favors. Some, like Daniel Carton of *Le Monde*, "carefully avoid all dinners" and refuse all "social events," making a clear separation between the "work day" and life after eight o'clock. Many use the formal (*vous*) rather than the informal (*tu*) "you" form in conversations with their sources, drawing a linguistic boundary between personal and professional relationships. Anne-Marie Casteret explains that she is "allergic to invitations" because it is "very difficult to gain distance once personal relationships have been established." Out of principle she refuses to write about her friends. Because collusion between journalists and the political establishment is strongly criticized (Rieffel 1984; Halimi 1997), an emphasis on the strict separation of roles is a very important component of the facework of French centrist journalists.

   Although reporters self-consciously avoid getting close to politicians, they also try not to be "too critical." Because words have power, journalists must exercise a "sense of responsibility." Several cited the tragic suicide of Prime Minister Pierre Bérégovoy (Bérégovoy had been the target of vocal press criticism) as an example of irresponsible journalism (Lemieux 1993). Along these lines, a journalist from *Ouest France* stressed the need for journalists to show restraint:

Writing an article which attributes blame to specific individuals is an action that can have great implications. We have to keep it in mind and view writing as an act that is performed responsibly. You can destroy people's lives. We have to keep this in mind and require thoughtfulness from ourselves and others.

Part and parcel of this commitment to responsibility is the notion that journalists must double-check their facts. According to a respondent from *Le Monde*, "there are always informants who try to make you write things that are not true." In his view, "the only way to avoid this is to use multiple sources."

The most important way that French centrist journalists have expressed their sense of professional detachment is through a commitment to "honesty." What do they mean by this term? Thierry Guidet of *Ouest France* offered this explanation:

I don't know if we can be totally objective. On the other hand, I think that we should be as honest as possible. First, this means presenting the facts as faithfully as possible. It also means that when there is a debate, we should describe both sides of the coin.

Rather than privileging one side or another in the parliamentary debate or in a social conflict, reporters must represent different viewpoints equally. Lemieux (1992) calls this attempt to juxtapose different versions of reality, "polyphony," arguing that it is the dominant form of detachment in French mainstream journalism. This commitment to polyphony was illustrated by Paul Meunier of *Sud-Ouest*, who said that one should "never go overboard in covering particular people," because everyone tends to "demand an equal say" (*exiger une part égale*).

Balance and fairness   In some ways, the French dedication to "honesty" (as expressed through polyphony) resembles the American notion of giving "balanced" coverage to "all sides" in a political debate. While the idea of balance may convey a more binary, dualistic meaning than polyphony, both metaphors emphasize the responsibility of the journalist to give equal time to a range of political perspectives (or as our French respondent put it, "both sides of the coin"). In the American context, Jack Kelley of *USA Today* illustrated this professional ideal when he stressed the importance of "reporting both sides of a story." Likewise, Robin Toner of the *New York Times* said it was important to give equal time to ideological adversaries in American politics: "You don't take sides. You try and give everybody a chance to be heard. I mean, in an abortion fight, for example, you listen to all sides and try to convey it."

Another similarity between French and American definitions of professionalism was expressed in the lengths many American reporters went to maintain a sense of professional distance between themselves and their sources. Although *Fortune*'s Don Holt has moved in élite political circles for thirty years, he has "never allowed" himself "to get on a first name basis" with prominent politicians, preferring a "more formal" relationship with his sources. In a similar way, Jeff Sheler of *US News* has tried to avoid the impression that he and his sources were "on the same wavelength," adding that at times he has "had to draw back."

Finally, American centrist journalists have emphasized the separation of professional journalism and political activism, arguing that the reporter must detach himself from his own political convictions in order to report the news. Don Holt has "never joined or even registered in any political party," adding that "one of the things" he gave up "in order to do this job . . . was political activism." Robin Toner said American journalists simply "don't talk about . . . partisanship" or "your stance on a particular issue," adding that "I wouldn't talk to fellow journalists about how I voted."

Not surprisingly, American centrist journalists were more willing to use the word "objectivity" than their French counterparts. At the same time, some American interviewees had trouble accepting the standard definition of journalistic objectivity. In the interview, former *UPI* foreign correspondent Wesley Pippert criticized what he called "mere objectivity" and "mere accuracy," adding that the idea of "value-free reporters" is "nonsense." By questioning the ideal of objectivity, reporters like Pippert have brought American journalism closer to its European counterpart.

The defense of democracy: involvement among French and American centrist journalists

While the principles of "balance" and polyphony can be easily be interpreted as expressions of detachment (requiring journalists to mute their own opinions), they can also be described as forms of involvement because they compel reporters to affirm publicly the value of fair and open political debate. As other scholars have noted, the journalistic emphasis on giving equal space to "both sides" of a debate is "itself a political perspective," in this case a "perspective most closely associated with political centrism" (Pedelty 1995, p. 171). Integral to centrist journalism's political "moderatism," is a commitment to democracy, the law, and a corresponding distaste for political and ideological extremism (Gans 1979, p. 51). In both France and the United States, centrist journalists have portrayed themselves as impartial moderators of the public debate who must occasionally defend the democratic process against potential threats.

Democracy and the limits of polyphony   While French centrist journalists have ordinarily stressed the need to separate private political commitments from the public task of reporting, they have occasionally moved away from polyphony towards outright advocacy of a point of view. Such a departure from routine has been deemed necessary when democratic procedures or respect for the law have been endangered by the participants in a public debate. In particular, journalists have abandoned a stance of total detachment in situations involving the extreme Right.

Despite their commitment to covering "both sides of the coin," many centrist journalists are divided on the question of whether to give equal space to members of the French National Front. While as "individuals, as citizens" they are in total disagreement with the racist and anti-democratic ideas of the Right, they cannot "refuse to give a voice to people who represent 15 percent of the electorate." A legal advisor for *Le Monde* recalls how upset a journalist was when he learned that the newspaper was set to publish a reply to an article from the National Front. The reporter opposed the idea in the strongest terms, arguing that the opinions of the extreme Right should be not be given space in democratic newspapers such as *Le Monde*. The lawyer replied that "from a strictly legal perspective," the Lepen supporters had a right to respond. The reply was published while the journalist in question was on vacation. Reflecting a similar perspective, a journalist from *Le Nouvel Observateur* said that Jean Marie Le Pen should not be treated by the press like other politicians: "All of us journalists, or almost all of us, share democratic assumptions. People who are not part of this consensus should be denounced as such by us. They are not ordinary politicians. They are a threat. Indeed, I believe that they threaten the normal functioning of democracy. If one day they came to power, they would threaten the proper functioning of the press."[8]

Another form of public involvement has come through the rise of American-style investigative journalism in France (Hunter 1997). Until the 1980s, *Le Canard Enchaîné* was one of only a handful of newspapers to unveil scandals on a regular basis. As a practitioner of this new form of French journalism, respondent Anne-Marie Casteret of *L'Express* became famous after having uncovered one of the greatest scandals of contemporary French history. Casteret revealed that people had become infected with the HIV virus after being exposed to blood known to be contaminated. Displaying a similar passion for investigative journalism, a reporter for *L'Evénement du Jeudi* said his interest in environmental issues is "not really for the benefit of flowers and birds, but because this is one of the sites where the absence of democracy in this country is most blatant." By combining attention to fact-checking and multiple sources with the denunciation of power, French journalists have balanced a commitment to detachment with active public involvement.

Moderating the American political debate   Although American centrist journalists have distanced themselves from the political platforms of the Left and the Right, they have been more than willing to describe themselves as advocates of democracy. While Robin Toner of the *New York Times* has concealed her partisan political leanings from her journalistic colleagues, she has shown no reticence whatsoever in proclaiming her passionate concern for what she calls "basic democracy issues." By asking, "How does democracy function? How connected are people? How much does their vote count? How much are they getting manipulated?" Toner has envisioned journalism as a way of monitoring the integrity of the democratic process.

In a similar way, E. J. Dionne of the *Washington Post* has praised what he calls "democratic, small 'd' civic engagement." Too often in American politics, argues Dionne, "there is very little engagement with the possibility that someone you disagree with might be right." Because journalists "have the luxury of being able to talk to very different kinds of people in some sort of odd relationship of mutual trust," Dionne feels they can help to identify "areas of consensus" in American politics where ideological opponents actually agree. As a journalist who has covered the culture wars over abortion, family values, and welfare policy, he has called for a renewed dialogue between Left and Right and "the creation of a new political center" (Dionne 1991, p. 27).

This mediating role has been particularly important during periods of intense political polarization. Recalling his years as a reporter for *Newsweek* during the civil rights and anti-war upheavals of the 1960s, Don Holt said that the "society seemed to be coming apart." Because of the "danger of the divisiveness of the debate," Holt felt that journalists contributed to the health of American democracy by mediating the debate between the establishment and the counter-culture.

Perhaps the most passionate display of public involvement on the part of American centrist journalists has come on the issue of racism. While centrist journalists are ordinarily not supposed to take sides in American politics, it is legitimate to criticize a politician for "playing a racial card," according to Robin Toner of the *New York Times*. Because racism is so widely regarded as a direct challenge to democracy, journalists can abandon a stance of detached neutrality in order to criticize the use of racially inflammatory language in American politics. By speaking out against racism, American centrist journalists proclaim their commitment to the values of tolerance and civility.

Towards convergence? French and American centrist journalists

Our interviews with centrist reporters document a partial convergence between French and American definitions of what it means to be a professional journalist in the mainstream press. Although American centrist journalists are still more likely to make use of the rhetoric of objectivity and the fact/value distinction, journalistic detachment has come to mean something quite similar in both countries. For both our French and American respondents, detachment has increasingly meant distinguishing between political activism and professional journalism, between friendships and sources, and between advocacy and reporting. As we argued above, the French dedication to "honesty" (through polyphony) and the American commitment to "balance" are strikingly similar in their emphasis on the need to give equal treatment to a wide range of political perspectives.[9] Such parallels are also reflected in the ways French and American centrist journalists have described their involvement in the public sphere. Reporters in both countries have viewed themselves as impartial moderators of the political debate rather than political activists, committed to the centrist political values of democracy, tolerance, and civil dialogue.[10]

How can we explain the similarities we have found in the ways French and American centrist journalists talk about their work? Recent historical scholarship on the profession of journalism in both countries may provide a clue. More specifically, the impact of "Americanization" on journalism in France and the questioning of objectivity in America may help explain the convergence in French and American definitions of journalistic professionalism.

In recent years, French scholars have called attention to successive waves of "Americanization" in the journalistic profession (Palmer 1983; Ferenczi 1993; Blondiaux 1998; Boltanski 1982). The first of these waves (during the 1880s) began the slow decline of the opinion press, and coincided with the industrialization of journalism (Delporte 1998). This newly industrialized press was more interested in conveying information and entertainment than in political issues (Palmer 1983; Ferenczi 1993), a development that shocked the French élite. The second wave of Americanization (during the 1960s) resulted in the reorganization of print media into large corporations, the development of journalism schools, the introduction of polling, and expert sources, and the rise of an American-style journalism (Blondiaux 1998; Boltanski 1982, pp. 179–87). A final wave of Americanization in the 1980s coincided with the emergence of a "French audio-visual landscape," increasingly competitive business practices, and the advent of continuous and live worldwide French news (akin to the American CNN). In the interviews, French journalists touched on the third wave of Americanization (in particular, the rise of "neo-liberalism" and laissez-faire economics), describing their own move away from the ideologies of the 1960s. Those respondents who came to mainstream journalism out of a background of activism were quick to distance themselves from what they see as the "rigid thinking" of the French extreme Left.

In a similar way, scholars have chronicled important changes in American conceptions of what it means to be a professional journalist. While "objectivity" was once central to American definitions of journalistic professionalism, there are growing indications that it has lost some of its grip on American journalism. With the breakdown of the post-war liberal consensus in the 1960s came a corresponding attack on objectivity, as American journalists questioned the possibility (and the desirability) of separating political judgments from the act of reporting (Novick 1988; Hodgson 1976). The rise of advocacy journalism, investigative journalism, alternative newspapers (such as the *Village Voice*), the new journalism (which used the devices of fiction to give a literary feel to reporting), and, most recently, civic journalism, has led to a gradual transformation in the way journalists perceive their roles (Mills 1974; Aultschull 1990; Schudson 1978). Surveys of professional journalists (at mainstream newspapers) show that reporters have increasingly seen themselves as participants in the events they cover rather than mere observers (Weaver and Wilhoit 1991). Although objectivity remains an important ideal for many reporters (and many of our respondents), the term does not appear in the most recent version of the Society of Professional Journalists' Code of Ethics (1996).

The historical scholarship on the "Americanization" of French journalism and the "simmering disaffection with objectivity" among American reporters (Schudson 1978, p. 193) is consistent with what we found in our interviews. While French reporters have become more Americanized in their emphasis on the need for professional detachment, the American de-emphasis on objectivity has brought them somewhat closer to their European colleagues. What is more, centrist journalists in both countries have developed a strikingly similar set of rules for governing the boundary between the public world of professional journalism and private life. The end result is a growing convergence between French and American mainstream notions of journalistic professionalism.

Professionalism in the service of conviction: French and American non-centrist journalists

The non-centrist journalists interviewed for this project have written for a wide variety of publications on the Left, Right, and center. What sets them apart is their open identification with a political stance outside the ideological mainstream (such as the religious Right or socialism in

America, or the National Front or Communism in France), or their employment at publications that are explicitly identified with the Right or the Left. Despite deep ideological differences (between Left and Right and between Americans and French), most of the non-centrist journalists we interviewed shared a common distaste for mainstream definitions of journalistic professionalism. Compared to their centrist counterparts, they were much less likely to stress the importance of journalistic detachment. De-emphasizing the boundary between the public world of journalism and their private convictions, they emphasized the need for the journalist to get involved in the public sphere. This section examines how non-centrist journalists talked about detachment and involvement in the public sphere, concluding with a comparative/historical overview of non-centrist journalists in both countries.

"Don't think like the Establishment": detachment work among non-centrist journalists

Not surprisingly, our non-centrist respondents rejected many of the separations that make up centrist journalists' notions of journalistic detachment (public versus private, professional versus political, news versus opinion, activism versus reporting). Believing that no sharp boundary should exist between their private political opinions and the world of journalism, they argued that journalists must bring their views into the content of their work. In both countries (but especially in France), opposition to journalistic detachment has been framed as a critique of mainstream *American* journalism and of "Americanization." While French and American Left- and Right-wing journalists have occasionally adopted mainstream definitions of professionalism (such as reporting a wide range of viewpoints or carefully verifying information), they have refused to embrace them wholeheartedly.

Rejecting "naive factualism"   The French non-centrist journalists interviewed for this project have categorically rejected the notion that it is enough to report the "facts" without commentary. For them, political convictions are necessarily intertwined with the act of reporting. To insist on a sharp boundary between public and private, facts and opinion, and political activism and journalism is unrealistic and undesirable. At the same time, most have engaged in some form of detachment during the course of their professional careers.

The French Left-wing journalists we interviewed argued that fact-gathering "is not enough." Rather, journalists must make an effort to escape the grip of conformity by systematically exposing the *structures of power* that hide behind the facts. In this spirit, Patrick Apel-Müller criticized the American press for its lack of critical perspective and political analysis, arguing that "Anglo-Saxon journalists are really weak on social and civil debates." Neither neutrality nor objectivity were a central part of the vocabulary of Left-wing journalists. The idea that it is even possible to gain access to pure "facts," outside a particular point of view, seemed absurd to them.

On the French extreme Right, Mathieu Pasquier expressed a similar disdain for American-style objectivity. While acknowledging that reporters must "determine the facts with a maximum of precision," he said there "is no such thing as objective interpretation." Criticizing mainstream journalism for its lack of frankness and its "hypocrisy," Arnaud Sobel argued that reporters at newspapers such as *Le Monde* are "pretending to do Anglo-Saxon journalism," while writing "articles that are actually . . . promoting specific political positions, even suggesting ostracism" of the National Front. In the same way, Gilles Preux described the separation of facts and commentary as "hypocritical and grotesque." For both Left- and Right-wing French journalists, American (and Anglo-Saxon) culture serves as a rhetorical foil, paralleling the findings of other contributors to this volume (Lamont 1992; Saguy in this volume).

Despite their sharp criticism of mainstream notions of professionalism, French non-centrist journalists acknowledged the importance of detachment in certain situations. Some Left-wing reporters went so far as to call for greater polyphony in the French Left-wing press. While acknowledging that a single perspective once dominated their newspapers, they said that the time had come for the Left-wing press to be open to a wide range of viewpoints. For example, Nicole Borvo of *Regards* said she was ready to use her column to engage "people on the Right." On the other hand, she ruled out any debate with "people who identify themselves with the National Front," arguing they do not share the minimal democratic values that make discussion possible. At *L'Humanité*, Patrick Apel-Müller was less receptive towards polyphony, while Françoise Galand said she was openly hostile to the idea of giving a voice to the Right.

In a surprising show of detachment, our Right-wing respondents were unwilling to describe themselves as members of the National Front. While Arnaud Sobel of *Présent* acknowledged that his "newspaper supports the National Front two hundred percent," he has not obtained a membership card in the party. "I'm held back by the fact that I'm a journalist," he explained, adding that "I wouldn't want the fact that I belonged to a party to prevent me from saying something." As an expression of this detachment, Sobel tells Right-wing politicians that he is a "journalist, so if you tell me something, it might come out in my newspaper!" In the same way, *National Hebdo*'s Mathieu Pasquier (who claims to be close to National Front leader Jean-Marie Le Pen) said that he does not belong to the party and "won't say" what his "political opinions are."

The most important differences within our sample of non-centrist French journalists emerged on the issue of "verbal violence." While our Left-wing respondents described their respect for the law and their firm opposition to verbal violence, our respondents on the Right expressed a cavalier attitude towards French laws against racially inflammatory language. On the Left, Jackie Viruega of *Regards* said she had "little tolerance for personal attacks" as a substitute for "debates about issues." By contrast, *Minute*'s Gilles Preux argued that is perfectly legitimate to publish a story without proof "if one has the conviction that it is true." Rejecting a posture of detachment, Preux said his paper weighed the risk of a lawsuit before deciding to publish a story. "If it could mean a $200,000 lawsuit, we'll hesitate to publish it. If it is more of a $2,000 lawsuit, we don't hesitate." Far from dissuading journalists on the Right, the risk of lawsuits has served as their greatest badge of authenticity and a sign that they have challenged taboos.

Questioning objectivity   Non-centrist American journalists on both the Right and the Left have rejected a total separation between political activism and journalism. Common to both is the conviction that the mainstream press (what we have been calling "centrist journalism") has failed to achieve the objectivity and balance it so often champions. Instead, so-called "objective journalism" has served to reinforce the position of the powerful (according to Left-wing journalists) or the anti-traditional morality of liberal élites (according to conservatives).

In the view of Left-wing respondents, mainstream journalism's ideal of detached objectivity is neither possible nor desirable. According to Victor Navasky of *The Nation*, it is impossible to separate political interpretations from the practice of journalism. While acknowledging that trivial facts such as "two plus two equals four" can be accepted by most people, he noted that most journalism is concerned with non-trivial matters such as "Who started the Cold War?" Daniel Lazare of *In These Times* took this argument one step further by asserting that "a fact as such doesn't exist." Rather, a "fact is an abstraction, is an artificial creation." In such a world, all journalism is inevitably politically and ideologically driven. Rejecting mainstream American journalism's emphasis on detachment, Lazare said he admired the politically engaged style of journalism practiced by European newspapers, articulating a critique that was remarkably similar to his French Left-wing counterparts.

Although Right-wing journalists were less critical of the *goal* of objectivity, they were equally adamant in criticizing the mainstream press for its bias. According to conservative Fred Barnes of the *Weekly Standard*, most Washington journalists are "out of touch with the rest of the population outside the beltway" (the highway surrounding Washington, DC). Besides harboring a liberal "ideological bias," the "press tends to be very secular and not even aware of how strongly religious a country the United States is."

Significantly, non-centrist American journalists have made some concessions to mainstream notions of professionalism. On the Right, syndicated columnist Cal Thomas said it was important to be fair to his political opponents, noting that "when someone like Charlie Rangel [a progressive African American congressman] comes on my television show, and in the middle of the show looks at me and says, 'You know, you're really fair,' . . . that really means a lot to me." Despite his opposition to gay rights, Thomas said that spokespersons from the gay community "get a fair hearing" on his talk-show.

On the Left, *The Nation*'s Victor Navasky conceded there were some benefits to mainstream journalism's focus on accurately reporting "the facts," arguing that "regardless of ideology," journalists should "avoid distorting the news on behalf of some pre-existing agenda . . . leaving out inconvenient facts, slanting the news," or "engaging in *ad hominem*. Those are all instances of what I would regard as bad journalism." Although he has worked in opinion journalism for all of his career (first as a columnist at the *Washington Post* and later as an occasional contributor to *The Progressive*), Colman McCarthy said that he tries to write "informed opinion," that is based on both "feelings *and* facts" [emphasis added]. Those who write "uninformed opinion" rely on their feelings alone, neglecting the "legwork" necessary for good journalism. By employing the language of fact, McCarthy and Navasky have illustrated the power of mainstream definitions of journalistic professionalism to shape the discourse of non-centrist American journalists.

The impossibility of impartiality: involvement among non-centrist journalists

Common to most of our non-centrist interviewees was the notion that journalists should be able to bring their ideological convictions into their professional lives. In most cases, they identified themselves as active supporters of political movements on the Right or the Left. Fusing the roles of journalist and activist, most were quite open about the ways their political perspectives influenced their writing. While our Left-wing respondents have described themselves as advocates of social justice, those on the Right have envisioned themselves as the defenders of traditional lifestyles and "national ideas." In both cases, non-centrist journalists have seen their work lives as bound up in a ideological critique of contemporary French and American society.

Social justice, frankness, and courage   In sharp contrast to their colleagues in the mainstream press, our French non-centrist journalists have refused to distinguish between their jobs and their political convictions. This fusion of activism and professional journalism was evident on both the Right and the Left. Our Left-wing respondents have defined themselves as both "professionals" and "polemically engaged people," without considering these two terms to be contradictory. Rather than concealing their political leanings, they have explicitly revealed their support for one political party over another. All have rejected the idea of working for a newspaper lacking a clear Leftist political line. As Françoise Galand explained, "I look at life and I say to myself: 'I take a side, I'm not objective.'" Galand described her own newspaper, *Politis*, as "firmly Leftist" and "clearly critical of the Socialist and Communist Parties."

French Left-wing journalists have justified their public involvement by arguing that social transformation is a moral necessity. Their principal goal has not been the pursuit of the scoop, but the denunciation of social injustice. In this respect, they have demonstrated a sociological sensibility. According to Patrick Apel-Müller, it is not enough to be alarmed about the suffering of the homeless. One must also "examine the social logics that produce and reproduce situations of exclusion."

By contrast, our extreme-Right French interviewees were somewhat less forthcoming about their political convictions. Unlike their Left-wing counterparts, they refused to describe themselves as members of a political organization. At the same time, they admitted having a decided bias regarding the news, expressing their strong support for what they call "national ideas" and the National Front. Rejecting "Anglo-Saxon" notions of objectivity, Right-wing interviewees described "honesty" as the paramount journalistic virtue. According to Gilles Preux, "honesty" means "not hiding your point of view," and taking responsibility for your own political position.[11] Among French Right-wing journalists, this political position has been articulated through a rhetoric of ethnicity, nation, and religion (Schain 1987). In defense of "*la France éternelle*" (the eternal France), they have lamented the influence of non-Catholic foreigners, cosmopolitan élites, and Americanization on French society.

The emphasis Right-wing French reporters place on "courage" is related to both a "culture of fighting" (one respondent is an aging paratrooper) and a deep-seated ambivalence towards the French Establishment. As journalists who crave social and professional recognition, they resent being marginalized by mainstream politicians and journalists. In the interview, Mathieu Pasquier claimed that he "hardly ever gets invited to" the most official and prestigious events. Although Pasquier often meets with politicians, even ministers, who "agree to answer questions, to talk, or to have lunch," this is always "with the understanding that their discussions are off the record." At the same time, such ostracism is not entirely unwelcome to Right-journalists because it allows them to present themselves as the victims of humiliation. By calling attention to their own marginality, they are able to confirm their own commitment to the ideals of "courage" and "anti-conformism." As Arnaud Sobel put it: "We are a bit like untouchables. We don't fit in the mold." For Gilles Preux, "It is important to learn how to stand up for oneself, even if one has to pay dearly."

Social transformation and "traditional values"   Like their French counterparts, Americans non-centrist journalists have de-emphasized the boundary between private political convictions and the public world of professional life. In very different ways, American Left- and Right-wing reporters have described their writing as a form of social criticism aimed at transforming American society. On the Left, this has taken the shape of a sociological critique of the dominant power structure. In the words of Daniel Lazare of *In These Times*, the purpose of journalism should be to "draw back the curtains to penetrate to the essence of American society," in order to "understand what's right and wrong . . . and what has to be done to fix things." By revealing how the routine "patterns of everyday life" help perpetuate relationships of power and domination, reporters can "change consciousness" and "change ways of thinking."

Our Left-wing respondents have seen no conflict between crusading for social change and reporting. Reflecting this activist conception of journalism, Colman McCarthy said he likes to "write about people who are on the margins, who are voiceless, who've been locked out of the power system, and do what I can to align myself with their hopes to reform." In a similar way, Victor Navasky said it was important for journalists to help readers interpret political events from within a coherent political outlook that explains "how the world works." In Navasky's opinion, "the job of alternative media" is "to report on stories that the mainstream media hasn't bothered to cover and doesn't even understand."

Though equally committed to an activist model of their profession, our Right-wing respondents have focused on a very different kind of public involvement. Rather than concerning themselves with questions of power and inequality, they have emphasized the importance of calling America back to "traditional moral values" on issues such as abortion, sexuality, and school prayer. Cal Thomas articulated this position when he described abortion as the "civil rights, slavery, and holocaust issue of our time" and "family breakup" as the "major contributor to crime, anti-social behavior, and all those other things."[12] Like their counterparts on the French Right, our American Right-wing respondents have articulated a binary rhetoric of "liberal" versus "conservative," and "religious" versus "secular," arguing that national élites are out of touch with the beliefs of ordinary Americans (see Hunter 1991 for an account of the binary rhetoric of the "culture wars"). According to Thomas, an "authoritarian élite" has taken over the "flow of culture" in the United States in science, the media, politics, and intellectual life. Using much the same language, Fred Barnes said "an upper-middle-class educated élite" now "dominates national journalism in a way that it didn't used to and that is not in line with the thinking of the rest of the country on political, on religious grounds, on values ground, on practically anything."

During the interview, Thomas said it was impossible to separate his religious convictions from his work as a journalist, adding that "faith informs, gives me an added dimension that those who are not serious believers don't have." Likewise, Barnes said that being an evangelical Christian has given him a "broader perspective about the world" and an "interest in issues that aren't about religion *per se*, whether it's abortion or whether it's illegitimacy, or family life." Like their colleagues on the Left, Right-wing American journalists have often refused to separate their politics from their writing.

Challenging mainstream definitions of professionalism

As noted earlier, there are vast differences between the French and the American Left, between the French and American Right, and between the Right and the Left in each nation. Because of such differences, there has not been a convergence in professional cultures parallel to what has occurred among centrist journalists. At the same time, French and American non-centrist journalists have articulated a shared critique of mainstream journalism (albeit from a range of ideological perspectives). Rejecting the separation of the private and the public, they have conceived of journalism as a form of active engagement in the public sphere.

To be sure, non-centrist journalists have made some concessions to mainstream definitions of journalistic professionalism. While French Left-wing reporters have called for greater polyphony, their American counterparts have acknowledged the benefits of accurately reporting "the facts." In a similar way, journalists on the French extreme Right have denied belonging to the National Front (although they have said they support the party "two hundred percent"). Despite such displays of detachment, non-centrist journalists on both sides of the Atlantic have strongly criticized the ideal of "objectivity," going so far as to argue that "there is no such thing." Although this has been especially true in France, where non-centrist journalists have accused the mainstream press of succumbing to Americanization and "pretending to do Anglo-Saxon journalism,"[13] even American non-centrist journalists (especially on the Left) have expressed admiration for European-style journalism.

Though we should be careful not to overemphasize their similarities, non-centrist journalists in France and the United States have used many of the same arguments to justify their involvement in the public sphere. On the Left, they have described themselves as advocates of social justice who must peel back the layers of the power structure. While this critique has been grounded more explicitly in Marxist sociology in France, both French and American Left-wing respondents have seen journalism as a way of critiquing the systematic oppression of subordinate groups. On the Right, they have attacked the "Establishment" for abandoning traditional values, morality, and (in France) national ideals, arguing that journalists must defend the cultural heritage of the nation from the threats of secularism (and Islam in the French case), foreigners (in the French case), and liberal élites. Together they have emphasized the impossibility of impartiality, collapsing the boundary between personal political convictions and professional journalism.

Conclusion

What does it mean to be a professional journalist? Too often sociologists have made comparative generalizations about the differences between American and European journalists without grounding them in cross-national data (Gans 1979; Pedelty 1995). Even Alexander's (1981) theoretically suggestive comparison of French and American journalism relies heavily on secondary historical sources and impressionistic observations, concluding that French journalists are less able to separate their work from the entanglements of class, party, and ideology.

As we stated at the outset of this paper, the juxtaposition of objective Americans and ideological Europeans does not adequately capture the ways French and American journalists talk about professionalism. Drawing on face-to-face interviews with twenty-four French and American journalists, our study challenges the conventional wisdom about the differences between European and American journalism. Instead of objectivity-oriented Americans and ideological Europeans, we found considerable overlap in the ways French and American journalists talk about what it means to be a professional. Although centrist American journalists were more likely to use the term "objectivity" to describe their work, several questioned the desirability (and possibility) of objective journalism. Likewise, French centrist journalists emphasized the importance of reporting "both sides of the coin," articulating a model of journalism that sounds remarkably like the American concept of balance. Finally, non-centrist journalists in both countries articulated a similar critique of mainstream definitions of journalistic professionalism, arguing that it is impossible (and undesirable) to separate political activism from reporting.

To be sure, national differences remain important. The greater access of French Left- and Right-wing journalists (and to a lesser extent French centrist journalists) to arguments challenging "Anglo-Saxon" empiricism has undoubtedly made them more resistant to American-style journalism. In a similar way, the widespread legitimacy of religious language in the United States has led Right-wing American journalists to couch their arguments in theological terms. Finally, widespread concern about the rise of the extreme Right in France has made French journalists less open to reporting "all sides" of the debate than they otherwise might have been. Simply put, the "cultural tool-kits" (Swidler 1986) of French and American journalists are filled with different cultural tools (arguments, stories, rhetorics).

At the same time, our interviews suggest there has been at least a partial convergence between French and American definitions of journalistic professionalism in the mainstream press. In both countries, centrist journalists have defined professionalism as the art of separating private political convictions from the practice of journalism. While differing in the terminology they have used to describe this separation ("objectivity," "honesty," etc.), French and American centrist journalists have been equally committed to the importance of journalistic detachment. While more research with a larger sample of journalists is clearly needed, our study shows that French and American notions of journalistic professionalism are closer together than previous studies have recognized.

APPENDIX   LIST OF RESPONDENTS

AMERICAN JOURNALISTS

Centrist
E. J. Dionne, *Washington Post*
Robin Toner, *New York Times*
Jack Kelley, *USA Today*
Don Holt, *Fortune*
Wesley Pippert, formerly of *United Press International*
Jeff Sheler, *US News and World Report*

Non-centrist (*L* = Left-wing; *R* = Right-wing)
Victor Navasky, *The Nation* **L**
Daniel Lazare, *In These Times* **L**
Colman McCarthy, freelance for *The Progressive* and *The Nation* (formerly *Washington Post*) **L**
Fred Barnes, *The Weekly Standard* **R**
Cal Thomas, *Los Angeles Times Syndicate* (formerly editor of the *Fundamentalist Journal*) **R**
Russ Pulliam, *Indianapolis News* **R**

FRENCH JOURNALISTS

Centrist
Daniel Carton, *Le Monde*
Jean Guisnel, *Libération*
Dominique Foing, *L'Evénement du Jeudi*
Paul Meunier, *Sud-Ouest*
Thierry Guidet, *Ouest-France*
Anne-Marie Casteret, *L'Express*

Non-centrist (*L* = Left-wing; *R* = Right-wing)[14]
Patrick Apel-Müller, *L'Humanité* **L**
Jackie Viruega, *Regards* **L**
Françoise Galand, *Le Nouveau Politis* **L**
Mathieu Pasquier, *National Hebdo* **R**
Arnaud Sobel, *Présent* **R**
Gilles Preux, *Minute* **R**

Notes

1 Like many of the other selections in this volume, we analyze the "boundary-work" that social actors engage in to preserve or to weaken cultural and moral distinctions (Lamont 1992), in our case the boundary between the public and the private spheres.

2 By "involvement" we mean the active display of political, moral, and emotional commitments by journalists in the public sphere. By "detachment" we mean the confinement of political, moral, and emotional commitments to personal life and the observance of a clearly institutionalized boundary between the public and the private spheres (our usage of these terms differs slightly from Elias 1987).

3 For an application of this approach to the specific case of French journalism see Lemieux 2000.

4 Alexander (1981) compared historical studies of French and American journalism, but did not look at American journalists outside the mainstream press. While Pedelty's (1995) comparison of American, European, and Salvadoran journalists included a section on American "stringers" who occasionally freelanced for the alternative press, it was not a major focus of his study. Neither looked at Right-wing French and American journalists.

5 While there are vast differences between Right- and Left-wing reporters in both countries, we group Right- and Left-wing journalists together in the "non-centrist" category because of their common distance from the professional culture of the mainstream press.

6 Alterman (1992) argues that Right-wing columnists dominate the opinion pages of American newspapers. The two Right-wing journalists in our sample who write for mainstream newspapers have close ties to the new Christian Right. During the 1980s Cal Thomas (*Los Angeles Times* syndicate) served as vice-president of the Moral Majority, the most important new Christian Right organization of the period. Another respondent, Russ Pulliam of the *Indianapolis News* (a cousin of former Vice-President Dan Quayle), has described himself as a member of the "religious Right." Moreover, the *Indianapolis News* is one of a handful of American daily newspapers known for being on the Right (Bethell 1991).

7 The lesser appeal of Right- and Left-wing publications in the United States ultimately reflects deeper differences between French and American political cultures. While the French Left has historically been rooted in a vast mass movement centered in the working class, the American Left has, on the whole, been more narrowly confined to the intellectual world (Lipset 1979). Although the United States has had a succession of extreme Right-wing movements during this century (such as the KKK in the 1920s), it currently has no exact parallel to the National Front in France (Bell 1964).

8 The quotation from *Le Monde*'s legal advisor is taken from an earlier interview by Lemieux (2000). The quotation from the *Nouvel Observateur* reporter is taken from a debate on French radio. They were included in this study because they closely parallel the attitudes of our respondents.

9 This does not mean that French and American centrist journalists always incorporate the same range of political and ideological perspectives in their news coverage. The French mainstream press undoubtedly contains a broader range of viewpoints than its American counterpart. Nevertheless, reporters in both countries talk about the ideal of representing all sides equally.

10 To be sure, French centrist journalists are more likely than their American counterparts to identify with "Center-Left" or "Center-Right" ideologies. Reporters at *Libération* are much more likely to identify as "*de gauche*" (radical) than their counterparts at mainstream American newspapers and magazines. At the same time, both French and American reporters stress the importance of basic democratic values.

11 Unlike French centrist journalists, journalists on the extreme Right do not see "honesty" as synonymous with polyphony.

12 See note 6 above.

13 This is despite the fact that French centrist journalists have rarely used the term "objectivity" to describe their work.

14 Our French Right-wing respondents will remain anonymous. The names given here are pseudonyms.

7   From rejection of contemporary art to culture war

Nathalie Heinich

Contemporary art shifts the boundaries that define what constitutes a work of art: mental or cognitive boundaries that mark the distinction between art and non-art; material boundaries such as the walls of museums, galleries, and auction houses or such as the pages of specialized reviews, catalogues, and art books (Heinich 1986, 1997a). There is no better way to study these shifts than via the negative reactions to works of art or proposals that breach the boundaries of common sense, shared references, and generally accepted categories. These rejections of contemporary art shed light on how a collective consensus as to the nature of things is achieved; on the modalities of decision-making – between relying on expert advice and the opinion of the majority – in a realm where the idea of "universal" judgment is thought to hold sway; and on the diverse levels of values involved in the evaluation of problematic subjects (Heinich 1990, 1993a).

In France, the topic of my research – the rejection of contemporary art spontaneously expressed by non-specialists – has encountered only skepticism or questioning. By contrast, in the United States, it elicits an immediately familiar, if not blasé, response: "Ah, you mean the culture wars!" Indeed I was somewhat disappointed to provoke so little surprise with a subject that was as decidedly *à la mode* overseas as it was hard to grasp, if not unwelcome, in France. On the other hand, I took comfort from the fact that my access to sources would present no difficulties because my interlocutors in the arts had identified me as an ally in their struggle against the forces of conservative reaction. In New York, Boston, Washington, and Philadelphia I was offered numerous interviews and meetings, archives were open to me, documents were sent to me without delay! Admittedly the asset of my French accent gave me the immediate privilege of being exotic, but accent cannot explain everything. My subject was timely, and the time was one of war. In wartime, all allies are useful.

This happy surprise was quickly to be tainted by my suspicion that the task of comparison risked becoming even more difficult, the more the differences in the status of the subject – and therefore the nature of the problem – made it easier to gather the facts. This suspicion was confirmed when an American political analyst to whom I was explaining my subject, with the help of several examples (Serra, Mapplethorpe, Serrano), replied without hesitation: "But that has nothing to do with contemporary art! It's a problem of the utilization of public resources!"

Methodology

When I left for the United States, I expected to find it necessary to repeat the slow fieldwork that had been required in France. But my research was infinitely easier on the other side of the Atlantic: I discovered an already well-constituted subject, and a corpus that was by and large already documented. In France, with the exception of a few major "affairs," there were scarcely any articles to be found in the mainstream press. I was therefore obliged to contact directly the directors of museums, and to attempt to gain their confidence so that they would allow me to see the visitors' books of exhibitions or the rare letters written by visitors, or tell me about any acts of vandalism that had occurred.

The cultural journals, in contrast, had made themselves the bastions of specialists with points of view critical of contemporary art. But these debates, virulent as they were, were confined to a small fringe of the intellectual world, and their analysis would have required a minute study of the current criteria of art criticism. Such was not my goal: the question of mental boundaries that delimit the artistic universe, and the values mobilized when they are shifted by contemporary art, is all the more relevant when it concerns the whole of a "culture" rather than just a small group of experts.

The decision to exclude from my study the specialists (defined as those who publish their opinions in specialized media) became, in France, something of a paradoxical choice similar to that of an anthropologist who chooses to focus on people without writing. In the United States, in contrast, where everybody – citizens, editorial writers, critics – writes to the press, this kind of limitation would have made less sense: the debate, at first broadened to non-specialists, had become a general confrontation of interest to everybody, a "culture war," as the title of Bolton's book indicates (1992). Articles of all kinds from the press could be found on the subject of various famous "affairs."

Bolton's book is by no means the only one on the subject: I discovered that there was something of a library on the question, whose serious and well-documented books were written by academics. Would there some day be a "culture wars" section in American bookstores, located some-where between "cultural studies" and "self-help"? In any case, a large part of my study of the question in the United States was possible while I was still in France, thanks to these books.[1] Even better, statistics already existed,[2] a dream come true for a sociologist who knew that such figures would be impossible to obtain in France – for there to be statistics there must be, minimally, a compilation of facts, and for there to be a compila-tion of facts, there must be a question whose existence is recognized as such.

The essential part of my documentation thus having been put together by others, my remaining fieldwork consisted of fleshing out these statis-tics, or the stories of "affairs," or accounts of incidents mentioned in the press with anecdotes, micro-reactions to be found only in the visitors' books of exhibitions, or the letters written to museums. The gulf between the two countries was striking. The French study comprised only a few "affairs" (and of these, only one attained national significance: that of the Buren columns at the Palais-Royal in Paris in 1986 [Heinich 1997b]), and some scattered "incidents" which had been mentioned in the press. The essential part of this documentation consisted of anecdotes, micro-reactions that could only be collected on the spot, which I had to place in some relation to their American equivalents. To do that, I had to check that such equivalents did exist on the other side of the Atlantic, even if hidden behind the immediate visibility of the "affairs" and incidents that received so much media attention and on which my American colleagues, better equipped with computer software and press clippings, had based their investigations.

It thus became clear that differences between the elements of the problem ("rejection of contemporary art" on the one hand, a "culture war" on the other) could not be extricated from differences in the methods of study. Although the American "culture wars" were aimed principally at the use of public funds, at least in the public domain of "affairs" and incidents covered by the press (notably by spokespersons for associations and letters to the editors in newspapers), at a somewhat less public level – of opinions expressed in guest books or in communications received directly by cultural institutions – the same kinds of specifically artistic questions posed by contemporary art emerged and were much like those in the French corpus. The two ways of approaching the subject, the two problematics – one taken from political science that adapted well to the American context, the other from the sociology of art that was better suited to the French context – each derived its relevance from the methodology adopted. It is impossible to dissociate the methods of study, the content of the protests, and their forms.

Table 7.1. *Methodological resources*

France	United States
no organized movement against contemporary art	"culture wars" against contemporary art
no statistics	statistics
few press notices	heavy press coverage
no studies of the subject	many studies of the subject
corpus = anecdotes	corpus = "affairs,"
local incidents without media coverage	incidents with heavy media coverage,
one "affair"	several anecdotes

The forms of rejection

Simple anecdotes collected on site, incidents given prominent media coverage, hotly disputed "affairs": the gamut of forms taken by the rejections of contemporary art ranges across the boundaries of public and private, from individual to collective expressions. In the United States, the "incidents" and above all the "affairs" clearly have a higher profile than in France. This is not simply the effect of method, as "anecdotes" are just as easily discovered by direct questioning of institutions. Street demonstrations, the creation of counter-movements, televised public debates – nothing like this occurred in France. With a few rare exceptions, the conflicts remained purely local and were limited to disagreements between experts about the relevance of aesthetic choices.

In the United States, an appeal was even made to the American Constitution itself when, in 1989, a resolution of the House of Representatives condemned the Art Institute of Chicago and its art school for having allowed "the presentation of an exhibition encouraging lack of respect for the American flag and abusing the right of freedom of expression guaranteed by the Constitution." This resolution referred to an artwork entitled "What is the Proper Way to Display a US Flag?" by Dread Scott Tyler, a student at the school. It consisted of a collage of photographs showing flag-draped coffins and demonstrators burning the American flag; an actual flag was placed on the floor of the gallery, and spectators were obliged to walk over it if they wished to write down their comments or questions. In response, several people, led by Vietnam veterans, organized a protest march in front of the Art Institute; President Bush and other Republican leaders proposed a Constitutional amendment (which was not adopted) to overturn the decision of *Texas v. Johnson* that protects acts profaning the flag in the name of freedom of expression.

Nothing better illustrates the intensity that can be found in civic protests about contemporary art in the United States than the Nelson affair, which had taken place in the preceding year in Chicago. Such a swift and effective mobilization – in this case organized around strongly held values such as the rights of minorities (blacks and homosexuals) and anti-obscenity campaigns – would have been unimaginable in France. The cause was a work by David Nelson, hung in the gallery of the Art Institute's school during its annual student exhibition. It was a "crudely executed portrait of an overweight Mayor Harold Washington dressed only in white lacy women's underwear – bra, panties, garter-belt, and stockings – holding a pencil in his right hand, staring dejectedly from the canvas. The title was *Mirth and Girth*."[3] This "affair," provoked by an argument the artist claimed was anti-iconoclast and anti-homosexual, clearly touched on values (racial and sexual minority rights) that were simultaneously strongly held and defended by an existing organized body. This type of vulnerability to different registers of indignation, and the existence of movements ready to take up the cause, explains the rapid build-up of the "affair" and the efficiency of the adverse reaction.

The only comparable French affair, at least from this point of view, was the Ping affair at the Pompidou Center in Paris. In 1994, after two months of agitation, animal rights groups managed to stop a project to display different species of insects and reptiles together in a glass case. However, the argument that allowed them to claim victory was entirely administrative in nature, and the publicity given to the affair never went beyond the small world of animal rights groups, Pompidou Center administrators, and the visitors who saw the few protestors gathered in front of the building on the morning of the show's opening (Heinich 1995b). The only "affair" that reached national level was that of the Buren columns at the Palais-Royal in 1986. It took place during an election campaign that pitted a socialist Minister of Culture first against a Right-wing mayor of Paris, and then against a new Right-wing Minister of Culture, during a period that saw the novel experiment of "cohabitation" between a socialist President of the Republic and a Right-wing Prime Minister (Heinich 1995a).

To see the major differences in the forms taken on by organized protests, it is enough to compare the Buren affair with a similar event in America. In the Serra affair in New York – which, like Buren, concerned a publicly funded project for a conceptual work in a public place – the protests, launched exclusively by local residents in the form of a petition, and relayed by the administrators in charge of the project, ended in a public hearing where the question of artistic authenticity was marginal

Table 7.2. *Buren versus Serra*

	France	United States
Cause	national heritage	city planning
Object	public project (installation)	public project (installation)
Context	only national affair	one among many
Place	Paris	New York
Duration	several months	seven years
Initiative	the press, an elected politician	local residents
Relays	associations for heritage protection, residents, citizens, the press	administrators in charge of the project for the city
Means	administrative procedures, press campaigns, petitions and letters, graffiti	petitions, public hearings
Counter-attack	ministry of culture, artists, intellectuals	artists, experts
Judges	Parliament, Commission on Historic Monuments, Administrative Court [*Conseil d'Etat*]	experts, artists, elected politicians, citizens
Result	victory for the artist (realization of the project)	defeat for the artist (dismantling of the project)

compared with functional considerations. The result was the dismantling of the installation and, correlatively, the defeat of the artist, who was not protected by the "moral law" found in Europe that gives authors the right to have a say in the presentation of their work to the public, independent of any financial consideration. This right allowed Buren to win his case in the end, despite the commitment to the contrary initially made by the new Right-wing Minister of Culture.

This comparison makes clear, first of all, the differences in procedures: on the whole, they are administrative and technocratic in France, while in the United States – where litigation is a frequent form of conflict resolution – they are legal and democratic. At the same time, we can see the link between the forms of rejection and the legal and political resources available to the two sides. The comparison highlights the gulf between them: French law tends to be permissive toward artists, who are protected by a moral right, while citizens' public utterances are severely curtailed by the rights to privacy, the protection of children, and anti-racist laws. American law, by contrast, is permissive toward its citizens thanks to the First Amendment rights guaranteed by the Constitution, but only allows artists a material right to the profits derived from the exploitation of their work (copyright) and no moral right (with the exception of two states which do make provisions for it) over the conditions under which their work is presented to the public.[4]

Thus a work is not protected in the United States unless it is clearly political, whereas in France it is protected simply by being recognized as artistic. Lawyer Barbara Hoffman concludes her remarkable analysis of the Serra affair by showing how the artist would have won his case if his work had contained even the slightest expression of a political position; because it was purely conceptual and abstract, it could not be treated as any kind of expression, and thus it could not be protected under the First Amendment.[5] In France, Daniel Buren won his case by threatening to sue the state for his moral right, as an artist, to complete his work.

Finally, the strong legal protection accorded to French artists is barely affected, politically or administratively, by control over subsidies (financial criteria are exclusively subordinated to expert judgments of artistic quality), nor by pressures from interest groups (which are relatively inactive with regard to the defense of values). In contrast, American artists are henceforth subject to the Helms Amendment which, since 1989, makes public financing of culture subordinate to moral criteria.[6] They are also subject to strong ethical objections on the part of powerful voluntary groups which militate for the defense of family and national values.

In this manner, differences in the legal and political status of artworks, linking legal resources and the potential to mobilize opinion in the name of a political cause, largely account for the differences we see in the forms that rejection takes. In the United States they are much more likely to be civic (major "affairs," court cases, petitions, demonstrations), in which artistic questions tend to be referred back to the more general problem of the freedom of expression, considered to be more important by all citizens, and strictly framed by legal and political (that is, constitutional) resources. In France these forms are more likely to be individual and private (sporadic protests by non-specialists, or debates confined to specialists), and the questions raised by artistic innovations are less immediately connected with causes that are susceptible of political mobilization.[7]

But, as we saw in the comparison of contexts, the seemingly more "civic" character of American rejections must be seen in light of the nature of the artworks in question, and the degree to which they touch on general rather than more purely artistic questions. For now, let us merely observe how the range of values defended by those who oppose contemporary art is divided between the two countries.

Table 7.3. *Legal and political situation*

	France	United States
General legal provisions	restrictive laws for citizens, permissive laws for artists	permissive laws for citizens, restrictive laws for artists
Protection of artists in law	law on artistic and literary property (material and moral rights)	First Amendment, Copyright (financial rights)
Legal control of public expression	Right of privacy, right to the image, protection of children, anti-racist laws. Expression is protected if it is artistic	Jurisprudence limiting the freedom of expression. Expression is protected if it is political
Administrative controls	no explicit criteria	Helms Amendment
Controls exercised by public opinion	weak organization in defense of values	strong ethical controls by interest groups

The defense of values

"I suppose a star of David set in excrement in a toilet bowl would be a wonderful expression of art, if the lighting was right! To think that part of the tuition is paid to support this supposed art expression in the name of free speech, at the expense of sensibility to the feelings of many, is appalling." This thought was written in one of the visitors' books at the Serrano exhibition in Philadelphia. Art, beauty, the use of public funds, sensitivity to feelings, common sense: these are quite disparate orders of value called upon to substantiate the indignation inspired by "Piss Christ." But this plurality of arguments is in no way synonymous with confusion, incoherence, or irrationality. Let us clarify the range of values that reactions to contemporary art invoke.

A first approach to this repertoire of values is the survey undertaken by the "Art Save" committee of "People for the American Way"; no equivalent French survey exists because there are no similar issues that would involve freedom of expression.[8] The following statistics were produced by taking into account only those cases which concerned the plastic arts, and following a typology that I established on the basis of the information furnished by the survey (see the notes to Table 7.4). The totals are larger than the number of cases due to the multiplicity of motives (Table 7.4) and protests (Table 7.5).

Motives related to sexuality are by far the commonest, mentioned in more than half the cases studied; after these come religion, civic values,

Table 7.4. *Artistic freedom under attack, 1994–1996: motives*

	1994 (n = 128)	1995 (n = 64)	1996 (n = 54)	Total (246)
Sexual morality[a]	92 (47%)	45 (54%)	47 (66%)	55%
Religion[b]	25 (13%)	12 (14%)	13 (18%)	15%
Civic values[c]	35 (18%)	13 (16%)	2 (3%)	12%
Minority rights[d]	26 (13%)	7 (8%)	2 (3%)	8%
Other[e]	19 (9%)	7 (8%)	7 (10%)	9%

Notes:
[a] E.g. "sexually explicit, nudity, inappropriate, pornographic, obscene, harassing, homosexual"
[b] E.g. "blasphemous, anti-religious, satanic, demonic"
[c] E.g. "desecration of the flag, violence"
[d] E.g. "racist, offensive to women"
[e] E.g. "misuse of public funds, insensitive to animals, no artistic merit, vandalism"

Table 7.5. *Artistic freedom under attack, 1994–1996: protest demonstrators*

	1994 (n = 128)	1995 (n=64)	1996 (n=54)	Total (246)
Individuals	64 (32%)	24 (29%)	18 (24%)	28%
Local authorities	37 (19%)	18 (21%)	17 (23%)	21%
Parents, educators, religious leaders	22 (11%)	10 (12%)	21 (28%)	17%
Cultural leaders	15 (8%)	6 (7%)	10 (13%)	9%
Students, academics	24 (12%)	9 (11%)	— —	8%
Voluntary groups	21 (11%)	10 (12%)	6 (8%)	7%
Business people	10 (5%)	7 (8%)	2 (3%)	5%
Vandals	4 (2%)	— —	1 (1%)	1%

and the rights of minorities. We can observe that the number of cases decreases from 1994 to 1996 (this is possibly due to the methods of information gathering); simultaneously we see a rise in the number of motives linked to sexual morality, to the detriment of civic values and the rights of minorities.

When it comes to types of protestors who have taken the initiative to react, the largest category is that of individuals acting independently, followed by local authorities, then parents or educators, cultural leaders, students (either high school or university), members of voluntary associations, and, finally, business people. Initiatives by parents and educators increased compared with those of students and academics: this probably reflects a fall in the level of liberal opposition in the name of "political correctness" and a rise in the motives related to sexuality. Indeed, an analysis of the correlations between types of motives and categories of protest shows that the initiatives of citizens and educators are highly concentrated around motives pertaining to sexuality, while the interventions of local authorities are more equally divided among the various categories of motives. Let us note, finally, that in 1996 there was a trend toward politicization or greater use of euphemisms in the motives invoked, particularly on the part of local officials: phrases like "inappropriate use of public funds" or, more vaguely, "inappropriate" and "potentially offensive" appear more frequently.

What about the aesthetic or artistic motives so often invoked in France? There are none: not that they do not exist in the United States – they had been deleted from the survey. This removal effectively constitutes a fundamental restriction: those incidents prejudicial to artistic freedom must be "based on content."[9] Thus excluded from the statistics was the case of the sculpture whose color was changed by the corporation who bought it, or that of the local mayor who used administrative regulations to remove from public view a work which he personally hated. A pre-selection of this kind strongly biases the results in relation to the French survey: because issues involving moral values are given privileged status, *the statistics cannot tell us anything about properly aesthetic problems*. But this lack of symmetry is itself highly significant of the ethical bias of the problem in the United States, where even those who defend artistic liberty do not defend it on artistic grounds, but rather for ideological or moral reasons.

To gain insights into values other than moral ones in protests against contemporary art, we are forced to abandon the "culture wars" arena, and with it the statistics, as well as the major "affairs" so well covered by the press, and instead to concern ourselves with simpler incidents, i.e. with those anecdotes that we could gather only through fieldwork. But it is at the same time necessary to give up any attempt to establish a statistical comparison between the two countries since we lack a sufficiently homogeneous corpus of material that would allow us to attempt such a comparative survey. Once again, the path we find ourselves obliged to take by qualitative methods is a function of the nature of the subject, whose degree of generalization has not yet achieved the status, so to say, of the "statistically correct" – that which can be surveyed and quantified (Desrosières 1993).

The comparison between the values that those who oppose contemporary art claim to defend in France and in the United States will therefore be established on the basis of their frequency not as it is precisely measured but as it is approximately evaluated in relation to the three categories of "affairs," incidents, and anecdotes (see Table 7.6). The rejections are classified first according to the object on which judgment is passed (the work, the work and the person, the person, relation to a context, the referent), then according to the register of value (in capital letters), of value (in bold type), and the type of criticism (in parentheses). The proper names refer to the most typical of the "affairs." Included in the "aesthetic" register are appeals to beauty and artistic authenticity (which is correlated with inspiration), while the "hermeneutic" register concerns the demand for meaning. We have taken into account the "purificatory" dimension of the appeal to integrity, as well as the "functional" dimension of the demands for utility, convenience, and security. The register of "reputation" is based on fame, with both its negative and positive connotations. We have classed under the heading "civic" all appeals to public interest, separate from arguments based on legality (juridical arguments), the economic rationale of public expenditures (economic/civic), and equity (ethics). Finally, we have imputed to the "ethical" register those values (sensitivity, decency, religion) which common sense tends to group under the heading of "moral" demands.[10]

Autonomous values: the work and its author

Let us begin with the grounds for rejection that appeal to the most "autonomous" values, that is, to those most specific to the art world:[11] those which are applied either to the work (beauty, meaning) or to the relation between the work and the person (authenticity). Although not included in the American statistics, these values nonetheless exist, even if they are rarer in the United States than in France, and used in a somewhat different fashion.

The appeal to beauty is not frequent in either corpus: either it appears too subjective to substantiate a complaint, or it has less force than issues pertaining not to the aesthetic value of a work (is it beautiful, in good taste, harmonious, etc.?) but instead to its artistic nature (is it a work of art?). In the American visitors' books, as in France, one finds very few protests made in the name of beauty: "Unfortunately, it's easier to be unique than it is to convey a sense of beauty" (List Visual Arts Gallery, Boston). The question of beauty is not enough to "create an affair" in the United States any more than it is in France; at most, it allows one to flesh out an argument. This is clear in the Serra affair in New York, where the petition "For Relocation," signed in 1980 by more than 1,300 people who demanded that "Tilted Arc" be moved, read as follows: "We the undersigned feel that the artwork called *Tilted Arc* is an obstruction to the plaza and should be removed to a more suitable location. (The individuals whose names are listed with an asterisk * find no artistic merit in the Serra artwork.)" In this case, the functional argument is the bulwark of the public protest, while the aesthetic argument – written in an ambiguous fashion somewhere between denying the work's aesthetic value and questioning its artistic nature – is reduced to a footnote, an asterisk placed next to some of the signatories' names.[12] Among the opponents brought in to speak at the public hearing, only one explicitly raised the question of aesthetics, regretting that the work interfered with the beauty of the plaza: "The *Tilted Arc* totally obstructs the architectural beauty of the court, the Jacob B. Javits Federal Office Building, and detracts from the view of so many the beauty, simplicity, and openness of the plaza and fountain."

One of the few (local) "affairs" that took up the question of aesthetics was the abstract sculpture commissioned from Gary Rieveschl for the city of Concord, California in 1989. Called "Spirit Poles" or "Porcupine Plaza," this installation, composed of vertical spears, won the prize for the "ugliest public sculpture ever financed by public funds in America" in a contest organized by the *National Enquirer*. A lack of harmony (aesthetic register) and dissonance with its site (purificatory register) were the principal complaints against the work, and it was ordered to be dismantled by vote of the new city government after a vigorous media campaign (the sculpture nevertheless remains in place because it is protected by California's "moral right" law).

Professional critics seem more likely to make aesthetic references to beauty because their professional expertise compensates for the subjectivity of the criterion. Thus, in the Mapplethorpe trial, the experts put on the stand by the defense to justify the exhibition of photographs depicting extreme homosexual acts argued neither for the autonomy of the artist, nor for the symbolic character of the images, nor for the ethics of transgression – all arguments that one might have expected to hear in France. Instead they insisted on the beauty of the compositions: a purely aesthetic argument.

Table 7.6. *Comparative frequency of the values invoked*

	France	United States
A. *Judgments about the work*		
AESTHETIC		
beauty		
("not beautiful")	★	★
	(Pagès)	(Rieveschl)
HERMENEUTIC		
meaning		
("it doesn't mean anything")	★★★	★
B. *Judgments about the work/person*		
AESTHETIC/INSPIRED		
authenticity		
("it's not art")	★★★	★★★ (Serra)
seriousness		
("it's a hoax")	★★★	?
reason		
("he's crazy")	★★	★
talent		
("a child could do as well")	★★★	★★
originality		
("it's already been done")	★★	?
inventiveness		
("he's repeating himself")	★★	?
disinterest		
("done for the money")	★★	?
interiority		
("trying to make a reputation")	★★	?
C. *Judgments about the person*		
REPUTATION		
fame		
("unknown artist")	★★	?
("trendy artist")	★	?
LOCALE		
proximity		
("foreign artist")	★	?
("neighborhood")	★★★	?
D. *Judgments on the relation to a context*		
PURIFICATORY		
patrimony, nature		
("maladjusted, degrading")	★★★	★
	(Buren)	(Heizer)
FUNCTIONAL		
convenience		
("it's in the way")	★★	★★ (Serra)

Table 7.6. (*cont.*)

	France	United States
security		
("it's dangerous")	⋆	⋆ (Serra)
utility		
("it's useless")	⋆	⋆
CIVIC/ECONOMIC		
economic rationales		
("it's too expensive")	⋆⋆⋆	⋆⋆⋆
market regulation		
("it's not up to the State to subsidize")	⋆	⋆⋆⋆
CIVIC		
the law of large numbers		
("the majority don't like it")	?	⋆⋆⋆
("the people don't understand it")	⋆⋆⋆	?
democracy		
("citizens were not consulted")	⋆⋆	⋆⋆⋆
CIVIC/JURIDICAL		
legality		
(law suits)	⋆	⋆⋆⋆
CIVIC/ETHICAL		
representativeness		
("other trends exist")	⋆⋆⋆	⋆⋆⋆
ETHICS		
equity		
("it's not just")	⋆⋆⋆	⋆
work		
("anyone could make it")	⋆⋆⋆	?
E. Judgments about the referent		
CIVIC		
ideals		
("Nazi, anti-American")	⋆	⋆⋆
	(Finlay)	(Tyler, De Maria)
CIVIC/ETHICAL		
minority rights		
("racist, sexist")	⋆	⋆⋆⋆
	(Bazile)	(Nelson)
ETHICAL		
decency, dignity		
("obscene")	⋆	⋆⋆⋆
	(Bazile)	(Mapplethorpe)
religion		
("blasphemous")	⋆	⋆⋆⋆(Serrano)
sensitivity		
("sadistic")	⋆	⋆
	(Ping)	(Yanagi)

Key: ⋆⋆⋆ = frequent; ⋆⋆ = possible; ⋆ = rare; ? = no meaningful example in the corpus.

The prosecutor, Frank Prouty, asserted that these photographs of what the *New York Times* called "anal and penile penetration with unusual objects" were without artistic value, an essential claim in obscenity charges. But Ms. Kardon [the director of the exhibition] disagreed. She pointed to Mapplethorpe's sensitive lighting, texture, and composition, calling "a self-portrait of Mapplethorpe with the handle of a whip inserted in his anus" almost classical in its composition . . . An image of a man urinating into another man's mouth was remarkable because of the strong and opposing diagonals of the design. Another photograph demonstrated Mapplethorpe's fondness for "an extremely central image," she said. "That's the one where the forearm of one individual is inserted into the anus of another individual?" Prouty asked. "Yes," she replied. "The forearm of one individual is the very center of the picture, just as many of his flowers occupy the center." (Steiner 1995, p. 9)

The denial of artistic autonomy by the moralists is echoed, symmetrically, in the denial of the transgression of moral values by the aesthetes. In each case, what is rejected is the possibility of more than one point of view, as well as the reality of the affect, according to a logic that, from a French standpoint, appears equally puritanical on both sides (on the conservative side, because they refuse to countenance any images with a sexual connotation; on the liberal side, because they deny the sexual aspect of the image).[13]

In France, arguments about beauty are willingly abandoned in favor of arguments about meaning: thus in the Ping affair at Beaubourg, which concerned the question of sensitivity to animal suffering, the organizers of the exhibition did not argue about the aesthetic quality of the work, nor even about its place in an avant-garde tradition, but about its moral and political symbolism (Heinich 1995b). The reliance on the hermeneutic register is little present in the American corpus; one finds it only occasionally: "I didn't understand. But it's probably just me" (visitors' book of List Visual Arts, Boston). Furthermore, the "meaning" in question seems to grow spontaneously out of the "message" that the artist personally would have wanted to communicate (and not, for example, the capacity of the work to symbolize the phenomena of its own time), as in this reaction to one of Calder's sculptures: "I must say that I did not really understand, and I do not today, what Mr. Calder was trying to tell us." Here we can see how art falls back into an ideological dimension, so that artistic creation becomes simply a way of expressing an opinion – a phenomenon that looks typically American to a French observer.

"It looks like a sculpture piece of junk that some doped-up artist calls art," argued a Concord native *à propos* the Rieveschl installation. Another said: "It shows that the inmates have taken over the asylum!" And yet another: "Aluminum poles? Downtown is not a high tech industrial park." Although these arguments also arise from aesthetic considerations, they no longer operate as a continuous evaluation of the work (is it more or less beautiful, more or less meaningful), but as a discontinuous classification on either side of the borderline between art and non-art. The issue here is that of artistic authenticity, with criteria that (often inextricably) encompass both the work and the artist, the object and the person of its creator. This question, an important one in the French corpus, was also at the heart of several of the American incidents. In 1983, in Boulder, Colorado, a project by Andrea Blum for a public sculpture in a park, consisting of three concrete pavilions, provoked a public debate that ended with the project being cancelled. In 1984, in Tacoma, Washington, citizens, infuriated by two abstract neon sculptures by Stephen Antonakos installed with municipal funding, voted to have them removed. In 1986, in Cleveland, Ohio, an outdoor sculpture by Claes Oldenburg, commissioned for the headquarters of a corporation and consisting of an enormous ink-pad bearing the word FREE in letters 5.5 meters high, was the object of a protest campaign when the corporation offered it to the city. There have been similar incidents involving multimedia installations in Georgetown, Delaware, Las Vegas, Nevada, and Silver Spring, Maryland.

The questioning of a work's authenticity may be confined to an unsubstantiated rejection of the artistic character of the work, often with reference to the emperor being naked in Hans Andersen's story of "The Emperor's New Clothes": it is the innocents who know the truth (the emperor is naked, there is no art), while the experts who rave about the works are suckers and snobs preyed upon by impostors. But there also exists a repertory of arguments that can support that accusation. In France, there are frequent accusations that refer to seriousness of intent, to reason, to talent, to originality, to inventiveness, to disinterest, to interiority; in the United States, these arguments seem less widespread (with the exception of arguments about "reason" or sanity which question the mental health of the artist). Better represented are the demands for the definition of limits, such as limits to the freedom of expression, to the private domain, and to transgression.

And here an essential difference between the two countries emerges. The question of aesthetic quality can be approached in two different ways: one discontinuous (the questioning of what belongs to the category of artwork, put in terms of "art versus non-art") and the other continuous (an evaluation of a work's place on a scale of values, put in terms of "more or less" good art, whatever the criteria used to make that judgment). In France, agreement that something is a work of art (discontinuous judgment) leaves open discussion, and therefore disagreement, about the quality of the work (continuous judgment), so that the question of authenticity gives way to questions of composition or symbolism. (Note that it was a French visitor who wrote in a visitors' book for an exhibition at the Wadsworth Atheneum in Hartford, in 1994: "It's good social work, but BAD ART!") In the United States, the heart of the conflict seems to lie in establishing the borderline between art and non-art, to the point that once a work is accepted as art by expert opinion, the question of artistic quality – and thus the legitimacy of public support for it – is no longer posed. If it is art, the work can be seen as nothing but art (and not, for example, as pornography), and it therefore merits total support and protection.

The emphasis on judgments of the nature of a thing rather than judgments about its quality was particularly evident during the Mapplethorpe trial, where the confusion between aesthetic value and artistic nature allowed the experts to evade the question of how criteria of quality were applied in selecting the works: the category of "art" was enough to mark the boundary between what was and was not acceptable, and it served equally as a rallying point for the liberals against the conservatives, or for the defenders of freedom of expression against the defenders of moral values. This discontinuous logic therefore rules out any subsequent questioning of the purely aesthetic aspect of curatorial choices: aesthetics becomes a matter of politics, ideology, and ethics without the possibility of further discussion about the competence of the experts or the quality of the artists thus defended.[14] This point is emphasized by a reader of the *New York Times* (July 30, 1989), who wrote in response to an article by critic Hilton Kramer that argued for the aesthetic qualities of Mapplethorpe's photographs and Serra's "Tilted Arc":[15] "Values in much that transpires in the art world are enhanced by inflated vocabulary, with the label 'art' sufficient to sanctify many works and blur them from clear scrutiny."

To sum up, the aesthetic register is present in the American "culture wars" as it is in the rejections of contemporary art in France, but in a different fashion. The question of beauty seems equally unlikely to be the basis for agreement unless it is used by experts. In France, these experts rely more on the hermeneutic register of meaning, based on a symptomatic analysis of the work; whereas in the United States, the question has more to do with an expectation of common sense relating to the ideological "message" consciously transmitted by the artist. And while the question of artistic authenticity recurs in both countries, the repertory of arguments seems less well developed in the United States. Topics such as the inspiration of the artist, which is central in France, are rarely mentioned; instead, one finds a questioning of the limits of art, reflecting a stance that has less to do with aesthetic judgment than with political and ethical positions.

Between autonomy and heteronomy: the relationship to the context

Less specific to artistic creation are those values exclusively centered on the relationship between the person of the artist, his or her work, and the context. In France, artists are dismissed for many different reasons: it can be a question of their reputation, either they have too much ("he's too much a creature of the media") or too little ("no one knows him"); it can be a problem of local connections, again either that the artist is too local ("he was chosen only because he's around and the choice had nothing to do with his talent") or not local enough ("he's from elsewhere"). Such arguments seem to be employed less frequently in the United States; in any case, they do not appear in my corpus.

But one does find many protests that focus on the relationship of an artwork to its context. The first register of values underlying these complaints is the one I have called "purificatory," that is, the appeal to the integrity or the purity of the place that the artwork has in some manner muddied, alienated, or disfigured. The place can be a natural site: an example would be the criticism of Michael Heizer's *Double Negative* – a project that involved an excavation by a bulldozer in an open space in Overton, Nevada in 1970 – as environmentally irresponsible. But the place is equally likely to be urban, as in the case of the Rieveschl affair in Concord, or Christo's Central Park project in New York, "Gates," which was the object in 1991 of a negative campaign by local residents (supported by a *New York Times* editorial) who were afraid of the crowds that it would attract and the "dangerous precedent" that it would set. Environmental activists and urban planners were also drawn into the struggle against such a profanation of the park, and in the end, it was their arguments that motivated the final rejection by the Parks Department, who wrote that it feared a "systematic and complete alteration of a landmark space" (we see here feelings not unlike those expressed in the Buren affair in Paris). Similarly, in the Serra affair, also in New York, several opponents argued that it was necessary to protect the site: as one regional administrator for the Health Department, who proposed several reasons for removing the "barrier that passes for art," said: "it constitutes a scar on the plaza and creates a fortresslike effect," "it's a target for graffiti," "it is too large for its present site and it violates the very spirit and concept of the plaza."

Another argument was that the work "destroys the previously open plaza by obstructing free passage across the plaza and blocking an open view of the fountain." This complaint takes us into another register, the functional one, which can concern not only ease of use – as it does here – but also utility ("I don't care for the spending of money on a mess of jackstraws dumped in the middle of the road and called art. Better to spend our taxes on something useful," objected one of Rieveschl's opponents), but also security, as in cases where the emphasis is put on the greater likelihood of risk, of graffiti, or of drug trafficking.[16] In a similar manner, a work by Carl Andre ("Stone Field Sculpture," a 1977 installation of rocks in a public space in Hartford, Connecticut) drew many complaints in the local newspapers like this one: "these rocks are dangerous – kids might injure themselves crawling all over them." Another objection holds that "muggers might hide behind these rocks and pop out at unsuspecting passersby." This security argument was occasionally employed in the Buren affair, notably that they were an obstacle to access by fire safety vehicles in the event of a fire.

While arguments about the inconveniences and security risks of contemporary art are relatively rare, the argument about uselessness is, in contrast, applicable to almost any public commission. The functional argument is here combined with another register of values based on both economic considerations and a civic duty to make rational use of community resources: here we see how the classic "voice of the taxpayer" is frequently invoked in both countries. In the United States, the value of the artwork is measured against the yardstick of money (economic register), which allows it to be compared with other possible uses of public resources (the civic register). Such arguments occur in France, but sporadically, and are limited to the general public, who are little inclined to bring purely aesthetic criteria into the debate. In the United States, these arguments appeared in force in 1995 *à propos* the budget restrictions proposed for the National Endowment for the Arts (NEA); they followed on from the national concerns of the last ten years: "They don't need to spend any more money on something they can't afford." "Not many people really enjoy that kind of stuff. I don't." "Spend money on education or the highways. The roads in my city are terrible. Maybe put money into homeless shelters." "The arts have some way of getting private money, whereas welfare, Medicare and Medicaid don't. I would hate to see those areas cut to allow for the arts"(*USA Today*, July 28, 1995).

This last point of view contains another line of argument – of regulation by the market – that also involves a conjunction of economic and civic concerns, and which, since it never appears in the French corpus, seems to be peculiarly American. It reduces the artistic question to a problem of freedom of expression, and subjects freedom of expression to the laws of supply and demand: "There are two very good reasons that art flourishes in this country. First, we offer true freedom of expression through our constitutional rights, and second, we have a free market that will support that which finds an audience. We have always honored our academic efforts in developing the arts, and I am sure we will continue to do so as long as there are people who want to express themselves" (*The New York Times*, August 13, 1995). The NEA debates elicited numerous interventions by citizens arguing that all support for artistic creation should be private.[17]

The demand that art be regulated by the market is readily followed by a denunciation of the élite status of subsidized art, based on a purely civic argument: that of democracy. Its first concern is the will of the majority, which takes different forms in the two countries. In France, the main argument is about the élitism of art that is incomprehensible to the ordinary citizen; in the United States, it is about the importance of pleasing the majority. In the first case, therefore, what motivates the protest is demand for equality; in the second, the motive is respect for the strength of the greater number. Consequently, the NEA's choices are violently criticized insofar as they offend the opinions of a large portion of the electorate ("Without being necessarily obscene, much of the 'art' funded by the NEA could certainly be called junk by most taxpayers and wouldn't stand the scrutiny of a public vote"), or the feelings of the middle class ("Many artists feel the creative need to ridicule middle-class sensibilities, and expect taxpayers to finance the effort"), or finally, and more generally, the consensus on the fundamental values of the community ("While I do not feel strongly about ending funding for the arts, I violently oppose spending dollars on cultural programs that are controversial. What is art to some is pure trash to others. If I am compelled to contribute, it will not be at the expense of my value system").

Close to this argument is the denunciation of the anti-democratic character of selection procedures and the public installation of artworks. Several protests were generated in response to installations financed by public funds that did not sufficiently benefit the community as a whole. In 1985 in Ottawa, Illinois, a large environmental sculpture by Michael Heizer on the site of an abandoned coalmine provoked violent disagreements between local users and the Federal Department of Conservation when, after a few years, the park was closed. In 1986 in Alexandria, Virginia, *Promenade classique* by Anne and Patrick Poirier, commissioned by a private corporation, attracted criticism for encroaching on public space. In 1991 in Langley, Virginia, *Kryptos*, a sculpture made of granite and copper commissioned with public funds for the CIA headquarters, was criticized first for its cost, then because it was inaccessible to visitors, and finally because it had an inscription in code that was unintelligible to the public. In 1992 in Canon City, Colorado, a sculpture designed in 1986 by Andrew Leicester for a prison, and financed by the State Arts Council's Percent for Art, and which was inaccessible to both prisoners and their visitors, was first not maintained for several years, and then destroyed.

In matters of selection, it is the failure to consult citizens that is condemned in the name of democracy. This argument exists in both countries, but is more often applied in the United States, where reliance on experts – a fairly well-accepted practice in France (Urfalino and Vilkas 1995) – is strongly counterbalanced by the civic requirement to submit choices to majority agreement, and by belief in the universality of aesthetic judgment. The Serra trial in New York gave rise to many of these kinds of objections: "What is really at stake here is a question of democracy. . . . The public is saying, we don't like it, and we are not stupid, and we are not philistines, and we don't need some art historians and some curators to tell us that we will like it. We don't like it . . . Democracy says we are not fools, we are not stupid, we don't like that piece of art. I say, in a democracy, why not let democracy rule."

These democratic civic requirements for the selection process can take on a legal character, though the recourse to trials is an extreme form that occurs only rarely in France but frequently in the United States where, as everyone knows, legal resources are exceptionally well developed. The appeal to the courts can occur more informally in both countries, in the name of equity to artists. These encounters combine the ethical register of concern for individual sensibilities and the civic register of respect for the diversity of aesthetic tendencies, in accordance with the general interest of art (in France) or to the nation (in the United States). In the Whitney Museum's archives there is a cartoon based on the theme of "When the Saints Come Marching In." It represents "The Blessing of the Clones by His Unctuousness from the Sacred Church of MOMA," and denounces the academicism inherent in institutions of modern and contemporary art. In spirit, it is similar to the complaints of one adversary of the NEA, who declared: "Still, American artists with more traditional styles have been completely ignored by the NEA, which spends the vast majority of its funding on questionable 'art,' sometimes called 'Contemporary' but often rejected even by critics and collectors of true Contemporary art." During the Serra affair, there was one artist who raised her voice against the monopolization of culture by a particular clique, against the domination of a certain type of minimalist and conceptual art (an argument much invoked in France over the last decade), against the absence of artistic value in the works thus favored, against the intimidation of a large portion of the public, and against the attack on the moral rights of the architect who designed the plaza. And *à propos* of the NEA, one artist, himself subsidized, complained that the organization, under the thumb of an academic élite, stifled creativity by favoring "aesthetically correct" art over traditional forms.

Under such conditions, it is not surprising to find a pamphlet in the United States calling for a public protest against the exclusion by a museum of non-realist artists which invokes a register that is doubly civic – both in its form and its content – appealing for representativeness in cultural choices. Protests like this one against exclusions by museums, or the curators of exhibitions, are nonetheless more likely to be expressed in terms of minority rights rather than in the name of art. We thus slip into arguments about "political correctness," which no longer concern contemporary art but, more generally, the link between cultural politics and the representation of diverse communities – as with the tract in question ("STOP RACISM AND SEXISM"), calling for a protest, accompanied by a petition to stop an exhibition entitled "Three Centuries of American Art" which included "no black artists and only one woman artist" (archives of the Whitney Museum).

In France, the denunciation of injustice, less able to appeal to legal resources and less interested in civic demands for representativeness, tends instead to rely on the informal mode of ethical indignation about a moral failure. The failure consists of granting to some what should be due to others and, in particular, in giving special treatment to artists of dubious quality while others, at least as deserving, are ignored. In this case, the democratic requirement of equality no longer has to do with providing access to art for the greatest number of those who appreciate it, but with allowing access to public resources to those artists who are most competent to benefit from it. We are thus no longer concerned with a defense of the public interest, defined as a function of the greatest number (whether egalitarian in the French mode, or majoritarian in the American), but with a defense of the rights of a given individual, in the name of a principle of justice sustained by the requirement of equity and indignation in the face of infractions experienced as immoral. The emphasis thus shifts from civic concerns to ethical ones, using an argument about the need for equity in public policies for culture; this argument is often found in France in denunciations of privileges unjustifiably bestowed and of the risks involved in making misjudgments in the eyes of posterity.[18]

Arguments about justice for artists appear sporadically in the American corpus, but they are more likely to be combined with other registers: either they are civic, in the name of fair representation, or they are economic, in the name of fair pricing (the visitors' book at the Guggenheim Museum has the following entry: "I'm disappointed in your number of artworks. For such a large museum you could have more ordinary *modern* art. There are probably thousands of young modern artists in NYC alone. For the price, have more art . . . Price is too much for such a limited display"). In France, they are more likely to take a form little found in the American corpus: that of the recompense that is due to each person in proportion to their finished work. This is an argument underlying the notion that "anyone could do it," which refers back to equity, a topic close to the aesthetic demand for specific artistic talent, which refers back to authenticity. This combination of ethical indignation and aesthetic skepticism is the most common expression of protests about contemporary art in France, whereas it almost never appears in the American "culture wars."

Fame or proximity of the artist, the integrity of the site, functionality, rational public expenditures, democracy, legality, equity: these different categories of arguments reflecting the relationship of an artist and his or her work to its context thus probably constitute an acceptable and rational formulation of the feelings of strangeness and exclusion felt by ordinary citizens when they view works that lie outside habitual frames of reference and so are unfamiliar and unintelligible. But only more sustained interviews would allow us to test this hypothesis, which is about what distinguishes contemporary art, the trigger for the "culture wars" which, not by chance, were provoked by precisely such objects.

Heteronomous values: the referent

Up to this point, the differences between French protests and the American "culture wars" have appeared only in the margins of the value registers discussed – globally similar so long as we looked only at the autonomous values connected with the work, or at mixed values that bear on the relationship to its context. But if we turn to heteronomous values, which concern the referent of the work directly, we shall see massive differences emerging between the two cultures. In essence, the problems that contemporary art raises in the United States lie in the civic and ethical domain of ideals that the works transgress. This is not usually a dimension of the problem in France.

What is meant by "values of the referent"? Let us take as examples the complaints of the citizens of La Roche-sur-Yon (Vendée) about a fountain commissioned in 1986 from Bernard Pagès consisting of battered oildrums; or the protests of the citizens of Cincinnati when they saw the four winged pigs in bronze that crowned a monumental gate conceived by Andrew Leicester in 1988 which, it was argued, would give a degrading image to the city. More typically American is the case of the murals commissioned in 1994 from Michael Spafford for the State Congress building in Olympia, Washington named the "Twelve Labors of Hercules," withdrawn after a group of congressmen and women complained that:

"Hercules killed his wife and children. And those murals are about rape. It's not what our visitors should be looking at"; "As a woman, I feel offended by them."[19]

These judgments about the referent of the work (i.e. the subject represented), without taking account of the mediation proper to artistic representation, are a long way away from the sphere of autonomy of art and of aesthetic judgment, whether expert or amateur. They may refer to the civic dimension of ideals about the nation ("As with our rivers and lakes, we need to clean up culture; for it is a well from which we all must drink. Just as a poisoned land will yield up poisonous fruit, so a polluted culture, left to fester and stink, can destroy a nation's soul," declared conservative leader Pat Buchanan, *à propos* of Mapplethorpe, in the *Standard Star*, June 19, 1989), or civilization ("If the extent of a city's civilization can be judged by its artistic displays, then Hartford must be in the Neanderthal boondocks. Now all we need is a statue of King Kong among the boulders," as one opponent of Carl Andre's installation wrote to the local paper), or humanity as a whole ("I, as an artist, hate to say that, but I have come to the conclusion that most of the monies given are just going into the destruction of a humanizing influence. It's going towards an art that I believe is basically dehumanized," declared one artist during the Serra affair). These ideals can even be diametrically opposed to patriotic traditions: in 1990, in San José, California, citizens protested against the erection of a monumental sculpture in bronze representing a captain in the nineteenth-century American army because it glorified militarism.

In France, there have been only a couple of rejections of contemporary art based on ideological motives. One, in Carmaux, concerned an installation judged detrimental to the memory of Jean Jaurès: the municipal council had ordered that it be displayed outside the town hall. Another case concerned British artist Ian Finlay, whom an assistant accused of harboring pro-Nazi sympathies because his work, commissioned for Versailles during preparations for the bicentennial celebration of the French Revolution, included a Nazi emblem. The artist brought a libel action, and won by showing that his assistant had personal and vengeful motives, and by arguing that including this emblem did not reflect any sympathy for the ideology it represented but was, on the contrary, an attempt to condemn it. In the United States, the cases are more numerous and clearcut. They may be no more than anecdotal – for example, several entries in the visitors' book of "The Tradition of the New" exhibition at the Guggenheim Museum in 1994 took offense at a work of Walter De Maria's which placed a swastika next to a Christian cross and a star of David – but they can also become national concerns, such as the Chicago exhibition of Dread Scott Tyler's work.

Somewhere in between the civic defense of democratic values and the ethical indignation at injustice toward citizens because of their membership in a community lie those protests which occur in the name of minority rights. These can be racial minorities (blacks, as with the Nelson affair in Chicago), national minorities (in 1991 in Pittsburgh, Pennsylvania, a glass-fiber sculpture by Luis Jimenez, "Hunky Steelworker," was the object of a series of attacks because it was taken as an insult to Americans of Eastern European descent), or sexual minorities (as in the case of the "Labors of Hercules" mentioned above). In this last instance, the protests were often ambiguously situated between feminism and moralism, between the defense of women and the defense of decency. Similarly, in New York, a sculpture commissioned from George Segal, called "Gay Liberation," that showed a lesbian couple and a homosexual couple, provoked mixed reactions: some found it too ugly, others too big for the site, others feared that it would attract tourist hordes and serve as "an invitation to public sex"; some homosexuals and lesbians accused it of being racist since it only showed white people (when it was installed on the Stanford campus in 1984, a passerby defaced it with a hammer). In France, too, one of the very few examples of an artwork being rejected because of its sexual character revealed a similar ambiguity between moralism and feminism: the exhibition by Bernard Bazile at the Pompidou Center in 1993 of three nude female mannequins aroused only a few comments in the visitors' book but prompted the (female) guards to refuse to guarantee the safety of this attack on the dignity of women and on the cultural vocation of the Pompidou Center.

The ethical rejection of obscenity occurs frequently in the American corpus, fed as it is by a considerable number of works that transgress the prohibition against representing the sexual act, or sometimes simple nudity. The tone of these reactions is particularly violent whenever the act depicted is homosexual: thus it is not surprising that the Mapplethorpe affair, with its photos of extreme homosexual acts and naked children, attracted the most virulent criticism and had the most lasting consequences. We find, in the diatribes against the exhibition, a recurrent theme of the need to maintain strict boundaries between art and pornography, art and non-art, between freedom of expression and license, between art worthy of public subsidies and provocations designed simply to shock: "THERE'S A BIG DIFFERENCE BETWEEN ART AND SMUT"; "A MERE LABEL CAN'T TURN PORNOGRAPHY INTO ART"; "OBSCENITIES TOO OFTEN DISGUISED AS ART"; "OBSCENE PHOTOS ARE NOT ARTISTIC" were headlines in *The Atlantic Journal, The Florida Times-Union,* the *Donathan Eagle,* and the *Roanoke Times.* James J. Kilpatrick criticized that "prurient junk, intended to shock the decent sensibilities of those who would come to a public museum"(*Taunton Daily Gazette*), and declared that "because I live by the First Amendment, I am prepared to go a long way in defending a right of free expression. But when it comes to free expression with public funds in public institutions, reasonable lines have to be drawn. In this appalling affair, the lines were trampled underfoot"(*Parkersburg News*).

The comparison between the two countries is particularly delicate when it comes to ethical reactions to artistic propositions which, for some, clearly involve sexual morality and, for others, are seen as being above all about aesthetic perception, i.e. as without any erotic content. A French person can certainly understand why Americans concerned to maintain sexual prohibitions would be upset that the 1990 performance of "Post-Porn Modernist," presented by Annie Sprinkle at The Kitchen in New York, in which she appeared naked and talked about sexuality, was paid for by the NEA and the New York State Council on the Arts, or that the NEA gave a grant to a feminist work called "The Dinner Party," considered by some to be obscene. But it is more difficult not to laugh when one hears that the Virginia Museum of Fine Arts in 1992 organized, at the request of certain schools, parents, and religious leaders, a guided tour of the Museum that avoided all the nudes in the collection (a task, admitted one employee, that turned out to be difficult); or that patrons of a certain store in Springfield, Missouri in 1992 removed a reproduction of the Venus de Milo because "it was too shocking . . . this is a family-oriented conservative area"; or that a junior high school teacher, with the support of the Commission for Women at her institution, demanded the withdrawal of a reproduction of Goya's *Maja desnuda* from a classroom wall because it constituted sexual harassment (this occurred in Philadelphia in 1992; the image was re-hung after the Art Department protested).

The borderline between puritanism and lack of discernment, or between hypersensitivity and underestimation of the erotic aspect of images – more generally speaking, between ethical and aesthetic perception – is particularly difficult to draw whenever the representation is of naked children, in which some see pedophilia and others see an awareness of the beauty of children's bodies. Several scandals testify to this: first was the case of Jock Sturges' photographs (he was arrested by the FBI in 1990), and the more telling case of Sally Mann, who photographed her own children in situations that could be described as ambiguous by some and frankly provocative by others. Are liberals, who defend the freedom of artistic expression, sexual obsessives who *want* eroticism everywhere (the conservative spin)? Or are conservatives, who defend moral values, sexual obsessives who *see* eroticism everywhere (the liberal spin)? Even in the

United States, it is difficult to draw a line between the two, including at the level of the courts, where the imputation of obscenity is strictly limited by jurisprudence, although the "compelling state interest" or the "clear and present danger" – which alone should allow the curtailment of the freedom of expression guaranteed by the First Amendment – is not clearly defined by the Supreme Court. Thus Mapplethorpe's accusers, convinced that the images in question were harmful, wanted to insist on the "obviousness" of their obscenity; and thus they lost the suit to his defenders, who were able to stress the subjectivity of this position while arguing for the objectivity of the images' artistic qualities.[20]

Let us look more closely now at a particular Franco-American case which demonstrates this ambiguity on several levels. It concerns an image commissioned in 1993 from Balthus to illustrate the labels that the Château Mouton Rothschild asks a contemporary painter to produce every year. The charcoal sketch of a nude girl posed no problem in France, while in the United States, various groups joined forces against this "kiddy porn." Eventually, the American distributor replaced the image with a white strip on the bottles intended for export. In a press release, the Baroness called this "censure" and said that she was "dismayed by this unhappy misunderstanding, having never imagined that this charming work of art could be perceived in a sexual fashion or linked to the even more tragic global problem of child abuse."[21] Up until that point, things seemed clear from a European perspective: the puritanism of American conservatives had once again reared its ugly head, to the great detriment of liberals. But things were actually somewhat more complex. On the one hand, the press handout destined for America was even more ambiguous than the image on the label: "The fragile and mysterious adolescent that he has drawn for the 1993 Mouton Rothschild seems to embody the promise, still secret, of a shared pleasure." Furthermore, one cannot determine the quality of the image in question without considering its context: should a wine label be considered a work of art that can be appreciated in a purely aesthetic manner, or a simple image unprotected by the mediation of art? Can one, more precisely, use images signed by artists for commercial ends, particularly if those ends involve the stimulation of the senses, while continuing to insist on their artistic character and denying the legitimacy of extra-aesthetic uses? Isn't it attempting to have one's cake and eat it too if one makes reference to "secrets" and "pleasures" in a marketing strategy while at the same time denying – in the name of art – that there is any ambiguity (doesn't the artistic element tend to be canceled, or at least obscured, by the context)? To put it another way, should one impute responsibility for this affair to the puritanism of the American leagues of virtue or to the duplicity of the French exporters, who are quick to hide virtuously behind "creative rights" the sensual and commercial dimension of the image? If there is a puritanical obsession on the one side, is there not also aesthetic hypocrisy on the other? And isn't the accusation of American puritanism here the very French over-interpretation of a reaction to a proposition that is objectively (if not intentionally) ambiguous?

The fact remains that protests about contemporary art in the name of sexual morality are more or less absent in France. When they do occur, they remain at an anecdotal, or even less coherent stage, being strictly constrained at the institutional level by the (moral) risk of being accused of censorship – a much more serious accusation than that of incitement to debauchery. That such cases are rare can largely be ascribed to the nature of the proposed works themselves; but in that case, the difference between avant-garde positions may tell us a great deal about the comparison between the two countries since the transgressions characteristic of contemporary art in each country involve very different kinds of values. We will verify this à propos one other type of value often invoked in ethical protests: religion.

We saw in the American statistics that the number of protests because of the blasphemous character of a work was second only to those linked to obscenity. Herein lies another clearcut contrast with France, where there were only two cases arising straightforwardly from the denial of a subsidy in the name of respect for the spiritual vocation of the site. In these cases, the conceptual art projects clearly did not have blasphemous intentions, but were attempts to find modern expressions of spirituality. In the United States, however, accusations of blasphemy are frequent and spectacular: the most prominent example was Andres Serrano's "Piss Christ," part of a traveling show sponsored by the NEA, which provoked a national scandal. As in the Mapplethorpe case, the artist chose to offer a defense entirely grounded in aesthetics without claiming either hostility toward Catholicism or the right to freedom of artistic expression. When asked about his motives and choice of a title, he replied: "I could just use piss for the beautiful light that it gives me and not let people know what they're looking at. But I do like for people to know what they're looking at because the work is intended to operate at more than one level." One visitor echoed this sentiment in a visitors' book in Philadelphia, illustrating once again this shift entirely into the aesthetic register, denying any emotional charge in the content of the image: "The liquids used in making the photos create some wonderful colors and effects. But I don't understand why the nature/source of the fluid matters at all; I find a plain minimalist white and red composition just as uninteresting when it's made from paint as when it's made from milk and blood. For me, color is color; I don't like needing to look at the label next to the painting to explain what I'm seeing."

From the opposition side, reactions were much less ambiguous. Christians went so far as to organize a candle-lit vigil in front of the Institute of Contemporary Art in Philadelphia during the show's opening. This allowed them to demonstrate their refusal even to visit the exhibition, an act of protest against the very principle of such images. This refusal was interpreted by the partisans of artistic freedom as proof of the protestors' obscurantism since they presumed to judge what they had not even seen. We can note that, unlike aesthetic questions about artistic authenticity, indignant ethical reactions to images perceived as blasphemous or obscene are relatively lacking in nuances. The fact of showing this work was interpreted by some as a declaration of war against Christianity ("Showing 'Piss Christ' has little to do with definitions of art or federal funding of any offensive works. Displaying this work is about the cultural war on Christianity and which side the ICA, and consequently the University of Pennsylvania, has decided to join"), and its only claim to beauty was condemned as outrageous: "As a Roman Catholic, I am outraged that the University would permit the Institute of Contemporary Art to exhibit this sacrilegious display of Jesus Christ crucified. Wendy Steinberg, ICA public relations coordinator, depicted this photograph as 'very, very beautiful – actually kind of reverent.' She can't be serious! Steinberg's statement clearly demonstrates a lack of religious sensitivity, and is an outright slap in the face to all Christians."[22]

There remain the cases, still in the ethical register, of reactions to those (rare) installations that display live animals. Such was the small scandal aroused in 1994 at the Pompidou Center by a project of a Chinese artist to have insects and reptiles of different species co-exist for the duration of the exhibition. The simple fact of putting insects on display is capable of arousing a revulsion that falls somewhere between disgust and the stirrings of an awareness of animal suffering: "I never realized how much I'd been affected by the animal rights movement until I saw Campopiano's installation. Is this necessary? The ants look happy, but the fish need room and the mice smell" (visitors' book of the List Visual Arts Gallery in Boston, 1989). Those already sensitive to the animal rights cause can equally invoke the Endangered Species Act, as some did at the Lyon Bienniale in 1993, where an installation by Annette Messager, in which stuffed birds were glued on spades, drew threats from an association for the defense of animals because one of the birds belonged to a protected species. In a similar vein, a visitor to the Guggenheim Museum, after having complained about the lack of ordinary modern art, added: "Also, if Rauschenberg's bird is real feathers it is illegal for him to have with bird feathers unless they are chicken or he is an amerindian [*sic*]."

One of the few cases that occurred in the United States had nothing particularly American about it, since it also provoked reactions at the Venice Bienniale. In September 1992, an installation using live ants by the Japanese artist Yukinori Yanagi, *World Flag Ant Farm*, became the subject of an investigation by the Italian justice system. They wished to determine whether the ants had "suffered in the name of conceptual art." The investigation was instigated by an association of vegetarians alerted by a visitor who had noticed dead ants, and who accused the work of being "highly uneducational, because it lacks the necessary respect for nature and for living creatures. The ants were dying because their highly organized life had been turned upside down."[23] This same installation, presented in 1995 at the Wadsworth Atheneum in Hartford, Connecticut, was the subject of a strongly worded letter to the editor in the local paper, headed: "FREE THE ANTS!"

Thus "affairs" are simultaneously more important, more numerous, and more homogeneous in the United States, where the causes are clearly identifiable (religion in the case of Serrano, sexual morality in the case of Mapplethorpe, the free disposition of public space in the case of Serra); this facilitates the task of the analyst faced with a "culture war" that contributes to hardening further the issues and resources. The French situation is more changeable, more diffuse, more fragmented. In sum, the essential difference between the instances of rejection of contemporary art in France and the "culture wars" in the United States lies in the content of the protests, which is linked to the degree of politicization of their forms of expression. The ethical registers (sexual morality, religion, sensitivity, minority rights, equity) and the civic registers (use of public funds, democracy, ideals) are much more frequent in America, while in France the values defended – when they do not refer to the civic question of public expenditures – are drawn more often from purificatory demands to defend national heritage, or from an aesthetic requirement to defend artistic authenticity and the symbolic intentions, or the plastic values, of the works. American rejections are more often phrased in terms of a *heteronomous* judgment on the referent of the works, or on their relation to their context, while French rejections tend to depend on a more *autonomous* judgment about the person of the artist or the work itself. The gap in the range of registers is particularly flagrant in the United States, where the disparity between aesthetic values and those of the ordinary world makes even more evident than in France, the problem of the "*différend*" in Lyotard's sense (1983) – that is, conflicts not about evaluations in terms of a given scale of values, but about the choice of such a scale or register of values, making any agreement unlikely, and making every discussion the occasion not of a possible consensus, but of an increase in dissension (Heinich 1995a).

Conclusion

It remains only to sketch a few hypotheses to explain these differences as functions of three explanatory dimensions: the object of the judgments (the works), the subjects (the protestors), and the context, in particular American culture.

What is most striking about the artworks that provoked violent reactions in America is that their transgressions (proper to most contemporary art) have nothing to do with formal characteristics, i.e. with the aesthetic and cognitive frontiers defined by the history of the plastic arts (medium, materials, modes of representation), but with the moral frontiers, i.e. with images representing forbidden acts or subjects (blasphemy, sacrilege, exhibitionism, sado-masochism). This conception, whereby art becomes more valid the more it transgresses common values, is explicitly expressed by ordinary people ("If art is not to provoke, then what purpose does it serve? – visitors' book at the Serrano exhibition in Philadelphia) and by art critics or historians: "The best art is often controversial, even confrontational – radical in style as well as substance. It's *supposed* to question the status quo, to shake us out of our complacency, to elicit strong reactions."[24] If "ethical" rejections are so much more numerous in the United States, it is primarily because opportunities to display moral indignation are abundant in artistic production there, whereas they are exceedingly rare in France. But this fact only shifts the problem back a stage, from reception to production.

If we turn now to those making the judgments, i.e. the protestors, the ethnological method chosen for this study ruled out any socio-demographic identification that would have permitted cross-references between the types of reactions, the values invoked, and the social category of the protestors (age, sex, level of education, etc.).[25] But we can establish a major difference in the political coloring of the protestors. In both countries they may be on either the Right (conservatives) or the Left (liberals or progressives): this is a relatively recent phenomenon which contributes to the clouding of the issue and makes any approach to it more complex. But in the United States, those who reject from the Left use "political" terms (so as not to specify whether civic or ethical) to express their values, defending the rights of minorities harmed by representations degrading to women or blacks. In France, by contrast, those who protest from the

Left tend to express themselves in the name of artistic authenticity and against the academicization of cultural policies.

It looks as if the American logic tends toward a permanent division into clans constituted once and for all, so that the various positions, once established (for or against, liberal or conservative), need no longer be discussed. Everyone simply defends his position against that of the opposing clan. This logic of sharing in a collective opinion, rather than affirming oneself through a personal opinion, is also found among art professionals when they defend the theory of the "cutting edge," that is, the idea that once an artist has "crossed the line," it is necessary to defend him or her. The only meaningful criterion is the artist's capacity to remain on the edge, flirting with the original, the innovative or the avant-garde – and the museum's only role is to ratify the artist's presence in the market.

In contrast, the art professional's French counterpart would no doubt practice the "narcissism of little differences," endeavoring to promote art that is more interesting than the rest, more innovative, and more likely to last. But in France, the professional would be involved in the internal competition between specialists to launch the best candidate, while in the United States it is primarily a question of choosing an *a priori* position against the traditionalists. And this defense of the avant-garde takes on a specifically moral tone: once an artist is identified as being an authentic innovator, it is the *duty* of artistic institutions to sustain him or her, whatever happens. This is less a matter of aesthetic evaluation than of moral commitment.

This moralization of the aesthetic issues brings us to the third explanatory dimension: the cultural context. We shall choose here only three characteristics to account for the differences observed. The first is the feebleness of the aesthetic register in the United States, even among supporters of contemporary art. Indeed, even if some do defend art by referring exclusively to arguments about beauty, and even if the work at stake clearly plays on affects (we saw this with the experts who testified at the Mapplethorpe trial), most pose the question in terms of "moral improvement," and reduce it to its ideological dimension. For example, "People for the American Way" declares: "The arts and humanities are the means we use to examine human existence. Government at all levels should seek to encourage their development and should not seek to suppress any idea, subject matter or point of view." This moralization of the aims of cultural policies would seem odd in France, where one would be more likely to talk about support for the arts and encouragement of culture (this raises again the eternal Franco-American misunderstanding as to the meaning of the word "culture," understood either as the totality of artistic goods or as the totality of features of a civilization). For the

American defenders of artistic freedom, it is not strange to reduce artistic creation to the formulation of a message, often treating works as "words" or "discourses," and identifying artistic work as the "expression" of ideas or opinions.[26] Even the most fervent partisans of artistic freedom are a long way from autonomy of art as an end in itself. Here again is a salient difference, this time not between the United States and France, but between American and French intellectuals. This is not a conflict between one aesthetic view (traditional art) and another (the avant-garde), nor even a *"différend"* between aesthetics and ethics, but a conflict between one ethical code (traditional moral values) and another (freedom of expression).

This minimizing of the aesthetic issues, not only by the adversaries but also the supporters of the avant-garde, takes on a more concrete form in the generalization that a French observer can draw from the American conflicts: with few exceptions, the conflicts concern works of little aesthetic interest, unworthy of all the fuss. This is, of course, a question of aesthetic bias: once one thinks that a work is of little artistic value if all it does is represent subjects or acts that would be shocking in reality (i.e. on the basis of the status of its referent in the ordinary world – a point of view evidently not shared by all French people, nor even all French specialists or amateurs), then the problem is no longer whether it is necessary to support Mapplethorpe, Serrano or Serra when they are attacked, but whether they should be subsidized or exhibited.[27]

This relationship to aesthetic perception can be extended to include the more general question of fiction. This is indeed a second "cultural" characteristic which, to a French eye, appears peculiarly American: that is, a viewpoint little concerned with the autonomy of representation, with the result that the image is reduced to its referent, fiction to reality, and art to ordinary life. Whence the impression that irony, the capacity to play with different frames of experience, has little place in a world so deeply concerned with things taken at face value, where the distance between representation and reality matters so little that a musician can refuse to play a piece of music because it projects a negative image of an animal. Even the liberal theoreticians remain ensconced within this paradigm of perception, including when their intention is to criticize it: to denounce the illusion of representation undifferentiated from reality, the supporters of freedom of expression promote a conception of representation as a reflection of reality – as if fiction can arise only from the imaginary and not from reality, or art from aesthetics rather than politics.[28] This "Leftist literalism" lies at the heart of radical feminism which, following Catherine McKinnon and Andrea Dworkin, demands that pornographic publications be banned because they involve not just images, but acts.[29] From this perspective, a sado-masochistic image is treated as a double reduction: of the imaginary to the real, and of the real to the symbolic:

imaginary	real	symbolic
image	oppressed woman	oppression of women
"key"	"primary frame"	interpretation
fantasy	power relations	politics

Here we have arrived at the heart of the problems posed by "political correctness."[30] This movement combines a "literalist" logic of de-fictionalizing and hyper-symbolizing representation (any utterance about an item is taken to refer to the whole of which the item is a part), and a "communitarian" logic of belonging to small groups (this community is immediately given the authority to control, via its representatives, any representation made of it). However, this literalism is criticized even in the United States, and by feminists, who insist on the fact that the imaginary is not the real, and who have pointed out the many ways in which Leftist literalism has paralyzed liberals.[31]

The question remains of whether it is moral commitment that makes differentiating among registers and aesthetic distancing so hard, or whether it is the difficulty of dissociating frameworks that leads to the hyper-moralization of experience (Heinich 1990). In either case, one discovers in this standpoint a question that lies at the heart of the problems posed by contemporary art, with variations in focus, as they bear either on the "art" mode (aesthetic appreciation), or on the "primary frame" of the represented action or subject (moral, civic, functional, economic). We can interpret this phenomenon in Goffman's (1974) terms, as a problem of assimilating many frames of reference: "modes" ("keys") seem to be systematically reduced to "primary frames" by detractors; while, conversely, once defenders have placed something in the category of "art" (or in the "mode" framework), they no longer imagine that it can be removed, or at least consider that it might be understood differently by others, or in other circumstances, or that the subject might be read from other perspectives. And the assertion "it's art" thus goes beyond being an ontological statement and becomes an evaluation that tends to protect the subject from any future dispute (Schaeffer 1996). It is as difficult for defenders as for detractors to relativize, to admit the plurality of registers, frames, or relations to the world. And this difficulty no doubt also plays a part in the uneasiness of the French observer who is confronted with situations where she would have problems choosing a "camp," because the camp that defends art and struggles against censorship seems to her to be rooted in issues with little relevance, such as the defense of moral laws or the rights of minorities.

A third characteristic of American "culture," at least to a French observer, concerns the relationship between public and private and, more precisely, the extension of public space. The possibilities for public debates are, as we have seen, greater in the United States than in France, which to some extent explains the differences in the nature of the material gathered in each country, and the methods applied. Furthermore, the problems of public funding – a marginal factor that merely supplements indignation in France – are central in the United States.[32] It seems probable that there would be no controversy in the United States if there were no public funding, whereas in France we can see indignation being expressed even in private galleries wherever artistic authenticity or proper recognition of artistic merit seems to be under attack.[33] Thus the public control of public aid granted to contemporary art is very strong in the United States, with the corollary of silence *à propos* any question that does not involve public finances. This means that there is no choice between the two approaches mentioned in the introduction – via contemporary art or via the use of public funds: they are complementary and mutually exclusive. The first is more French and the second more American.

In conclusion, the extension into public space (and so the tendency toward public "affairs") is clearly more pronounced in the United States than in France, but only if public resources are involved. In France, private conduct can result in virulent controversy whenever it involves a value that can be considered universal. At the same time, protests are more often dominated by groups rather than by individuals in the United States, where the defense of rights is more likely to be based on struggles against racism and sexism; in France, it is more often a question of defending equity for artists. Correlatively, the subjects in the American controversies tend not to be autonomous, but instead concern *heteronomous* issues, i.e. that affect society at large (notably by way of moral rules), whereas in France, they are more specifically about art, with its autonomous issues, which refer to universal questions that exceed the frame of any given society. Finally, the problem of authenticity, linked to the artist's qualities, reveals a different form of the "rise of generality" occurring in America, where the artist's capacity to give objective expression to common experiences is valued at the expense of subjective expression, which is criticized as narcissism. On the French side, the demand for authenticity is directly linked to ideas of interiority and originality, qualities indispensable in order to "authenticate" the artistic process by placing value on singularity, which guarantees its connection to a universal experience beyond the boundaries of any one "culture." Thus we see how differences between France and America are based on variations in the way shifts from the particular to the general occur: from private to public, as regards the context of the controversies; from the individual to the group, as regards the subjects of controversy; and from the subjective to the objective, when it concerns the artists.

Notes

Translated by Debra Keates. I would like to thank Denise Fasanello, Brian Goldfarb, Arfus Greenwood, Tobbie Falk, Julie Melby, Elizabeth Weinberg, Martha Wilson (New York), Milena Kalinovska, Katy Kline (Boston), Andrea Miller-Keller (Hartford), Jennifer Dowley, Ann Green, Marisa Keller (Washington), Carrey O'Eagle, Judith Tannenbaum (Philadelphia). This project was aided by the Fulbright Foundation, the cultural services section of the French Consulate in New York, the Department of Sociology of Princeton University, the Groupe de Sociologie Politique et Morale at the Ecole des Hautes Etudes en Sciences Sociales (Paris), and the Centre National de la Recherche Scientifique. The French sections were written with help from the Delegation on Plastic Arts at the French Ministry of Culture and the association ADRESSE. Thanks are due as well to Eric Fassin, Michel Feher, Peter Meyers, Jacques Soulillou, Ari and Vera Zolberg, and to the contributors to this volume.

1 See Bolton 1992; Doss 1995; Dubin 1992; Heins 1993; Jordan et al. 1987; Mitchell 1990; Pally 1994; Raven 1989; Steiner 1995; Weyergraf-Serra and Buskirk 1991.

2 See *Artistic Freedom Under Attack* 1994, 1995, and 1996, edited by the "Art Save" project (against censorship) of People for the American Way, an association that defends freedom of expression.

3 Becker 1989, p. 233. Harold Washington, who died on November 23, 1987, was the first black mayor of Chicago. His election had represented a historic but precarious victory.

4 There is, however, a federal law, in existence since 1990, called the Visual Artists Rights Act (VARA), based on the Berne Convention, which allows some moral rights to the artist for a period of 50 years: "right of attribution (right to claim authorship) and the integrity of the work (right to prevent prejudicial modification and the destruction of a work)." It replaces, at the federal level, the California ARA of 1979 (Art Preservation Act) and the New York ARA of 1983 (Artists Authorship Rights Act).

5 Hoffman 1987, 1990.

6 In 1989, as a result of the Serrano and Mapplethorpe affairs, the House of Representatives imposed budgetary restrictions on the National Endowment for the Arts (NEA), and approved the amendment by Senator Jesse Helms which forbade the disbursement of its funds for:

the dissemination, promotion, or production of (1) obscene or indecent objects, particularly sadomasochistic, homosexual or pedophile representations, or those representations which show individuals committing sexual acts; or (2) objects which denigrate works or beliefs of any religion or non-religion; or (3) objects which denigrate, vilify, or degrade a person, a group, or a class of citizens because of their race, their beliefs, their sex, their handicap, their age, or their national origin.

7 Steven Dubin (1992, p. 255) has made a list of the major demonstrations in favor of contemporary art: 200 artists in Chicago, and rallies in Los Angeles, New York, Philadelphia and Minneapolis in August 1989 for Arts Emergency Day; 2,000 demonstrators in New York in May 1990 demanding that Congress authorize the NEA to continue its activities without restrictions; 400 protestors in Kansas City in August 1990; 5,000 demonstrators in Chicago on the day after Labor Day in 1990, proclaiming that "Creativity is our greatest natural resource." No similar movement has ever appeared in France, either for or against artistic freedom.

8 The data, which cover the whole of the United States, come from "art activists" (there are approximately 3,000 names) who set up a hot line, as well as from the perusal of the press by the movement's leaders. The latter checked each incident and retained only those in which an agreement to mount an exhibition had been first received and then rescinded – excluding cases in which a single work was not chosen for exhibition, any [organism] having in principle a right of selection. Only cases in which the government was involved were considered as censure.

9 "The common link among all of the catalogued incidents is that they involve an attempt in 1995 to limit access to a form of artistic expression because of its viewpoint, message, or content, or that they amount to a violation of the artist's access to a forum for expression that had previously been understood to be available. Without exception, the incidents documented in the report are grounded in the content of the "message" of the art" (*Artistic Freedom Under Attack*, 1996, No. 4, p. 12).

10 These different registers of value are inspired by the model proposed by Luc Boltanski and Laurent Thévenot (1991), but extends it so as to allow certain categories of argumentation to appear which previously were included only at a secondary level (this as a result of its compact nature and its high degree of formalization). The typology thus obtained has no ambition of being carried forward – the model does – by a theory of orders of worth (Thévenot and Boltanski call them *"cités"*) that commands the different orders of justification. But it permits us, as compensation, a description of the values invoked by the actors that is at once finer and closer to common sense, if we take into account the differences between targets of judgment (object, person, relation between object and person, relation to context, referent) which are determining factors in artistic matters (Heinich 1997a). This typology is compatible with the model of the orders of worth, to which it can at any point be assimilated.

11 On the concept of "autonomy" as it applies to the arts, see Bourdieu 1992.

12 It would have been interesting to know what percentage of the names listed were marked by an asterisk, but the petition seems to have scarcely captured the attention of the critics who wrote about the affair in numerous publications: only one publication reproduces the text, while the majority of the

commentators (who, with one exception, took up the defense of the artist against his opponents) only make inexact references to it, without taking account of the precise nature of the arguments it invoked.

13 The double puritanism was also pointed out by American observers: "This puritanism led to some extraordinary claims in court. The CAC's director, Dennis Barrie, swore under oath that works are 'striking, not titillating.' . . . Over and over, the jurors . . . were told to judge the quality of the works by 'looking at them as an abstract, which they are, essentially'" (Steiner 1995, p. 56).

14 Wendy Steiner (ibid. pp. 54–5) notes that:

Janet Kardon [director of the exhibition] claimed that the Mapplethorpes were art because they had certain formal qualities that experts could recognize as artistic, regardless of the subject matter that was so formed. This, of course, is justification for the authority of the experts: that they have the experience, the training, and the sensitivity about formal issues to distinguish art from non-art. Interestingly, though, this is an issue having to do not with whether a photograph is art but whether it is good art . . . The decision about worthiness is not ontological. Unworthy art is still art. Thus, the formal argument is a matter of quality, not ontology . . . The Mapplethorpe trial, because of the framing of the obscenity law, made the question "What is art?" replace the question "Why do we (or they) like this art?" And thus, the expert's partiality, their contextuality, their humanity were all elided into a true–false issue – art or non-art? – which obscured the real issues of the case.

15 "Failed art, even pernicious art, still remains art in some sense" (H. Kramer, "Is Art above the Laws of Decency?" *New York Times*, July 2, 1989, quoted in Bolton 1992, p. 54).

16 Security risks and inconveniences were also cited by the art critics opposed to the work: Hilton Kramer invoked the "sculptor's wish to deconstruct and otherwise render uninhabitable the public site the sculpture was designed to occupy" (ibid., p. 56); Anna C. Chave (1990).reminds us that

Serra's arc, enormous and dangerously curved, formed a barrier that was too high (3.66 meters) to see over, and a long detour (36 meters) for pedestrians crossing the plaza. The severity of its material, the austerity of its form and its gigantic stature seemed to provide an oversized caricature of the rhetoric of minimalism's power. One can guess some part of the public reaction by noting that the work was covered with graffiti and urine as soon as it went up.

17 This topic of the "market" recurs several times in the leaflet put out by the NEA, and reprinted by Art Save in its defense manual on the freedom of artistic expression, when it came time to denounce "myths," that is, critical commonplaces about the public financing of culture:

1. Support for the arts is not a legitimate function of the Federal Government. 2. At a time of fiscal restraint, the arts are a luxury that we simply cannot afford. 3. The Arts Endowment is "élitist," a subsidy of the upper class. 4. The loss of public funding for the arts will be readily replaced by the private sector. 5. The states are better suited to support the arts. 6. The best of the arts will survive in the open market.

On the different references to the market in publishing, see the Chapter by Daniel Weber.

18 This argument is typical of the "Van Gogh effect" (Heinich 1996).
19 *Artistic Freedom Under Attack* 1994, p. 212. There is also the case, unimaginable in France, of a cellist who refused to play Prokofiev's "Peter and the Wolf" because the work projected a negative image of wolves.
20 See Heins 1993; Pally 1994; Soulillou 1995; Steiner 1995. For a historical perspective, see Beisel 1993. For a more general reflection on the problems that surround the definition of pornography, see Arcand 1991.
21 Edgar Roskis, "L'éthique et l'étiquette," *Le Monde-Radio-Télévision*, May 12–13, 1996.
22 In American history, the emphasis of censorship has moved from blasphemy (criticism of the Church) and sedition (criticism of the state) to obscenity, a category that does not appear in law until the nineteenth century (Heins 1993, pp. 16 and 19). That "puritanical" censorship of obscenity is a recent invention is proof of the historicity of "puritanism," which belongs less to American "culture" than to a particular moment in its history.
23 "The work consists of almost 200 transparent Perspex boxes filled with colored sand representing the national flags of the world. The boxes are connected by clear plastic tubes. A colony of ants moves freely through the whole maze, carrying grains of sand from flag to flag until the recognizable symbols evolve into a single, universal flag. At least that was Yanagi's concept. The artist procured a colony of ants from an entomologist in Bassano del Grappa in northern Italy" (*Art News*, September 1992).
24 Heins 1993, p. 117. The author employs the expression "flag art" *à propos* of the Tyler affair, suggesting that transgression of a prohibition is enough in itself to constitute a genre of art.
25 For an approach that complements ours here, and which takes into account the social determinations of cultural differences towards "symbolic borders," see Lamont 1992.
26 "Creative works are constitutionally protected in large part because of the critical role they play in a society that values individual autonomy, dignity, and growth. Artistic expression not only provides information and communicates ideas; it also expresses, defines, and nourishes the human personality. Art speaks to our emotions, our intellects, our spiritual lives, and also our physical and sexual lives. Artists celebrate joy and abandon, but they also confront death, depression and despair" (Heins 1993, p. 5). This point of view is confirmed by the courts: "No one seriously contests the proposition that an artist's work is sufficiently imbued with elements of communication to fall within the scope of the First Amendment. The protection of the First Amendment is not limited to ideas. The landmark case of *Cohen v. California* established that the First Amendment protects expression that appeals to the emotions as well as to the intellect" (Hoffman 1990, p. 126).
27 Should we consider this reduction of aesthetic concerns to a secondary status an aspect of puritanism? Max Weber formulates a similar hypothesis:

> Concerning the opposition between the form and content of art objects, Max Weber emphasizes that "all sublimated redemptive religions interest themselves only in the things and the acts which may be of importance to redemption, and not to their form." This latter is, on the contrary, all the more indifferent from a religious point of view, if

not completely devalued, when sent back to the accidental, a register foreign to meaning. In this case, it seems that the complicity between art and religion remains possible so long as the creator hides himself behind his creation, and his creation remains on the order of "know-how." If the signification of the work is transformed, if the notion that an artistic creation is attached to its forms emerges, then conflict appears between an artistic sphere which understands itself to create meaning and a religious sphere which considers itself threatened on the very territory it once monopolized. (Bouretz 1996, pp. 151–3).

28 "The mistaken notion, so common among advocates of censorship, that the images, ideas, and stories shown on the big screen (or in any art form) actually *cause* the difficult, painful realities of modern society, instead of reflecting, confronting, protesting, or examining those realities" (Heins 1993, p. 43).

29 MacKinnon's argument, which is legal, comes back to the position that pornography cannot be by the American Constitution under the rubric of free speech: pornography must be itself (because of its direct effects) qualified as a crime; it is neither an idea, nor a fiction, nor a representation: it is a criminal act. It is not even the spectacle of the discrimination against women, it is that discrimination itself and should therefore be forbidden" (Angenot 1995, p. 20). See also Fassin 1993 and Feher 1993.

30 In spite of the care one must observe when using this concept. As Eric Fassin justly remarks: "French for Americans, American for the French, *political correctness* is always essentially foreign. It is always in the image of the other intellectual" (1994, p. 34).

31 Pally 1994; Steiner 1995, p. 60: "The current hostility to pornographic art like Mapplethorpe's cannot be explained simply through conservative fundamentalism. Leftists are exerting a similar pressure to take art as real-world speech ... If liberals are irritated by right-wing fundamentalists, they tend to be paralyzed by feminist and minority extremists who engage in such literalism." On the collusion in fact between the conservative Right and the multiculturalist Left, see Robert Hughes 1993, especially p. 199. On different constructions of sexual harassment, see the work of Abigail Smith.

32 Arthur Danto summarizes the four possible positions of public funding and censorship: (1) neither funding nor censorship: the position of market partisans and free expression advocates (liberals in the French sense); (2) no funding, but censorship: the position of conservatives and some feminists; (3) funding, but not censorship: the position of liberals in general; (4) funding and censorship: the position of the NEA.

33 This is the theme of "Art," a play by Yasmina Reza which has had long runs in Paris and New York. The play looks at how the purchase of a minimalist painting thoroughly upsets the relationships among three close friends.

Part III

Political cultures and practices

8 Community and civic culture: the Rotary Club in France and the United States

Agnès Camus-Vigué

Most people in France think of Rotary Club members along the lines suggested by Guy Hocquenghem in his "Open Letter to Campus Radicals Who Have Crossed Over to the Rotary" (Hocquenghem 1986): they are seen as provincial notables who routinely parade their self-importance during overly indulgent dinners. According to their bye-laws, however, the members of Rotary International strive to serve a more laudable purpose, namely public service in support of humanitarian causes. While the activities of this organization are not well known in France, their deeds are recognized in the United States, where the group was founded at the beginning of the twentieth century.[1]

My motivation to study the Rotary International in France stems from a desire to understand better why this organization loses so much of its validity on crossing the Atlantic. Upon reflection, it has become apparent that the perception of the group in France highlights prominent traits characteristic of the organization. Rotary International combines recruitment of members based on professional criteria of standing and competence with a public service goal, specifically the support of humanitarian causes like immunizing children in Africa or creating infrastructures in underdeveloped regions.[2] Critics such as Hocquenghem challenge the ability of a group of people selected on the basis of professional competence and position to create civic solidarity; they suggest that although these people claim to help others, in fact, they are merely serving their own interests, which are the specific interests of the privileged class. To understand this type of tension, we might turn to Luc Boltanski and Laurent Thévenot's *De la justification.* (1991), which suggests that this critical shift has its roots in the civic equality and solidarity central to France's political tradition. In this model all specific interests must be subsumed in and superseded by the search for the common good.[3] Boltanski and Thévenot analyze the ways in which people try in their daily lives to make their behavior consistent with the common good. In their discussion of the "reality test" underlying such evaluations, they link the practice of evaluation with issues of political philosophy. They

213

demonstrate that one can arrive at justice not through the intermediary of transcendental law, but by following pragmatic constraints regarding the coherence of practical arrangements which guide the evaluation (Boltanski and Thévenot 1991)

The criticisms of Rotary International are not directed at the principles on which the organization is founded. Rather, these criticisms are leveled at a world of objects, practices, protocols – such as tables covered ceremoniously with fine food and wines – and influential local figures and pleasure-seekers showing off their social status during worldly social functions. These criticisms highlight the images which our sense of "commonality"[4] has trouble reconciling with commitment to a service organization, namely disinterestedness, dedication and altruism. Rotarians, like their critics, have a sense of morals that dictates what their conduct should be, befitting members of a service organization worthy of the name. In a brief visit to the organization's newsletter office, for example, I saw the ways in which the editor, a Rotarian himself, operates a type of censorship by selection. He pulls out all the photographs of club dinners that show club members eating and even goes so far as to crop photographs of dinner ceremonies so that only the upper body and faces remain, thereby suppressing the images of dinners and gastronomic pleasure. Despite the fact that the editor allows himself to be guided by this common sense urge to censor activities best removed from the public eye, and which, as he confided to me, give a negative image of the Rotary Club, this club member continues to participate in activities which to some seem incompatible. The juxtaposition of these activities gives rise to criticism since the ceremonious dinners may be considered trivial[5] and centered on individual corporeal self-interest or even on the superficiality of social-climbing, while public service has a universal goal. How do Rotary Club members attempt to reconcile two such incongruous worlds? This question has led me to analyze closely the associative nature of club life in France and the United States.

The study of daily life in fraternal organizations belongs to the field of investigation vaguely designated by the term "sociability." It was Simmel who first treated sociability as a subject of sociological study. This term designates the fun aspects of socialization which are "divorced from reality" in the sense that "they have no practical purpose" (Simmel 1981 [1910], pp. 125 and 123). They allow the individual to detach himself from values, ideas, and beliefs, in a congenial setting that promotes social contacts. Sociability as defined by Simmel offers a relational model to describe the members of clubs, fraternal organizations, and other associations that exist alongside larger social institutions. In reflecting upon this form of social relations, however, Simmel, like the majority of sociology's founding fathers, places social relationships outside the political sphere. In contrast, I propose that in order to elucidate the problems plaguing the Rotary International in France, we must question the basis for such a separation. Furthermore, we need to understand how different kinds of social and political contact are formed in France and in the United States.

Let us imagine American society as described by Tocqueville in the early nineteenth century. According to Tocqueville the customs of a society can be defined as "the set of intellectual and moral endowments that human beings bring in a certain state of society" (Tocqueville1980 [1835], p. 451) which "contribute to the preservation of political institutions." These social customs support and invigorate all institutions from the family to groups of citizens acting as local councils. The "public spirit" that Tocqueville claims characterizes Americans is at work in all American social patterns, whether private or public. Following Tocqueville's lead, I would like to attempt to elucidate these customs in order to demonstrate that the Rotary International activities in the United States are rooted in a model of community that does not exist in France.[6] In the United States the notion of "community" combines social interaction [*convivialité*] with expressions of civic commitment and service, whereas the idea of civic commitment is less important in the French notion of the locality.[7] A large number of the difficulties encountered by Rotarians in France stem from the fact that they try to contribute to the local common good using practices defined by the American organization. French Rotarians are given literature in the form of handbooks and circulars presenting guidelines for implementing various programs like service projects or for organizing meetings. In addition, club presidents receive regular training organized by the central administration.

In the following pages I will describe the projects undertaken by the Rotary International as public service. I will then discuss the activities of American Rotary International Clubs. This will allow us to understand the extent to which the definition of public service differs in the two countries.

My analysis is based on extensive research carried out over a period of several months in Rotary Clubs in France and the United States. Two clubs were chosen in France. The first, in Saint-Aubon in Normandy, had been in existence for only a year.[8] The second, in the Parisian suburb of Luzon, was formed in the 1950s. In the United States I lived in two communities where I studied the local Rotary Internationals. The first club is located in Chelley, Massachusetts, a suburb of Boston, and the second in Welmont, Vermont.[9]

Communal activities in France

We currently observe a variety of social activities in the Rotary Clubs in France. In Saint-Aubon, for example, the weekly meeting as well as the business meeting are both held during meals in a hotel restaurant that serves as the club's headquarters. At first glance, nothing save the absence of women[10] distinguishes these meetings from any of the semi-domestic, semi-professional encounters, like business meals or socializing with colleagues, that take place every day. More than a year after the creation of this club, however, there remain a number of questions regarding the proper organization of these meals. For example, how should the formal side of these meetings, which must occur weekly according to central administration mandate, be handled? How are simple meals – frugality being recommended by the headquarters in Evanston – to be prepared when the culinary traditions of this region in the fertile Normandy countryside encourage the consumption of sausages, smoked meats, pâtés and other rich, elaborately prepared foods? From the very beginning of my observations, I took note of the trivial domestic incidents brought to my attention, like cases of food poisoning, the omission of important guests or the inclusion of undesirable ones. One Rotarian's wife spoke to me about the anxiety and concern that seems to have accompanied the choice of menus favoring a simpler country-style fare with cold meats and raw vegetables. Over the course of the study it became obvious that this task of choosing menus that simultaneously evoke the abundance of food as well as its freshness and simplicity resulted from the specific need to tailor local hospitality and social customs [*convivialité*] to the central administration's requirement of frugality. In an attempt to create and foster local and personal ties, Rotary Clubs resort to the customary forms of hospitality that normally structure their domestic universe by organizing the type of meals that would usually promote close social contact. These traditional customs favor a form of socializing centered around abundant food and wine, which in turn encourage familiarity. Rotarians are forced to invent new models of social functions, like meals at members' homes or "country-style buffets" in which the guests serve themselves in order to reconcile two seemingly incompatible constraints, namely the creation of a warmly welcoming atmosphere for all members in a lively setting in which the abundance of food promotes intimacy, and the avoidance of an ostentation that ill befits members of a service organization. The club members thus create a universe of objects like rustic tables, wine in casks, and fireplaces in order to evoke a warm, simple setting where one feels "at home" because one is among friends.

In addition to these questions, another preoccupation for the clubs centers around the choice and implementation of service projects. Sometimes all of these issues are discussed during the same business meeting. An agenda might include planning a menu and planning a service project. Another concern involves the problem of raising the funds that must be sent regularly to the international association and therefore whether to institute regular monthly dues or collect money at each dinner. There is also the problem of the form of local service projects. The Rotary handbook in fact advises undertaking works in collaboration with other local bodies. In Saint-Aubon, Rotarians have enjoyed little success in instituting programs in cooperation with other organizations involving the municipality, schools, the Church and local clubs. Establishing a potential collaboration with the schools has failed in part because the teachers publicly reject what they see as the Rotarians' inflated sense of self-importance as local leaders. Hence the reaction of the principal of the local vocational high school in Saint-Aubon, who explained that in his opinion, one cannot simultaneously have one foot in a service project and the other in a social function. The Luzon Rotary International suffers from this same image. For the past eighteen years, the club has tried in vain to build a center for the handicapped. They have struggled with insurmountable obstacles raised by local municipalities who, for example, refused a building permit on the grounds that this club is not recognized as an association oriented towards a civic "public interest" [intérêt public]. They have received no support from other service organizations since the Church views the Rotary Club with the same suspicion that it views freemasonry.

Let us turn now to the question of the specific types of project undertaken and the criticisms regarding them by looking at a concrete example that illustrates these difficulties. In keeping with recommendations from brochures distributed by the central administration, members of the club attempt to initiate a local and personalized service project. Their program would offer financial assistance enabling lower-income children to participate in the class ski trip during winter vacation. Instead of providing one contribution for the entire class, as the teacher would prefer, the Rotarians choose to personalize their project by writing checks to the needy families who cannot afford to send their children on the trip. The teacher criticizes this type of personalized contribution by stressing that it violates the dignity of these families. In the absence of any established procedure, the Rotarians must take personal responsibility for collecting information regarding income, household expenses, and needs in order to determine which children in the class should receive financial assistance. Interviewees such as the school teacher believe that this raises the problem of how to process such information. What happens to this personal information about these people's private lives? As a body, the Rotary Club does not guarantee the confidentiality of the information gathered. Sharing this confidential information in meetings, i.e. in a public place, potentially exposes personal concerns that should be private. In addition, it potentially undermines the validity of information collected, since a personal sense of dignity may lead some people to hide certain facts that suggest financial inadequacy or poverty. Rotarians could even be suspected of deliberately trying to expose people's misfortune. One could accuse them of manipulative intentions. Furthermore, in acquiring this information, the Rotary becomes very close to the people it hopes to help, thus creating an ambiguous intimacy. A more anonymous gesture, like a contribution for the entire class, would have guaranteed a detachment between donors and recipients that would have established the nature of the project as incontestably altruistic. Luc Boltanski (1993) has demonstrated that the fewer the connections between victims and those who defend them, the greater the possibility that the defense offered will be deemed acceptable. By attempting to adhere to the central organization's definition of community service, in this instance, the Rotary has constructed the reverse of this paradigm.

Social functions and service projects in the United States

Social events like luncheons or the annual dinner-dance, which constitute the daily life of Rotarians in the United States, are organized differently there than in France. In the United States, the menus are not the result of specific deliberation and they are served without ceremony. These dinners comprise food prepared according to local culinary traditions and served individually by waitresses with trolleys. A typical menu would be stewed lamb with peas followed by jelly and apple pie accompanied by tea and coffee. Moreover, in the United States fund-raising does not present a problem. This activity is naturally integrated into the course of the meal. A large number of games, and in particular, raffles, provide an occasion for raising money for service projects. In Welmont, at the beginning of the meal, for instance, Rotary club members buy numbered tokens. One person then draws a certain number of corresponding tokens and calls out the winning numbers. Members holding winning numbers receive different prizes, like books or serving dishes. Other games are also played. For instance, the chief of police might ask all the members whose names appeared recently in the local paper, for example in a wedding announcement, to donate a certain sum for the general treasury. In addition, on their birthdays, each Rotary club member gives a check to the group as an annual contribution to the charity fund.

In the United States, Rotary International activities also include the public. The Rotary Internationals of Welmont and Chelley regularly invite certain local figures to participate in their activities. For example, a meeting in Chelley was devoted to discussing a problem raised by the Chief of Police, namely the need to improve traffic conditions in the city. After the discussion, the members decided to participate with the police administration in creating traffic regulations. In the archives of the Welmont club, we also find evidence of talks given during weekly luncheons by a priest, a minister, the mayor and members of other organizations. Rotarians also invite to their meals people who help them to organize local activities like prize draws[11] or charity sales.

The club's daily events include activities directed towards the collective celebration of citizenship and patriotism mixed with activities connected to a more domestic sphere, like songs or games. In each club hall we find an American flag, in front of which club members end each meeting by "pledging allegiance to the flag." When listed in the bulletin summarizing the Welton Rotary's activities, luncheon events form part of club life, which combines both social events and service projects. Thus, by lunching together, Welton and Chelley Rotarians are not merely enjoying themselves. They are also contributing to the public good. We know, for example, that during the financial crisis in 1927, 1928 and 1929, Rotarians limited themselves to milk and crackers while still paying the full price of the meal in order to save money for service projects paid for through their Welfare Fund. Frugality and ascetic self-denial, which as we have seen are encouraged by the central organization, were in this instance spontaneously expressed and specifically directed towards community service.

Let us now compare the service projects carried out in a club with the activities carried out in a French city or town.[12] Club minutes record the works carried out over the years. Examples include payment for dental work, prostheses for various people, and baskets of food for families in need. Potential acts of service are suggested, debated, and decided upon by vote. Unfortunately, the minutes do not record the arguments advanced in this sort of collective deliberation. All we know of the decision to help a well-known young woman to find a job is that the motion was carried. The task was then turned over to the Public Affairs Committee. When financial assistance was decided upon so that another person could have dental work done, the money was given, as would happen in France, according to a principle of equity that apportioned the available funds according to individual needs. Here, however, we are dealing not only with an act of charity between privileged and needy individuals, but also with a collective action of solidarity rooted in a common universe. In the club halls of the Rotary International – in the American flag, in the songbooks, in the piano on which grace is played at the beginning of a meal, in the Masonic-style symbols – we find traces of this common universe. For the Rotary, a local service project fits into the notion of community which plays a central role in the polity.[13]

In the United States, public service requires proximity to a specific base and highlights the local and the personal as the grounds for a network of connections based on a domestic logic of trust (Boltanski and Thévenot 1991). Hence, the civic existence of a group is compatible with its personal connections. Therefore, in order to maintain close contact with the people they hope to help, the Rotary Club collects personal information regarding lack of financial resources, health conditions, and marital status which they then process as members of the civic group constituted on the basis of proximity known as "the community." Such a method of processing information circumvents the effect of publicly exposing personal information gathered from the private sphere since the collective body of the community simultaneously ensures and guarantees the deliberations on decisions: communal ties provide the very basis for a collective decision regarding the sharing out of local resources.[14] In the United States, the existence of this communal collective that simultaneously combines civic solidarity and a "domestic" trustworthy orientation fosters a relationship between the public and the private sphere since this collective community constitutes an intermediary between the two domains. Although in France philanthropy is linked to Catholic religious traditions and thus may be condemned as being a form of private interests, in the United States philanthropy constitutes civic participation.[15] As Tocqueville suggests, civic altruism has often been central to the American definition of a good citizen because such civic public service springs from the very existence of the collective community.

Good business and good deeds in France

In France, most members of the Rotary Club I interviewed, when asked whether improving their social status or performing a public service was a more central motivation for joining, mentioned instead practical motives, such as social advancement or the possibility of networking. Thus, as one Luzon club member explains:

The most praiseworthy way to justify belonging is to say that the Rotary Club is a service organization that carries out a number of charitable works and that you want to participate in a specific program. Mostly I think people join because being a member of the Rotary gives you a certain prestige and the kind of pride that comes from belonging to a certain caste.

Rotarians anticipate the everyday sense of justice of the person who is questioning them. Thus, they carry out their own critical disclosure of their secret motivations.

Furthermore, although discussion of the Rotary International's philosophy is encouraged in France by the literature put out by the central administration – which suggests, for instance, considering club members' professional practices in a collective discussion on how to promote the ideal of community service in the business world – no activity of this kind has been observed in the clubs. On the contrary, service takes on a whole new meaning in France, where it consists primarily in the organization of talks given by members about their own professions. These talks may be given during the initiation of a new member, during a trip, or even in the course of a meeting of a professional organization.

Why does the French Rotary International experience so many difficulties in reconciling "public service" and "professional interests"? These two goals appear to be particularly antithetical in a French context. Indeed, because of the tendentious history of relations between professional and political institutions, Rotarians do not have the cognitive resources that would allow them to see their group as a service organization. A brief historical overview demonstrates that the relationship between political and professional institutions has always been problematic in France. After the dismantling of the trade guilds at the end of the eighteenth century in response to the Le Chapelier Law, there was no further provision for the political representation of professional interests. Indeed, political citizenship was conceived of in true Jacobin spirit as the state to which individuals "stripped of every partisan interest" acceded when they demonstrated that they belonged to the nation by voting (Furet 1988). Later in the nineteenth century and in the first half of the twentieth century, the question of the role that business professionals should play in political institutions came to occupy a more central place in the French political debate. At stake were the issues of whether the economic and social position enjoyed by businessmen provided them with a more visionary perspective than that of other citizens, and whether a businessman whose identity is defined by his occupation is capable of representing the people politically. This political debate was particularly heated during the 1930s and 1940s, when various solutions to the financial crisis – like the institution of corporatism during the Occupation – came into conflict (Boltanski 1988).

The professional dimension of the Rotary Club which the handbook terms as "ethical service" fits poorly with the definition of business and political interests in France. Despite the strength of certain agreements,[16] the marriage of business and politics remains contested within the French political tradition. Thus, despite the implementation of actual programs, the problems raised with the creation of the first Rotary International in France regarding the appropriate form of service projects remain unresolved. Answers to these questions, although apparently similar to the issues raised by American Rotary International concerning, for instance, ethical behavior in business, are not provided by undertaking practical projects.

Good business and good citizenship in the United States

When asked about the reasons why the Rotary Club recruits people of high social standing, members of the Rotary International in Chelley and in Welmont explained that they believe the social position of club members increases their capacity to serve. One of our interviewees emphasized this by saying that "the Rotary develops friendly relations between community leaders" and "offers them a chance to give something to their community."[17] Helping others is an expression of solidarity and commitment based on the belief that members of the same group are equal and owe each other mutual assistance.[18] Helping others, however is also a matter of emphasizing one's privileged position within the community. Here in this composite sketch of a successful individual and a pillar of the community, we find an image that does not exist in France.[19] In the United States, holding a position of prominence and prestige in the community is harmoniously blended with the responsibility to serve the community and act for the public good.

Moreover, the image of the professional is also granted an ethical and political dimension since the professional's activities can include community affairs. Indeed, at the beginning of the twentieth century the Rotary Clubs in the United States participated in a campaign that took shape around the Federal Trade Commission.[20] In this campaign they publicly disseminated codes of ethics in businessmen's organizations. The attempt was geared to persuading these organizations to apply a code of ethics like those governing professionals such as doctors, lawyers, and judges in their business life, and in particular in business transactions. This service ethic refers to the same concrete measures that Rotary Club members evoke today in interviews. These codes of ethics are the same as those found in American professional and businessmen's organizations. Their emphasis on conventional moral standards led the Rotary to take part in the movement for moral reform that began in the early years of the twentieth century. The Rotarians drew up a general method of publicizing their major ethical principles by using examples drawn from the experiences of club members. Thus, the Rotary offers a set of moral guidelines for businessmen in industry. For the Rotary Club, this ethical mission consists of using practical wisdom,[21] or in other words, exercising reason by using their ethical standards as guidelines. Each person's actions should be governed by private reflection using the ethical codes as a means of making proper decisions. These ethical codes can be interpreted as methods that industrialists can follow in order to actively monitor their behavior according to the Puritan ethic described by Max Weber.[22]

A closer examination of these manuals of ethics demonstrates the existence of concrete propositions regarding the way in which an action must be performed. In making professional decisions, Rotary Club members are encouraged to respect certain procedures. For example, one should ask oneself the following questions several times a day: is this honorable and does it obey the Rotary International's law of service? By respecting these criteria, members apply general rules to their professional conduct. They submit their activities and actions to group approval. Such a code of ethics offers each and every citizen the right to monitor any activity, even those beyond his power to intervene. In this sense, the ethical codes are the means through which professional activities are projected into the public sphere. The methodical format of the code of ethics allows such a projection by creating the conditions for a public debate on proper professional conduct. An example of this would be the detailed description of the different tasks like financial management, or public relations involved in business activities.[23] While respecting these rules ensures a certain democratic validity in business practices, it has the added effect of promoting the prosperity of the company. Professional and businessmen's codes of ethics like those of the Rotary Club highlight this aspect. In fact, as the Rotary International's history indicates, the first club motto, "He profits most who serves best" and all the criteria that supposedly regulate the behavior of club members were established as much as an effort to help resuscitate failing businesses as an effort to combat unethical business practices. The Rotary Club's code of ethics thus combines rationality, procedure, democracy, and efficiency.[24]

Conclusion

In this study I did not directly address cultural differences between the United States and France but focused on the problems that arise when an American cultural pattern is transplanted to France. This sheds new light on the ways in which the social and the political bonds are expressed in these two countries. The difficulties and criticisms confronting Rotarians in France can be explained by the fact that this service organization combines proximate relationships [*convivialité*] and civic commitment that are seen as incompatible in France. Indeed, in France clubs and social activities tend to be local in character and thus difficult to reconcile with the more general aims of the Rotary. In the United States, however, this combination works because the club is also a community of citizens. The community defined by American Rotary International includes both civic and religious points of reference which have no equivalents in France. Thus, during meetings in America, all members bow their heads while somebody says grace and, as mentioned earlier, in America the members close meetings by reciting the "Pledge of Allegiance" together in front of the flag.

The validity of this conflation between a universal goal and proximate forms of socialization [*convivialité*] in the United States and its rejection in France can be understood by looking at the historical relationship between local forms of interaction and citizenship that has evolved very differently in the two countries. In France, the civic dimension at the local level, the *commune*, is diametrically opposed to the local social ties associated with the village community. From the very beginning it is obvious in Revolutionary debates[25] that the civic and administrative dimension of the *commune* seeks to play upon the anchoring of the *commune* in the web of mutual acquaintance and domestic relationships; the nascent institution of the *commune* was hard to accommodate to the Rousseauian definition of the nation. In the United States, on the other hand, the first colonial settlements were groups of individuals bound together simultaneously by civic and religious ties as well as social and neighborly connections. There was no sharp break between the status of citizen and that of a setting based on mutual acquaintances. Here, citizenship is not defined in opposition to the body of society, as was the case in France, where the Republic was constructed in opposition to the social order of the *ancien régime*. Rather, in the United States citizenship is based on membership in a religious community. This aspect has been highlighted by Max Weber when he described American citizenship as founded on belonging to a community of faith.

In addition to these distinctions, we find differences concerning the relationship between professional and civic sense in the two countries. In France, public service in connection with professional life and business has always been problematic, in part because initiated by the privileged classes – who by definition cannot represent the general will. It is seen as antithetical to the definition of citizenship. The whole history of political representation of professions is marked by this tension between two incompatible schools of thought. The first accords people a specific position in the body politic by virtue of qualities like vision or competence associated with their professional standing. The second, in keeping with the Rousseauian model, refuses to recognize the existence of a privileged élite whose interests potentially conflict with the general will. In the United States, the question does not occur in the same manner since businessmen are seen as capable of performing public service because of their specific codes of ethics forged through professional organizations. More generally, it would appear that in France the values currently associated with the upper-middle class carry a negative valence, and wealth in particular serves to undermine the legitimacy of a person's charitable actions. In the United States, however, possession of personal capital is not incompatible with public service. In part this is connected with Protestant traditions according to which wealth is not morally corrupt as long as it is used within the disinterested context of helping the community. Thus, businessmen can serve the community without conflict of interest. There is no incompatibility, as in France, between strategic individual interests and the general interest, but rather a more nuanced articulation between these two levels, precisely because the collective community includes a wide range of people and interests.

Notes

Translated by Michelle Cheyne. I wish to thank Michèle Lamont, Michael Moody and Laurent Thévenot for their helpful comments.

1 On the history of the Rotary Club, see Nicholl 1984; on Service Clubs in America, see Charles 1993.
2 We note that the standards for recruitment combine morals and competence. In *Money, Morals, and Manners* (1992) Michèle Lamont suggests that this pairing is characteristic of the American workplace, where certain people go so far as to claim that competence serves to insure against dishonesty. This notion of competence, as Lamont stresses, is central to the American cultural model and is increasingly mobilized in the strategies that delineate symbolic boundaries and, in particular, moral boundaries.
3 This orientation towards the common or public good also exists in the political tradition in the United States. Americans, like the French, may denounce individual or specific interests with respect to certain conceptions of the public good. Some accuse Rotarians of greed and selfishness that serve in their eyes as evidence of their strategic self-interest. Despite this, however, the public service goals of the group are not called into question. In fact, it would appear that in the United States reference to specific interests might be connected with a certain notion of the public good, as well as orders of justification which are oriented towards substantive common goods (see Thévenot 1996d; and Chapter 10 in this volume).
4 Nicolas Dodier in his review of Boltanski and Thévenot 1991 (Dodier 1991) underscores the fact that people demonstrate just such a sense of what is common *[sens du commun]* during disputes. This expression, which he

borrows from Boltanski and Thévenot (1991, pp. 101 ff.), denotes both a sense of what is "natural" that, in a given situation, allows us to recognize the appropriate elements to ground an argument; and a "moral sense" that allows us to assimilate the circumstances of a particular situation to the general imperatives of a justice applicable to all.

5 These dinners are, however, as Albert Hirschman has demonstrated, completely different from the egotistical activity which consists of "stuffing one's belly." Indeed, what is important is not so much the fact of ingesting the food, but of coming together in pursuit of a common goal. Eating together at the same table, or "commensality," thus constitutes a form of social contact, "a link between two very different spheres, that of the selfish individual and that of social collective" (Hirschman, 1997, pp. 137 and 147) From our perspective what is interesting to note is that the dinners are reduced to a trivial activity, probably because in the same publication they are in close proximity to the charitable humanitarian goal of the Rotary Club.

6 On the relations between Rotary or other service clubs and the American notion of community, see Lynd and Lynd 1929; Rossi 1961.

7 On these questions, see also the concluding chapter in this volume.

8 Saint-Aubon is an invented name for the purpose of anonymity.

9 These cities were chosen based on comparable size and population density. An anthropological study was carried out over the course of several months during which approximately sixty French Rotarians and twenty American Rotarians were interviewed. In the United States research centered primarily on archival documents which were made available to me by members of the two clubs. This research was supplemented by a series of interviews and a number of ethnographic observations.

The Rotary International in Chelley has approximately fifty members, the Welmont Club has approximately thirty members.

10 Until recently women were not admitted to the Rotary Club as full members. They could, however, accompany their husbands to certain meetings.

11 The Rotary Club of Chelley regularly features the results of such draws in the column "Raffle News" in its bulletin, *The Fellowship News.* The column lists the prize and names of both the donor and winner.

12 This type of information is reported regularly in the Club's minutes which we have considered as sufficient proof of its validity.

13 For an analysis of the relation between an allegiance to a local community and citizenship, especially with regard to the notion of "community of memory," see Bellah et al. 1985. See also Varenne's (1977) analysis of communal allegiance and the forms of cooperation that it implies, namely modes of mutual assistance that are sometimes extremely sporadic and that can be combined with individualistic and competitive relationships.

14 The American notion of "community" gives political weight to the local interests that exist in other public arenas. Thus, in their study of the movements that give rise to planning conflicts in France and in the United States, Michael Moody and Laurent Thévenot demonstrate that in California a local coalition can have a legitimate public voice in a political debate precisely because the coalition tailors itself to the notion of community and more specifically to the notion of a "fundamental community." In France, on the contrary, the local

and therefore partisan nature of a group minimizes its potential to represent (Thévenot 1996b, 1996d; Chapter 10 in this volume).

15 See Wuthnow 1991. On the different conceptions of help and philanthropy in France and the United States, see Lamont 1992, chap. 3.

16 These agreements were established notably in the long tradition of union action which contributes to the representation of professional interests. For further discussion, see the work of Philippe Corcuff (1991).

17 "The Rotary is more than a help, it is making a commitment to be part of a community, it is to give back, to respond to the need because we are the leaders in the community" (Mr. Crane, member of the Chelley Rotary International).

18 "Life is not a one-way street," and "If society is good to you, you should be good to society" (ibid).

19 This is the image of the professional that has been so widely described in the American sociological tradition. Originally by granting the professional a moral function, Talcott Parsons makes this function one of the central tenets of his theory on social structure. The professional can act for others because the very nature of his activities, all of which are guided by logic and efficiency, mean that he is disinterested. See especially his "Professions and Social Structure" (Parsons 1958 [1922]). More recently, Magali Larson in referring to the professional's ethics criticizes Parsons' theses by stating that professionals, far from being opposed to the idea of profits, actually facilitate the establishment of bureaucratic capitalism (Larson 1977).

20 This agency was established in 1914 to combat monopolies.

21 This is according to the Aristotelian definition of ethics, see Ladrière 1990.

22 These codes of ethics were conceived of as a series of questions guiding the user through a methodical interrogation of the morality of their behavior. Max Weber's analyses of the Puritan ethic can shed new light on the specific format of this series of propositions. Weber underscores the fact that the individual is engaged in personal reflection at the same time as he is placed in a double bind. On the one hand, all of his behavior should be directed towards celebrating the glory of God. On the other hand, the very way in which he carries out his work appears to confirm the effects of Grace. A Christian, thus, must "systematically examine his conscience" by continually questioning his state of Grace in order to verify that his actions are in line with the will of God. Weber refers to this constant process of self-monitoring as methodical.

23 Here we find the basis for the association between the notion of competence and morality/ethics. A task that is completed correctly or according to certain rules is legitimized and the person who accomplished the task is seen as having proved his good morals.

24 This rational and methodical format for ethical principles recalls the managerial procedures set out by Taylor, especially insofar as these ethical codes, like Taylorist principles, seek to define a fair means of accomplishing professional tasks. The format results from "investments in forms" which are necessary to "establish a stable relationship for a specified length of time" (Thévenot 1984) These "invested forms" put constraints on the establishment of relationships while also ensuring the stability and legitimacy of the coordination devices. By taking these norms into account, the "investor," as a person

engaged in an act which claims to be legitimate, renounces immediate profit. Daniel Nelson, although from another perspective, also underscores the fact that scientific management claims to act justly by virtue of its interest in the nation's prosperity, despite the fact that scientific management itself is geared towards profitability (Nelson 1984).

25 For further discussion on this point, see Claudette Lafaye's dissertation (Lafaye 1991).

9 Forms of valuing nature: arguments and modes of justification in French and American environmental disputes

Laurent Thévenot, Michael Moody and Claudette Lafaye

This chapter and the next compare political practice and culture in the United States and France through detailed analyses of specific environmental conflicts in each country. We study comparative politics as enacted in a range of public arenas and sites of conflict, but rooted in local participation and particular controversies, rather than focusing on specialized political institutions or actors. In carrying out such a broad comparison of political culture and practices through specific case studies, we need to avoid the risk of merely reinforcing macro stereotypes of the two "cultures" and of looking for comparative evidence on only one level such as "discourse." We do so by relying on precise analytical categories, which have been developed to account for the complex requirements of all actors in public disputes, and by analyzing both the arguments and the actions of a range of disputants in these particular cases. In this way, our approach to studying comparative politics can provide a precise analysis of the cultural models and practices found in political disputes in each country.

We compare primarily the claims and arguments made by the conflicting entities during the course of the two environmental disputes. And we take seriously the pragmatic requirements of making such claims in the public arena, including the necessity of providing a legitimate "justification" for an argument or evaluation (i.e. a reference to some kind of general interest or common good), the potential for similarly legitimate critiques and denunciations of these justifications, and the requirement of offering proof for the claims made. But the analysis of both cases investigates not only the dynamics of argumentation, but also the institutional, technical, legal, and material arrangements which support or complement the argumentation. Through this multi-level approach, we get a detailed picture of what the disputants in each country consider valuable or worthy (e.g. "untouched wilderness" versus "productive use of resources"), and of the cultural models governing how they go about expressing and implementing these criteria of worth and shared modes of evaluation.

We chose to focus on public disputes involving the environment because – of the range of causes and types of modern political disputes – conflicts such as those over proposed "developments" of nature (roads, dams, tunnels) in "pristine" or relatively remote "natural" areas are among the most complex and revealing. These conflicts yield insights into political culture and practices on many levels – from local communities to national traditions – and involve a great variety of modes and themes of argumentation, a wide range of innovative tactical interventions, and complicated arrangements of people and organizations.

This chapter and the next together explore the comparative findings from field research on two such cases of conflict over proposed infrastructure projects in remote "natural" areas, one involving the Somport Tunnel project in the Aspe Valley in France and the other a proposal to build a hydroelectric dam on the Clavey River in the United States. The first of this chapter presents background information and summary descriptions of each case and an overview of the data and their collection in each country that serves as a general introduction to both chapters. The rest of this chapter then compares the types of arguments which are made by the various protagonists in each case, and the dynamics of making a range of generalized "justifications." Chapter 10 attempts to place the findings of this chapter in a larger context by comparing the "strategy" of argumentation displayed by the disputants, and by moving to the level of comparing broader cultural models of interests and the common good underlying the evaluative dynamics in each country. Our analysis is particularly concerned with explaining key comparative findings, rather than with analyzing each case individually.

Summary of cases

The French case – the Somport road and tunnel project

The French dispute under study here is a heavily contested road and tunnel project being built through the Aspe Valley and the Somport Pass. The Aspe Valley is located south of the city of Pau in the Pyrenees mountains, near the Pyrenees National Park, between the Basque country and Aragon. It lies at the heart of the Béarn region of France, historically a highly independent, rural, and isolated cultural enclave. The valley, through which the Aspe River runs, is narrow and cliff-lined. It is a primary access route connecting France with Spain through the Somport Pass, which was in fact an important route used in the Middle Ages by pilgrims heading to the shrine of Santiago de Compostela in Spain. The

Aspe Valley is considered to be one of the last relatively wild valleys of the Pyrenees, yet despite its isolation, there are several small villages. The valley is home to some of the last Pyrenean brown bears, which are protected (hunting them is forbidden) but are nevertheless nearly extinct, with only five or six surviving in the wild. The Ministry of the Environment has recently planned a gradual introduction of similar brown bears from Central Europe. A favorite of the media, the bear is a famous symbol of the Aspe Valley, but environmentalists also point to other rare species in the area, such as the wild chamois goat and a native vulture whose name in Spanish means "bone-breaker." The Aspe River is also protected by various governmental orders, as it is the habitat of trout and migratory salmon.

From the economic point of view, the Aspe Valley has long been mostly a sheep-herding and farming valley known for producing goat cheese. Dominant in the past, the pastoral economy has in recent times become more marginal: the shepherds are less numerous and they spend less time than before in the mountains. On the other hand, the creation of the national park has boosted tourism, which is now the main activity of the valley. The valley attracts skiers in winter and hikers, climbers, canoeists, rafters, and trout anglers during summer time.

The plans to build the road from Pau (France) to Saragossa (Spain), and to construct a road tunnel under the Somport Pass, began in 1987/88. In 1990, the European Council in Brussels adopted a regulation declaring the "E07 truck road" a priority. This aroused strong opposition to the project, which grew steadily in subsequent years. The first "public utility decision" on the project, adopted in 1991 by the French government after the statutory process of public hearings, was followed by an intense mobilization of opposition, which was both local and supported by nationally known artistic and environmental personalities. The opposition was led by Eric Pététin, who became a prominent figure in the media after being jailed several times for obstructing the construction site. In addition, some inhabitants of the valley formed a committee and appealed against the official decision. This decision was then overturned by the national administrative tribunal, on the grounds that the environmental impact study had been too limited. This tribunal also called for more study before considering a new decision.

The opponents also organized a collective [collectif], grouping together all organizations opposed to the project on many levels: local (e.g. the "Committee of the Inhabitants for Life in the Aspe Valley," "Aspe-Nature," "My Land"), national ("France-Nature") and international (World Wildlife Fund and Greenpeace). Big demonstrations were organized every year, during the Whitsun weekend. This opposition campaign proposed the reopening of an old railway and tunnel, closed in 1970, as an alternative to the new project. The opponents feared that the road would become a major highway or "truck corridor" that would harm the valley's human and animal inhabitants.

However, many local officials and some residents are supporters of the project, arguing that it is important for local development. A new public inquiry took place in the spring of 1993; it gave a favorable recommendation and a new official decision (DUP). Construction started again immediately afterward. At the end of 1993, Somport opposition committees were created all around France; they made a variety of legal appeals and continued other types of opposition. Meanwhile the construction of the tunnel through the Pass progressed and was recently completed, but the widening of the road and its connections to other highways are still under dispute. The opposition campaign's arguments are now focused on preventing the tunnel from becoming a main truck route, and on promoting the use of train tunnels there and elsewhere in the Pyrenees.

The American case – the Clavey River dam project

The Clavey River is a remote stream running through a steep canyon on the western slope of the Sierra Nevada mountains, just west of the famous Yosemite National Park in eastern California. It flows south through the Stanislaus National Forest for 47 miles before emptying into the Tuolumne River and creating a challenging set of rapids known as Clavey Falls, revered by some to be among the best white-water "rides." Unlike most rivers in the Sierra range, the Clavey has no major dams along its course and is heralded by environmentalists as "one of the last completely free-flowing, wild rivers" in the region, indeed in the entire American West.

The local area around the Clavey – Tuolumne County, including the main town of Sonora, the classic western town of Jamestown, and the tourist outpost of Groveland on Highway 120 – is part of California's Gold Country, the areas around Sutter's Creek where the 1849 Gold Rush began. Many of the local residents are direct descendants of gold prospectors and many still work in the so-called "resource extraction" industries, mostly timber instead of mining these days. But tourism is fast becoming the dominant industry of the area, serving the flood of visitors to Yosemite as well as a growing number of people braving the white-water rapids of the Tuolumne River with one of several local rafting companies. The Clavey is not itself a major tourist draw, but it is very important to the people who do venture to its banks, including trout fisherman, hunters, hikers, and native plant aficionados who see the Clavey as an "untouched wilderness" containing old-growth forests and some endangered species, and a nearby native American tribe, the Me-Wuk, who trace their cultural heritage to seasonal migrations along the Clavey. But the remote Clavey could not remain in "untouched" obscurity forever. A proposal in 1990 to build a large dam and hydroelectric plant on the Clavey began a rancorous dispute which played out on the local, regional, state, and national levels over the next five years. The dam was proposed by the Turlock Irrigation District (TID), the water and utility company for the town of Turlock in the San Joaquin Valley about 70 miles (and two counties) away from the Clavey. TID had previously tried to build a dam on the Tuolumne but failed when that river was declared "wild and scenic" in 1984 (see Pertschuck 1986, for a summary).[1] Turning its attention to the Tuolumne's main tributary, the Clavey, TID submitted a proposal to the Federal Energy Regulatory Commission (FERC) – which regulates all hydroelectric dam projects – detailing a $700 million project that would affect water flow on 19 miles of the river and be used primarily during peak summer months when the increasingly suburban residents of Turlock (historically an agricultural region) turned on their air conditioners. The Tuolumne County local government (where the Clavey Dam would have been located) signed on as a minor partner in the venture, after TID agreed to pay the locals a share of the revenues from the project, even though all the electricity would be sent down to Turlock.

Building on the coalitions that had been so successful in "saving the Tuolumne," an opposition force quickly mobilized to "Save the Clavey" by stopping TID's dam project. The opposition included a heterogeneous mix of groups and individuals on many levels. In Tuolumne County a grassroots opposition coalition was formed that included the rafting companies and other tourism interests, local environmentalists, and other local people who wanted to Clavey left wild. In Turlock a former river rafter started an opposition campaign among TID's ratepayers, and TID's main industrial customers also opposed the higher electric rates they would pay to fund the project. And on a state and national level, environmental groups concerned with river protection lobbied in Washington DC and assisted the local opposition. But the project also had its proponents, TID and its "silent partner" Tuolumne County were able to mobilize other supporters for the project, including the Tuolumne Chamber of Commerce and a local pro-development, "wise use" group supported by the local timber company.

During the period when FERC was considering TID's proposal, the two sides in the dispute rarely debated openly (let alone negotiated) in public, but often submitted dueling comments to regulatory agencies like the Forest Service, lobbied national legislators, sought endorsements from the same local groups (including the Me-Wuk tribe), and sought ink in the same state and local media. In July 1994, the FERC recommended against licensing the project as outlined by TID, claiming that the economic benefits did not outweigh the large environmental costs of the project, but suggested a couple of more expensive alternative designs. The TID Board of Directors then decided in January 1995 to "shelve" the project, citing a number of factors that had reduced the demand for power, as well as the impending de-regulation of the electricity industry which made other supply sources cheaper. Since this decision, TID has not pursued its plans on the Clavey further, while the environmental opposition has continued to push for federal protection for the river.

Methods and data

Data from extensive field research on the two cases orient the analysis and are offered as evidence throughout both chapters. The data consist of various sorts of "texts" and observations collected from several sources: in-depth interviews with the major participants in the Somport and Clavey conflicts, documents and public statements put out by the opposing organizations or governmental agencies involved (e.g. planning reports, legal petitions, opposition campaign flyers and press releases), media coverage and quotations, any available private papers or other materials, etc.[2] Our analysis of these texts is targeted on a few themes and topics of specific analytic concern, but our findings within each topic come from reviewing and comparing these texts in the two cases. We focused the comparison particularly on areas in which the data were directly parallel (e.g. comparing interviews with local opponents in the Aspe Valley to similar interviews with local opponents in Tuolumne County), and care was taken to collect similar data when possible. We also consider the relation of the texts to their complex context, but we are careful to recognize that the "setting" for an argument or action is multi-layered and often ambiguous.[3]

The data for the Somport tunnel case were collected during fieldwork in the Aspe Valley (March and April 1995) by Claudette Lafaye, Marie-Noël Godet, Jean-François Germe and Laurent Thévenot, with additional fieldwork in 1997 completed by Eric Doidy. A total of 17 activists and other local actors were interviewed in sessions ranging from one to two hours, in their homes or offices in the Aspe Valley and Oloron. Other data included observation of a demonstration in the Valley and Oloron (April 8, 1995) which brought together a variety of styles of expression and contestation – from trade union members' marches to animal spokesperson's speeches – and of a meeting of the "Collectif Alternatives

Pyrénéennes à l'axe E7" where public positions and strategies were discussed. An extensive file of national and local media accounts was assembled by Godet, with the generous help of Jean-Luc Palacio's own documentation brought together for the purpose of the "Collectif." This was supplemented with a Nexis database search for English-language newspaper reports. Various other reports and documents were collected and analyzed also, including the government's impact study report, which was analyzed in detail by Germe.[4]

The data for the Clavey River case were collected both during a joint research trip by Michael Moody and Laurent Thévenot in June 1995, and during visits and the on-going research efforts of Moody during 1995 and 1996. A total of 21 activists and interest representatives were interviewed in sessions ranging from one to three hours, usually in their homes or offices in Tuolumne County, the Turlock area, or in San Francisco and Sacramento. A large collection of other materials was assembled from several sources. Nexis and other database searches yielded much of the public and media record of the dispute, and the major activists provided additional public and some internal documents in response to phone and mail research queries. Materials were also gathered while in the field (e.g. from government offices or while conducting interviews in organizational offices). Two sources in particular were most beneficial: the vast files of the Tuolumne River Preservation Trust, and the personal files of Wally Anker (who founded the local grassroots opposition group), including his notes, minutes of group meetings, correspondence, reports, and materials from TID and his opponents.[5]

This chapter and the next were written in a time-consuming but rewarding joint writing process. The two main authors, Michael Moody and Laurent Thévenot, wrote and revised primary drafts of the texts in English during several intensive periods of coordinated work in Paris and in Princeton, discussing each new section of text in depth and making revisions together. This face-to-face writing dialogue between scholars native to the two countries forced each to clarify more extensively to the other highly nuanced interpretations, reduced the risk of unintended stereotyping or misunderstanding, and, we believe, resulted in a more balanced presentation of the two "cultures." A third co-author, Claudette Lafaye, wrote some original sections of the Somport analysis (in French) and participated in the development of Chapter 10.

Analytical approach

Our comparative approach to studying political culture and practice in France and the United States takes seriously the complexity and diversity of the argumentation dynamics when actors and organizations are engaged in important public disputes. We focus on a specific environmental dispute in each country, but explore these cases with an analytical focus which allows us to consider the array of voices, actors, and issues in a variety of public arenas and discursive settings.

In this chapter, we take a first step by sorting through the complex public debate over the disputed projects. We systematically categorize in rich comparative detail the argumentation dynamics and types of "justification" utilized by the disputants. Our analysis explores the ways in which these disputants attempt to defend their positions through various types of "generalized" arguments – that is, arguments which make some claim to general applicability by reference to different sorts of values, principles, or models for judging what is good, worthy, and right (e.g. equality, tradition, the free market, or environmentalism). We compare the frequency of certain types of arguments and "modes of justification," as well as the dynamics of their use in national and cultural contexts, paying particular attention to argumentation that involves combining various modes or justification. We also consider the material or organizational arrangements which support the justifications found in each case.

Disputes that ostensibly pit infrastructure projects "against" nature, or economic goals "versus" environmental goals, are particularly revealing subject matter for comparative cultural analysis. The activists, planners, and others who advocate a particular position on the development projects at the center of our two cases rarely offer only one sort of statement of their claim, or one description of the project or of their opponents. Instead, the public claims and portrayals are quite diverse, and any one participant in the conflict routinely varies the form and content of his or her arguments, making the task of comparing argumentation a complex one, irreducible to the broad characterization of cultural contexts. We employ a rigorous analytical approach to accomplish this complex task.

The comparative approach employed here builds on the analysis of modes of "justification" developed by Boltanski and Thévenot (1991), which examines the type of appeal to a common good characteristic of a set of different "orders of worth" regarded as particularly legitimate.[6] A justification in this theoretical view is an attempt to move beyond stating a particular or personal viewpoint toward proving that the statement is generalizable and relevant for a common good, showing why or how this general claim is legitimate. Disputants involved in debating the resolution of a public problem are charged with this task of justification.

Each order of worth offers a different basis for justification and involves a different mode of evaluating what is good for a common humanity (in terms of market worth, or efficient technique and method, for instance).[7]

Justifications can involve positive "arguments," claims, or position statements, but might also be critical "denunciations" of opposing views in the dynamics of public disputes. The critique of justifications from one order usually rests on the evaluative basis of another order (such as the denunciation of bureaucratic planning from a market flexibility perspective, for instance).

Justifications involve more than "just words" or "accounts"[8] – they rely on the engagement of objects or other elements of the situation (as relevant backing for an argument), and they must meet the requirement of offering proof for their assertions.[9] The form of proof that is considered legitimate, and the way objects or events are evaluated as relevant to sustain the justification, varies with each kind of worth. In order to be engaged as a probe in justifications, objects (or persons or events) need to be "qualified" according to the particular order of worth.[10] For example, the Somport road is qualified as an "international highway" in one order of worth and as a "local access road" in another order. This qualification of entities is more than a rhetorical characterization, but also involves material features, such as the number of lanes of highway.[11]

Boltanski and Thévenot describe in detail six orders of worth in this regime of justification: "market" performance; "industrial" efficiency based on technical competence and long-term planning; "civic" equality and solidarity; "domestic" and traditional trustworthiness entrenched in local and personal ties; "inspiration" expressed in creativity, emotion, or religious grace; and "renown" based on public opinion and fame.[12] More recent work has pointed to the contemporary emergence of an additional order of worth, "green" worth, which is gaining specificity but is still often used in combination with other types of justification (Lafaye and Thévenot 1993). We are particularly interested in comparing how such "green" arguments are employed or expressed in the two cases. Using this range of justification types as a starting point, we compare how an array of arguments and generalized justifications are expressed in the two countries. Not all justifications fit easily into one and only one order of worth, however, and Boltanski and Thévenot use the term "compromise" to denote these attempts to overlap and make compatible justifications from two orders of worth. Like the justifications themselves, these attempted connections differ from one country to the other, and bring about distinctive argumentation dynamics. Making clear such differences will help provide a more acute understanding of the distinction between the cultural repertoires of each country.

Our analytical approach relates to recent work in cultural sociology (Lamont and Wuthnow 1990) and connected fields like practice theory and the "new institutionalism" approach to organizational analysis

(Powell and DiMaggio 1991), as well as the "turn" toward cultural analysis of social movement discourse or "framing" and toward narrative and argumentation in policy analysis (Throgmorton 1996; Rowe 1994; Fischer and Forrester 1993). But we also seek to fill some prominent theoretical and methodological gaps in these "cultural" approaches to rhetoric and public debate.

Current approaches to the use of "repertoires" or "cultural resources" in the justification, preparation, or explanation of action attempt to move beyond a static and determinist model which assumes an overarching layer of values and "culture" to an approach which considers values and culture "in use" and examines the way actors creatively employ certain resources in practice (Knorr-Cetina and Schatzki forthcoming) and in varying contexts (Eliasoph 1998; Lichterman 1996; Steinberg 1995; Alexander and Smith 1993; Lamont 1992; Wuthnow 1992; Wilson 1990; Schudson 1989; Swidler 1986). We also focus on the usage of cultural elements or repertoires in practice, but with an eye toward the nature of the constraints on this usage, including the fact that different arenas of debate and justification have variable requirements for generalization. We pay close attention to the pragmatic requirements of demonstrating proof of one's argument (e.g. by pointing to the real world), and to the possibility of critique as a consequence of open debate about public problems (Tricot 1996). In this way, we also seek to bridge analysis of "cultural repertoires" and "repertoires of contention" (Traugott 1995; Tarrow 1994; Tilly 1978) or action.[13]

The recent spate of work on "framing" in social movements focuses primarily – at times exclusively – on the strategic manipulation (the "business of persuading others") of appeals to resonate and mobilize an intended audience (McAdam et al. 1996; Morris and Mueller 1992; Snow et al. 1986; for critiques of the instrumental approach, see Goodwin and Jasper 1999; Jasper 1997; Emirbayer and Goodwin 1996) although some work (e.g. Gamson 1992) does examine how frames are used or interpreted by the audience.[14] While we consider at length in Chapter 10 the nature of the "strategy" involved in constructing arguments, we approach argumentation not simply as a rhetorical assertion but also a provision of evidence involving more than one speaker, one intended audience, or one mode of claiming a common good.[15] In this way, we also go beyond the standard "social construction of social problems" perspective (e.g. Best 1989; Hilgartner and Bosk 1988; Spector and Kitsuse 1977).

We are concerned with examining the pragmatics of public space and discourse through an analysis of a plurality of regimes of action. Habermas' (1984) normative theory of the linguistic pragmatics of communicative action, and Arendt's (1958) theoretical understanding of the maintenance of a public realm through the "disclosure" of unique individuals also approach the study of politics through a close examination of multiple modes of action.[16] Similarly, we seek to uncover common requirements shared by all orders of worth, and to account for a variety of modes of acting which may qualify for public legitimacy. As we shall see from the comparison, the configuration of public space and the dynamics of discourse depend heavily on the mode of acting privileged in a political culture.

Comparative issues

Utilizing this analytic approach, we provide fresh insight into a number of important areas of substantive comparative research on the dynamics of political dispute. In particular, our findings contribute to the understanding of locality in the two countries. In addition to general discussions of environmental movements, policy, and politics in the United States (e.g. Dowie 1995; Fiorino 1995; Gottlieb 1993; Dunlap and Mertig 1992; Paehlke 1990) and France and western Europe (e.g. Axelrod 1997; Dalton 1994; Prendiville 1994), much existing American research on local political or environmental disputes focuses on the tactics of local, or so-called "NIMBY" ("Not In My Back Yard"), groups in fighting corporate power, infrastructure development, or toxic waste disposal (e.g. Walsh et al. 1997; Gould et al. 1996; Williams and Matheny 1995); on the NIMBY phenomenon as a national movement (Mazmanian and Morell 1994; Freudenberg and Steinsapir 1992; Piller 1991); or on the differential determinations of "risk" in various communities or localities (Douglas and Wildavsky 1982). We expand on this work by considering the more general question of whether threats to a local areas in our two cases are rejected based on NIMBY-sorts of arguments or not, and by closely comparing how such arguments are specifically expressed and considered as legitimate in the two countries.[17]

In exploring the category of "green" justifications, we contribute fresh insight into the literature on environmental discourse or rhetoric, particularly the understanding of the different conceptions of wilderness and nature in the United States and France, and of the relations of humans (and human communities) and nature (Dupuis and Vandergeest 1996; Spangle and Knapp 1996; Bennett and Chaloupka 1994; Killingsworth and Palmer 1992). And our analysis adds an important comparative dimension missing from most previous work on environmental rhetoric by asking what differences might exist in the content or use of "green" arguments or images in these two countries, which have different environmental histories and movements.

More generally, our analysis also contributes to the literature on comparative political culture, specifically by opening to empirical investigation the basic characterizations of American political culture as individualistic and market-oriented, and of French political culture as collectivistic and civic-oriented.[18] While we address some basic comparative questions along these lines – such as whether market arguments are used more commonly in the United States, and whether "solidarity" arguments are used more in France – we also try to make more nuanced comparisons of how these general political-cultural orientations are played out in practice, such as comparing the dynamics of connecting different types of justifications in each country.

Comparison of arguments and modes of justification

Justifications based on the market ["market" worth]

Arguments involving market justifications evaluate worth based on the price or economic value of goods and services in a competitive market.[19] Relevant pieces of evidence brought in support of these arguments only "qualify" for market justifications as long as they can be treated as exchangeable goods or services. These justifications consider the worth of things only in terms of price, and support a very short-term construction of time in which the market competition "test" is the basis for evaluation. Market arguments for the projects in dispute in our cases might include, for example, claims that the project will boost revenue for a region's commercial areas, or that it is the cheapest method of providing a service for which there is demand. In general, the use of market arguments are more common and well developed in the United States case. In the French case, market arguments come "from above" (from Brussels) rather than emerging "from below" as in classic market economics. Market arguments are endorsed by local actors only when they are "compromised" within the idea of "local development," i.e. articulated with arguments based on traditional trustworthiness entrenched in local and personal ties (another order of justification dealt with in detail in a later section).[20]

In the French case, the road and tunnel were conceived and defended by the European Community (EC) in Brussels as an integral part of the Pan-European transportation network intended to foster the "free circulation" of goods and people, which is the main reference point in the construction of the EC. Supporters of the tunnel claim it will integrate and provide access to previously isolated or "landlocked" areas – the French term *"désenclavées"* is used to express this process – which are situated at the periphery of the EC. The road is defended as a way to reduce the cost

Table 9.1. *Schematic summary of orders of worth*

	Market	Industrial	Civic	Domestic	Inspired	Opinion	Green[a]
Mode of evaluation (worth)	Price, cost	Technical efficiency	Collective welfare	Esteem, reputation	Grace singularity creativeness	Renown, fame	Environmental friendliness
Test[b]	Market competitiveness	Competence, reliability, planning	Equality and solidarity	Trustworthiness	Passion, enthusiasm	Popularity, audience, recognition	Sustainability, renewability
Form of relevant proof	Monetary	Measurable: criteria, statistics	Formal, official	Oral, exemplary, personally warranted	Emotional involvement & expression	Semiotic	Ecological, ecosystemic
Qualified objects	Freely circulating market good or service	Infrastructure, project, technical object, method, plan	Rules and regulations, fundamental rights, welfare policies	Patrimony, locale, heritage	Emotionally invested body or item: the sublime	Sign, media	Pristine wilderness, healthy environment, natural habitat
Qualified human beings	Customer, consumer, merchant, seller	Engineer, professional, expert	Equal citizens, solidarity unions	Authority	Creative being	Celebrity	Environmentalist
Time formation	Short-term, flexibility	Long-term planned future	Perennial	Customary past	Eschatological, revolutionary, visionary moment	Vogue, trend	Future generations
Space formation	Globalization	Cartesian space	Detachment	Local, proximal anchoring	Presence	Communication network	Planet ecosystem

Notes:

[a] This column presents indications of a possible new order of green worth. This category is currently being developed and is far from being as well illustrated or strongly integrated as the others (see text for comments on this; also see Lafaye and Thévenot, 1993).

[b] The specific meaning of "test" and other terms here – e.g. "qualified" – is explained in the text.

of transit traffic. The funding for the project was proposed in Brussels as a way to promote competition and free markets in Europe through better transport of goods. However, the sorts of evidence that are most characteristic of the way market arguments are put to a "test" – e.g. comparative prices and actual competition – are not provided in the course of debate over the merits of the Somport project.[21]

While the French case begins with market arguments but contains no consequential market evidence, the American case seems to end with market arguments, and market evaluations seem to have considerable consequences for the eventual fate of the project. Throughout the dispute over the proposed Clavey dam, the opponents attempted to characterize the project as "economically unfeasible," while Turlock Irrigation District (TID) and its allies continually claimed the dam was the "cheapest" way to meet the long-term energy demand of Turlock residents. Market evaluations were particularly salient in the Turlock area of debate, as the local opposition group, Turlock Ratepayers' Alliance, emphasized the impact of the project on the electricity bills of county residents.[22] Several opponents acknowledged this emphasis on economics as a keen strategic move on their part, designed both to avoid being labeled as "environmentalists" (in an area where environmentalism has little public support) and to appeal to the sensitivity of politicians to economic arguments. As the organizer of the Ratepayers' Alliance, Mike Fuller describes their choice of arguments, ". . . it was anything that we could really grab onto within reason that had to do with economics." Also, market evaluations seem to have largely determined the decision to halt the project. TID maintained from 1990 through the end of 1994 that the dam was the cheapest way to meet rising electricity demand, while its opponents claimed other sources were clearly cheaper (and less environmentally damaging); both sides judged the project on market criteria. In announcing the decision to shelve the project in January 1995, TID offered as its primary reasons the declining cost of natural gas and the impending deregulation of the electricity market which would make other sources more accessible.

A different example of market justifications found in both cases involves the tourism and recreation industry, which is important to the regions in which both projects were proposed. In France, the market argument of improving tourism is carefully blended with arguments promoting local and traditional activities. According to this "compromise," the road should not be an axis for improved trade markets (as Brussels would have it) but should give access to local trades and tourist sites.[23] The road, say the locals, should not be a "truck corridor" (as a pan-European market argument would propose it), but rather should be a road going to and ending at points within the valley – the road should be a way to access the valley, not pass through it. One local mayor, Jacques Lassalle, presents this in terms of the desire by locals to control any infrastructure projects built in their area (in explicit challenge to control from above): "It is necessary to build transportation networks[24] that will remain in our locale and that we will therefore dominate [maîtriserons]." So the local businesses propose a sort of mitigation of the project, a "compromised" road – they will accept a road if it is not a superhighway truck road. To demonstrate the problems with the current proposal, locals cite an example of a valley in the Maurienne region, where a small road has been connected by tunnel to Italy, and the whole valley has become exactly the "traffic corridor" feared in the Aspe Valley. The road cuts across historic old towns, people have left their homes because of the traffic and the accidents, etc.

In the United States case, the frequent references to tourism are more directly framed as market justifications. Representatives of the tourism industry in the Clavey area, led by an active group of river rafting companies and employees, repeatedly argue the dam would lead to a decrease in tourist dollars for the local economy. A group of tourism business owners, the Highway 120 Association, was strongly opposed to the project, which they considered a threat to their "livelihood." Tourism supporters claimed fishing, hunting, and camping on the Clavey would be diminished when its status as a "free-flowing, wild river" was lost. However, proponents of the dam, such as the Tuolumne County Chamber of Commerce, argued the opposite, claiming the dam's reservoir and new roads would provide better access for other sorts of tourism that would benefit the local economy even more.

Justifications based on technical efficiency and planning ["industrial" worth]

Another category of justifications includes arguments where evaluations depend on technical efficiency and professionalism, planning, and long-term investment in infrastructure. This category relates to the "industrial" order of worth in the Boltanski and Thévenot (1991) scheme, but "industrial" here is not limited to the industrial economic sector. While technical competency and planning arguments are sometimes connected as such to economic outcomes, the bases for evaluation in this category are different from market criteria. Market justifications place value based on the competitive price of goods while technical competency justifications place value based on the efficiency of investments, professional planning and expertise, and long-term growth. In addition, the form of proof involved in market justifications is short-term profitability, while the form of proof for planning justifications is long-term investment and technical or scientific competency.[25]

In their beginning stages, both cases show a predominance of technical and planning arguments, as evidenced by the treatment of each project as an "infrastructure investment." In the Clavey case, TID describes the project as part of a long-term planning effort to ensure continued growth in the Turlock area and argues that further hydroelectric power development is necessary "for the future of California" – they characterize the dam as a well-planned and scientifically sound investment.[26] Most often these planning arguments are made (by both sides) in combination with other types of justifications, particularly in terms of the now common American dispute over whether to use nature as a resource for human benefit or to preserve nature in its pristine state. The "wise use" movement has emerged as an explicit counter to what their supporters view as the excesses of the environmental movement, with wise use advocates claiming nature can be "conserved" while still serving useful purposes for human development (Dowie 1995; Echeverria and Eby 1995).[27] The wise use movement found a local expression in the Clavey dispute through a group called TuCARE (Tuolumne County Alliance for Resources and Environment), which characterized the opposition to the dam as an attempt by "preservationists" to "lock up" the resources of the Clavey and deny local residents the benefits of their use. TuCARE's perspective is a good example of an explicit "compromise" of planning or technical efficiency (and market) justifications and environmental justifications: they envision nature as both an environmental and a scarce economic "resource" with multiple potential uses – energy, recreation, income for the county – which must be used efficiently.

Interestingly, both sides in the Clavey dispute claim to be advocating what is "best for the future,"[28] but present competing visions of what is best: the environmentalists say preserve wilderness for the future, while the dam proponents say build infrastructure. Also, both sides utilize a form of proof which is congruent with technical competency justifications – the use of scientific expertise and evidence – to validate opposite arguments, for example on the question of whether the dam will hurt or help the Clavey fish populations.

Another important connection between planning and environmental justifications is the notion of "mitigation": making up for or minimizing the project's impact on the environment. The idea of mitigation rests on the acceptance of both technical and environmental criteria of value as legitimate, and provides the basis for a compromise between them through, for instance, features added to the project to make it more "environmentally friendly." At one point in the Clavey case, both sides discussed possible mitigations, including additional releases of water at times when the fish most need it, placing the dam further upstream so it would not be visible to rafters on the Tuolumne, a faux-wooded path across the top of the dam for deer to cross, and even diversion intakes made to look like rocks. However, the environmental opposition continued to oppose the dam categorically, implying that no amount of mitigation was possible to "make up for" the damage caused by a dam in a cherished wilderness. This continued opposition angered the dam proponents, who touted their project as a model compromise. The project director, John Mills, praises the dam proposal in a way that nicely shows the attempt to use both green and infrastructure justifications: "a project that would leave the smallest footprint on the river and get the highest returns to the county and to Turlock."[29]

In the French case, technical and planning arguments are also found most significantly in the beginning of the conflict. The project is defended because of the necessity of providing roads, tunnels, and other infrastructure in order for there to be economic growth in the future. This sort of industrial planning argument is extremely influential as an argument for the tunnel project in France, and reflects the well-documented embrace of an "engineering mentality" or "technocratic" approach by the French state (Jasper 1990; Lamont 1992). This strong compromise of technical-industrial and "civic" justifications (see the next section also) closely connects technocratic planning by the state with the general interest, and this approach is perpetuated through the training of élites in "engineering schools" [*Grandes Ecoles*] for high positions in the state.

Providing relevant proof for a technical and planning argument became a very prominent point of contention in the French case, as the market proof did in the US. Specifically, the initial plans contained a very extensive report projecting the level of traffic on the new road, but then an ecologically minded geography professor from Pau, a city near the Aspe Valley, produced a counter-report projecting much higher levels of traffic. What is significant is that while this report refuted the other report, they are both based on the same type of "test" – the long-term efficiency of the project – with the same criteria of proof and instruments of evidence (technical evidence from modeling and statistical analysis).

The effectiveness of the infrastructure planning arguments in France might also explain a primary difference with the United States: in France, these evaluations are not as frequently mixed with environmental evaluations as in the United States in terms of "wise use" or mitigation or "renewable" energy sources. On the one hand, the process of trying to make up for environmental damage is certainly found in the Somport case. For example, planners of the proposed Somport road included a great many innovations in their impact study to make the road more "environmentally friendly" (to use the American term), such as using "local species of trees" and "techniques of ecological engineering" in "landscaping the roadside" and rest areas, building "bear bridges" and "bear-ducts" over or under the road, and modifying the work schedule to avoid interfering with "sensitive nesting sites" during the "reproductive periods" of birds. On the other hand, there is no comparative term for "mitigation" in French, nor a legal requirement for it, as in United States environmental regulations. In France it is much more common to stay within the realm of infrastructure planning and efficiency evaluations rather than trying to compromise this with environmentalism. For example, hydropower projects in France were not normally defended by reference to their relatively green, renewable quality (as the Clavey project was), but rather were judged based on their efficiency as long-term investments.

Justifications based on civic equality and solidarity ["civic" worth]

Justifications based on civic equality or solidarity refer to the collective welfare as the standard of evaluation, and propose or oppose projects based on such goals as equal access and protection of civil rights.[30] Various forms of these "civic" justifications are found in both cases, and equality or solidarity is often the guiding logic underlying the modes of engagement or organization, especially in the Somport case. There are comparative differences also, relating generally to the fact that in the United States the emphasis is more on equal rights, while in France the emphasis is on solidarity against inequality (but not as much on civil rights: cf. the contributions of Michèle Lamont and Abigail Saguy in this volume, who find the same differences in the implementation of civic justifications).[31] There are also many examples in both cases where equality and solidarity justifications are combined or integrated with other types of justifications, although in different ways in the two different cases (e.g. combinations of civic and technical – industrial worth – arguments in France, combinations of civic equality with opinion, market, and environmental justifications in the United States).

In the Somport case, both proponents and opponents make a range of equality or solidarity arguments: the project, like other infrastructure developments, is very often defended by the state and by other proponents as a way to meet the common needs of citizens, and as a way to maintain equality of access and communication between regions. The opposition campaign makes different sorts of civic arguments, but they also engage in modes of protest and organization which embody these civic goals. For example, there has been an attempt to make connections between the Somport struggle and other similar disputes in Europe, in the Alpine region including Switzerland, which involve the choice of building a railway tunnel for the transportation of cars and trucks (*"fer-routage"*) versus a road or traffic tunnel (the opposition prefers a railway). This attempt to generalize the cause is couched in civic language of "solidarity between struggles" during meetings where spokespersons provide testimonies of comparable experiences. The opposition to the Somport project also organized many demonstrations and used the high level of participation in their demonstrations and their unitary slogans as proof for their arguments against the project.[32]

In the Clavey case, civic justifications are utilized by the various players on both sides of the dispute (as in the Somport case), but are more commonly employed by the opponents of the dam project. The local "grassroots" opposition coalition in Tuolumne County often emphasizes their representation of a diverse array of local people (not just the rafting interests or the environmentalists), and the silent solidarity of many more uninvolved but concerned local citizens. The proponents of the dam, however, also lay claim to this silent support of the locals. Both sides at different times collected thousands of names on petitions and submitted them to either the local Board of Supervisors or the national FERC officials. This dispute over who has "public opinion" on his side reveals the connections in the United States between two modes of arguing: a "civic" mode of arguing based on a figure of "majority" commitment to one's side and on the need to "raise consciousness" for gaining more active supporters; a mode of arguing (to be reviewed in detail later) based on "renown" attempting to gain media attention or to "put the issue on the national agenda," as environmentalists explicitly tried to do with the Clavey dispute. In the US case (as in other domains investigated in this volume: cf. chapters by Cyril Lemieux and John Schmalzbauer, and by Nathalie Heinich) frequent references to the "majority" offer a bridge between civic and renown justifications. This connection has historically been a highly legitimate argument in American political culture. Whereas in France, the civic reference to the "general interest" or "solidarity" is not indexed on the number of supporters or some measure of public opinion (see the next chapter for further exploration of this also). The debate over the Clavey in the Turlock area, the valley agricultural region where the power from the dam would be used, provides additional insight into how solidarity is conceived in terms of opinion in the United States Both sides in this arena – Turlock Irrigation District proposing the dam versus the opposition from corporate "ratepayers" and the "Ratepayer's Alliance," a group claiming to represent the residential customers – claim to be doing "what's best for TID's ratepayers" and to offer evidence that "public opinion" is in their favor. For example, the opposition groups compiled lists of groups opposed to TID and tried to make the list as diverse and as public as possible.

It is also notable that the environmentalist-sponsored opposition group called itself the "Ratepayers' Alliance." This name shows the connection often made in the United States between civic equality concerns and market concerns, which were seen as more effective and generally resonant than strictly environmental arguments (or environmental-sounding group names). The term "ratepayer," which is commonly used throughout the United States, is in one sense a market identity – a "customer" of the power "company" – but it also signifies a civic, non-market identity – a citizen (or citizens as a group) being served by a "public utility" which they usually cannot abandon for another competitor utility for the market reason of lower price. The Alliance leaders often utilized this dual connotation because it allowed them to emphasize market arguments at some times and civic equality arguments at others.

The same sort of combination of equality and market arguments is usually rejected in France (see also Camus-Vigué in this volume). In contrast, it is more common in France for equality and solidarity justifications to be connected with justifications concerning infrastructure planning and technical efficiency ("industrial" rather than market worth). Projects like the Somport tunnel are often defended by their developers as meeting the needs of citizens (collectively and equally) through the most competent technical planning. In fact, the civil servants of the Ministry of Public Works (*Ministère de l'Equipement*), charged with planning and building infrastructure projects, denounced local opponents of the Somport project as trying to protect their own piece of land and remaining stuck in the past, while resisting "progress" and denying the benefits of the project to all others.

A durable "compromise" between equality arguments and environmental arguments has been developed in the United States earlier and to a greater extent than in France. The great concern with protecting everyone's equal right to access to nature (at least on "public lands" such as national parks or forests) is both promoted and regulated with the goal of keeping individuals from appropriating nature for their own exclusive use. United States programs and devices to promote equal access to nature include interpretive nature trails, nature education centers, and, in the Clavey case, United States Forest Service regulation of rafting capacity on the Tuolumne River designed to protect the river from overuse and to preserve the pristine wilderness experience for others to enjoy. The debate over the recreational uses of the Clavey reflects the importance of "making nature available to all people," but also shows a further connection to market arguments in the US (similar to the one observed in the publishing industry, where popular access means both general availability and market distribution).[33] In fact, both sides in the Clavey debate claim to be concerned with marketing recreational services so that many people will be able to enjoy nature. The opposition groups maintain damming the Clavey will take the Clavey away from the people who want to enjoy it recreationally through rafting or fishing or hiking. TID and other dam proponents, on the other hand, retort that the Clavey is currently so remote that only "wealthy yuppies" who can pay the high price for a rafting trip or for wilderness gear can now enjoy it, while their project will provide new roads into the Clavey canyon and many more opportunities for "flatwater recreation" on the reservoir and camping on its shores.[34]

The attempt to reconcile civic equality arguments with environmental arguments is also at the core of the much-disputed "wise use" movement and the wise use group involved in the Clavey conflict, TuCARE (described earlier). TuCARE argues that their populist approach to environmental protection ("wise use" of resources, not abuse nor complete preservation of them) is a better reflection of local public sentiment (in an area where many residents work in "resource extraction" industries), and a better representation of what is good for all local citizens, than that of the environmentalists (who, they claim, care little about the good of most local citizens). Both of these examples of connections between equality and environmental arguments are not nearly as well developed in France – where there is no institutional equivalent of the "wise use movement" – but the land-use planning of protected areas has been recently growing in France.

Justifications based on tradition and locality ["domestic" worth]

Another distinct category of arguments relies on justifications where traditions are valued and are constantly being revisited in making judgments about the present, and where locality and ties to a place are revered. Evaluations of this type support hierarchies of reputation and trustworthiness. These justifications relate to what Boltanski and Thévenot (1991) term the "domestic" order of worth in which the claim of a general value is warranted by personal tie or local attachment, so that personal character or proximity are considered the source or building blocks of universal goods. In the French case, arguments of this sort are found in the call by project opponents to protect the region's treasured culture and heritage (*patrimoine* in French), of which the valley's landscape is a significant part.[35] In the American case there are many similar arguments pointing to the preservation of a place close to one's home and hearth, and references to the region's heritage. But these arguments are oriented less around the idea of heritage and patrimony in the United States and more in terms of the protection of one's "backyard," either as a protection of private property (a compromise with market arguments) or a rejection of non-local authority.

Justifications based on tradition and locality are utilized extensively by opponents of the Somport project in France, and there are a variety of rich testimonials from the inhabitants of the Aspe Valley on the need to preserve a patrimony and way of life cherished by many and upheld in various ways by existing traditions of the region. This local view is summarized in a report on the project, "This project will confiscate the best cultivated land. The movement of animals [*transhumance*] by shepherds will be impeded by the new transportation axis. The tourism industry, which is presently harmoniously integrated in the area, will suffer from the proximity of a heavily used road. The local trades and craftsmanship which give life to the villages will be forced to disappear." This shows the consideration of the French "landscape" of villages – with their distinct cultures, traditions, and crafts that are highly differentiated across regions (*régionalisme*) – as a tourist attraction threatened by the project.

When local officials and some residents support the project with these sorts of justifications, they compromise local patrimony with market or infrastructure arguments. They claim the project is important for local development: it will improve tourist access to the area, open markets for local trades, etc. As the mayor of the small valley town of Borce explains, "It [the project] is the only possibility we have at present to develop handicrafts, trade, industry, and tourism in our isolated region, which is becoming more and more depopulated." The "compromise" is made in proposed restrictions to the width of the road: "We only need a two-lane road with three-lane sections for passing. This will create the necessary and indispensable exchange among nearby locals," says another local mayor who supports the project.

Many of the arguments in the Somport case, in both camps, refer to the harmonious existence of "living on the land": "what was really significant for me was this land; I did not want to betray this land . . . We have a fabulous land" (a pro-project local mayor); "My valley is so beautiful, I pity those who left" (an anti-project shepherd). Close connections between people and their land, from villagers who reside in the small valley communities to the shepherds who make their living traveling to remote and rugged mountain pastures, through fishermen and hunters. In France, the idea of "domesticating nature" includes nature and animals as parts of the broader human community or "*habitat.*"[36] Also, the idea of a "landscape" in France is not simply used to refer to a wild area or a vista; rather, a landscape specifically includes the human community, the towns, the networks of trails and roads around the villages, scattered but integrated groups of houses, etc. Even the old railway running through the Aspe Valley is now seen as a part of the "domestic" landscape and is favored as part of the heritage of the area – a past infrastructure project has been transformed into a patrimonial value.

In the Clavey dispute there are also many examples of arguments, almost exclusively among the local opposition activists, calling for the preservation of a treasured local place which is a valued piece of the local history and heritage as well as a location of special meaning for the personal history and lives of many inhabitants. For example, Wally Anker is a retired banker who now raises horses on land near the Clavey that has been in his family since they were early settlers in the nineteenth-century Gold Rush. He spearheaded the founding of the Clavey River Preservation Coalition and he would begin his speeches with a story about how he first visited the Clavey in 1944 as a teenager, at a time when the Clavey was legendary among the local "old-timers" as the most remote and wild stream for trout fishing.[37] Upon returning to the area in the 1980s, Mr. Anker resolved to help keep it that way for his grandchildren. Talking about the Clavey, another activist muses, "You know, there's a certain thing to be said about a sense of place, and that's hard to put into words. Pride, sort of." He goes on to say the river has since taken on this familiar meaning, this "sense of place," for his son and daughter whom he took to the Clavey's banks throughout their childhood. These personal stories are made public and assumed to have a public (not simply private) value because of the general legitimacy made possible by this order of worth based on locality and tradition.

Another comparative difference in the ways local attachments are valued and made general are the references to the good of protecting one's personal home or "backyard," which reveals divergent ideas about ownership, property, and individuality between the United States and France. In the United States the defense of one's property is strongly stated and tied to an individual identity, and it rests on private ownership and property rights (which also sustain market worth) (Perin, 1988). The acronym NIMBY ("Not In My Backyard") is first a rejection of any intrusion on personal property but also has a broader usage as a rejection by a community of an unwanted development or an environmental health risk.[38] Clearly, though, NIMBY is a powerful conceptual tool and motivating force for United States activists. For example, Marty McDonnell describes his intense involvement with the opposition coalition in these NIMBY terms: "We had a personal interest in it, this is our backyard . . .

This is my home. You know people will pick up guns and defend their home . . . I will go to the wall [for] my backyard." He determines what he will fight for, then, based partly on locality, partly on a notion of individual possession or even property – "*my* backyard" – that is not found in similar justifications in France. In France the attachment of a human to property is, in law, dealt with in this liberal way (the individual is the owner of property and locus of privacy), but there is also a different sense of a shared attachment to the land within a local community, particularly in agricultural areas, where local heritage and integration of people with the land are the issues, not private individual ownership. In the United States, where individualism is strongly defended even at a community level (Bellah et al. 1985; Varenne 1977), often in opposition to federal (or other non-local) intervention, it appears more legitimate for someone to argue on the basis of private ownership or NIMBY. Whereas in France, there appears to be a greater tendency to appeal to values more general than NIMBY such as tradition, *la patrie* (Wiley 1974), or nationalism (see Brubaker 1992, on the evolution of a national conception of "citizenship" in France); for example, saying "my backyard" is part of "our" local or national heritage.[39]

Justifications based on inspiration and emotion ["inspiration" worth]

A less obvious but often quite significant category of justifications involve judgments based on inspiration, passion, and emotion, and often point to the singularity or creativity of a person, object, or action which is the source of inspiration. The "proof" for inspiration justifications is the display of an emotion, or otherwise showing that one is moved or overwhelmed or awed. Although these sorts of arguments often lead to the critique that they are unable to be discussed or challenged as general (more than personal) claims, and that they are irrational or unreasonable, we find that emotionally inspired (or inspiring) gestures and claims can be publicly displayed, commonly evaluated, and criticized within a specific order of worth.[40] They can be the proof of some valuable attachment beyond mere personal feelings, of people making the step from personal passion to a kind of generalized argument where inspiration is valued as a common good.

In both the Somport and Clavey cases participants make crucial moves from inspiration arguments to environmental arguments in terms of an emotional or even spiritual attachment to nature. In the French case, the expression of inspiration arguments are best illustrated through the actions and rhetoric of the main opposition figure, Eric Pétetin. Pétetin is

often portrayed in quasi-religious terms, e.g. as "an English preacher ser-
monizing alone in the desert" who presumably preaches his opposition
message from a spiritual inspiration.[41] Pétetin gives impassioned
speeches with artistic flair and gestures; he lives in an abandoned railroad
car in the Valley and, in a similarly avant-garde way, has transformed the
derelict railway station into a café to welcome hip, non-touristy travelers.
The radical singer-songwriter Renaud also protests against the project
from an emotional or aesthetic standpoint: "The Aspe Valley is really one
of the most grand landscapes, one of the most overwhelming that I have
had the privilege of seeing." There is also a local shepherd, Labarère, who
has been an active opponent of the project and who writes poems in the
native dialect of Béarnais extolling the beauty of his land. One of his
poems reads: "The Bedous peaks, what a grandiose place / Hidden in the
heights of the Aspe Valley / Two giants watch over it, the Audà and the
Soperet / Two stone giants clothed in red / Who, since eternity, look at one
another like a couple in love." Another quote from Pétetin reveals the
inspirational value placed on the "harmony" of man and nature: "The
Aspe Valley is a stone cathedral, unique in the world. Because it is narrow
and winding, it is impossible to build anything without destroying its
balance and its beauty and harmony."

In the Clavey case, inspiration arguments almost always relate to the
sacred value of nature and many in the United States talk about the highly
emotional, even spiritual experience they have in the wilderness of the
Clavey area. People refer to the Clavey canyon as a special place evoking
personal tranquillity, and they talk about the transformative "feeling" of
being a mere human in the rugged wilderness of the area.[42] This is particularly true of the professional river rafters who became involved in the
opposition campaign (they spend more time physically near the Clavey
than anyone else), and of the members of the Me-Wuk tribe who attach
not simply an emotional but a religious importance to the Clavey canyon.
Finally, like Pétetin, Clavey activists refer to the natural "harmony" of
man and nature, an equilibrium that is beautiful and inspiring, that is
found in the remote canyon. Clearly the examples in this section from
both cases involve not merely inspiration justifications about the awe or
passion to be derived from nature, but also environmental or green justifications which imbue "nature" and "wilderness" with some measure of
inherent value beyond its effect on humans.

Justifications based on renown and public opinion ["renown" worth]

While all orders of justifications involve arguments designed to garner
public support, the standard for judgment and evaluation of arguments in

the other orders is not the extent of public knowledge or renown itself. There are arguments and evaluations, however, which do point to the importance of public knowledge for determining the worth of a cause. In the cases under review here, the mechanisms specifically designed for generating this valuable renown and fame are much more developed in the United States than in France, and arguments about the extent of public concern are more common in the United States There is even a sort of division of labor among the project opponents in the Clavey case so that one organization, the Tuolumne River Preservation Trust (TRPT), is primarily responsible for promoting and managing public knowledge about the dispute (on a state and national level). However, both cases involve attempts at gaining media attention or influencing the impressions of an audience who might not know the issues in-depth. More significantly, both cases involve denunciations of these sorts of "publicity" moves.

In the Clavey dispute, advocates for both sides had at their disposal a well-developed set of tools (used in political disputes of all sorts in the United States) for generating public and media attention, such as a fax network for press releases, slick bumper stickers (the opposition's read simply: "Save the Clavey"), guest editorials sent out to newspapers for consideration, slide shows, newsletters and mass mailings, endorsement campaigns and announcements, and a distinctly American form of pamphlet, the "alert." Interviews with key environmental leaders in the Clavey dispute reveal they were explicitly concerned with making the Clavey a well-known issue, particularly among environmentally minded citizens in San Francisco and nationwide, and among key elected officials such as national Democratic congressional representatives who might endorse the opposition campaign. TRPT worked with national environmental groups including American Rivers, which publishes an annual list of "The Ten Most Endangered Rivers" in the United States and generates a great deal of national media coverage. The head of TRPT, Johanna Thomas, said the national groups acted "kind of like a public relations firm for the river, because they had the ability to put out materials and reach a huge audience, much like advertisers do." This advertisement for the river then paid crucial dividends in the form of pressure on the dam proponents to recognize that not just the politicians were against the dam but also masses of people from throughout the state and nation, many of whom wrote letters to government calling for a halt to the project. She contends, "I think it was very threatening when [TID] saw that the Clavey was getting this kind of attention."

The denunciation of these publicity efforts by the dam proponents also suggests the relevance and power of opinion claims. Mills attempts to play down the national renown of the Clavey by pointing out that most of the people who wrote opposition letters were "outsiders" who would never see the river and had no "stake" in the dispute. He characterized them as professional adversaries of any dams, who for that reason should have no weight in local decision-making. Mills goes further to argue against judging the project in terms of opinion at all; he believes opinion evaluations are dangerous because opinion is so fickle and so easily manipulated by "public affairs gurus" and "spin doctors" who know how to "push buttons" on "whatever's popular right now." Another project supporter, Shirley Campbell, also acknowledged the importance of opinion on a local level. She helped start the wise use group TuCARE partly because she wanted to counter the loud publicity from the environmentalists. Thus, the Clavey dispute in the local area took on the appearance of a "public opinion war" because both sides effectively utilized the many tools available to them.

While public opinion is also at stake in the Somport case, the goal of generating media attention and public notoriety is less explicitly pursued by the participants, and the mechanisms for renown are much less developed. The famous singer of protest songs, Renaud, made headlines when he came out against the tunnel, and he has continued to make dramatic public statements denouncing the tunnel. Also, there has been quite a lot of national and international press coverage of the large protests against the project. But there has been some reaction against the press treatment of the project, partly because the press were considered "Parisian" and not local. Finally, the Minister of the Environment, Brice Lalonde, has been denounced by opponents as being overly concerned with managing his image through his prominent role in the dispute. The influential valley mayor, Jacques Lassalle, says in an interview: "Mr. Lalonde feels compelled to shine [*il a besoin de briller*] in Paris." Overall, opinion judgments have not played the same central role in the Somport dispute as they did in the Clavey.

Attracting the attention and influencing the opinion of politicians is another area of comparative difference. This is an essential goal of both sides of the Clavey conflict, and both sides were active in lobbying both directly and indirectly. The opposition coalitions actively sought the endorsement of key legislators, and even took many legislators on rafting trips with the goal of letting them personally "experience" the Clavey. Much attention was given by the media to a visit by Senator Barbara Boxer to the region, when she came out against the dam. Again, the denunciations of these renown tactics also reveal the significance of public attention in contributing to the fate of the project. Shirley Campbell and other local dam supporters saw Senator Boxer's public endorsement as a "purely political" ploy to win her votes by portraying her as the champion of everyday local folk and environmental awareness.[43] Activists in the Clavey case even developed ingenious methods for informing the public and prompting "ordinary citizens" to write to their legislators. For example, rafting companies active in fighting the dam had their guides talk to the customers about the dispute and (when they felt they had convinced them) ask them to write letters to their representatives and to FERC. John Mills denounced this tactic also; he even sent in "spies" to take the rafting trip and report back on what the other side was telling the public.

Lobbying is a much less common activity of either side in the Somport case, and this is partly due to the fact that in France there are fewer direct budgetary or other ties between legislators and specific agencies like the Ministry of Environment[44]. But also the idea of lobbying – trying to influence legislators outside of public settings or even publicly announcing endorsements of any one side in the dispute – would rarely be considered legitimate in France, while it is often (but not always) considered a legitimate tactic in the United States[45] An example of the denunciation of lobbying in France comes from someone (quoted in an English-language news report) who believes lobbying had an influence in the French case: "It is incredible that as a consequence of the pro-road lobby, comprised of lorry drivers, public works construction companies, and local politicians, work has begun on building a tunnel like this without having made a complete study of the project."

Justifications based on "green-ness" and environmentalism ["green" worth]

Many examples in previous sections refer to nature or the environment within an evaluation based on non-environmental justifications and principles, e.g. when nature is marketed as a tourist attraction. Other examples move to the next level: when environmental justifications, based on principles of what might be called "green-ness" (as described below), are presented for their own sake or are combined with other sorts of justifications, e.g. when mitigations to infrastructure plans are proposed to make them more environmentally sensitive.[46] These types of justifications – which might add a new "order of worth" to the Boltanski and Thévenot (1991) scheme (see Latour 1995; Lafaye and Thévenot 1993; Barbier 1992) – have become more refined and widespread since the rise of the global environmental movement in the past few decades, but they also have important historical and cultural precursors (Oelschlaeger 1991; Nash 1982; Moscovici 1977; Collingwood 1945).

Actions or entities are worthy, with regard to this "green" justification, when they support or reflect the principles of environmentalism or "green-ness", e.g. clean/non-polluting, renewable, recyclable, sustainable, and in harmony with nature. Justifications based on environmentalism consider the general good of humanity to be advanced through a sensitivity to environmental issues and consequences, protection of wilderness, stewardship of environmental resources, and cultivation of various attachments to nature, the land, or the wild. Strictly green arguments, beyond the level of integrating the environment into other sorts of non-green justifications, posit a unique type of dependency which assumes more than simply a spatial interaction of humanity with the natural world, but also a temporal extension of humanity by way of an implicit or explicit reference to future generations (Goodwin 1992; Dobson 1990; Larrère 1997; Larrère and Larrère 1997; Naess and Rothenberg 1989; Taylor 1986). The green order of worth is revealed in distinctly "green" qualifications, such as the "health" of trout in the Clavey River valued as something that is good for humanity, which are not considered relevant in any other order. At a further level, some environmental evaluations depart from the political and moral requirements which are shared by all orders of worth – where common humanity is the group of reference for the evaluation – and propose an extension of the "community" of reference to include non-human entities (a move to "ecocentrism" rather than "anthropocentrism"; see, for example, Eckersley 1996; Devall and Sessions 1985; Stone 1974).

The subsections which follow compare the expression and frequency of a number of green or environmental arguments found in the comparative survey, and explore the different modes of the relation of humans and the environment revealed by these arguments.[47]

Unique and endangered   Perhaps the greatest similarity between the two cases is the extent and nature of arguments about the uniqueness or singularity of the natural places in dispute, and about the threat to "endangered species" (plant and animal) posed by the projects. In the Clavey case, uniqueness arguments are perhaps the most prevalent environmental justifications offered by dam opponents. There are several senses in which the river is characterized as a unique natural place: in terms of being the "last" undammed river in the ecosystem, in terms of its specific role in local heritage and its historical importance, in terms of being a "rare" ecosystem not found elsewhere and in terms of the number of endangered species which live in the ecosystem. The environmentalists who opposed the dam on the Clavey were constantly referring to a long list they compiled of all the "officially threatened or endangered" plant and animal species, such as the rare "wild trout," found within the Clavey canyon and presumably further endangered by the project.[48] The other side for their part constantly tried to refute this justification, either by denying the danger to these species or proposing to mitigate for any potential harm (but never explicitly by denying the importance of protecting endangered species).[49]

Arguments in the Somport controversy focus on the singularity of the Aspe Valley and the scarcity and uniqueness of the animals in the area. Evaluations of the uniqueness of the valley are not so much concerned with it being the last wild place of a certain type, but rather concern the singularity of the entire "landscape" of the valley, including the animal and human inhabitants and the special integration between the people and land found there. The bears became a famous symbol of the project opposition – they were described as the "last of their kind" and "endangered," and were considered deserving of protection because they had lived in the area for a long time (a somewhat different characterization to the legal sense of "endangered species" in the United States).[50] The attachment to the Pyrenean bear is understandable because it holds a special place of honor in this region – it plays a central role in local customs such as carnivals, and it was a feared threat to humans, particularly farmers and shepherds, but also the prized prey of local bear-hunting heroes. An exhibition on the bears in the valley town of Accous tells the "fabulous story of a mythical animal." The use of the bear as a symbol attractive to the media has also been denounced by project supporters. In addition to the bears, other animals were put forward as endangered by the project, including a unique sort of amphibious mole.

Untouched wilderness   In the Clavey case, there are numerous arguments about keeping the Clavey "free-flowing," "untouched," "pristine," and "the way it was long before humans arrived." These claims became crucial points of contention and debate, and were given explicit consideration in the decision-making by the government agencies involved – e.g. the Forest Service rated the river partly on its value as an undisturbed habitat. Dam proponent John Mills spent much of his time attempting to disprove the claims that the Clavey is "free-flowing" and "untouched" – for ewample, he argues there have been non-wild, hatchery trout released into the river, and that there are small dams near the headwaters of the river.

When used by environmentalists, however, these arguments generally mean "untouched by development" rather than untouched by man at all. While they are accused by Mills and others of taking a "preservationist" or deep ecological stance that wilderness should be locked up and unused by any humans, many dam opponents making these "pristine" arguments are in fact fisherman, hunters, and rafters who enjoy "using" the "untouched" Clavey. So these green arguments in the United States about pristine wilderness imply a view of the relation of humans and nature whereby humans can get great benefit from "participating in," "experiencing," or "struggling against" wilderness (or preserving untouched wilderness for others in the present or future to experience). So wilderness is valued (by dam opponents) because of its non-human qualities, but the pristine quality of wilderness is used as a justification (against building the dam) because pristine wilderness has a benefit for humanity.[51]

In France, the notion of a "sublime" and "wild" nature is commonly found in the Somport dispute, as in the Clavey dispute.[52] Renaud provides a nice example of this view: "If you touch the Aspe Valley, if you want to make it more accessible, if you give it over to concrete and trucks, it would be a crime against beauty, an acid facelift of the noble visage of a distinguished old lady." However, the relation of man and the wild is not described in terms of a struggle so much as in the United States, and there is less attention to the "experience" of wilderness. In France the idea of "domesticated nature" is not necessarily set against "untouched wilderness" as in the United States[53] While the Clavey debate often concerns separating what is to be untouched and what is not, this is not always the case in the Somport debate, and there are instead connections made between the domestic life of the valley and its natural life. For example, one reason offered against the road-tunnel project was, "The survival of the large Pyrenean scavenger birds depends on the perennial continuation of traditional practices such as mountain transhumance."

The "wilderness industries" in the United States are more highly developed commercial enterprises than in France. These industries explicitly market a struggle of man against the wild and an escape from domestic life, and in the Clavey dispute they are a primary source of the environmental arguments against the dam. In France, the tourist activities oriented toward nature were not, until recently, nearly as heavily equipped and are not geared toward a "struggle" of man against the wild, but rather a contemplation of the landscape by man. We can distinguish in the arguments made by wilderness industries between explicit green arguments – wilderness experiences are good for people – and the compromise of these arguments with market concerns, i.e. selling this experience to tourists.

Wild places as heritage and habitat   In the earlier section dedicated to justifications based on tradition, we saw how evaluations of the projects based on "*patrimoine*" or "heritage" sometimes refer to "green" attachments to a place – "inhabiting" a wild or natural place. The green characterization of "natural" heritage is particularly oriented toward future generations. In the Clavey case, for example, dam opponents made the arguments that wild places like the Clavey must be preserved because they have been entrusted to our stewardship by past generations and we must pass them on the future generations[54]. Other times, these sorts of heritage arguments are also careful combinations of justifications based on tradition or locality ("domestic") and green justifications. For example, there are similar arguments in both cases about the value of being attached for a long time to a land that has been passed down through several generations of one's family, and these are then combined with arguments about the natural value of the land and the need to preserve it for the future. The Clavey activist Wally Anker combines arguments in this way by saying first that the Clavey is "the only place I know that is the same today as it was during the Ice Age," then saying that his family has lived near the Clavey for generations, and he wants to preserve the Clavey so his grandchildren can have the same attachment to it.

Animals can of course be included in these evaluations of wild places as part of our heritage, but animals have their own attachment to the wild place in terms of their "habitat," an attachment which environmentalism wants to preserve as part of "heritage." This raises the problem of arranging for "cohabitation" of humans and animals in making green arguments. This cohabitation problem is found in both cases, but is perhaps more central in France, where the connection between wild nature and domesticated nature has been built up over time. A voluntary association in the Aspe Valley, FIEP, is in fact entirely dedicated to promoting harmonious "cohabitation," particularly by working to "let shepherds and bears live together in the Pyrenees." FIEP arranged for helicopter transportation of supplies to shepherds in their mountain outposts as a way to avoid building new roads that would threaten bear habitats, while still retaining the shepherds' way of life. They promoted numerous mitigation measures such as wildlife road passages to allow for cohabitation. They emphasized the integration of valley habitats: "The bear is an integrator. We cannot take care of bears without taking care of the forest or the pastures, because the bears are demanding." The problem of cohabitation of humans and animals is also used in an ironic way by the prominent project supporter, Jacques Lassalle, who at one point states his goal as having "both genuinely wild bears and genuine humans." He contrasts wild bears with non-wild bears put in zoos, and compares this to the contrast between genuine humans and non-genuine humans who are forced by environmental restrictions to live in a "reservation of humans like a reservation of Indians" – in this way he uses cohabitation ironically as a defense of the project and at the same time denounces his opponent, the "Indian" Eric Pétetin, who often identifies himself with the native Indian ideal of living in harmony with the land.

Native "Indian" attachments to sites Pétetin's identification with the native American "Indians" makes an ideal of the intimate connections of native Indians to their culturally significant sites. Pétetin often dresses up using some symbols of American Indian costumes like a feather in his hair, and holds up Indian culture as an exemplar of a sustainable and harmonious relationship with the land – this attachment is then used as a green justification for his position against the Somport project (although there is also a significant element of inspiration justification). Pétetin says, "The Indian culture is a culture shared by men and women who lived in harmony with nature all year around, without spoiling it, while using its richness, while loving it, while knowing it." Pétetin's reference to the "Indian" orientation to nature points to the important overlap between the native political and moral viewpoint, which emphasizes the integration and dependency of humans with non-human entities, and the viewpoint of modern environmental politics which emphasizes this dependency also.

In the Clavey case, the involvement of the Me-Wuk Indian tribe in the controversy meant there was a more direct consideration of Indian attachments to their land in this case. The tribal member most active in the Clavey controversy is a grandmother named Phyllis Harness, who expressed her attachment to the Clavey in many ways, including the fact that her grandson is named "Clavey." One of her primary self-descriptions is as a "gatherer" – one who collects plants, particularly mushrooms, from the ancestral lands which surround the Clavey – and she often describes her gathering as a ritual, "sacred" cultural practice (something her elders taught her).[55] The sacredness of her attachment to this place is in some ways "proved" only through being present in the place, and she prizes the experience of being near the Clavey. This sort of presence is an intimate attachment to the natural place that Phyllis compares to the connections of animals to specific locales or habitats: she compares the Me-Wuk historical migrations through the Clavey canyon with the migratory routes of a particular deer herd.

The recognition of the power of this sort of native attachment to the Clavey site as a general good (and so as a possible justification for or against the dam) was revealed in the rigorous competing attempts by both sides in the dispute to gain the endorsement of the Me-Wuk tribe. The spokeswoman for the tribe originally endorsed the project (without an official tribal vote) after project supporters promised that the tribe could operate campgrounds on the dam's reservoir. When the rest of the tribe found out about this, however, Harness and others vigorously objected and eventually passed a tribal resolution against the dam. Thereafter the Me-Wuk were often touted by the opposition campaign as key opponents of the project. The courting of the Me-Wuk tribe's endorsement was clearly important both because of its political appeal (politicians are known to be sensitive to "native" issues), and because their attachment to the land makes them the most legitimate "spokespersons for the land."

Deep ecology   A particular variant of "green" standards of evaluation known as "deep ecology" has been developed, primarily in the United States but initially in Europe (Naess and Rothenberg 1989; Devall and Sessions 1985; Lovelock 1979), which makes a very important move away from the common moral requirements found in the other types of justification we have been considering. The justifications – environmental or other types – discussed so far refer to the good of humanity as the primary basis for assigning value: the goal is "good for everyone." But in the deep ecology philosophy and movement, the community of "everyone" that is the basis for evaluations is extended beyond the human community to include the good of non-human natural entities (e.g. trees, animals); they refer to this as a shift from "anthropocentrism" to "ecocentrism."[56] Green arguments based on a deep ecology perspective value a healthy environment or the preservation of species not because of their benefits for humanity, but for their own sake, for the benefit of the integrated ecosystem (which includes humans) itself.[57]

Deep ecology arguments are explicitly made only rarely in the Clavey case; they are never made seriously in the Somport case, but there are a couple instances when they are used sarcastically. One example from the Clavey case is a statement made by the rafting company owner with a deeply personal connection to the river, Marty McDonnell. In talking about reasons to preserve the river, he discounts the human definition of a clean environment and privileges the animal's concerns in determining what's really important: "Throwing a beer can out the window doesn't really harm the health [of the environment]. It may look bad, but I'm sure that the deer that walks by could care less if he sees a beer can on the side of the road or not. It offends my sense of natural order, but that's just a human thing."

In the Somport case, there are a couple of instances where deep ecological arguments are used sarcastically, mocking the radical environmental notion that the good of animals on their own should be the criteria of worth or evaluation. One instance of this is a letter to the editor of an important paper in the Pyrenees region which is in fact a parody of efforts to protect the bears. The author mentions all the money to be spent on

Somport mitigation measures such as bear-ducts and bridges, and he pro-poses to spend as much money to protect a species of glow-worm from devastation by the road and tunnel. He ironically praises the efforts of Americans to save species in peril (stranded whales rescued by an ice-breaker), by suggesting the construction of an underground tunnel for the worms to avoid the road is a similar but more modest effort of a less wealthy country. This parody is partly also a denunciation of the influence of "radical" American environmentalist views in the Somport controversy.

Conclusion

This detailed review and classification of the range of legitimate critiques and justifications in two environmental disputes adds precision to our understanding of the differences between French and American patterns of evaluation and constructions of what is generally good. We found com-parative discrepancies in the generality or scope of different types of eval-uations in each culture, in the ways that arguments were combined or "compromised" (in the sense of making different forms of evaluations compatible), and in which arguments were in tension with which others in each case.

Rather than finding that market evaluations were only – or more – important in the United States, we found more interesting and specific differences. Market evaluations were common in the United States and were often combined with other sorts of evaluations, often with "civic" arguments (see Chapter 1 in this volume) and also with "green" argu-ments (which is surprising, given the anti-capitalist tendency of some environmental movements). Market arguments for the project were also used in France, but primarily came from Brussels and were not endorsed at the local level, except in connection with contributions to "local devel-opment", in a combination with "domestic" arguments grounded on the value of locality. Claims based solely on the value of the free market were much more commonly criticized in France.

Arguments based on planning and technical competency evaluations ("industrial worth") were important in both countries and were employed in similar ways, particularly at the beginning of the disputes. The biggest difference was that in the United States, as with market crite-ria, there is a more developed and accepted combination of planning arguments with green arguments, particularly as embodied in the "wise use" movement for which there is no real equivalent in France.

Both cases also involved plenty of attention to civic equality and soli-darity as standards of judgment, but here the difference in application was significant. In France civic equality arguments were tightly bound with planning arguments (as the technocratic defense of the state and the role played by engineers would suggest). By contrast, in the United States equality judgments are more commonly tied to market judgments, making what in France would be considered an odd association between one's status as a free consumer or "user of nature" and one's status as a citizen with equal rights to access nature and wilderness (in opposition to élitist control of nature).

As would be expected in disputes involving local communities, we found the debate about local development and local heritage or "patrimony" ("domestic worth") to be of central concern in both countries. But there were interesting differences in the ways that local attachments were shaped and the models of community in which they were placed. In France the arguments were oriented toward a defense of a shared local "patrimony" and local tradition, while in the United States the arguments tended to be oriented toward a defense of a "backyard" (although not always). Even though the American political trope of the "backyard" can be extended to include the collective "backyard" of a community, the model is still based on a private property model, whereas the French notion of patrimony is more general and explicitly not private.

Both cases involved similar wars over "public opinion," and there were very similar denunciations of opinion-seeking. However, the tools for and attention to generating media renown or publicity are more developed in the United States, particularly as a preferred means of influencing public officials and of making a connection, expressed by the demonstrations of "majority" support, with a civic expression of a collective will – this sort of civic expression is not tied to opinion so much in France.

Finally, we found significant evidence in both cases for recognizing a distinct category of generalized justifications based on "green" or environmental evaluations. For example, the protection of "endangered species," reverence for the natural beauty and harmony of the land, and especially for the harmonious attachment to the land of "natives," were important as arguments against the projects in both countries. However, in the United States there were more arguments relating to "wilderness," and even a whole well-developed "wilderness industry," based on the notion of humans struggling against a "pristine" wilderness that stands outside man, while in France there is a stronger connection of the domesticated life (and patrimony) of the valley with the wild life of the valley.[58] So the issue of the "cohabitation" of humans and animals is much more central in France (where the bears are seen as long-time inhabitants of the valley alongside the shepherds and valley folk) than in the United States (where the fish are also long-time inhabitants, but are valued for their "wild" habitation and not their cohabitation with humans).

The differences we discovered in our comparative analysis are grounded in (and help us specify) the political culture and traditions of France and the United States. For example, we found some evidence for the standard comparative finding of the "classical liberal" orientation of American political thought versus the "republican" orientation of French political thought, but we showed how these orientations are manifested in complex patterns of justification in each case (e.g. the various compromises of market evaluations with other types in the United States). To specify our understanding further, we need to situate the types and patterns of evaluations that we have identified here within a broader perspective by considering the "strategy" of argumentation displayed by the disputants, and by comparing the conceptual models employed in each culture for connecting the actors' "interests" with some configuration of the "common good" or some vision of "community." We address these tasks in the next chapter.

Notes

In addition to the NSF-CNRS grant providing for the meetings between American and French researchers involved in the project, the fieldwork on the Somport case (and part of the Clavey fieldwork) was covered by a grant from the Ministry of Environment to the International Institute of Paris – La Défense. The fieldwork and research expenses for the Clavey case were covered primarily by a dissertation grant from the Nonprofit Sector Research Fund of the Aspen Institute, and by small grants from the Center of Domestic and Comparative Policy Studies at Princeton University. Other presentations of the research include: (in French) Thévenot 1996b, d, e; Thévenot and Germe 1996 (involving a game based on the French case); (in English) Moody 1999, Thévenot 2000b. We wish to thank for their helpful comments Michèle Lamont, James Jasper, Peter Meyers, Eric Doidy, and all the members of our working group.

1 The Tuolumne was dammed upstream of the Clavey confluence long ago to create Hetch-Hetchy Reservoir and provide a good portion of the drinking water and power supplies for the distant metropolis of San Francisco.

2 Translations of French quotes from the Somport case used in Chapters 9 and 10 are the authors'. At times the original French word or phrase is also given for statements that convey a particular meaning in French that is lost or awkward when translated.

3 "Setting" or context might include such factors as real or imagined audience, objects, place, history, past or present or planned relations of people involved, political and national climate, etc. We pay particular attention to instances

when the participants themselves point to a particular feature of the context as relevant.

4 We are also indebted to Olivier Soubeyran (Université de Pau) for giving access to the unpublished results of research he carried out with Véronique Barbier.

5 Johanna Thomas generously opened and copied the Trust's files when requested, and Mr. Anker provided full, unsupervised access to his box of materials, which yielded an extensive documentary record of the dispute. Anker's files are now located in the Water Resources Center Archives in Berkeley, California.

6 For a short presentation in English, see Boltanski and Thévenot 1999. While we started from this pre-developed set of general categories, we maintained an open empirical perspective which actively looked for variations in the frequency and type of arguments in the two countries, including the possibility that some category of justifications might be entirely absent in one or the other country. This led us to identify and analyze significant differences and second-order elaborations of the justification types rather than merely confirm the existence of the categories.

7 Each order of worth has been "built" historically to address public problems through an order that ranks people or things while also maintaining equal human dignity, and each derives its legitimacy as a basis for evaluation from this (e.g. a eugenic order that ranked people based on genetic qualities would not meet this requirement of common humanity and would not address the need for justice). See Boltanski and Thévenot 1991 for a precise analysis of the shared specifications and matrix of justification common to all orders. For a comparison of this analytical framework to theories of justice (Rawls and Walzer, in particular), see Thévenot 1992b, 1996a. For a general perspective on justification and evaluation, see Chapter 1 in this volume.

8 While our approach benefits from ethnomethodological or other research on "accounts" (Orbuch 1997; Mills 1940), our analysis seeks a more systematic treatment of modes of evaluation beyond situational context. Instead of analyzing the consistency of the process of making accounts under situational constraints, we consider the cross-situational constraints imposed by the fact that one is attempting to produce a generalized argument and to refer to a certain extra-situational value or justification. Instead of considering all claims as only locally valid, we consider the different ways to make a claim generally valid.

9 Reality may be engaged in the proof of a generalized justification in many ways, e.g. presented as a chart or table of statistics, embodied in a highly recognizable sign, or pointed to in terms of lived experience or displayed emotion. Following Latour's (1987) and Callon's (1986b) seminal work on the "enrollment of non-human entities," Boltanski and Thévenot (1991) deviate from them in highlighting the plurality of ways this association is made, in relation to orders of evaluation, and the critical tension or compromises that result from this plurality. John Law (1994) accounts for a plurality of "modes of ordering" within an actor-network perspective.

10 In an extension of the ordinary usages of the word "qualify," we use it to designate the characterizations which are intended to make people and things

general and relevant to public issues. On the "investments in forms" that are needed for such generalizations by means of standards, grades, criteria, customs, etc., see Thévenot 1984. On the relation with the ways facts need to be "qualified" in court to justify the enforcement of law, see Thévenot 1992a; on a comparison between these everyday "qualifications" and the construction of artificial "moral entities" in law, see Thévenot 2000b.

11 This process of qualifying relates to what Boltanski and Thévenot (1991) call putting the argument to a "test." A "test" in this sense is a creative and dynamic process of demonstrating what is relevant in a particular situation (and de-emphasizing or ignoring what is not relevant), and attributing "worth" to the relevant entities.

12 The orders of worth taken into account in the regime of justification do not encompass all possible kinds of evaluation, as the eugenics example given in n. 7 above suggests. For a short presentation of the theoretical and empirical agenda of this research orientation, and commentary on its position within on-going debates, see Thévenot 1995c. For a discussion, see Dodier 1993a.

13 Our approach to argumentation is different from the tradition of "Rhetoric" practiced and studied since Aristotle and the Sophists, revisited in the "new rhetoric" (Perelman and Olbrechts-Tyteca 1988) and continued in recent work (Hirschman 1991; Billig 1987; Simons et al. 1985). Perelman and Olbrechts-Tyteca updated and refined this classical approach by arguing rhetoric is more than simply manipulating opinion, but is part of understanding reasoning and reasonableness more generally. However, they are concerned only with discursive evidence and not with the technique of pointing to the real world or to objects. On the relations between rhetoric, justice and justification, see Thévenot 1996a.

14 The notions of "frame resonance" and "alignment process" account for variability in subjective meanings among a target audience and raise the issues of the credibility and ideological relevance to personal identities (Hunt, Benford, and Snow 1994; Snow et al. 1988).

15 Referring to Kenneth Burke's analysis of irreducible "God terms" (Burke 1969 [1945]), Jasper (1992) argues there are types of rhetoric which claim unquestionable grounding and are employed in rhetoric to stifle any critique. By contrast, Boltanski and Thévenot (1991) study orders of justification that involve an inevitable process of questioning within each of them, or in their mutual critical relationship. When the generalized rhetorical claims made within any order fail to be questioned, it leads to a sense of injustice. On the requirements of a third party evaluation for democratic debate, see Meyers 1989.

16 Both Habermas and Arendt carefully distinguish different types of human activities (e.g. Arendt delineates fine distinctions among labor, work, and action) and types of action (e.g. Habermas contrasts communicative action explicitly with instrumental action).

17 On the modes of generalization used to escape NIMBY in the French context, see Lolive 1997a, b. For a discussion of the challenges for democratic theory presented by NIMBY environmental disputes, see Press 1994.

18 For attempts to specify these general characterizations see Bellah et al. 1985 on the United States; Brubaker 1992 on France; and Lamont 1992 on both.

19 See Table 9.1 for a schematic summary of the different orders of worth and types of justification.

20 Recent work in economic sociology (e.g. DiMaggio 1994; Zelizer 1994) argues that markets and a market orientation are socially constructed and embedded in social networks and cultural norms. Along these lines, our aim is to consider how the market can be used as a generalized argument in different contexts and is combined or articulated with other sorts of general arguments in the two countries.

21 There is no competition for the production of the road and tunnel or discussion of it as the "cheapest" alternative, and the service provided by the project is only considered as a means to improving competition (or lowering prices) rather than the object of competition itself.

22 James Jasper (personal communication) draws a parallel with the way arguments about high costs eventually stopped the construction of nuclear plants in the United States. He also observes that "ratepayers" differ from other "customers" because the rates charged by utilities (as "natural monopolies") are set by public utility commissions. So the only way of negotiating with their electric utility is by organizing politically, without the possibility of switching brands or boycotting.

23 To speak of natural areas as "tourist sites," as is done in both France and the United States, is to transform nature into "goods and services" which qualify for market justifications.

24 In French the term *"voie de communication"* – translated here as "transportation networks" – actually implies a broader sense of the connection between the transportation of goods and the possibility for communication between cultures or communities. The same official makes this connection explicitly when he says, "We realized that we had a culture which made us distinctive while allowing for communication with the entire world."

25 This distinction is made explicitly by some of the disputants in our cases. John Mills, a principal dam proponent in the Clavey case, argues against focusing on short-term profitability (market) and for evaluating the project as a long-term, reasonably planned investment. Electric utilities were traditionally run by engineers, and it is only recently that they have adopted this sort of more market-oriented thinking. The tension between short-term market evaluations and long-term "industrial" evaluations is a well-developed subject in economics, and the dominance of the short term over long-term evaluations is seen as a recurrent problem in market economies.

26 In defending the dam in these terms, TID reflects what has been called the "engineering ethos" (Espeland 1998) that guided most dam-building projects throughout American history (see Worster 1985). Paterson's (1989) history of TID demonstrates that the District was historically one of the greatest champions of this ethos. (A similar ethos is common in French history, but tied more directly to the national level and the state-owned Electricité de France or the national railways company SNCF (Dobbin 1994).)

27 Environmentalists, in turn, challenge the wise use movement as merely a grassroots façade for large resource extraction industries who seek to exploit and over-use resources, not use them "wisely."

28 These claims might be seen as compromises between orders of justification also, since both technical planning and environmental justifications focus attention on the long-term future. However, although these two types of justifications are temporally oriented toward the future, which helps support the combinations of the two, they propose different ways of building that future – in "industrial worth," the future is supported by the regularities of technical investments while in "green worth" the future is supported by ensuing human generations and ecological evolution.

29 Mills is an interesting case study in the art of making strategic connections between types of justifications. He clearly prefers to operate in the realm of "industrial" judgments, and sets up the dam project as the product of rational and scientifically sound planning while characterizing its detractors as unscientific and unconcerned with the long-term needs of the public. However, he also makes much of the fact that hydropower is a "clean, renewable source of energy" in order to make connections with green concerns.

30 Struggling against the lack of precision in the contemporary usage of the term "civil society," Alexander (1997) conceptualizes a "solidary sphere" of "universalizing social solidarity" which "transcends particular commitments, narrow loyalties and sectarian interests" and where protests against injustice become social movements. In such a definition, civil society is deeply grounded in this order of worth that Boltanski and Thévenot (1991) identify as "civic."

31 See also the penultimate section of Chapter 1 above on "The relative salience of some criteria of evaluation and how they are brought together.".

32 Certain engagements in protests and demonstrations may also qualify for the worth of "inspiration" which values "emotional" elements (see section on this order below), as passionate or creative expressions of outrage. Fortunately for our comparison, the rafting company owner and anti-Clavey dam activist Marty McDonnell happened to witness a protest against the Somport project while visiting the Pyrenees. He recalled the protest as "incredible" and "one of the most impressive, emotional demonstrations I'd ever seen," while this same protest was viewed, in France, as a nearly standard expression of solidarity to the cause.

33 See Chapter 5 above; see also similar connections for artworks in Chapter 7.

34 This later argument reveals a tension concurrent with the acknowledged benefits of civic access to nature: use can quickly become overuse, and too much human access can "disturb the wilderness." This problem is often illustrated by reference to the heavily visited Yosemite National Park near the Clavey. The Me-Wuk tribal member most active in the Clavey campaign, Phyllis Harness, nicely illustrates this tension when discussing the possible increased use of the Clavey: "I'm kind of bitter for having to give up Yosemite [their ancient habitat: Godfrey 1977 (1941)], and to see it the way it is now. But, I mean, that's progress." Later she acknowledges that moderate human use is the ideal because she wants people to be able to see the "breathtaking" beauty of the area, rather than leave it completely "untouched."

35 For a French-German comparison of the "*patrimonialisation*" of nature, see Trom 1997.

36 On the concept of *habiter* [inhabit] and its political implications, see Abel
    1995; Berque 1986, 1996; Bréviglieri 1998. On the possible politicization of
    attachment to the earth into conservative and Nazi politics, see Ferry 1992;
    Alphandery et al. 1991.
37 Similarly, the rancher Ian McMillan became a powerful symbol of opposition
    to the Diablo Canyon nuclear power plant in California (Jasper 1997, chap.
    5). For an illustration of the depth of attachment to a local or "family river"
    that can result from trout fishing, see Norman Maclean's passionate account
    in *A River Runs Through It* (1976).
38 See Walsh et al. 1997; Gould et al. 1996; Williams and Matheny 1995;
    Mazmanian and Morell 1994; Press, 1994; Freudenberg and Steinsapir 1992;
    Piller 1991.
39 Of course, this sort of generalization happens in the United States also –
    NIMBY groups often try to argue a particular development should not be in
    anyone's backyard (see Williams and Matheny 1995, on "NIABY") – and
    there is certainly a great deal of reverence for local ties and celebration of local
    community in the United States (Fischer 1991). But there seems to be more
    of a standing imperative to generalize to locality or tradition justifications in
    France. For an example of such an extension, see the autobiographical
    account, titled *Saint Concrete: A War Diary*, of one person's singular and
    ardent fight in France against the "concrete builders" who "ruined our pas-
    tures and our forests, who raped our sacred land" (Antigona 1995).
40 For approaches to studying social movements and protest which take emo-
    tions seriously, showing how emotions are part of almost every collective
    action and do not make that action irrational as some critics claim, see
    Goodwin 1997; Jasper 1997; Emirbayer and Goodwin 1996; Jasper and
    Nelkin 1992.
41 In his discussion of Pétetin's activism, Eric Doidy (1997) mentions that, as a
    student, Pétetin wrote a paper on "Faith and Activism [*l'engagement*]."
42 In his survey of American Christian ethical codes and practices, Stephen Hart
    (1992) describes the decisive religious experience of a man facing the sublime
    of an inspired nature: attending a camp meeting as a youth, he experienced an
    intense storm that blew the tents down. However, inspiration worth does not
    always coincide with religious engagement. There can be non-religious
    expressions of inspiration in a creative experience, whether artistic or entre-
    preneurial. There can also be kinds of religious engagement which relate not
    to inspiration, but rather to other orders of worth. Hart shows that Christian
    faith can lead in the United States to other forms of evaluation which depart
    from inspiration and include a "civic" fight for equal rights and social welfare,
    or a "domestic" respect for authorities, sustaining paternalism and corpo-
    ratism.
43 Congress did control the funding of the agencies ruling on the Clavey (e.g. the
    Forest Service and FERC), so beyond the mere opinion benefits of getting
    political support there were other strategic concerns for lobbying.
44 By contrast, lobbying is very active at the level of the European Community
    (Mazey and Richardson 1993).
45 There are quite different traditions and definitions of "lobbying" in the two
    countries, and different conceptions of what is legitimate contact between

legislators and citizens. For instance, in the United States citizen letter-writing is often considered a legitimate form of lobbying alongside more traditional "interest group" lobbying, whereas in France citizen-letter writing is directly opposed to interest lobbying by corporations or other groups. In both countries, much private influence exerted (or attempted) on politicians take place outside the public realm that we focus on here.

46 The difference between these two levels of environmental reference can be seen clearly when we compare two sorts of justifications of hydropower projects in the Clavey case. In one instance, hydropower is seen as a way to bring nature in as another "resource" to be "developed" – a justification based solely on planning and technical efficiency criteria – while in another instance, hydropower is seen as a "clean and renewable" energy source: a combination of planning and efficiency justifications with environmental justifications based on criteria like "renewability."

47 Various forms of valuing nature result from placing value on different types of "attachments" to nature which involve both material and emotional dependency (Thévenot 1996b). On the "social construction of nature" and the cultural, ideological, and rhetorical frameworks used to make sense of the natural environment, see Fine 1997; Eder 1996; Cronon 1995; Hannigan 1995; Douglas and Wildavsky 1982.

48 Both the state and national governments in the United States make "official" designations of individual species as either "threatened" or "endangered."

49 For example, a great deal of the debate over protecting rare species focused on whether the dam would hurt the populations of "wild trout" or whether the dam and its mitigation measures would actually be "better for the fish."

50 The threat of legal action and entanglements regarding endangered species protection in the United States makes these sorts of arguments more threatening than in France.

51 There is obviously a range of American conceptions of "wilderness" – and the relation of man and nature – which in fact were developed historically in direct comparison with the ideas about nature in Europe (Nash 1982). Wilderness is considered "terrible" and savage but also sublime with its "splendidly sculptured rocks and mountains" (Muir 1970 [1918]). The geological or biological features of wilderness are emphasized, and man's interaction with the wild is valued for its benefits to human health and well-being. The construction of the "wild" is also closely connected to the "frontier" mentality of the settlers of the western United States, who struggled to control the wilderness they found (Walton 1992; Turner 1920).

52 Mid nineteenth-century French painters developed the idea that a landscape "only has grandeur if it is uninhabited" (du Camp 1861, quoted in House 1995).

53 In La Nouvelle Héloise, Rousseau distinguishes between "wild nature" [nature sauvage] – "huge rocks" and "eternal torrents" – and "cultivated nature" [nature cultivée] – a "cheerful, peaceful [ranch] pasture" – but emphasizes the "striking blend" of the two one finds in the world: "houses found close to caverns" (Rousseau 1959, p. 77). He shows the integration of the two rather than the radical separation of them that we find in the "sublime" tradition (Pseudo-Longinus 1965; Burke 1990 [1757]) and German Romanticism, but

also in Chateaubriand (*"les tempêtes ne m'ont laissé souvent de table pour écrire que l'écueil de mon naufrage."*: Chateaubriand, *Mémoires d'outre-tombe* 1997 [1850], p. 64), and in the American exaltation of wilderness (e.g. Thoreau 1997 [1854]; Muir 1970 [1918]; see Nash 1982, Oelschlaeger 1991).

54 On the notion of "patrimony" in relation to the environment, see Godard 1990.

55 The tribal legends of the Yosemite Me-Wuk clearly reveal dependencies to places and animals (who are said to have gathered in a council to create man). See La Pena et al. 1993 [1981].

56 On the use of the notion of "community" in the history of ecology, and its resurgence in sociology (and to Robert Park in particular), see Acot 1988.

57 Deep ecology writer Gary Snyder (1985), for instance, urges people to see a country as a "natural biological region" governed by "parliaments or soviets" which include "the voices of trees, rivers, and animals, as well as human beings," so that "the world of nature penetrates the political meeting-chambers of mankind" (for a similar idea of a "parliament of things" which would represent non-human actors, see Latour 1995). Snyder argues that this is partly achieved with ritual dances (as we can learn from the Ainu people): "She who becomes a bear in the bear-dance for a brief while can speak for the bear." A French participant in a Somport demonstration acted the part of the bear in order to speak for the bear among other demonstrators. Similarly, an American participant in a public hearing on the Clavey wore an owl costume.

58 These differences in the nature and employment of "green" judgments can be partly explained by the different form and extent of environmental movements in the two countries, and their very different environmental histories, particularly the fact that the United States has (relatively recently from a French viewpoint) engaged in the development of a massive "frontier" in the West which left substantial marks on the political and cultural life of the entire nation (Walton 1992).

10 Comparing models of strategy, interests, and the public good in French and American environmental disputes

Michael Moody and Laurent Thévenot

To expand our comparative understanding of local disputes, political culture, community, and the public good in French and American cases of environmental dispute, we need to supplement the previous chapter's comparison of the content of argumentation and modes of justification in several ways. In this chapter, we compare facets of the same two cases of environmental disputes in France and the United States (presented at the beginning of Chapter 9) which illuminate further how the disputants approached the work of defending or opposing the projects.

Specifically, we compare the disputants' varying "strategic" practices of selecting and using arguments, and the models of coordination and the public good which inform their advocacy of their causes and "interests." We begin by considering in what sense the disputants in both cases were "strategic" (or were denounced as being strategic) in constructing arguments, switching between or combining arguments, or creating complex organizational arrangements to distribute or diversify the types of arguments and rhetoric each person or group employed. Then we explore in depth the conceptual models – either explicitly stated or implicitly displayed by the disputants in each case – of the connection between the actors' "interests" and some configuration of the "public good"[1] or some vision of "community," comparing how the use of these models varies within cases and between the two countries.

Analytical approach

The arguments and arrangements discussed in the previous chapter all involved some type of "justification" that required the political actors to demonstrate the general worth of their position by reference to a universal principle or collective good (e.g. equality, the free market, "green-ness") and occasionally by explicit "compromise" of their goals with the goals of others. This connection to a collective or general good is a necessity of public debate about public problems (even in cultures where self-interest is often a legitimate motive for action), yet we must also accept that public

273

involvement and justification are part of a larger sequence of actions, some of which involve instrumental or strategic decisions.[2] How do we account for the need to make public good justifications along with the need to make tactical moves and create an instrumental plan of action to advance one's particular goals? What models underlie the way political actors in the United States and France go about meeting these dual needs?

Empirical social science analyses of these tensions too often reduce the collective justification into the framework of the instrumental stance. They look for some pre-existing, particularistic "interest" which drives the manipulation of rhetoric and organizational arrangements, and they call into question the validity of the public good claims made by these strategic, interested political actors. The problem is often deferred to normative political and social theory. Our analysis, in contrast, seeks to open these dynamics of extending the scope of interest up to a comparative and empirical review. We do not claim to be able to answer definitively the question of whether all argumentation or action in these cases is, in fact, "really self-interested" or whether all public good claims are "true" or "honest."[3] Rather, we consider the boundaries of, for example, "special interest" versus "public interest" to be a point of contestation and cultural construction.

The common social science perspective on "strategic" political action and debate is limited by its assumption of the dominance of instrumentality and the objective nature of, and ultimate determination by, "interests" (for similar critiques, see Ringmar 1996; Mansbridge 1990; Wolfe 1989; Etzioni 1988). In particular, the perspective suggests that being strategic about argumentation means manipulating words or rhetoric merely to maximize and legitimize one's interested goals. Even studies that seek to take culture seriously in explaining collective action, such as the recent work on "framing" processes in social movements (e.g. McAdam et al. 1996; Benford 1993; Morris and Mueller 1992; Snow et al. 1986), tend to talk about rhetoric as the instrumental manipulation of language and arguments to mobilize support, without examining the practical constraints on this manipulation or its context.[4] Alternatives to this instrumental view emphasize the constraints on strategic choice of rhetoric of the structured, institutionalized set of "codes" or "themes" of political culture (Emirbayer and Goodwin 1996; Gamson 1992; Tarrow 1992; Alexander and Smith 1993), but this work occasionally under-emphasizes the instrumental and the possibilities for rhetorical and practical creativity (Jasper 1997) and fails to pay "serious attention to strategy" (Goodwin and Jasper 1999, p. 53).[5]

As in the last chapter, our approach considers rhetoric as partly creative and instrumental – e.g. in the choice or mixing of arguments to fit the situation – but also partly constrained in several ways, for example by the cultural repertoire, by the requirements of demonstrating relevant proof, and by adjusting the argument to the context. The repertoire of political culture – e.g. the available models of the public good and community – both constrains and enables the use of political rhetoric (Steinberg 1995, Williams 1995), as does the complex context for the discourse (Diani 1996; Ellingson 1995; Fine and Sandstrom 1993; Wuthnow 1987, 1992; Schudson 1989; Hilgartner and Bosk 1988).[6] Our perspective also builds on work that looks at the dynamics of "switching" between repertoires, "borrowing" logics, or mixing multiple arguments and accounts in "multi-vocal" ways (Stark forthcoming; Swidler forthcoming; Boltanski and Thévenot 1991; Friedland and Alford 1991; Burke 1989; Griswold 1987a, b).[7] We assess the varying capacities for "versatility" of particular actors or groups, while also acknowledging that this versatility is at times a source of denunciation in particular contexts.

We are not concerned just with how arguments are constructed or framed but also with comparing how arrangements are devised to develop and deploy these arguments in the two countries, and how this strategic deployment of arguments is practically coordinated and whether it is denounced for being too strategic. There is some work which analyzes how "discourse coalitions" (Hajer 1993, 1995) or "advocacy coalitions" (Sabatier and Jenkins-Smith 1993) share common beliefs and at times coordinate their argumentation, sometimes through a learning process (Gariepy et al. 1986). And there is also some important recent work that suggests cultural analyses of political action and debate should focus on the "practice" of various "political styles" in everyday activity, rather than merely analyzing rhetorics and values (Eliasoph 1998; Lichterman 1996).

Our approach also seeks to avoid the limiting assumptions that all action is oriented toward some enduring, objective "interest" or bundle of interests, and that the political process is dominated by groups only concerned with "special" or non-public interests. The assumption that all action is to be explained by reference to underlying interests has become, according to Ringmar (1996), the "modern orthodoxy" of social science, and there have been numerous attempts to challenge the strict interests view (e.g. critiques of materialist Marxism and of rational choice alike). While we cannot deny the fact that much action is guided by specific interests at some level, we seek to contribute to the development of a less narrow conception of interests, recognizing cultural or contextual differences in how interests are conceived and defined in different practical settings, and seeking to explain variability in the level and manner in which interests are attributed or conceived, especially cross-culturally.[8]

Much of the work on "interest groups" in political life seeks to explain how these groups go about trying to influence political outcomes, or how groups form alliances and maintain membership.[9] Other work seeks to defend or critique the system of "interest-group liberalism" or "pluralist democracy"[10] that is said to operate in the United States. While "faction" has long been seen as a central (but necessary) threat to civic life in the United States (Madison 1961 [1788]), it is important to recognize that conceiving of American political life as predominantly controlled by interests and interest groups (versus political parties only) is a relatively recent historical development (Clemens 1997), and that the degree to which interest groups are seen as influencing the political process is partly a cultural construction that varies considerably across national (Dobbin 1994; Brubaker 1992) and institutional (Espeland 1994, 1998; Minkhoff 1995) contexts. And there are significant conceptual as well as cultural differences in the way interests are defined across time and context (Connolly 1993 [1974]; Hirschman 1977, 1986). Building on this work, we see interests as an object of contention and variable interpretation rather than an objective unchanging motivation, as a grounded "stance" taken at various points in the debate and elaborated upon in ways that are open to empirical review.[11]

The most important extension and elaboration of interests for political actors is toward the level of the public good or public interest, since this move – extending the expression of one's interest beyond the particular to the general – is often necessary to give broad legitimacy to the group's claims (although at times the particular interest of an individual or a group is certainly legitimate on its own, especially in the United States).[12] Much of the scholarly work dealing with how particular interests relate to the public interest is normative debate about how to achieve an acceptable debate about, or conception of, the public good in an interested world. Not surprisingly, much of this work calls for a substantive, fully collective public good independent of the taint of any particular interests (e.g. Sandel 1996; Barber 1984). This normative goal is achieved through improved democratic deliberation focused on so-called "generalizable interests" (e.g. Habermas 1975, 1990; Dryzek 1990). While this normative and theoretical view is essential, it requires a more rigorous empirical grounding and a more complex view of interests and the public good, one which avoids what Lichterman (1996) has called the "see-saw" model, in which any emphasis on one personal or group interest necessarily detracts from emphasis on, or the possibility of, the public good, consensus, or community.

Influential empirical analyses on the subject see a lack of any adequate debate about the public good (Bellah et al. 1985, 1991), or conclude that the debate is merely competing attempts by special interest groups to portray their interest as *the* public interest (Madsen 1991). Other work, however, sees the debate about the public good as a continual project of the public sphere that cannot be simply reduced to posturing by particular interests (Mansbridge 1998; Calhoun 1998), and that must be investigated empirically rather than (only) normatively (Moody 2000).[13] As Calhoun (1998) puts it: "the public good is not objectively or externally ascertainable. It is a social and cultural project of the public sphere . . . It is created in and through the public process, it does not exist in advance of it."

This process of creating a continually evolving public good is informed by a plurality of culturally variable conceptual models of interests and of the public good (Williams 1995; Williams and Matheny 1995; Dobbin 1994; Morone 1998, [1990]; Bellah et al. 1985; Barry 1990 [1965]) which are more diverse than the notion of "self-interest properly understood" which Tocqueville 1980 ([1835]) praised in American political culture (see Moody 2000; Kalberg 1997). Accordingly, our approach looks comparatively at how activists in the two countries pragmatically shift from one model to another and accommodate particular interests within the models.[14] We focus in particular on the level of "group interests," since this might reveal interesting differences in the level of generality at which interests are "public enough" to be evaluated as legitimate. We also take the crucial next step by comparing how these models for the connection of particular interests with the public good – and the implied models of community (see Fowler 1991 for a review) – are manifested in the creation of organizational arrangements, such as "coalitions" or "collectives," which provide perhaps the most telling insight into how these cultural models are practiced in each case.

The relation of central concern for us – how the different sides in each country relate their own goals to the goals of others and/or to the public good generally – is a relation which, as Tocqueville (1980 [1835]) and others have shown, reveals much about national differences in political culture. The simplistic view of how this relation is manifested in political life in each country is: (1) the United States is a land of "liberal pluralism" where "special interest groups" compete for influence[15] and the only possible public good is found in the procedure to mediate or balance these particular interests (Sandel 1996; Dahl 1989); whereas (2) France is a land of "republican collectivism" where everyone is concerned only with a state-controlled universal or national general will (informed by a "civic" order of worth), and any particular interest is excluded from inclusion in the common good. We intend to open this simplistic view up to empirical specification toward a much more complex and nuanced picture.

"Strategy" in arguments and arrangements

Versatility, multiple competency, and the strategic mixing of arguments

The first sense in which political debate and action are said to be "strategic" is in terms of the intentional construction or use of arguments themselves. The basic view is that actors or organizations in a dispute will craft an argument or a set of rhetorical emphases which will appeal to the proper audience, couch the position in the most legitimate terms, and/or deflect potential criticism. This presumably instrumental manipulation of the justifications offered might occur in several ways: combining several arguments; switching readily between arguments; focusing on a specific form of justification to attract a specific audience. Such manipulation of argumentation is often denounced as being "strategic" in that it merely seeks to advance particular interests under the guise of public good justifications.

Both individuals and organizational entities can be said to engage in strategic argumentation, and each person or organization is variable in their degree of both versatility and multiple competency. We define *versatility* as the ability to switch between modes of justification or types of argument quickly and frequently, while we define *multiple competency* as the capacity to engage expertly and deeply in many different realms of worth and arenas of argumentation. Of course, these abilities overlap in many cases, and they can both be the focus of denunciations. Extreme versatility and switching between arguments, in particular, can raise suspicions about the effective engagement in each of them. Actors sometimes determine that the best strategy is not to display their versatility or wide competency, but rather to stick to their primary argument and to resist engaging with their opponents on the terms which the opponent critiques them (even though they could). The different capacities of people and unequal access to the resources for being versatile means that being strategic in this way is not always a choice, and that power dynamics are involved. Versatility and multiple competency should not, then, be viewed as always normatively good or practically efficacious.

We found evidence of both great versatility and multiple competency in both cases, and observed that these capacities are not equally distributed among all actors in each case. Often the statement or message involves repeated shifts between more than two realms of value. For example, in the stylish information packet created by the Tuolumne River Preservation Trust primarily for lobbying trips to Washington DC, the environmental group summarizes its case for declaring the Clavey "Wild and Scenic": "Rather than dam the river for a single purpose – to produce unneeded, over-priced power for the Turlock Irrigation District – the Clavey will serve the greater good by continuing to provide healthy habitats for wildlife, as well as recreational and spiritual refuge for our own species." Multiple switches in one sentence are quite evident here. Many other examples involve shifts among arguments across time and setting. For instance, the Trust or its allies dealt in more depth with each of the various arguments in the statement quoted above – "over-priced," "single purpose" versus "greater good," "habitats for wildlife," recreation, and "spiritual refuge" – at different points in the dispute. But the fact that they packed all these justifications together in a single key statement – with evidence presumably offered elsewhere – demonstrates their recognition of the strategic benefit of being versatile and mixing arguments.

There are examples of versatility and multiple competency from the Somport case also. For example, a young shepherd active in opposing the project displays his diverse competency in an interview statement on how best to promote their cause, "It is necessary that the bear be an asset, a brand name for our products, a sign of recognition of the quality products made by shepherds who, at the same time, are protectors of nature and bears." He is clearly trying to demonstrate a market sensibility while also shifting easily from this market realm to his more traditional and local competency as a shepherd, as well as his "green" competency as a protector of nature.

However, the primary comparative difference in strategic argumentation in the two cases is that fewer of the main characters in the Somport case display a high level of versatility. For example, the main opposition activist, Eric Pétetin, has remained very focused throughout the conflict on a particular style of expression and protest, and on a bounded set of preferred themes and issues. He prefers to express his views in what we have called "inspirational" terms, and has steadfastly refused to respond to scientific studies in support of the project with his own scientific critique, as many prominent Clavey opponents did, even though he probably had the competency and skill to be versatile and to engage in many forms or topics of debate (see below). Others in the Somport case (e.g. the valley mayor Jacques Lassalle) were not as singular in focus, but in general we see much less variability presented by single people or groups in the Somport dispute. By contrast, in the United States it appears that most of the main actors (on both sides of the dispute) saw it as a benefit to display their versatility and multiple competency, and worked hard to cultivate these abilities. For example, several anti-dam environmental organizers told of working hard to develop the expertise to engage with TID regarding the economics of the project. The dam project director John Mills also emphasized his own range of abilities, from dealing with engineering specifics, to understanding the regulatory process, to being savvy about energy market issues. However, in the Clavey case there was also some unwillingness to display one's multiple competencies. For opposition figures, some competencies were hidden in order to focus on a particular argument in a particular setting. For example, Mike Fuller of the Turlock Ratepayers' Alliance said he switched from operating exclusively in the mode of economic debate in the Turlock area to operating exclusively in the environmental mode, displaying his "expertise" on the river's ecology and beauty, when acting as guide on the rafting trips which the opposition used to lobby national politicians.

The observed differences in the displayed variability in the two cases might be explained by different cultural understandings of what is effective or acceptable as strategy, and of what it means to be "professional" in advocating one's political goals. In the United States, versatility and multiple competency are more commonly considered marks of professionalism in political advocacy, in the sense of being "savvy" about what is required in various situations. The ability to distance oneself enough from a singular or overly passionate defense of one's cause allows one to know when switching to another (also legitimate) defense is more effective.[16] It is not surprising, then, that versatility and switching between, or mixing, multiple competencies are displayed more often in the Clavey case than in Somport, particularly by "outsider" and more "professional" activists such as the representatives of environmental groups from San Francisco. Interestingly, these same activists acknowledge that hiding an expertise, *appearing* to be less versatile, is often the most "versatile" move in a particular situation, and is a valuable professional skill to learn.[17]

In France these capacities are not considered marks of "professionalism" in the same way and – more than in the United States – tend to raise suspicion about one's commitment or the depth of one's development of a particular position. Accordingly, we see a much less diverse range of arguments, and less switching between various modes of justification, among actors on both sides in the Somport dispute. Rather, we see more attempts to demonstrate competency and commitment in a particular field. Again, Eric Pétetin is the most obvious illustration of this comparative difference. He is a former student of a prestigious school of political science – the Institute of Political Studies [*"Sciences Po"*] in Bordeaux – which means he is fully aware of and probably competent in such forms of political debate as administrative or organizational efficiency assessments, and the language of policy and planning. But his involvement in the Somport case belies any such skill or knowledge, since he chooses to avoid just these sorts of administrative or policy planning arguments and to engage in physical and emotional protests which are the explicit opposite of the preferred practices taught by a prestigious school of political studies.[18] It is important to note that Pétetin's corporal engagement in the cause (he has been put in jail several times) is seen even by his opponents as a demonstration of the authenticity of his commitment, and as contributing to the strength of his claims and critiques. For instance, Pétetin's main opponent Jacques Lassalle says: "The only one who is sincere in this whole case, because he is a bit crazy, is Pétetin. Pétetin, he believes viscerally in the cause, and he has served the cause well because he has courage. When there are policemen, when there is a big fight, then there is no one else [left] but Mr. Pétetin."

Strategic division of rhetorical labor and the diversity of arguments

The second sense in which argumentation might be "strategic" is in terms of the arrangements developed deliberately to coordinate how and when arguments are made. This coordination involves first a consideration of the extent to which the groups involved will seek an explicit diversity in the arguments they make, and then how (or whether) they will go about creating organizational, legal, or other types of arrangements either to divide up and/or to coordinate the range of claims. We are interested in detailing how the participants in the United States and French environmental disputes sought (or not) to deploy a diversity of arguments, and how they defended this diversity and strategic coordination. We are also interested in how and why the strategic arrangements were denounced by opponents.

In the Clavey opposition campaign we can see a very deliberate division of rhetorical labor among the various different groups and their "arenas" of involvement: Tuolumne River Preservation Trust in San Francisco, Clavey River Preservation Coalition in Tuolumne County, and the Turlock Ratepayers' Alliance in Turlock.[19] The groups were assigned a particular type of argument or rhetoric to present, based on a mostly deliberate assessment of such factors as perceived political opportunity and the receptivity of certain locales to certain arguments. The local, grassroots Coalition focused mainly on domestic arguments about their "backyard" or certain types of green arguments relating to close attachment to one's environment. The Trust, being an "outsider" in the local area, intentionally focused on more scientific types of green arguments, such as attacking the biological studies in TID's proposal and also making opinion arguments about the extent of national and state-wide opposition. Finally, the Turlock Ratepayers' Alliance focused very explicitly on economic arguments, such as the high cost of the project and low demand for it, and strategically avoided any sort of green argument which would have little resonance in the agricultural and industrial Turlock area. Johanna Thomas, the leader of the Trust who worked closely with local Coalition leaders in planning the opposition campaign, explains how this division of labor came about: "In the beginning, when I first started, I drew up a lengthy memo of how to divide responsibilities [among several groups] . . . Mostly it was kind of informal . . . You know, beyond that memo, beyond the first meetings, it was mostly just a case by case basis where we would try to figure it out. And eventually there wasn't even a question in some instances, it was kind of natural."

This division of rhetorical labor arrangement was denounced by the dam proponents, who pointed out the close working relationship of the local groups and the outside environmental groups, and painted the opposition campaign in conspiratorial terms as a small cadre of environmentalists using non-green arguments and organizations to fool the public into thinking there was broad and local opposition. The groups employing this strategic arrangement, however, counter this attack by saying that all the justifications they deploy are valid arguments against the dam, and their decision to deploy them strategically does not change their public good validity. Coordinating the opposition campaign by dividing up the argumentation tasks was defended as a necessary and effective pragmatic move, not merely the instrumental pursuit of a special interest, that did not dilute or falsify the arguments themselves.

Some coordination of argumentation is found in both cases, but the extent to which this strategic process is explicit and developed into a common tactic used in many such campaigns differs somewhat between the two cases and countries. In the United States there are many formalized instruction guides, handbooks, or other practical assistance tools (some geared to "organizers" generally, and some to environmentalists specifically) available across the country, and these were used by activists in the Clavey case to help them develop and implement their strategic plan.[20] The professionalized national organizations American Rivers and Friends of the River provided organizing guides, materials from other river campaigns, and provided other "expertise" to assist the coalition opposing the dam. These sorts of explicit practical "activists'" guides and other tools are not found in the Somport dispute, or in French political disputes generally.

In the Somport case, we do find examples of seeking a diversity and coordination among the opposition groups, but the division of rhetorics is less an explicit plan from the start. For example, as we mentioned above, Eric Pétetin specifically stayed within an inspirational mode of justification and favored dramatic actions and tactics. In many instances, alone or with a few friends, Pétetin has borrowed tactics from non-violent activists like Gandhi and physically impeded the construction work on the tunnel by sitting in front of the bulldozers or even by passively resisting the policemen charged with removing the protesters. He tries to rile up the crowd with fiery speeches during demonstrations, and to incite their emotions by playing the guitar and singing. His messages and language refer to the beauty of the Aspe Valley, the harmonious and emotional connection of a "native" to his land, and so on. Another opposition body is the *Comité d'Habitants*, a group of inhabitants of the Aspe Valley who appealed against the report recommending the project, claiming it did not sufficiently survey all of the project's local impacts – environmental, social, economic. In developing their opposition plan, they decided to focus on legal concerns and activities.[21] What is significant is that the *Comité* chose this focus in explicit response to the singular style of engagement and mode of argument of Pétetin. The President of the *Comité*, Paule Bergès, acknowledges this when she says, "We did realize that we had chosen a good mode of mobilization, something very legal, in contrast to Eric [Pétetin]. We said to ourselves, 'Now we are going to commit ourselves to something very legal, a kind a legalistic struggle'."[22] Sometimes the *Comité* was critical of Pétetin's message or method, but many other times they sided openly with him. The *Comité*'s choice of argument focus was not an attempt to distribute various justifications across the various actors or groups or locales (as in the Clavey arrangement), but rather they sought to broaden the range of modes of opposition to the Somport tunnel and to resist the reduction of their cause to one type of argument.

Another deliberate strategic arrangement found in the French opposition campaign is more similar to the United States in its attempt to utilize a diversity of arguments, but very different in the extent and manner in which the different arguments are distributed among groups. To block the expropriation of the parcels of land in the Aspe Valley necessary to build the highway, the coalition of opponents (both local and non-local organizations) created a scheme whereby this land is purchased from the farmers who live on it under a special legal agreement. Only the ownership of the land is sold, but the rights to use the land are not (so farmers continue farming as before); the agreement includes the provision that the ownership of the land is sold back to the farmers after ten years. The new buyers of the land are recruited only through advertisements in the environmental publications of groups like Greenpeace and the World Wildlife Fund, so they are generally green-oriented foreigners (from Germany, Holland, etc.) who the opponents know will never sell the land to the government for development of the road. The purchases are mediated through respected elder residents of the Aspe Valley, so that the farmers can trust the agreement. This strategic arrangement represents a sort of integrated montage of many distinct arguments and groups (local elders, international environmental groups) into a sequential whole, each piece relying on the other.[23] So in both cases there is some attempt to coordinate the "rhetorical labor," but in the Somport case, the division of rhetorics is less explicit or backed by professionalized tools or guide, and the coordination of arguments is more designed to seek compromises or combinations of many arguments by different actors, rather than a division and separation of arguments (and groups making them) from one another.

In sum, our comparative analysis of these two sorts of "strategy" (strategic switching and mixing arguments, and strategic arranging and dividing argumentation) in the two cases suggests the need for a more complex perspective on strategy in political debate and action, a perspective that avoids the simplistic view that any public good claims made by partly instrumental actors must be insincere or reduced to interested posturing. Instead, we need to rethink strategy in terms of a sequence of moves, in which the so-called instrumental move is a necessary but not all-corrupting complement to the move of providing a public good justification.[24] We argue it is analytically necessary to avoid collapsing these two moves, in order to escape the reductive (and somewhat unfalsifiable) claim that all action and rhetoric is controlled by particular interests. It also makes it possible to analyze empirically the complex tensions and reactions of others caused by the existence of both instrumentality and justification (both an interest and an appeal to a common good) in one actor's sequence of actions. The reaction of others to this sequence is particularly important since this reaction is often a critique which tries to reduce the two moves, to "expose" the public good claim as merely a mask for the instrumental goal.

"Interests," coordination, and the public good

The critique that strategic pursuit of an interest corrupts the public good claims may be less of an issue in the United States than in France, because it is apparently more acceptable in the United States to operate solely from an interested position. Previous research suggests that the advocacy of particular interests is generally considered a more integral part of the political process in the "liberal" system in the United States than the "republican" system in France. However, not all debates or actors in each country fit this profile. The models of connecting interests with the public good are diverse in both countries, and different between them, and so these models deserve further empirical scrutiny if we are to better understand the evaluative process and standards in the two countries.

Often the conflict, identification, and the mutual denunciation of the people, groups, or coalitions of groups involved in these disputes are framed in terms of competing "interests" or related concepts. While groups or coalitions sometimes describe themselves in terms of their interest (private or public), more often the attribution of an interest is found in the attacks on one's opponent as a private or "special interest." In this section, we look explicitly at the comparative use, frequency, and extension of the notion of interests in the judgments and arrangements in the two cases.

While the idea (positive or negative) of personal benefits accruing from public projects has some resonance in both France and the United States, we find that the notion and language of "interest" is much more broadly applied in the United States (perhaps because of the greater legitimacy of a market perspective in which social relations are governed by private interests), and that there are different types of connections made between particular interests and the general interest in the United States. However, we find only partial support for the cultural stereotype that considerations of self or private interest dominate United States political debate, while evaluations in French debate are all oriented toward a republican public good.

Interests and the public good in the United States

In the Clavey case, there are some instances where participants defend their involvement or position in the dispute on the basis of having a legitimate "interest" or personal or organizational stake in the outcome, but most of the references to a particular interest occur when one person or group seeks to denounce another. The positive claims of having an organizational stake in the dispute came primarily from industrial representatives, who argued that their business (and perhaps the economic health of the area) would be effected in some way by the decision to build or not build the dam. These claims to a financial interest varied from the concerns by Turlock area industrial ratepayers (individual businesses, or as a group) that their electricity rates would be raised significantly to cover the expense of building the project, to concerns by local tourism industries (collective represented by the Highway 120 Association) that their hotel, restaurant, and recreation businesses would decrease if another river were dammed in the area they serve. There were other claims of interest beyond merely financial or business, some involving a sense of personal or proprietal interest in the local area. The rafting company owner and active opponent Marty McDonnell claimed many of the most energetic participants in the opposition coalition were involved at least partly because they would be personally affected by the outcome: "And when we write down our list of concerns as who we are, we are landowners that are going to be affected, directly affected by this project." However, on the whole there are few instances where someone explicitly admits having a "self-interest" in the Clavey's fate.[25] There are even occasions in Clavey interviews when activists make an explicit attempt to prove that their self-interest would lead them to act in the opposite way than they in fact did. For example, McDonnell, somewhat contradicting his earlier statement, claimed that his financial self-interest would in fact be better served if the Clavey were dammed, because water over the main rapids, Clavey Falls, would be evened out over a longer period of time. "So," he says, "if I were totally greed-motivated, then I would probably have supported the project. Because it would have made, just for me personally, I would have made more money."

More common in the Clavey interviews and debate, however, is the attribution of interest for purposes of denouncing one's opponent, demonstrating their self-interestedness and lack of concern for the interests of others or for some public interest. Often the same sort of interest that was considered legitimate to provide as a reason for involvement is used by others in a negative way. For example, George James, a retired Forest Service official who was an active board member of the pro-dam "wise use" group TuCARE, repeatedly claimed that the "rafting interests" were fomenting opposition to the project because of their greed. James lays it out directly in an interview: "And all of this effort that was coming in so far as the so-called Tuolomne River Preservation [Trust] and everything, the lead strong emphasis came from the rafting interests, largely the commercial rafting interests. And it's a very, very lucrative activity, and they need this kind of water . . . " "Exposing" the "hidden" interest of another in this fashion is seen as a way to show the falsity of the other side's "rhetoric," and in particular to cast doubt on the sincerity and legitimacy of the public good claims of the "interested" party.

As these examples show, it is quite common in the United States for the debate over interests to move to an extra-individual level – to group interests, organizational benefits, or the stakes of other collectivities that are still less broad than the level of "the public" or "the community." The group-level interest might be either an identifiable organization, a collection of individuals based on class (e.g. the "wealthy yuppies" denounced below), a collection of individuals not based on class (e.g. residents of Tuolumne County who sign a petition opposing the dam), an industry or business community (e.g. the tourism industries mentioned above), or a "coalition" of individuals or interests. These group interests, while they are usually seen (at least in the United States) as having a greater degree of connection with a public good, are still exclusive to some degree and often involve material benefits accruing only to a particular subset of people or a particular organization. And some group interests (e.g. local businesses) are considered more legitimate than others in that they can more easily make a defensible connection of their group goal to the general good than can other groups (e.g. the "wealthy yuppies").[26] In fact, it is much more common for a group in the Clavey dispute to offer a financial stake as a good reason for their concern or involvement than it is for an individual to do so. An example of this comes from a leader of the industrial opponents of the project in Turlock, Phil Green, who responded to a question about whether his company was active because of a "special interest" in this way: "I don't think it gets as narrowly focused as, you know, it [the probable rate increase because of the dam] just isn't good for my [company's] bottom line. I mean, we operate in a community, you know, and we provide jobs to a community. We have a lot of employees in the community. And the businesses – several of them are involved – are the same way."

A somewhat different example of the attribution of group-level interests found in the Clavey case is the denunciation of the "outsiders" by the "locals." In the Clavey debate, this denunciation was made by locals in support of both sides of the dispute. On the one hand, some locals argued *against* the project because they wanted to stop outsiders from "stealing" their water (water that "belongs" to locals as a group exclusively), as outsiders had done repeatedly in the past. On the other hand, other locals argued *for* the project because they claimed the people who wanted to "save the Clavey" were actually urbanites ("wealthy yuppies" from San Francisco) who wanted to prevent the rural local area from development so that the urbanites could have a nice "backwoods" area to visit, recreate, and use as their "personal park." The reference to "wealthy yuppies" brings in a nascent class element to this denunciation of outsiders in terms of group interests. Similar sorts of denunciations of outsiders and of classes [e.g. "Parisians"] are found in the Somport dispute, but on the whole the debate and argumentation on the level of group interests is more present in the United States case, and there is a wider range of types of collectivities considered in terms of their interests in the United States

The multiplicity of the usage and meanings of interest terms in the United States explored so far gives some idea of the diverse American cultural repertoire regarding these political concepts (see Mansbridge 1998; Kalberg 1997). While "self-interest" in United States political debate usually means an individual (often a material) stake in a preferred outcome, related terms like "private interest" or "special interest" are more commonly used on the group level.[27] "Special interests" is used to describe, at times, both non-profit and for-profit organizations (or, more commonly, groups of these organizations with shared interests, such as tobacco companies), but the term "special interest" more commonly identifies a group or set of groups attempting to influence legislation through lobbying – a practice which is less common and less legitimate in France (though it is prominent at the EU level, see Axelrod 1997; Mazey and Richardson 1993).[28] The designation as a special interest may also signify that a group represents the concerns of only a portion of "the public" and is unconcerned or adverse to the concerns of the other parts.[29] (The meanings of "public good" in the United States are discussed later.)

Looking at the debate and interviews in the Clavey case, we see how actors and groups seem to take advantage of this ambiguity in interest terms and meanings, particularly in attempting to characterize an opposing group as a "special interest," even if that group explicitly claims to be working for a common or public good. For example, John Mills and others characterize environmentalists opposing the dam as a "special interest group" because they represent the concerns of only a part of the populace and ignore the legitimate interests of a much larger public (even though the dam proponents also admit that conserving the environment of the river is a public good). On the other side, the environmentalists respond to the special interest charge by emphasizing the fact that their goal of preserving this unique wild river is something that will benefit everyone and will even be materially beneficial for people other than themselves.

Here we see support for our view of "interests" as constructed and disputed in the course of political debates, and the need to look empirically at the moves made to express or attribute an interest to one's own group or one's opponent. As we have indicated, one of the most significant "moves" that political disputants engage in is the move toward generalizing or extending interests (in a positive sense), not just to a group or class level, but also to the level of the "common" or "public" interest, specifically to demonstrate a relation between one's interest and some conception of the common good. Of course, sometimes a "special" group interest is presented as a legitimate claim on its own level (e.g. the interests of a "Mom-and-Pop" tourism business), but often even these claims contain an implicit connection to a larger common interest (e.g. the economic health of a community). The goal often seems to be to show that a particular interest is "public enough" to be considered legitimate, and this goal is accomplished in different ways across contexts and (we find) in the two cases. In the United States case, we find multiple types of models for extending or connecting particular interests with the public good.

The first type of public good claim found in the Clavey case is one based on some sort of universalistic principle or shared good, where a group's particular "interest" is made to seem fully and substantively public. An example of this is when the environmentalists claim in their brochure, quoted earlier, that leaving the Clavey wild will "serve the greater good by continuing to provide healthy habitats for wildlife, as well as recreational and spiritual refuge for our own species," while damming the Clavey will only serve "a single purpose." The "greater good" here is defined in terms of the principle that preserving the environment (e.g. "healthy habitats" for all species) is good on its own terms, a goal we can all agree on as always good (and that this environmental "public interest" group is promoting). Another example of this type of public good claim are the competing assertions from both sides that they are in fact advocating what is "best for the future" (as opposed to only good for some person's or group's future, or only good for the present). The dam proponents claim the future is best served by building adequate infrastructure to meet future power needs, while dam opponents claim the future is best served by preserving wilderness for generations to come.[30]

A second type of public good model found in the United States case is based on the number of people supporting a particular position or goal, so the public good is determined by whatever many, or maybe a majority of, people agree is good. Numerous activists on both sides of the Clavey dispute defended their goals by saying that a majority of some relevant public or some large constituency (e.g. the local community residents, the "ratepayers," the membership of a large group), agreed with them and supported their opinion. Many respondents in their interviews set up a sort of continuum of support in which there were "extreme" fringes on either side, and then claimed that while they appealed to the vast majority of reasonable people in "the middle," their opponents in the dispute tended to come from or get support from only one or the other fringe.[31] Another example of how different sides in the Clavey conflict both offered this second type of public good claim are the competing arguments in the Turlock area about who – TID or the Turlock Ratepayers' Alliance – was in fact doing what was best for, or supported by, TID's "ratepayers." On the one hand, TID throughout the dispute maintained that it was merely doing what was best to meet the needs of its constituency, its consumer and industrial ratepayers. On the other hand, the Ratepayers' Alliance also claimed to be representing the concerns of all ratepayers. TID's reaction to the Ratepayers' Alliance efforts also reflects this model. A TID board member, Randy Fiorini, summarily dismisses the Alliance as "an absolute joke" because it involved only a "few people" so "there was no foundation."

A third model of the public good found in the United States debate is an aggregate or procedural one, where the public good is achieved by bringing together all the diverse, but legitimate, "interests" or "stakeholders" and combining their goals in some equal way. This model of public good can be created in different ways: for example, by creating an "omnibus" solution that "balances" or "combines" the requests of all interests or public goods in some way, or by allowing access and providing voice to different claims for a public good in a fair and inclusive procedure and letting them deliberate toward a consensus solution.[32] The model implies that the greater the number of different interests invited to "sit at the table," or the greater the number of public good proposals included in the aggregation, the greater the likelihood of achieving the overall public good. This model cannot be reduced to the view of the public good found in the classic "liberal pluralism" or "interest-group liberalism" form of politics (Berry 1996; Lowi 1969; Dahl 1967), because multiple public or common goods (not simply multiple special interests or specialized groups) might compete for attention and inclusion in an aggregative result, and because the concrete solution reached through a procedure might be a substantive synthesis or "compromise" (Boltanski and Thévenot 1991) of multiple public good visions which not only conglomerates but also integrates them (see Chapter 9).

While there were no formal deliberation or negotiation procedures among the Clavey disputants, there were several instances where all sides were invited to present their comments to various decision-makers. Many times the environmentalists invoked the procedural model by forcing governmental agencies to receive and respond to their comments, often through a series of detailed legal maneuvers and formal documentation requests. TID, which was seen by its opponents as an advocate for a particular interest rather than an adjudicator of interests, argued in contrast that its position itself had aggregative public good credibility. In an editorial provided for a local newspaper, the president of the TID board defended the project on the following grounds: "We invited every environmental, conservation, and other special interest group we could find into the design process ... We incorporated every one of their recommendations into the project's design – not some of them, but every one of them" (Clauss 1993, A-13; see also Paterson 1989, for the historical sources of this viewpoint in TID's planning ethos).

The key conclusion to be emphasized here is that in the Clavey case we find a variety of models to connect a particular interest or position with some model of the public good. These models either transform a particular interest into a "public interest" by extending it into a universal good or connecting it to a large number of supporters (e.g. saving the environment is a general value, or is supported by most community residents), or by placing a partly public, partly special interest alongside other such interests in an aggregation or procedural negotiation leading to the public good (e.g. all groups gave input to our decision, so it is the best public good solution). For ease of comparison, we can call these types of public good models "*substantive*," "*constituency*" (or most frequently "*majority*") and "*aggregative*" or "*procedural*". All of these models appear to be well developed and shared in the United States, and we will see in the next section how they are found in different forms and frequencies in France.

Interests and the public good in France

The evidence from the Clavey case suggests that in the United States there is great variability in the use and connotation of the term "interests," and the concept is frequently extended to several intermediate (group) and general (public) levels. In contrast, there is not such a general applicability or diversity in the usage of "interest" in the Somport case. Nevertheless, the term is used in France, and claims about personal benefits from or stakes in public projects are often set in contrast to public benefits in ways similar to the United States.

One significant difference in the evidence from the two cases is that the attribution of an interest or a personal stake is almost always negative in the Somport case. No one justifies their involvement, at least publicly, on the basis of a personal, individual benefit they want to "protect" or "advocate" in some way. And any sort of material benefit accruing to an individual from the project is never self-attributed in public. Perhaps the most obvious comparison is between shopkeepers in the Aspe Valley who might see an increase in business from the new road and the tourism industry mobilized against the Clavey project. As we saw, the interests of tourism businesses was at times a preferred argument for participation among the tourism industry in the Clavey case, but among Aspe Valley shopkeepers this sort of justification for involvement is much less likely. They appear similar to the United States business owners in speaking with some authority about the consequences for the industry or trade group they are a part of (e.g. craft shops as a local economic group), but unlike their United States counterparts, the French businessmen involved in the dispute tend not to speak in terms of how their personal interest is connected to the interest of the region as a whole through jobs or economic prosperity (Lamont 1992, and Camus-Vigué, in this volume, find similar American-French differences). Even those with the most apparent material stake in the project's outcome refer to a more general level of patrimony and the good of the valley.

On the other hand, the rejection of positions or opponents is often framed in terms of interests or personal concern. It is a potent argument in France to claim one's opponent in a dispute is motivated by financial gain, or that the government officials proposing a project are motivated by anything but the general good. The first type of interest denounced is financial or material interest. One of the more blatant denunciations of material interests is the message on a placard in an anti-Somport demonstration which reads, in French, "*Ni camions ni trains pour les intérêts du fric!*" This might be best translated as, "No trucks, no trains for cash interests!," which can be seen as a general denunciation of the market and its focus on private material benefits. While this rejection of material interests is similar to those found in the Clavey case, the general critique of the market and an emphasis on distributive equity is much more frequent in the Somport case. Challenges claiming that one group or person will benefit disproportionately (not just whether they will benefit) seem to be more standard in France. Other examples show denunciations of non-material but still personal interests. For instance, the local mayor Jacques Lassalle denounces the Minister of the Environment as using his public, media role in the controversy for his own personal advantage. While the Minister, Brice Lalonde, is required to represent his position in the media as a representative of the government, the mayor claims Lalonde's involvement is guided by his need to be in the spotlight. In contrast, Paule Bergès, the woman in charge of a local "*Comité d'Habitants*" opposing the project, makes the same charge about Mayor Lassalle. She says Lassalle is making personal use of the media to "make insults" against the environmentalists, particularly Greenpeace, whom he calls the "scavengers of the sensational," when he should be "behaving as the spokesperson and listening carefully to what people have to tell him." Clearly this involves setting up some type of personal advantage (not financial) in contrast to the public good (e.g. the "real" concerns of the people).

Perhaps the most significant difference in the debate and evaluations about interests in the two cases is on the group level. In general, the group interests that are attributed legitimately in public debate usually pertain to much higher or generalized level collectivities in France, such as at the level of "*socio-professionnel*" categories (broad groupings of people which have been institutionally recognized in, for example, national or industry-wide labor negotiations). At the level of the interests of organizations, groups of individuals in a city or region, or industries, any attribution of a group interest in the Somport case is usually a denunciation of the exclusivity of claims at this level and their detraction from the overall public good (rather than their connection to the public good, as such group interests are often seen in the United States). In fact, the denunciation of group interests is quite prevalent in the Somport debate, particularly in rejection of the industries which will benefit from the new road and tunnel. The shepherds who see their livelihood at risk from the road never proclaim the need to consider the "shepherding interests" or "farming interests." They do, however, proclaim the importance of protecting the patrimony of the valley or of the Béarn region, which can only be framed in terms of interest or good at a much more general level, if at all.

The interest or good of a region ("*communauté*" is rarely used in French to delimit the scope of a local good) is not seen as divisible into the specific group interests that collectively would make up a region's interest. The idea that the interest of a "locale" ("*localité*," "*pays*," "*région*") is a conglomeration of "divergent interests" is rarely found in French discourse and any divergent interests are seen as antithetical to the idea of a collective interest of that local community. The term *intérêt valléen* (the interest of the valley as a whole) is generally used to designate not merely the interests of the Aspe Valley residents as a distinct population, but also the valley as a natural and historic entity. There is much debate in the French case about what will in fact benefit the valley's interest. For example, the project proponent and mayor Jacques Lassalle uses the term *intérêts valléens* in denouncing the "outside powers that are enemies of valley interests," such as Parisians or environmentalists fighting the project. A local project opponent, Jean-Luc Palacio, responds to this challenge by retorting that while Lassalle claims to be an advocate for the valley's interests, in fact his support for the project ignores the genuine interests of the valley inhabitants. Palacio says the inhabitants are the "guardians of the valley patrimony," and so the real "common interest" [*intérêt commun*] is to "conserve a rich patrimony and the power to attract tourism which is getting more and more significant." Palacio claims the tourism development is in the "real" interests of the valley, not the supposed development from the road. He asks, "Why waste in such a manner public funds with no possibility of return [to the valley]? Because specific interests [*intérêts particuliers*] want to buy the valley, not for the sake of the valley itself, but because it is specifically necessary for the realization of a certain plan and for the making of certain profits." Finally, he rejects the project using the most general level of the "public" interest, while still acknowledging this public interest is "complex": "The public interest [*intérêt public*], which is by definition global and complex, specifically cannot be reduced only to the imperative of economic efficiency, expressed by a capitalist group."

The exchange about the *intérêts valléens* also reveals a significant similarity in the two cases: the rejection of "outsiders" attempting to impose their will on the locals, or attempting to tell locals what is in fact in their best interest as a collectivity. Specifically similar to the United States case is the denunciation of supposedly "wealthy" outsiders, especially environmentalists, for their lack of concern for the development of local, rural areas. Farmers in the Somport area, who want the road to help them in their agricultural development, respond to the opposition from environmentalists by asserting, using colloquial phrasing, "We ain't gonna keel over in our clogs for the pleasure of wealthy environmentalists."[33]

While this denunciation of outsiders is an important commonality between the two cases, there are noticeable differences here as well. The rejections of outsiders in France rarely take the form of "their interests versus ours," as in the United States, but more commonly are framed as "outside specific interests versus the collective interest," such as the interests of *"bétonneurs"* [literally "concreters," those who want to cover everything with concrete]. A good example of this is found in a tract put out by the Socialist Left movement: "We prefer the collective interest [*intérêts collectifs*] to the interest of *bétonneurs*, particularly with regard to the utilization of public funds, and the preservation of nature."

The terms used in the examples above suggest there is also a diversity of interest and public good language and concepts in French political culture, but the range of usage is different than in the United States. In general the term *intérêt* is used in France to signify a range of particular interests, including non-financial personal stakes. The French term closest to "special interests" is *intérêts particuliers*, which is always pejorative and seen in direct contrast to the common good or collective interest. So the interest of a large collectivity like the *intérêt valléen*, generally attributed positively, would not be considered an *intérêt particulier* in most uses. The term *intérêt collectif* used in the Socialist pamphlet above signifies a general interest or will (of the public as a whole) rather than the interest of a specific collective, but there are other common terms for this level of general or public interest in French, such as *intérêt commun, intérêt général,* and *intérêt public*. These terms are always positive concepts in France, as in the United States, and are often appropriated to add legitimacy and influence to an argument. Of course, in French political culture the idea of the "general will" [*volonté générale*], as promoted by Rousseau (1987 [1762]), holds a place of special honor in the predominant "civic" definition of public or governmental action.[34]

What we called earlier the "substantive" model of the public good – as based on a universal principle or oriented toward a general good – is much more common in the Somport case than the "constituency" (or "majority") model of the public good based on the numbers of supporters, or any "aggregative" or "procedural" models.[35] While in the United States there is a tendency to accept the idea of a plurality of interests and public goods, each represented and advocated by an advocacy group, and then to consider how much support there is for each of these (or debate who represents the majority), in France the focus on support is not the issue and the plurality of competing public good conceptions are not tied to specific groups. The question in the Somport debate, as in French political and public debates generally, is not one of who has more support for their view of the public good, but rather what is best for everyone as a whole.

Coalition, coordination, and local community

The cultural models of the relation of particular or special interest to a public good compared above – models which underlie language, concepts, and arguments used in the two cases and countries – are also manifested in the organizational arrangements developed and used by the activists in each case (and the reasons they give for arranging their activities in this way). As one would expect from the comparative differences described so far, we find different arrangements of people and groups in the two countries – in simplest terms, "coalition" in the United States, and "coordination" in France – governed by different logics of organization and justifications. These different arrangements also embody different visions of local community and local attachments, and different ways the activists conceive of their responsibilities and roles in representing or perpetuating their community's public good.

In the Clavey case, the primary grassroots institution developed in opposition to the dam project, the Clavey River Preservation Coalition, is described by organizers as a "coalition" of distinct, disparate "interests" brought together into an intentionally diverse, "broad-based," and ever-expanding group which offers its "diversity of interests" as evidence of its authority to make public good claims and to speak as the voice of the local community. The main organizers of the Coalition saw this as a key strategic move which lent their enterprise crucial legitimacy. The rancher and volunteer conservationist Wally Anker, who did the initial organizing and was the first chair of the group, emphasizes the need for breadth and a local focus: "And we said the way to really be successful was to get as broad a coalition as we possibly can . . . So this was our tactic. It had to be locally based, even though we might not do as good a job as the professionals, and as broadly based as possible. [Interviewer: So that was a definite goal, to get different people with different interests in the Coalition?] Absolutely. Coalition. This was the emphasis from day one." The very definition of coalition involves for him a diversity of local interests, and this diversity is a necessity for success. The rafting company owner Marty

McDonnell, talking about why the Coalition format was chosen, echoes this belief: ". . . when you're looking at fighting a political battle, you collect a list of special interest groups, and then expand on that . . . when you're trying to influence elected officials or people who are trying to be elected, the more people that you represent and the more diverse your group is, the much more influence you have." He states the formula clearly – the more special interests, the more influence – without regard to the nature of, or differences among, the interests themselves. Eric White, a young rafting guide who co-chaired the Coalition after Wally Anker, points to the need to collect diverse interests as a way to avoid denunciation as a special interest: "So I think you can't just look at the issue and say that one group . . . There's a special interest that is really pushing and driving this whole thing, or only one reason why people are driven to protect this river. I think the reasons to protect it are as diverse as the members in the Coalition are." White's view reflects most directly the American conceptual model of the public good as an aggregation of interests.

The Coalition evolved according to these logics over the course of the opposition to the project, with anyone expressing any concern or inclination being invited to join the Coalition board, either as an individual or as a representative of their group. The Coalition eventually included representatives from the local Sierra Club and Audubon chapters, the Me-Wuk tribal council, a local Coalition for Better Government, various rafting companies and other tourism business, the local California Trout chapter, and others. In many cases the individuals or groups become involved explicitly out of what is or can be called a self-interest in protecting the river, or at least out of a highly personal commitment or local connection. For example, some fishermen and hunters were active in the Coalition campaign because they wanted to continue to pursue their recreational activity in the Clavey area undisturbed. They were considered assets to the Coalition because they could provide expert or personal knowledge of the river and its habitat, and they were direct examples of customers of the tourism industry who would not patronize the local establishments if the dam were built. Other members of the Coalition were interesting hybrids of different identities and interests, people who could claim to be more than mere environmentalists or rafters – in other words, more than single special interests – and who might be seen as coalitions of interests within themselves. The primary organizer Wally Anker, for example, is a retired banker with business expertise, a respected local landowner, a rancher with long family ties to agriculture, and a volunteer for various conservation organizations like Audubon. His identity as a rancher was particularly emphasized in the media and by other members of the Coalition, since this implied he was not some environmental ideologue.

In general, the goal of the Coalition approach was not to avoid talking about the interests that drove people to oppose the project, but rather to be "broad-based" enough to avoid being labeled as one particular interest. There were occasional tensions between members who were very different politically or took opposite positions on other community issues, but it was seen as significant that they all chose to join together on this cause. The logic and arrangement of the Clavey Coalition is not surprising given that this type of coalition approach is a preferred form of collective organization in the United States, particularly among Left-wing or multicultural organizers (Jesse Jackson's famous "Rainbow Coalition" is the prototypical example). The Coalition approach clearly reflects the "aggregative" model of the public good shown earlier to be important in the United States, as well as the American vision of the local community as itself (partly) a collection of interests.[36] The Coalition was designed to have the authority to speak to decision-makers as a "voice of the community," a microcosm encompassing the diversity of the community at large.

The Coalition also had to be local in both membership and orientation. The Coalition's putative authority to speak for (or as) the community's "interests" reflects the American notion of the local community as a self-governing political entity in which local residents concerned about "backyard" issues such as this project consider their participation as part of their duties and role as "citizens" (not just as "advocates" with interests). This vision of local commitment helps explain the rejection of "outsiders" who are perceived to be taking control of local decisions or resources. In fact, the importance of the Coalition as a local community body caused some tension with other "outside" groups also opposing the project, such as the San Francisco-based Tuolumne River Preservation Trust. The two groups, however, were quite aware of the importance and appeal of having a local focus, and so explicitly tried to avoid being perceived in local venues as too closely associated with one another, even though they worked closely together and strategized an overarching plan (as discussed earlier). They also promoted their local focus and membership outside the local area, particularly when lobbying national politicians who want to be seen as supporting local concerns (especially small towns) whenever possible. The rafting guide and dam opponent Eric White said he emphasized his local ties when he traveled to Washington DC: "I think it was good . . . to have this little hometown boy out there, this little local kid from small Tuolumne County, living eight miles outside of a tiny little city in that county."

Given that we noted earlier how the model of the public good as a collection of interests had little currency in France and in the Somport case, we would not expect the organizational arrangements and alliances of the Somport opposition to be similar to the coalition approach of the Clavey opponents. And in fact, the French alliances are better characterized as based on "*coordination*," a logic more in line with a substantive and generalized model of the public good, and with a vision of local community in terms of a local common good or patrimony rather than interests. Two levels of organizational arrangements within the Somport opposition campaign provide some comparative insight: the trans-local alliance translated as "Collective for Pyrenean Alternatives to the European Highway E-7," and a local Aspe Valley group known as the *Comité d'Habitants*.

The Collective is designed in line with a common French organizational form, the *collectif*, which seeks "coordination" between a number of (usually political) groups. Like the coalition approach in the United States, the *collectif* approach is the preferred form of coordinated organization of the Left in France.[37] The Collective organized against the Somport project included groups such as the local Socialist party (separate from the national party), the Communist Party, the Greens, Greenpeace (international), WWF (international), other wildlife groups concerned with the bears or other particular species, and the local *Comité d'Habitants*. The Collective is designed as an alliance of distinct groups, but not as a "coalition of interests." The organizational logic is not to bring in a broad range of diverse particular interests or to demonstrate a representative membership, but rather to coordinate the work of the many opponents and avoid overlaps. There are no shopkeepers or business representatives in the Collective, for example. The Collective does not promote its diversity or broadness as its source of legitimacy, but rather seeks to demonstrate solidarity and to present a united confrontational and adversarial resistance in a more significant way than we find in the United States case. And the Collective does not claim to represent the "voice of the community" because it is more than local, but also because a "community" is not conceived as composed of diverse interests to be collected together.

The *Comité d'Habitants* based in the Aspe Valley is perhaps a closer analogue to the Clavey Coalition, but it is also very different in logic and design. The membership of the *Comité*, like the Coalition, cuts across multiple social and political divisions. This diversity was partly intentional, insofar as the organizers did not seek out just a few types of people and wanted to allow space for cross-cutting divisions, but the membership was not specifically designed to make the divisions into a public issue and certainly not to tout this diversity as the source of legitimacy of the group. Rather, the members of the *Comité* are seen collectively in terms of their shared identity as "inhabitants" of the valley, emphasizing the fact that they are local people with local ties. The group's activities and goals are centered around a set of shared concerns considered relevant and important to all the members (and to all inhabitants of the Aspe Valley). The members are involved in their capacity as inhabitants, not as interests.[38]

The *Comité* shares with the Clavey Coalition a conscious identity as a specifically "local" organization which was designed to avoid the control of the Aspe Valley by "outsiders" or "outside powers," and to avoid the denunciation that it was only non-resident environmentalists who were opposing the project (a denunciation common to both disputes). However, unlike the Clavey Coalition, the *Comité* members do not claim to be a representative "voice of the local community" or to embody the diversity of local interests. Their legitimacy is backed by a more patrimonial vision of locality [*"localité."*] The typically French idea of local community is both (1) a resident people (*"habitants"*) with shared customs, family connections to the region and land, and mutual ties to a patrimony which must be cultivated and preserved; and (2) the *"collectivité locale,"* which is less an autonomous, self-governing political entity than a piece of a much larger collective and national political unit, which is justified on civic grounds. These two visions of French localities are in constant tension because the first emphasizes local attachments while the second supersedes local attachments. However, the "local" (in terms of patrimony and "domestic" worth) is still an important point of reference in France, as the influential role played by an explicitly local committee of inhabitants points out.

An example of a tension within the *Comité* illustrates the differences from the Coalition in the *Comité*'s self-conception and orientation. Like the Coalition, there are a range of environmental sensibilities among the members of the *Comité*, some oppose the project because they want to protect the bears or preserve nature, while others oppose the project because they are anti-Parisian and concerned with local patrimony (but not so much with bears). The preferred style of argumentation and language used by the members is often quite different. These differences, however, are not promoted as a source of legitimacy but are rather seen as a source of tension which must be overcome through a consolidated focus on the "common interests" of all members. Again, the modus operandi is coordination, not coalition. One member of the *Comité*, Jean-Luc Palacio, is concerned that the vocabulary of environmentalists does not "speak to" the inhabitants of the valley or some other *Comité* members, and also that he strongly opposes the xenophobia of many locals against foreigners. He responds by trying to turn their attention to the common interests of the valley. Quoted in a local newspaper, he says the people who live along the intended road, the shopkeepers, farmers, and others should all see their "common interest" in spite of their differences in "logics which look irreconcilable at first." He says, "we should not ignore that each of these groups has its logic and its interest to defend, but the problem [*le drame*] comes about because we don't know how to talk about our common interests despite these differences. Our common interest is to maintain our patrimony, and [being] a tourist site is also important." So while he first acknowledges a diversity of stakes, logics, or interests, in a pluralist American-style perspective, he proposes to resolve this problem by moving beyond differences and adopting a language and logic of the common interest that is more "substantive" than "aggregative."

Conclusion

This second part of our comparative analysis of American and French environmental disputes built on the review of the argumentation dynamics and classification of evaluative patterns in Chapter 9 in two ways: (1) by considering how the justification processes discussed previously were articulated with "strategic" instrumental moves; and (2) by moving to the level of comparing broader models of interests and the public good underlying the evaluative dynamics of the cases. We were specifically interested in how to deal with the fact that the disputants in the cases were both making generalized, public good arguments and instrumentally pursuing a specific goal (and critiquing the goals of others). We compared the differential ways actors in each country used "interests" as a standard of evaluation and the manner in which they extended this notion to more general or collective levels. Finally, throughout this chapter we sought to analyze organizational arrangements as significant manifestations of underlying cultural models and political grammars. Our findings add considerable specificity to our understanding of the nature of local political disputes and the notions of community and the public good in France and the United States.

Comparing the ways in which actors in each country were "strategic" in their argumentation, we found that, while versatility was a mark of professionalism in the United States, this capacity tended in France to raise suspicion about one's commitment. Comparing the strategic arrangements and plans for dividing or coordinating the arguments, we found that the division and assignment of rhetorics among organizations was explicit or backed by professionalized tools in the United States, while in France the coordination of arguments was more designed to seek compromises or combinations of many arguments by different actors. We concluded there were analytical advantages to rethinking "strategy" in political debate and action in terms of a more extensive and segmented sequence of "moves," including both an instrumental move and a public good justification move but not reducing these moves into an explanation that considers the instrumental strategy as always corrupting the common good claim.

Next we turned to a comparison of the conceptual models of interests, the public good, and local community, focusing in particular on comparing the extension of interests in each country and the relations between interests and the public good made in each case. We find only partial support for the cultural stereotype that self- or private interest is the common basis for evaluation in the United States, while general or public good (or "will") is the common basis for evaluation in France. Instead we found more specifically that at times personal or self-interest was attributed positively in the United States, but it was usually negative and used as a denunciation, while personal interest was always used negatively in France, and was more often generalized into a denunciation of the market as a whole. Further, while it was common for the debate about interests to move to an extra-individual level, this was done in quite different ways. While in the United States group interests at the level of an organization, an industry, or a segment of a local community were often used as legitimate defenses of participation, in France group interests at this level were more likely to be denounced while collective interests at a more general level – such as a region (e.g. the "valley's interest") – were commonly defended.

At the most general level of the public good, we found significant differences in both the language and the implicit models in the two countries. We found a wide variety of complex connections made between particular interests and the public good in the Clavey case, where the public good was based variously on universal principles, majority support, or the aggregation or procedural collection of all the separate, specific interests. In the Somport case, there were quite different emphases on these various models, with most examples reflecting references to a "substantive" public good model based on principles valuing what is good for everyone collectively. There was also little evidence in France of an American-style view of the community or the public good as a collection of specific interests, nor of the need for majority support.

Reflecting these different models of the public good, we found similar differences in the forms and logics of organizational coordination (and local community activism) in the two countries. The local "coalition of interests" opposing the Clavey dam was explicitly oriented toward collecting a maximum of the discrete "interests" of the community together into a "broad-based" group of citizens which could speak with some political authority as the voice of the community's diverse groups. In contrast, the various alliances of *"coordination"* developed by the Somport opponents are not designed to collect disparate interests but rather to coordinate an integrated opposition. The local *Comité d'Habitants* in the French case was oriented around a set of concerns shared by the members not as interests but as inhabitants, and it rests on a vision of local community and attachment in terms of patrimony.

In general, these findings suggest not simply a rethinking of the standard view of "strategy" but also of the view of "interests" as enduring, all-determining qualities of individuals or groups, and of debate about the public good as either normatively separated from interests or as merely a disguise for special interest claims. Instead, our analysis shows the need to look closely at the way the logic and language of interests is extended beyond the individual and beyond the particular in culturally patterned ways, and at how a particular type or level of interest is attributed to others (to denounce them) or to oneself or one's group (as a legitimate "stance" in certain contexts). Further comparative research should explore the historical sources of these interesting cultural differences as well as examining how cultural conceptions of community, interests, and the public good are played out in other sorts of disputes.

Notes

1 The distinctions in meaning among terms such as "public good," "common good," and "public interest" are blurred in ordinary English usage and vary significantly across academic disciplines and subfields, with no single set of meanings gaining widespread authority and recognition (see Barry 1990 [1965] for an illustrative attempt to make definitive distinctions among the terms). We use the term "public good" primarily in this chapter, but occasionally we use "common good" and "public interest" as well. "Public good" has the widest range of uses and meanings in social science, and for this reason is perhaps the most appropriate to use in an empirical study of how practical actors use the term or define the concept. We should be clear, however, that what we mean by "public good" is much broader and open to variation and abstraction than what economists or public choice theorists mean by public good (i.e. a valued good that is potentially beneficial for and available to everyone, regardless of whether they contributed to its provision: cf. Olson 1971 [1965]). We allow for many more uses of the term than this, including ones in which something very intangible, like a sense of fairness or the procedural inclusion of many groups, is said to be "in the public good."

2 In such sequences, actors do not only shift among, but also combine, different pragmatic regimes (Lafaye 1994; Thévenot 1995a, 1996d; in English: 2000b, 1996c) such as familiar acquaintance (Thévenot 1994), planned instrumental action (Thévenot 1995b) and public justification (Boltanski and Thévenot

1991; for a short presentation in English see Boltanski and Thévenot 1999). The grounds of this *sociologie pragmatique* of regimes of action and coordination are presented in Boltanski 1990, with special regard to the regime of "*agapè*" as love without judgment, and in Thévenot 1990b, forthcoming. For a discussion from the perspective of a sociology of modernity, see Wagner 1994a, 1999.

3   This does not mean we cannot identify in some cases that the basis for a denunciation of someone is that they are driven primarily by a hidden interest. This is an important part of approaching the problem empirically.

4   Even a useful and detailed typology (Cress and Snow 1996) tends to put "instrumental resources," moral arguments, and material equipment on the same level.

5   As Hans Joas (1993) argues, pragmatist philosophy moves American sociology in just this direction, toward an examination of the creative aspect of human action.

6   As we stated in Chapter 9, our focus is on the "pragmatic use" of cultural repertoires within a set of constraints, including the differential access to repertoires (see Lamont 1992 on access to repertoires).

7   On the pluralization of logics as a crisis of organized modernity, see Wagner 1994b.

8   Many interest approaches, such as newer rational choice theories, have refined their view to leave the definition of interests open to individual interpretation and changes over time. What we object to in these approaches is the view of people only in terms of their interests, when in fact this is just one of many ways to characterize or evaluate people (see Espeland 1998 on this point).

9   See Berry 1996; Heinz et al. 1993; Petracca 1992; Scholzman and Tierney 1986. See Ingram et al. 1995 on interest groups and environmental policy specifically.

10 E.g. Dahl 1967, 1989; Lowi 1969; Schattschneider 1975 [1960]; Offerlé 1994.

11 Our question is similar to the one which Clemens (1997) addressed, which she developed out of the new institutionalism theory in sociology (Powell and DiMaggio 1991). New institutionalism, Clemens says, "does not deny that politics may be driven by self-interest but asks how 'self-interest' is constructed and *under what conditions* it becomes the dominant script guiding political action" (1997, p. 9, italics added).

12 Again, our view of interests as malleable and extendable does not mean we think the public good claims that groups make are false or merely strategic ploys.

13 We treat the public good as an "essentially contested concept" (Gallie 1956), and hope that by exploring how it is contested we can gain crucial insights into larger social, cultural, and political dynamics; this is the benefit of studying such concepts.

14 This approach seems most appropriate to analyze political disputes in which two or more legitimate, common goals (not just special interests) come into conflict. Environmental disputes have historically been important cases of such conflicts, when meeting common environmental goals (e.g. preserving

natural resources) potentially conflicts with meeting common economic goals (e.g. sustaining industrial production). See Hundley 1992; Walton 1992; and Worster 1985, for good historical reviews of these dynamics in previous water conflicts in California. For French literature on the political implications of environmentalism, see: Acot 1988; Alphandery et al. 1991; Berque 1996; Ferry 1992; Godard 1990; Kalaora and Savoye 1985; Larrère and Larrère 1997; Lascoumes 1994; Latour 1995; Mathieu 1992; Moscovici 1977; Serres 1990.

15 See Hunter 1994; Rauch 1994; and Navarro 1984 for the popularized version of this view.

16 See Jasper 1997 on the "virtuosity" and creativity of American protesters and movement organizers, and Brint 1994 on the "particularizing refinement" frame in professional culture. Also see Lemieux and Schmalzbauer in this volume.

17 The multiple competencies displayed by the Clavey disputants is not adequately explained by the relatively more technical nature of the debate in that conflict. Many defenders of the Somport project presented predominantly technical arguments.

18 On the relations between forms of knowledge and regimes of engagements, see Thévenot 1996c, 2000b.

19 The "division of rhetorical labor" involves not simply assigning "rhetoric" (in the pejorative sense) to different allies, but rather involves the complex distribution of all aspects of public argumentation: issue focus or specialty, fact gathering, development and employment of proof, etc.

20 In fact, the main San Francisco environmental lawyer involved in the Clavey dispute, Richard Roos-Collins, had previously co-authored a book titled *Rivers At Risk*, which gave explicit instructions on "how to save your local river" – how to build a working coalition and craft a strategic plan, how to make effective arguments and make sure your allies make similar arguments, and how to respond to your opponent's attacks (Echeverria et al. 1989; see also Owens 1991, Crowfoot and Wondolleck 1990).

21 They pursued legal challenges to the report up to the highest court of administrative law in France, and eventually got the report's recommendation nullified.

22 Pétetin considered this legalistic orientation treasonous and disqualified it because of the lack of any physical and emotional engagement.

23 In contrast to the Clavey case, the arguments in a single realm of the Somport dispute sometimes directly tie the many pieces of the arrangement together and make "compromises" (Boltanski and Thévenot 1991) between types of arguments. For example, farmers in the Aspe Valley are not persuaded to sell to foreigners simply because the arguments are offered by village elders or because it would advance the local public good, but also because they are made aware of the broader public good being served by the whole arrangement. The farmers' concern with "cultivating nature" is shown to be overlapping with the environmentalists' concern with "protecting nature," in a way that is much less common in the United States.

24 This sequential combination of private goals and public justification does not always imply the justification is fake (Lafaye 1994). We want to consider the

possibility that the two moments are distinct. A distinction made by Philippe Corcuff (Corcuff and Sanier 1995) between "Machiavellian" action and "Machiavellic" action is useful in this regard. "Machiavellian" action involves references to the common good which are serious even if combined with a very instrumental plan, while "Machiavellic" is strictly instrumental and calculating without reference to any common good except perhaps as a purely self-interested rhetorical move.

25 This is partly a result of the pragmatic constraint of the interview setting, which tends to push people toward describing their positions in terms of their general application and hence away from reference to possible self-interest. The interview setting is similar to other public arenas of argumentation in this sense. On the relations between the mode of survey and the "pragmatic regime" which tends to be induced in each mode, see Thévenot (1996d, 2000b).

26 In some cases, the interest of an individual (e.g. of a common citizen, acting as a citizen) might be considered more publicly legitimate than the interest of a collectivity (e.g. of a specific company, or of a heavily polluting industry).

27 The "private" in private interest can mean personal (not public), or individual, but may also mean non-governmental either in terms of "non-profit" or corporate.

28 So the label "special interest" might be attributed to all three of the following groups: an organization of trout fishermen seeking to conserve rivers in its members' domain (non-profit group, semi-private goal); a national environmental organization seeking to conserve all "endangered rivers" nationwide for the good of future generations (non-profit group, public goal); and a rafting company lobbying in Washington DC to conserve the river they raft on (for-profit group, private goal perhaps presented also as a public good).

29 Sometimes the less pejorative term "specific interest" is used in this instance, to clarify that the interest or goal of the group is one among many existing interests or goals.

30 The common good justifications reviewed from both cases in the previous chapter would be classified in this basic category of "substantive" public good claims.

31 These sorts of arguments often involve an attempt to give some sort of evidence in support of the claim of widespread support, which in the Clavey case usually consisted of references to the number of signatures on a petition or the number of people giving supportive testimony in a public hearing. While this category of public good claim seems similar to the justifications based on renown and public opinion described in Chapter 9, the important difference is that the central basis for the claim here is on the *number* of supportive people, rather than on the extent of public knowledge, attention, or fame.

32 See Moody 2000, for an exploration of the important distinctions between "aggregative" and "procedural" models, which are loosely combined here (for ease of comparison) but which must be kept analytically distinct in order to accurately depict the diversity of models used in practice. An aggregative argument is based on the collection of many public good proposals together, but the procedure used in this collection is not itself the key to why the aggregation is defended as in the public good (as it would be in a procedural

model). In addition, relying too heavily on the classical, simplistic "procedural" versus "substantive" distinction misses the point that different types of procedures unequally facilitate different types of goods or outcomes, and some procedures lead routinely to substantive rather than aggregative goods (see also Thévenot 2000a).

33 *"Nous n'allons tout de même pas crever dans nos sabots pour faire plaisir à des écolos nantis."*

34 Gunn (1989) shows how French discourse about the public interest evolved through many stages during the seventeenth and eighteenth centuries, even at times considering aggregative conceptions quite different from the now dominant conception of a "general will." For example, he notes Turgot's use of a formula for the public interest as "la somme des *intérêts particuliers*" (1989, p. 201), and similar views among the Physiocrats.

35 In the French case, there has been an attempt to build an institution to sustain a procedural composition of common goods, the "Institution patrimoniale du Haut Béarn." But it was criticized for being highly skewed by the personality of the chairman, Jacques Lassalle, a fervent defender of the road-tunnel project, and by the insistence on the "patrimonial" good of domestic worth (Thévenot 1996d).

36 This Coalition approach points to the importance of the distinction between the aggregative and procedural models that are loosely combined in this paper, because it involves the collection of interests without the necessity of a procedural adjudication or compromise. On these distinctions, see also the Conclusion to this volume by Thévenot and Lamont.

37 The *collectif* form of organization arose historically out of the New Left and May 1968 reforms, which sought to develop civic, solidarity-oriented, decentralized organizations outside the traditional, bureaucratic and technocratic model of the big political parties. On the transformation of political activism in recent French social movements, see Thévenot 1999.

38 The *Comité* is decentralized like the *collectif* and oriented toward the "grassroots," but it is less directly tied to the New Left reforms.

Conclusion: Exploring the French and American polity

Laurent Thévenot and Michèle Lamont

This chapter offers a reflection on the implications of our findings for understanding the social bonds that link members of the French and American polity. There are a number of perspectives that we could have used to describe the thread that runs through our various case studies. In the introduction, we identified some major trends in the relative salience of boundaries across national contexts. The centrality of market arguments in the United States, and of solidarity (civic) arguments in France are cases in point. In our conclusion, we could focus on the conditions that support the frequent use of such criteria across national settings. We could also trace their impact on French and American collective identities as they are formulated, for instance, around issues of sexual harassment. Instead, we have chosen to speculatively explore how our various criteria of evaluation are typically combined and sometimes conflict, and how they are used to define the polity and maintain a political community in the two national settings. In the process, we bring together various themes that emerge from our specific case studies, elaborate on them, and suggest directions for further explorations.

In the first section, we address the drawing of boundaries and the closure of the communities of reference they suppose – in particular, the weight given to race as a mechanism of closure within humanity. This is an important dimension of the definition of "common-ness" (or sociality) and as such, is essential for understanding evaluation and how people are construed as belonging together (Jenkins 1996). In the second section, we return to the question of the weight of criteria of evaluation and are concerned with how civic solidarity and market performance are typically brought together as principles of evaluation in France and the United States. We describe this process as it appears in our case studies, ranging from the definition of literary and artistic values to environmental conflicts, issues of sexual harassment and racial inequality. Here again, we pinpoint the primacy of market evaluation over other types of evaluations in the United States as compared to France. In the third section, we turn to national differences in the articulation between the public and the private manifested around issues of self-presentation and in the place given to personal ties in public debates. We also consider national differences in the limitations put on state intervention in the realm of private relationships. Finally, in the fourth section, we examine the rules and frames that characterize the functioning of a pluralist polity in France and the United States. We point to differences in the place given to majority opinion, the hearing of the diversity of positions, bargaining by interest groups, and reaching political consensus (or compromise) around the definition of common good. We also discuss differences in the place and the meaning given to multiculturalism in the shaping of France and American polity. These discussions can be viewed as attempts to explore available repertoires of forms of sociality and the impact of national political traditions on them.

Who is being compared? The community of reference in evaluations

Our case studies reveal variations in the groups of reference that are implicitly or explicitly taken into consideration when people evaluate others. In some cases, the group is all-encompassing and based on the sharing of basic traits, such as the simple fact of being a "human being." In others, it is more limited and based on specific characteristics having to do with race or gender. Moreover, our case studies reveal differences in the extent to which the various criteria used to draw boundaries are typically used in conjunction with narrower or wider communities of reference across some of our case studies. From a political perspective (the perspective of the "polis"), the most legitimate criteria of evaluation (or closure) are those that can be met by the largest possible groupings (e.g. "all humans").[1] We should also note that the size of the community of reference has implications for issues of social justice. For instance, in our study of American environmental conflicts, activists who define their community of reference in such a way that it includes even spotted owls aim at ensuring the protection of the moral rights of these non-human beings.

The chapter on French and American racism and anti-racism speaks directly to the question of the boundaries of the communities of reference. Evaluations of differences between races suppose that the drawing of boundaries among human beings is on the basis of a hierarchy of innate biological and genetic differences. As such, they challenge the notion of common dignity for all human beings central to the Enlightenment tradition or to Judeo-Christian religious traditions. This type of evaluation is absent among the French workers Lamont interviewed, but it constitutes an infrequent yet significant trope used by Euro-American racists. A few African American interviewees also rebut white racism by pointing to their greater resilience as compared to Euro-Americans, using physical differences between races to buttress their belief in the superiority of blacks.[2]

In contrast, anti-racist arguments often presume a *common humanity*, or common dignity among all human beings, and as such can be described as universalistic. For instance, anti-racists in both countries point to physical evidence of similarities across racial groups (*"we are all passing like clouds"* [i.e. are all mortals]; *"if you and I cut ourselves, red blood will come out"*). Moreover, anti-racism based on a discourse of human rights (absent from Lamont's interviews but central in the literature on the topic)[3] also presumes a common humanity, against far Right discourse promoting community boundaries based on cultural closeness or likeness (see, for instance, Schain's analysis [1987] of the political platform of the National Front).

An enlarged community of reference potentially involving all human beings is also present in arguments pointing to the role of *market performance* and consumption as a basis of equality or inequality (although they both vary across classes). Market references are often used to ground more basic arguments about human dignity in the United States, but never in France: American workers who are racist point to the inability of blacks to make money (or consume) to demonstrate their difference from whites, while American anti-racist workers point to blacks' ability to make and spend money to establish racial equality: *"money makes people equal."* Blacks, like whites, *"want a decent paying job, a few credit cards, a car that's decent, a nice place to live . . . their thinking is just about* equal *or the same."*[4]

Communities of reference can also be defined more narrowly on the basis of *cultural similarity* or likeness. Such boundaries are drawn by American and French racists alike when they point to their moral and cultural superiority in relation to African Americans or North African immigrants (who are described as lazy or backward). Conversely, North African immigrants and blacks rebut French racism by privileging their own spiritual and moral values, or the warmth of their familial relations, which they find lacking among French natives. However, moral principles of evaluation are not necessarily particularistic: they can also be used to show similarities among all human beings, as when anti-racists in both countries argue that *"there are good and bad people in all races."*

Finally, a narrow definition of the community of reference is generally incompatible with civic solidarity, which we view as fundamentally universalistic because it is grounded in notions of common humanity, irrespective of cultural membership. Hence, French participants in our project were surprised that American anti-racists could offer evidence of equality by stating *"we are all equal because we are Americans."* This statement refers to nationality, a form of cultural particularism,[5] to demonstrate equality. As such, it denies universal equality based on a common humanity.[6]

Historically in France, the state has often adopted solidaristic measures to reduce inequality, allocating benefits only to members of the national community. In periods of crisis, xenophobic groups such as the National Front attack these policies by challenging the civic notion of solidarity: they argue that the French should prioritize helping those who are least different from themselves. Hence, they support an "uncivic," because limited, definition of an ethnically French population worthy of the benefits of social policies, a population that of necessity excludes "parasites" (cf. Chapter 2). Both France and the United States have been the site of several episodes where such "uncivic" definitions of the community gained in legitimacy.[7] However, interviews with French and American workers suggest that overall, French workers put more emphasis on extending solidarity to the human race as a dimension of morality than do their American counterparts. African Americans simultaneously largely define a worthy person by his or her ability to show solidarity toward all human beings and emphasize racial solidarity within the black race (Lamont 2000).

How is the polity defined in civic terms?

To clarify the last paragraph, we need to turn to differences in the political culture and in the construction of the individual in the two societies and examine more closely how the polity is defined in civic terms in the two national contexts. After taking on this issue, we turn to national differences in the articulation of various criteria of evaluation in France and the United States, a topic related to that of their relative salience across national contexts.

A first difference is that in the United States, civic equality is more often primarily framed in terms of citizenship entailing legal rights, whereas in France, it is more frequently expressed in terms of solidarity. A second contrast is that while a market logic and civic equality are intertwined in the American case, civic solidarity is opposed to market inequalities in France. These differences are apparent in our analyses of environmental conflicts as well as processes of evaluation of cultural and artistic goods. Although the French Revolution promoted the universalistic individualism of the Enlightenment,[8] in the French context the polity often equates individual interests with egoism and lack of civil solidarity (or the common interests of all citizens).[9] This conception of the individual as particularistic and antithetical to "common good" is foreign to

American liberalism. In the latter, the individual is both the main actor in the market and the entity to which civil rights are given. Moreover, each person is his/her own center of evaluation (Walzer 1984) such that values can be understood as simultaneously subjective, expressing individual interests, and legitimate. Individual opinions compete in the "market-place" of ideas and are selected for their merit and contribution to the collective good, instead of being equated with private (i.e. illegitimate) interest.[10] This is why one can state that in the United States, civic solidarity (defined in legal terms) is compatible with market competition.

Such a strong association between these two principles of evaluation is not present in France (Boltanski and Thévenot 1991). Here, civic legitimacy is more associated with the defense of solidarity defined as action aimed at reducing inequalities. This is expressed in large-scale demonstrations and in attempts to mobilize allies by using a language of "solidarity across struggles." (cf. the conflict of Somport in Chapter 9). This solidarity is also expressed through collective groupings (especially "classes") that have been historically construed in the context of the workplace. It is there, in the workplace, that group membership is primarily manifested and where solidaristic policies and movements are developed (and not in the civic/legal realm, as in the United States). And in the workplace, individuals are framed as members of a group sharing equal status, as opposed to being framed as independent individuals functioning within the logic of the market.[11] A tradition of group solidarity is, of course, also visible in American labor history, but it is not framed in contradistinction to market mechanisms as radically as is the case in France. Moreover, this tradition does not structure the overall functioning of the polity as powerfully it does in France.[12]

Our case studies also indicate that the use of market demand as the principle of distribution of culture in the United States is interrelated with the civic notion that culture should be democratically available. In other words, cultural criteria of evaluation are subordinated to economic ones, and this is justified by democratic principles. For instance, as Daniel Weber shows in his study of the publishing industry in Paris and New York (Chapter 5), American publishers do not as readily use the distinction between high-brow and low-brow culture, which is common in France. They appear to be comparatively more reluctant to judge the value of cultural products in themselves, and instead point to the presence of differentiated market niches and to market performance to describe value – hence favoring the development of mass culture as open to everyone. In France, by contrast, although references to market value are becoming more common, including among "high culture" publishers, they remain comparatively rare. Even the most commercial French publishing houses denounce market pressures and profit motives (*"just making money"*) in the name of the cultural value of their product (*"traditions and qualities"*). Moreover, both literary publishing houses and those with a more commercial purview readily employ the distinction between "creative literature" and "mass market" literature. Commercial houses have recently begun to recruit "intellectual" editors, and literary editors are trying their hand at more commercially viable texts. Similar trends also appear in Heinich's comparative study of contemporary art: French artists are less likely to accept to judge the value of art by the demand for it than their American counterparts are (*"We have a free market that will support that which finds an audience"*). Note, however, that a romantic anti-market tradition remains characteristic of segments of the American art world.

Finally, our case studies suggest that market and civic arguments are more often used in conjunction with one another in the United States, as is the case when groups claim to represent collective interests. It is notably the case in the discourse elaborated by American activists involved in environmental disputes as compared to the French: Americans emphasize market arguments concerning the price of deregulated electricity. "*Ratepayers*" are a hybrid of *customer* and *taxpayer* and they claim a collective interest (as *citizens being served by a public utility*) – not only an individual economic interest. They eventually succeed in blocking the construction of the California dam studied by Moody and Thévenot, partly by using such culturally potent arguments. In the case of the French environmental conflict, by contrast, there is no connection between opposing the project in the name of the interests of the citizen and opposing it in the name of market prices. Instead, a movement of international civic solidarity brings together European and American environmentalists to buy land together in order to deter the construction of a super-highway (see Chapter 9). Similarly, Camus-Vigué's study of Rotary Clubs (Chapter 8) shows that philanthropic gestures typical of American members of this club are viewed as altruistic and truly solidaristic, although these gestures are frequently carried by local businessmen. By contrast, when made by French businessmen, the same kinds of gestures are denounced by their recipients as economically motivated and hence not reflecting genuine civic solidarity.

The constructions of a public space and the place of personal ties: the boundary between the public and the private

In this section, we offer some insights into the constructions of a public space in the two countries. We have noted that the discourses studied in this book (including our interviews) are generally made by actors in public settings. As such, their legitimacy is subject to the judgment of others, which creates specific constraints on how people present their opinion. This is particularly true for rules of participation in political debates, and for how conflicts over moral and aesthetic matters are framed (it may be less important in the realm of work and business, where entrepreneurial aggressiveness is more of an asset than in public debates). Drawing on our comparative case studies, we discuss: (1) the ways in which democratic norms set limits on self-referential or singular forms of aesthetic expression; (2) the place of local and personal ties and of private interests in public life; and (3) the boundary between the public and the private.

Democratic civility and moral evaluation

Above we suggested that in France the personal (or the individual) is often strongly construed as illegitimate and opposed to "the public," which is associated with the general interest. In contrast, American definitions of individualism, largely shaped by the liberal doctrine, conceive the individual as a kind of "public being" who by definition contributes to giving birth to the public interest. This requires that s/he submits his/her position to the evaluation of others according to the rules of liberal democratic space.[13] The latter creates constraints on rules of self-presentation.[14] More specifically, this democratic space exists alongside codes of democratic civility (in the public sphere and elsewhere) and requires that citizens contribute to creating conditions for communicating with one another, by being responsive to the needs of the audience and by avoiding idiosyncrasies.[15] Such codes of civility are documented in the literature and by our case studies. For instance, Americans frequently criticize others for not respecting the audience by being *"too pushy," "too abrasive,"* or *"too opinionated"* (interview analyzed in Lamont 1992, p. 37).[16] Similarly, in academia, scholars are comparatively more frequently stigmatized for not presenting their work in an accessible format, and for not adequately playing by the rules of a democratic intellectual space in the United States than in France.[17] In the arts, Heinich's study clearly demonstrates that avant-garde work is more frequently criticized in the United States for violating democratic rules (which is sometimes construed as immoral).[18] In particular, artistic products are more often criticized for not being accessible to all, and artists are more frequently attacked for being egoistic, self-indulgent, or self-centered. Moreover, while in France, artistic merit is typically examined through exclusively aesthetic lenses (based on criteria *of "seriousness," "talent," "invention,"* "*disinterest,*" or "*authenticity*"), in the United States, it is more often questioned because the artist has violated democratic rules of public civility, by, for instance, desecrating the American flag, insulting minorities, or spoiling a public place. Heinich suggests that the forms of rejection are also far more public in the United States (scandals, trials, petitions, demonstrations) and rely on the legal, political, and constitutional resources available to the citizen. Hence, she proposes that public opinion effectively limits the autonomy of the creator (or at least how and where s/he can present his or her work). In other words, democratic culture rests on a conception of individualism that weakens the boundary between the public and the private in the aesthetic realm. The most powerful counterweight to this subordination is found in civil rights, and particularly the right to freedom of expression guaranteed by the First Amendment of the United States Constitution.[19]

Creating a public space out of local and personal attachments

Our case studies also reveal cross-national differences in the role given to personal ties, local embeddedness, or tradition in public life in claim-making and as bases for public action. How are such relationships brought into the public space? The answers are different in the two countries, depending on the principles around which the public space is shaped. Intimate relationships or familiar acquaintances are not appropriate in such a space. Yet, these personal relationships can be at the basis of public reputations and hence become legitimately institutionalized as bases for public action.[20] In the two countries, we found such appeals to tradition and to personal and local attachment in claim-making.

In the California environmental conflict studied by Thévenot, Moody, and Lafaye, activists who fight development projects oppose them in the name of the preservation of a treasured local place: the value of "place" is grounded in its relationship with the local history and heritage, and its meaning for the personal history and lives of many inhabitants. This type of emphasis on neighborhood and local ties is more often related to the political construction of the local "community" in the United States (this last notion having no equivalent in France,[21] as noted by Tocqueville 1980 [1835]). Moreover, in American society ties to a local environment are often framed in terms of property ties and rights (following a market logic). For instance, Americans involved in the environmental conflict more often make claims in the name of their economic interest and those of their neighbors, using "*Not in my backyard*" (or NIMBY) types of arguments that privilege evaluation based on private ownership and on small and particularistic communities of reference (to go back to the issue we raised at the beginning of this chapter).[22] In contrast, French activists studied by Thévenot, Moody, and Lafaye more often promote environmental solutions in the name of a *shared* cultural tradition, a patrimony or a regional good – as opposed to their individual economic interest. All this points to different ways of valuing locality in the French and American cultural repertoires of justification.

In France, we also find a strong tension between public evaluations based on tradition, locality, and personal ties ("domestic" worth) and the impersonal relationships that prevail between formally equal citizens ("civic" worth). Since the Revolution, the latter has been used to denounce "local" and personal dependencies that are frequently associated with the hierarchical orders of the *ancien régime*.[23] As we saw, the local continues to be viewed as potentially leading to particularism, paternalism, clientelism, or corruption.[24] One such example can be found in the case of a schoolteacher who refused a donation from the local Rotary Club because it was targeted on a particular student and solicited through personal channels (Chapter 8). The proposed donation was rejected because it was perceived to encourage paternalism, an illegitimate personal tie.[25] In contrast, again, as suggested by Tocqueville (1980 [1835]), in the United States, the local community is central to the *Res publica* and within it, individuals exercise their citizenship in proximate relation to one another, in their neighborhood (see the discussion of the meaning of community and local in the two countries in Chapters 8 ad 9). This local American community, where civic solidarity and local ties are legitimately linked, eschews the ever-present tensions between a general civic solidarity and the "domestic" kind of bond based on local attachments that we find in France.[26]

The boundary between the public and the private

Finally, two of the domains we studied illuminated cross-national differences in the construction of the boundary between the public and the private:[27] the comparison of definitions of sexual harassment and the comparison of journalistic objectivity. Feminist understandings of what constitutes sexual harassment in the two countries (Chapter 3) call into question a defense of the private sphere against the invasion of the state, which defense is viewed as contributing to the perpetuation of domination and discrimination.[28] In the United States, anti-discrimination legislation is the instrument *par excellence* used to fight gender discrimination. The latter is condemned because it excludes people from equal access to market opportunity. This legislation extends the sphere of intervention of the law to areas (sexual relations) that often escape legal regulation because they are perceived as being located in the private domain. In France, these juridical regulations appear primarily under the aegis of the *droit du travail* (labor regulations), and aim at protecting workers against the abuse of official authority within the hierarchical structures of professional relations. Penal law also condemns abuse of authority in other realms such as professor-student, doctor-patient, or landlord-tenant relationships. Looking more closely into how feminists assess whether specific situations constitute cases of sexual harassment, as Saguy does, generates nuanced evidence concerning the legitimate sphere of state intervention. American feminists include in the category of sexual harassment actions such as jeers, derogatory statements about femininity, and jokes with sexual connotations. The American judicial category of "hostile environment" is favorable to this expansive definition. Some French feminists, however, adopt a narrower definition of sexual harassment, excluding even persistent efforts by one partner to reestablish a consensual relationship. Some of the French participants believe that personal relationships of this type are beyond the purview of public institutions and should be dealt informally by the concerned parties. A position of this type is concordant with the notion that the workplace should be the site for a plurality of types of relationships, public as well as personal or intimate. In the United States, we find some evidence that the maintenance of a professional frame of reference and the need to protect co-workers from illegitimate sexual pressure are central to aspects of American cultural repertoires.[29] Indeed, Saguy finds that American respondents develop arguments about professionalism that are not found in France.[30] The arguments about professionalism create a higher standard for the workplace (no dating, no naked photos, no sexual jokes, etc.) than elsewhere.

Finally, the comparative study of journalists (Chapter 6) also bears on the relation between forms of personal commitment and the requirement for personal and interpersonal detachment that characterizes the professional workplace. The difference between mainstream reporters and politically engaged journalists is neatly expressed by the ways in which they evaluate the boundary between private and public (professional) life. The former enforce a clear boundary between the two spheres: they mention the dangers of "dinners out," and of "social events," and they are wary of the "trap of friendship" that could lead them to be obliged to exchange favors. If Americans highlight a straightforward commitment to "objectivity," French journalists frame the issue more in terms of setting apart their personal opinions from the news, and of explicitly taking distance from personal relationship and friendship when reporting, thus expressing the need to separate the public from the private.

The political grammars of pluralism

We now use our case studies to speculate about national differences between the French and American democratic polity concerning how positions are constructed as promoting the common good. We are interested in national differences in the ways members produce and experience pluralism and proceed to validate their positions. Some of these political grammars are described in the literature on the liberal polity, from Madison to Tocqueville, while other are discussed in the European political writings on social criticism and on the defense of the common good and the general interest.[31] Most of these grammars are found in both countries, although with very different weights. They can be analyzed under the following headings: (a) the voice of the majority; (b) the democratic expression of individual opinions; (c) the balance between interest groups; (d) the reference to and combination of different conceptions of the common good; and (e) the use of multiculturalism to voice pluralism.

The voice of the majority

In the conflicts over evaluation we have studied, Americans are more likely than the French to justify political positions by referring to public opinion and to the opinion of the majority. Respect for the majority often serves to invalidate controversial minority opinions that are considered extremist. This is evident in the rhetoric used to reject contemporary art, and in the ways in which French and American journalists legitimize their position concerning the necessity to keep personal opinion private. Moreover, whenever public spending is discussed, the "taxpayer" is a trope frequently used to point to the power of the majority (Heinich on public endowments for the arts; Thévenot, Moody, and Lafaye on the Clavey dam project).

The democratic expression of individual opinions

In classical political liberalism, a healthy polity requires that individuals air their opinions (while following the democratic rules) and that their autonomous capacity to judge as independent individuals be respected. In the United States, one finds clear illustrations of this form of liberal democratic civility in the manner in which journalists characterize their profession, as described by Lemieux and Schmalzbauer. American journalists located in the political center insist that anyone be given "*a chance to be heard*" and pride themselves on their respect of diversity (e.g. on presenting the "pro" and "con" perspectives.) Also defending professionalism, French centrist journalists emphasize the need for "polyphony" (Lemieux 2000) in journalistic coverage and want to represent multiple viewpoints. The recent effort of some French Left-wing journalists to repudiate the Marxist-Leninist notion of "propaganda" in favor of journalistic polyphony is a good example of the influence of mainstream criteria of professionalism. Stronger cross-national differences are found in the comparison of the French and American environmental conflicts. In the United States, the procedures used to manage such conflicts require that citizens be consulted by way of "public hearings" where the diverse opinions of the concerned citizenry are heard. By contrast, the French "public survey" ("*enquête publique*") consists in a series of individual interviews conducted by a government employee, in order to write a report on the public utility of the project. Here, the term "public" as it is used in the United States refers to procedures by which individual opinions are collected and expressed to others (i.e. made in public – as in "public hearing"), whereas in the French case, what is "public" is the utility of the project, i.e. the fact that it serves the collective good. This leads us to believe that the democratic confrontation of individual opinions is more central to the grammar of the American pluralistic polity than to the French, where the reference to substantive common goods is more significant.

The balance between interest groups

The political model of bargaining and of balancing group interests and power has become a *common locus* of American political science to the point where it constitutes the vocabulary most often used in contemporary descriptions of the functioning of the polity. This model is often associated with the efficiency of supply and demand in politics.[32] Some have criticized this "bargaining" terminology for being reductionist and have argued that we need to distinguish between diverse ways of framing private interests in the public sphere.[33] Accordingly, from our comparative case studies we have identified various types of interest formats used by participants in environmental conflicts, namely self-interest, special interest, particular interest, and public interest (Chapter 10). Among these types of interests, we have found that American activists view group interests as more legitimate than the French do: "commonality" is built by aggregating particular interests, i.e. by blurring the line between particular and general interests. Hence, American activists use a "bargaining" terminology more readily than their French counterparts, who denounced "interest" as benefiting exclusively to one individual or one group. Moreover, in California, activists opposing the dam legitimize their position in discussions with state representatives by calling attention to the fact that their "coalition" speaks for a large number of disparate voices, or particular interests. Similarly, in classical liberalism, the reproduction of the polity results from the transformation of opinions into interests and from the balancing of interest: this model has been part of the classical liberal doctrine from the time of the American founding fathers (see Lowi 1987; Manin 1989a, 1994a, 1994b), as a defense against what Madison (1961) and Tocqueville (1980) defined as the risk of "tyranny" of the majority.

The combination of different conceptions of the common good

As an alternative to the other grammars we have mentioned, especially the "balancing of interests" approach, actors often resort to various ways of combining conceptions of common good. However, the identification and confrontation of these conceptions is made difficult by the fact that standard categories used in political and social science are often biased towards grammars. Most analyses that bear on the notion of "interest" are skeptical of references to "general interests" (widespread in social sciences) and often offer "realistic" debunking of the true interests hidden behind a reference to the common good or to values.[34] It is therefore difficult to study the ways actors demonstrate the generality of their own interests, or the fact that their position or action benefits the common good, as opposed to special interests.[35] By comparing how, in the two polities, actors legitimize their positions as serving the common good (Boltanski and Thévenot 1991), we find that both in France and the United States, actors frequently depart from just "bargaining" between interests and attempt to reach a compromise between various forms of the common good. The use of technical procedures observed by organizational theorists interested in legitimation processes (e.g. Meyer and Rowan 1977) can be viewed as one way of integrating such common goods.[36] We have identified several instances of the use of such procedures in the United States, particularly in cases where actors come together to discuss or establish regulations (see the comparative studies in this volume of journalists, sexual harassment, and environmental conflicts).[37] In contrast, the French are more likely to view the use of such apparently neutral modes of combining evaluations of what is worthy as reflecting a lack of authentic commitment or a strategic or cynical stance toward the common good (on this topic see the chapters on contemporary art, journalism, and environmental conflict).

The use of multiculturalism to voice pluralism

We also find important cross-national differences in the way particular-ism is framed in the construction of the pluralistic polity. This is especially salient in the use of multiculturalist arguments in the two national set-tings. In areas of concern as varied as racism (Lamont), sexual harass-ment (Saguy), literary studies (Duell), publishing (Weber), and art (Heinich), multiculturalist arguments are commonly made by Americans and infrequently, or not at all, made by the French.[38] Indeed, the contrast between American multiculturalism and French republicanism has become a common theme in the socio-political characterization of the two countries.[39] Multiculturalism has strong affinities with the liberal balance of interest groups discussed above.[40]

Multiculturalism "against" or "for" universalism   Multiculturalism challenges the notion of a single polity made up of similar and equal members and questions the possibility of universalism. Indeed, one of the characteristics of multicultural claims is that they presume relatively strong group boundaries, especially when claim-making is based on ethnic characteristics or sexual orientation. In this context, universalism is framed as one particular cultural set of beliefs among others. Liberal formulations of pluralism described above (namely, the democratic con-frontation of individual opinions and the balance of interest groups) can act as a bulwark against this radical pluralism. The presentation of all sides in a debate valued by professional American journalists, particularly those in the political center, is thus presented as an effort to counteract the danger of a society coming apart because of lack of communication (Chapter 6). As argued by Gitlin (1995), the American Left questions multiculturalist claims and the "balkanization" they might trigger by defending the importance of maintaining a notion of common good and a certain civic solidarity against inequalities and discrimination. He also points to the dangers of the "aggrandizement of difference" that jeopar-dizes the existence of a unified polity, and suggests that the "Culture War" has reversed traditional political roles by allowing conservatives to appeal to the common good instead of defending the special interests that they used to support.[41]

Multiculturalism does not result only in a fracturing of the polity. Indeed, it often proceeds from a critique of inequality grounded in civic solidarity that is, by definition, universalistic: the widespread use of a vocabulary of "discrimination" posits a universal community of human beings sharing primarily a right to equal opportunity and sometimes explicitly refers to human dignity.[42] Jason Duell's analysis of literary studies departments in France and the United States shows that American academics often denounce unequal treatment on the basis of race, class or gender, unlike the French. Minorities fighting for equality while affirming their common humanity create a paradox. They affirm differences that may lead to the decomposition of the polity.[43]

Multiculturalism and social protest   Multiculturalism also informs our understanding of national differences in the forms taken by social criticism (or social protest) in the two countries. First, we find an important temporal lag across the two countries, evidenced by the comparison of activism against sexual harassment (Chapter 3) and by the comparison between the modes of political engagement found in literary studies in France and the United States, one of the main sites for the American debate on multiculturalism (Chapter 4; Bryson 1999). The intensity of conflicts in American universities around issues of identity politics is comparable to the one found in the humanities and social sciences in the French academy during the 1970s, which is now viewed as part of the past (see also Chapter 6). Moreover, in contemporary France, literary studies departments are no longer the locus of protest movements, the latter centering now on unemployment, social benefits, and immigration laws, issues around which artists, by contrast, have been very active.[44]

But the differences between social protest in France and the United States go beyond the time-gap and contrasts in sites of mobilization. On the American side, protest is often organized around civil rights, i.e. around calling into question discrimination, to which affirmative action has been one response. Claims for equal opportunity (an argument having to do with equal access to market benefits) are central in anti-discrimination struggles. In France, on the contrary, social movements that take a stand against different kinds of inequality attempt to establish solidarity with, and continue to organize around, the inequalities generated by the market (Chapter 9; also Lamont 2000).[45] In other words, while in the United States, anti-discrimination law is organized around equalizing market opportunities so that they resemble what they would be in a "true market" (or a level field), in France, it is organized around mitigating the effects of the market.

Finally, the question of multiculturalism also illustrates how evaluations produced in each country are shaped by perceptions of the other society. For instance, French rejections of multiculturalism often refer to the perils of balkanization as exemplified by the alleged decomposition of American society. The construction of a national identity via the drawing of boundaries against the other society (Lamont 1992) plays a pivotal role in many of the assessments found here. Thus debates in France on the definition of sexual harassment refer to "American excesses," "hysterical" and "exaggerated concern" in a "general climate of suspicion," that is said to be unbearable "for the Latin people" and "French seduction" (phrases gathered in Saguy's interviews).

The approach we use presumes that we do not privilege the cultural norms of one country over the other. This analytical symmetry is at odds with the uneven cultural influence of French and American societies internationally. Not only do France and the United States occupy very unequal places in global markets, but communication infrastructures and the diffusion of neo-liberal models in Europe also show the traces of American ideological influence.

Conclusion

This brief panorama of the crosscutting themes emerging from our eight case studies offers direction for future sociological research on national repertoires of evaluation. Of course, much remains to be done in terms of systematic comparison between our findings and the literature on the topics we have addressed. Nevertheless, the value of our collective contribution will be measured not only by its promise, but by the concrete and grounded knowledge of the cultural dimensions of French and American societies that it offers in our specific case studies. And this judgment is, of course, in the hands of our readers, both French and Americans. With some trepidation, we leave the product of our collective adventure in their hands, with the hope that the criteria of evaluation they bring as readers will correspond to some degree with the ones we set for ourselves.

Notes

This chapter has benefited from reactions from Jeffrey Alexander, Thomas Bénatouïl, Luc Boltanski, Frank Dobbin, Eric Fassin, Riva Kastoryano, Paul Lichterman, Peter Meyers, and Renaud Seligman. Among the contributors to the volume, Cyril Lemieux, Michael Moody, and Abigail Saguy also provided us with detailed feedback.

1 Cf. Boltanski and Thévenot 1991. Such an assumption about legitimacy is also found in many theories of justice and in moral conceptualization (e.g. Kant's "golden rule," or Rawls' (1971) "veil of ignorance").

2 The declining importance of biological and genetic arguments in the rhetoric of racism is a major theme of sociological writings on racism (see the literature on symbolic racism, modern racism, and laissez-faire racism cited in Chapter 2 above). This literature does not discuss what this decline implies for changes in the community of reference used by racists and non-racists alike. (For an

alternative discussion of biological and genetic arguments in France and the United States focusing on the writings of social commentators, see Fassin 1997a.)

3 This puzzling absence might be explained by the low level of education of Lamont's interviewees. Gaxie (1978) and others have shown that cultural distance from official and legitimate political culture, of which the legal discourse is part, varies with level of education. Hence, the discourse that workers use to demonstrate or rebut racial inequality might be more exclusively grounded in personal everyday experience and less in abstract democratic ideals than is the case among college-educated people.

4 In particular, Molnar and Lamont (forthcoming) analyze how specialists in African American marketing understand that specific objects can be used to demonstrate racial equality.

5 Note that the American Constitution defines equal civil rights as a consequence of membership in that nation. Civic equality is thus fundamentally tied to membership in this national community, and not to cultural similarity. Hence, in this example, the reference to "Americans" does not necessarily imply a nationalist argument. This connection between rights and membership explains why Alexander (1997) can ground civil society (in general) in the "we-ness of the national community," as a kind of proxy for a more extensive civic solidarity, stating that it transcends particular commitments, narrow loyalties and sectarian interests.

6 Along the same lines, as French collaborators understand it, when the French Right stresses the Frenchness of French republicanism, it makes the latter incompatible with universalism by accentuating cultural particularism.

7 One should note that the theoretical frameworks that were brought together in our collective research endeavor favored one side or the other of these tensions. More specifically, "justification" as defined by Boltanski and Thévenot (1991) is viewed as having to answer to a requirement of universalism, whereas the boundary or cultural repertoire approach pays less attention to these issues.

8 Dumont (1991) stressed the difference between this French individualism and the German kind of "singularism" which is compatible with a holistic notion of culture.

9 Rousseau's political construction opposing "general will" and "particular interests" has clearly been influential in this regard. This opposition also permeates French social sciences. Michel Crozier and Erhard Friedberg's individualistic sociology of organization might be viewed as a reaction against the pre-eminence and valuation of collectives in other French sociological currents (Lafaye 1997).

10 Note, however, that we should not confuse the liberal balance of opinions with market competition of supply and demand (Manin 1994a, b).

11 Status and rights are institutionalized in a specific corpus of law, labor law ("*droit du travail*"), and it is through labor law that the French typically claim rights in the name of civic solidarity. In contrast, in the United States, the polity is organized less around civic solidarity than around the protection of civil rights. Of course, work also determines access to many social benefits in the United States (Dobbin and Sutton 1998). However, the historical literature on

the meaning of poverty in the United States suggests that there, dignity is given to workers because they contribute to society and are able to take advantage of opportunities in the labor market, which is taken to be proof of morality, i.e. of being self-sufficient and responsible (e.g. Katz 1989; on the relationship between work and American citizenship, see Shklar 1991). In contrast, in France, dignity is given to workers because they are members of productive organizations and as such are protected by labor law and unions. This protection is part of collective agreements sustained by group identity and solidarity. The unemployed receive benefits because they are compensated for being temporarily out of work. The increase in the number of permanently unemployed people threatens to crack this civic solidarity based on insertion in the workplace. The tension between such "social" solidarity and market principles is particularly visible in the construction of the European Community (Lyon-Caen and Lyon-Caen 1993).

12 For an illustration, see in particular the place given in French and American contemporary political discourse to the importance of socially reinserting in the social fabric the poor and the "excluded" (i.e., roughly speaking, victims of long-term unemployment) for the survival of the American and the French polity (Silver 1993; Lamont 2000).

13 Larmore (1987) opposes this kind of tie to the "mutually entwining bond" that is supposed by familiar acquaintance, the latter involving much "deeper" or "thicker" connections.

14 On the changing public-private boundaries, and especially of the social and political significance of "public" talk about "private" issues in the United States, see Josh Gamson's (1998) work on the presentation of sexual identity on television talk shows.

15 Quoting Horace Kallen (1924), who believed that the United States "has a peculiar anonymity," Walzer (1992) writes in *What it Means to be an American?* that "maybe cultural anonymity is the best possible grounding for American politics" (p. 23).

16 This criticism is easily addressed to the French, who are viewed by Americans as "arrogant."

17 This might be related to Jason Duell's finding (Chapter 4) that literary work is evaluated in more public or political terms in the United States, whereas it is evaluated in more aesthetic terms in France.

18 On the predominance of moral over aesthetic criteria of evaluation in the United States as compared to France, see also Lamont 1992, chap. 4.

19 Interestingly, unlike French artists, American artists are not protected by moral rights (only two states make this provision), but by a material right not to be exploited (*copyright*).

20 This is what Boltanski and Thévenot (1991) designate as "domestic worth."

21 This American local "community," unlike a traditional order in the Old World, is based on interaction of an essentially voluntaristic character and is highly compatible with market bonds. In contrast to Europe, the localism of the polity is not an obstacle to nationhood in the United States (Silver 1990).

22 Note however that NIMBYs often insist that they are not NIMBYs; they work hard to find general grounds for opposition, and attempt to shy away from

purely local arguments having to do with property value. We thank James M. Jasper for his comments on this point.

23 For instance, French representatives at the Assemblée Nationale are supposed to represent the whole nation and not a territorial constituency, and imperative mandates are forbidden (art. 27 of the Constitution, October 4, 1958).

24 For a classical analysis of local power, see Grémion 1976.

25 However, the French participants in our project were surprised to see the American literature interpret the Welfare State as "paternalist" (Lipset 1979). Social policies and institutions of the French state are mainly justified by civic solidarity, in contrast to the types of genuine corporatist institutions put in place by the Vichy government (de Foucauld and Thévenot 1995).

26 Allan Silver (1990) showed that the core religious culture in America that informed the secular sociology of face-to-face relations and social control provides simultaneously for individualism and community. We thank Luc Boltanski for drawing our attention to this contribution.

27 This discussion of the boundary between the public and the private builds on a rich sociological tradition that considers public relationships in the context of rationalization (Weber 1978), cosmopolitanism (Simmel 1971), detachment/involvement (Elias 1956), and communicative action (Habermas 1990). For an analysis of the different regimes of engagement that are involved in the definition of this boundary, see Thévenot 1990b, 1996c.

28 Alexander (1997) thematizes the need to extend the civil sphere to "non-civil spheres" such as family.

29 Distinctions between modes of engagement led a militant French feminist to find an employer's demand for weekend work unreasonable, a position that was not expressed by her American counterpart.

30 French and American upper middle class people also differ as to the importance that they attach to professionalism in their judgment of moral character (Lamont 1992).

31 The explicitation of differences between such grammars is made possible by the confrontation of American Republicans with the contrasting views of Condorcet and Siéyès (Manin 1989a, 1989b).

32 For the statement of the question in the 1950s, see Dahl 1958; Key 1958; and Latham 1952, amongst a growing literature on the subject. The split between two forms of liberalism – the liberalism of balancing interest groups, and the liberalism of market and of separated domains (Manin 1989a; Lowi 1987) – is manifested by critiques of the latter in the name of the former, such as those formulated by Hayek (1976). The mediation by interest groups can be either criticized as a group-driven domination of individuals or, on the contrary, favored as a condition of self-development, as long as an association with others takes place (Dewey 1927; Eisenberg 1995).

33 Schattschneider states that the "distinction between public and special interest is an indispensable tool for the study of politics" that cannot be abolished without making a "shambles of political science"; within private organization "discussions might be carried on in terms of naked self-interest, but a public discussion must be carried out in public terms" (1960, pp. 27–8.) We thank Peter Meyers for directing our attention to the critique of pluralism which was

already appearing at the end of the 1950s from the socialist, Marxist, and moderate Democratic Left, and which continued through the New Left.

34 This mainstream stance found in American sociology is also pervasive in French sociology, particularly where the influence of Bourdieu (1972) is strong.

35 Symmetrically, paying attention to the format of general interests should not prevent us from taking into consideration personal interest; for their articulation, see Chapter 10 above and Thévenot 1996d.

36 Actually, procedures are not as independent of the substantive conceptions of the common good as their proponents might claim them to be. Formal procedures are favorable to the most codified ways of "making things general." Conversely, defining the common good requires framing persons and things, i.e. specifying how they are understood in terms of "qualifications" (Boltanski and Thévenot 1991). Walzer relates each kind of social good to a distinct mode of distribution (Walzer 1983).

37 The use of formal procedures (as well as of professional codes of interpersonal interaction discussed above) might be more frequent in the United States than in France because construed as central to the American public civility mentioned before.

38 Renaud Seligmann (personal communication) observes, however, that the 1997 report of the French "Conseil d'Etat" echoes "Anglo-Saxon" policies of "affirmative action" and suggests domains where French public policies already have this orientation, such as "zones d'éducation prioritaires." In addition, the 1981 law which allows the creation of civic organizations of foreigners ("associations d'étrangers") encouraged the politicization of identities. This law is double-edged: it can contribute to the integration of immigrants into political society, because it gives them representatives; it can be used by communities to develop a collective consciousness (Kastoryano 1996).

39 For French contributions to this debate, see Lacorne 1997; Schnapper 1991; Touraine 1992; Wievorka 1996b; and the analyses of the mirror effect by Eric Fassin (1993, 1997a).

40 François Furet has insisted on the similarities between "multiculturalism" and the "liberal utopia" embodied in nineteenth-century America: immigrants settled in an a-national space but remaining attached to their communities of origin, united by the market and democratic individualism (Furet 1997). On the differences between this "ethnic/civic" nation and the French nation, see Lacorne 1997.

41 This reversal is commonly viewed as the price to be paid for the inability of American society (or its refusal) to incorporate African Americans to the same extent that other groups have been (Glazer 1997).

42 Walzer observes that "multiculturalism as an ideology is a program for greater social and economic equality" and that religious and ethnic activists end up "talking (at least) about the common good." This is the reason why he pleads for "a defense of group differences and an attack upon class differences" (Walzer 1997). For a defense of multiculturalism as "deep diversity," see also Taylor 1992.

43 Joan Scott observes that the decomposition of the polity is potentially the vehicle for rectifying inequalities (such as gender inequality) that persist despite the acquisition of formal rights (Scott 1996).

44 In the case of sexual harassment, American and some French interviewees present a reversed time-lag, stating that France is ten or twenty years behind the United States (Saguy). However, time-lag arguments obscure the important national differences that make it unlikely that one country will follow the other, even with a time-lag.

45 French gay rights groups recently marched in demonstrations supporting the rights of the unemployed without taking this opportunity to express their distinctive collective identity. The debate between a communitarian culturalism and a universalistic civic spirit cuts across the gay movement. In the French context, Jean-Loup Amselle (1996) sees the rise of chosen identities (*"identités de consolations"*) as the consequences of the decline in the political representations of class differences.

References

Abbott, Andrew. 1988, *The System of Professions*, Chicago: University of Chicago Press.

Abel, Olivier. 1995, "Habiter la cité," *Autres Temps* 46: 31–42.

Acot, Pascal. 1988, *Histoire de l'écologie*, Paris: Presses Universitaires de France.

Adams, Laurie. 1976, *Art on Trial. From Whistler to Rothko*, New York: Walker and Co.

Alexander, Jeffrey. 1981, "The Mass Media in Systematic, Historical and Comparative Perspective," in Elihu Katz and Tamás Szecskö (eds.), *Mass Media and Social Change*, Beverly Hills, CA: Sage, pp. 17–52.

(ed.). 1988, *Durkheimian Sociology: Cultural Studies*, Cambridge University Press.

1992, "Citizens and Enemies as Symbolic Classification: On the Polarizing Discourse of Civil Society," in Michèle Lamont and Marcel Fournier (eds.), *Cultivating Differences: Symbolic Boundaries and the Making of Inequality*, University of Chicago Press, pp. 289–308.

1996, *Fin de Siècle: Relativism, Reduction, and the Problem of Reason*, London: Verso.

1997, "The Paradoxes of Civil Society," *International Sociology* 12 (2): 115–33.

Alexander, Jeffrey C. and Philip Smith. 1993, "The Discourse of American Civil Society: A New Proposal for Cultural Studies," *Theory and Society* 22: 151–207.

Alphandery, P. P. Bitoun, and Y. Dupont. 1991, *L'équivoque écologique*, Paris: La Découverte.

Alterman, Eric. 1992, *Sound and Fury: The Washington Punditocracy and the Collapse of American Politics*, New York: Harper Collins.

Amselle, Jean-Loup. 1996, *Vers un multiculturalisme français. L'empire de la coutume*, Paris: Aubier.

Anderson, Benedict. 1991, *Imagined Communities: Reflections on the Origin and Spread of Nationalism*, London: Verso.

Anderson, Jervis. 1994, "The Public Intellectual (Profile of Cornel West)," *The New Yorker*, January 17.

Angenot, Marc. 1995, "L'esprit de censure, " *Discours social/Social Discourse*, No. 7.

Antigona. 1995, *Saint Béton, Journal de guerre*, Caudiès-de-Fenouillèdes (66220): Fenouillèdes Impression.

Apostles, Richard A., Charles Y. Glock, Thomas Piazza, and Marijean Suelzle. 1983, *The Anatomy of Racial Attitudes*, Berkeley: University of California Press.

Appiah, K. Anthony. 1994, "Identity, Authenticity, Survival: Multicultural Societies and Social Reproduction," in Charles Taylor with Amy Gutmann (commentary, ed.), *Multiculturalism and "The Politics of Recognition,"* Princeton University Press, pp. 158ff.

Aptheker, Herbert. 1992, *Anti-Racism in U.S. History*, New York: Greenwood.

Arcand, Bernard. 1991, *Le jaguar et le tamanoir. Anthropologie de la pornographie*, Quebec: Boréal.

Arendt, Hannah. 1958, *The Human Condition*, University of Chicago Press.

Arnaud, Remey. 1986, *Panorama de l'économie française*, Paris: Bordas.

Art in America 1985: 9 and 1989: 5.

Artistic Freedom under Attack 1994, 1995, 1996, Washington: People for the American Way.

Assemblée Nationale. 1992, *Rapport No. 2809*, Paris: Assemblée Nationale.

1997, "Projet de Loi relatif à la prévention et à la répression des infractions sexuelles ainsi qu'à la protection des mineurs," presented in the name of M. Lionel Jospin, Prime Minister, and Mme. Elisabeth Guigou, Garde des Sceaux and Minister of Justice, September 3, p. 202.

Aultschull, James. 1990, *From Milton to McLuhan: The Ideas behind American Journalism*, Baltimore, MD: Johns Hopkins University Press.

Austin, Regina. 1992, "'The Black Community,' its Lawbreakers, and a Politics of Identification," *Southern California Law Review* 65:1769.

AVFT. 1990, *De l'abus de pouvoir sexuel: le harcèlement sexuel au travail*, Paris: La Découverte/Le Boréal.

Axelrod, Regina. 1997, "Environmental Policy and Management in the European Union," in Norman Vig and Michael Kraft (eds.), *Environmental Policy in the 1990s: Reform or Reaction?*, third edition, Washington, DC: CQ Press, pp. 299–320.

Badinter, Elisabeth. 1986, *L'un est l'autre*, Paris: Odile Jacob.

1991, "La chasse aux sorciers," *Nouvel Observateur*, October 17.

1992, *XY: De l'identité masculine*, Paris: Odile Jacob.

Baker, Houston Jr. 1992, *Black Studies, Rap, and the Academy*, University of Chicago Press.

1993, "Introduction" to "Presidential Forum on Multiculturalism: The Task of Literary Representation in the Twenty-First Century," *Profession 93*.

Balibar, Etienne. 1991, "Is There a 'Neo-Racism'?," in Etienne Balibar and Immanuel Wallerstein (eds.), *Race, Nation, Class: Ambiguous Identities*, London: Verso, pp. 17–28.

Balibar, Etienne and Immanuel Wallerstein. 1991, *Race, Nation, Class: Ambiguous Identities*, London: Verso.

Banton, Michael. 1994, "Effective Implementation of the UN Racial Convention," *New Community* 20 (3):475–87.

Barber, Benjamin. 1984, *Strong Democracy: Participatory Politics for a New Age*, Berkeley: University of California Press.

Barbier, Rémi. 1992, "Une cité de l'écologie," Mémoire de DEA in Sociology, Ecole des Hautes Etudes en Sciences Sociales, Paris.

Barker, Martin. 1981, *The New Racism*, London: Junction Books.

Barry, Brian. 1990 [1965], *Political Argument*, Berkeley: University of California Press.

Barth, Fredrik. 1969, "Introduction," in Fredrik Barth (ed.), *Ethnic Groups and Boundaries: The Social Organization of Culture Difference*, London: George Allen and Unwin, pp. 9–38.

Barthes, Roland. 1957, *Mythologies*, Paris: Editions du Seuil.

Baudrillard, Jean. 1986, *L'Amerique*, Paris: Grasset et Fasquelle.

Beck, Ulrich, Anthony Giddens, and Scott Lash. 1994, *Reflexive Modernization: Politics, Tradition and Aesthetic in the Modern Social Order*, Cambridge: Polity.

Becker, Carol. 1989, "Private Fantasies Shape Public Events: And Public Events Invade and Shape Our Dreams," in Arlene Raven, *Art in the Public Interest*, New York: Da Capo Press.

Becker, Howard. 1963, *Outsiders: Studies in the Sociology of Deviance*, New York: Free Press.

Begley, Sharon and Adam Rogers. 1996, "'Morphogenic Field' Day (Academic Journal *Social Text* Falls for A. Sokal's Hoax Debunking Postmodernist Literary Theory)," *Newsweek*, June 3.

Beisel, Nicola. 1992. "Constructing a Shifting Moral Boundary: Literature and Obscenity in Nineteeth-Century America," in Michèle Lamont and Marcel Fournier (eds.), *Cultivating Differences: Symbolic Boundaries and the Making of Inequality*, University of Chicago Press, pp. 104–30.

1993, "Morals Versus Art: Censorship, the Politics of Interpretation, and the Victorian Nude," *American Sociological Review* 58: 145–62.

1997, *Imperiled Innocents. Anthony Comstock and Family Reproduction in Victorian England*, Princeton University Press.

Bell, Daniel (ed.). 1964, *The Radical Right*, New York: Doubleday.

Bellah, Robert N., Richard Madsen, William W. Sullivan, Ann Swidler, and Steven Tipton. 1985, *Habits of the Heart: Individualism and Commitment in American Life*, Berkeley: University of California Press.

1991, *The Good Society*, Berkeley: University of California Press.

Bénatouïl, Thomas. 1999a, "Critique et pragmatique en sociologie; quelques principes de lecture," *Annales, Histoire, Sciences Sociales* 2: 281–317.

1999b, "Comparing Sociological Strategies; the Critical and the Pragmatic Stance in French Contemporary Sociology," *European Journal of Social Theory* 2(3) 379–96.

Benford, Robert D. 1993, "Frame Disputes within the Nuclear Disarmament Movement," *Social Forces* 71 (3): 675–701.

Bennett, Jane and William Chaloupka (eds.). 1994, *In the Nature of Things: Language, Politics, and the Environment*, Minneapolis: University of Minnesota Press.

Benneytout, Mirielle, Sylivie Cromer, and Marie-Victoire Louis. 1992, "Harcèlement sexuel: une réforme restrictive qui n'est pas sans danger," *Semaine Sociale Lamy* 599: 3–4.

Benson, Rodney. 1996, "Constructing the Immigration 'Social Problem' in France and California, 1964–1995," unpublished, Department of Sociology, University of California at Berkeley.

Berezin, Mabel. 1997, "Politics and Culture: A Less Fissured Terrain," *Annual Review of Sociology* 23: 361–83.

Berger, Bennett M. 1995, *An Essay on Culture. Symbolic Structure and Social Structure*, Berkeley: University of California Press.

Berkovitch, Nitza. 1994, *From Motherhood to Citizenship: The World-Wide Incorporation of Women*, PhD dissertation, Department of Sociology, Stanford University, Stanford, CA.

Berkowitz, Peter. 1996, "Science Fiction (A. Sokal Perpetrates Hoax in *Social Text*)," *The New Republic*, July 1.

Berman, Russell A. 1995, "Global Thinking, Local Teaching: Departments, Curricula, and Culture," *Profession 95*.

Berman, Sheri. 1998, "Ideas and Political Analysis," presented at the 11th International Conference of the Europeanists, Baltimore, MD.

Bernstein, Richard. 1990, "The Rising Hegemony of the Politically Correct," *The New York Times*, October 25.

Berque, Augustin. 1986, *Le sauvage et l'artifice. Les Japonais devant la Nature*, Paris: Gallimard.

1996, *Etres humains sur la Terre*, Paris: Le Débat-Gallimard.

Berry, Jeffrey. 1996, *The Interest Group Society*, third edition, Reading, MA: Addison Wesley Longmans.

Best, Joel (ed.). 1989, *Images of Issues: Typifying Contemporary Social Problems*, New York: Aldine de Gruyter.

Bethell, Tom. 1991, "Fighting for the Union; 'Sacramento Union' Newspaper," *National Review* 43 (16).

Billig, Michael. 1987, *Arguing and Thinking: A Rhetorical Approach to Social Psychology*, Cambridge University Press.

Bird, Robert C. 1997, "More than a Congressional Joke: A Fresh Look at the Legislative History of Sex Discrimination of the 1964 Civil Rights Act," *William and Mary Journal of Women and the Law* 3 (Spring): 137–61.

Blau, Judith R. 1996, "The Toggle Switch of Institutions: Religion and Art in the U.S. in the Nineteenth and Early Twentieth Centuries," *Social Forces* 4: 1159–77.

Bleich, Erik. 1998, "Ideas and Race Policies in Britain and France," presented at the International Conference of Europeanists, Baltimore, MD.

Blondiaux, Loïc. 1998, *La fabrique de l'opinion*, Paris: Seuil.

Blumenthal, Sidney. 1988, *The Rise of the Counterestablishment*, New York: Harper & Row.

Blumer, Herbert. 1958, "Race Prejudice as a Sense of Group Position," *Pacific Sociological Review* 1: 3–7.

Bobo, Lawrence. 1995, "The Color Line, the Dilemma and the Dream: Racial Attitudes and Relations in the Twentieth Century,", Russell Sage Foundation (Working Paper 87).

Bobo, Lawrence, James R. Kluegel, and Ryan A. Smith. 1996, "Laissez-Faire Racism: The Crystallization of a 'Kinder, Gentler' Anti-Black Ideology," in Steven A. Tuch and Jack K. Martin (eds.), *Racial Attitudes in the 1990s: Continuity and Change*, Westport, CT: Praeger.

Bobo, Lawrence D. and Ryan A. Smith. 1998, "From Jim Crow Racism to Laissez-Faire Racism: The Transformation of Racial Attitudes," in Wendy F.

Katkin, Ned Landsman, and Andrea Tyree (eds.), *Beyond Pluralism: The Conceptions of Groups and Group Identities in America*, Urbana, IL: University of Illinois Press, pp. 182–220.

Body-Gendrot, Sophie. 1995, "Models of Immigrant Integration in France and the United States. Signs of Convergence?" in M. P. Smith and Joe R. Feagin (eds.), *The Bubbling Cauldron*, Minneapolis: University of Minnesota Press.

Body-Gendrot, Sophie and Martin A. Schain. 1992, "National. and Local Politics and the Development of Immigration Policy in the United States and France: A Comparative Analysis," in Donald L. Horowitz and Gérard Noiriel (eds.), *Immigrants in Two Democracies: French and American Experience*, New York University Press, pp. 411–38.

Boli, John and George M. Thomas. 1997, "World Culture in the World Polity: A Century of International Non-Governmental Organization," *American Sociological Review* 62 (2): 171–90.

Boltanski, Luc. 1982, *Les cadres*, Paris: Minuit.

1987, *The Making of a Class. Cadres in French Society*, Cambridge University Press and Paris: Editions de la Maison des Sciences de l'Homme.

1990, *L'amour et la justice comme compétences*, Paris: Editions Métailié.

1993, *La souffrance à distance. Morale humanitaire, médias et politique*, Paris: Editions Métailié. (English translation: *Distant Suffering. Morality, Medias and Politics*, trans. Graham Burdell, Cambridge University Press, 1999.)

Boltanski, Luc and Laurent Thévenot. 1983, "Finding One's Way in Social Space; a Study Based on Games," *Social Science Information* 22 (4/5): 631–79.

1987, *Les économies de la grandeur*, Paris: Presses Universitaires de France.

(eds.). 1989, *Justesse et justice dans le travail*, Paris: Presses Universitaires de France.

1991, *De la justification. Les économies de la grandeur*, Paris: Gallimard.

1999, 'The Sociology of Critical Capacity,' *European Journal of Social Theory* 2 (3): 359–77. (special issue on "Contemporary French Social Theory").

Bolton, Richard (ed.). 1992, *Culture Wars. Documents from the Recent Controversies in the Arts*, New York: New Press.

Bourdieu, Pierre. 1972, *Esquisse d'une théorie de la pratique*, Geneva: Droz.

1976, "Le champ scientifique," *Actes de la Recherche en Sciences Sociales* 2 (3): 88–104.

1983, "The Field of Cultural Production, Or: The Economic World Reversed," *Poetics* 12: 311–56.

1984, *Distinction: A Social Critique of the Judgment of Taste*, Cambridge, MA: Harvard University Press.

1987, "L'institutionnalisation de l'anomie", *Les Cahiers du Musée National d'Art Moderne* 19–20.

1992, *Les règles de l'art: Genèse et structure du champ littéraire*, Paris: Seuil.

Bourdieu, Pierre, and Jean-Claude Passeron. 1977, *Reproduction in Education, Society and Culture*, trans. Richard Nice, Beverly Hills: Sage.

Bourdieu, Pierre and Monique de Saint-Martin. 1978, "Le patronat," *Actes de la Recherche en Sciences Sociales* 21: 6–82.

Bourdieu, Pierre and Loïc Wacquant. 1998, "Sur les ruses de la raison impérialiste," *Actes de la Recherche en Sciences Sociales* 121/122 (March): 109–18.

Boureau, Alain. 1995, *Le droit de cuissage: la fabrication d'un mythe XIIe-XXe siècles*, Paris: Albin Michel.

Bouretz, Pierre. 1996, *Les promesses du monde. Philosophie de Max Weber*, Paris: Gallimard.

Bouvaist, Jean-Marie. 1991, *Pratiques et métiers de l'édition*, Paris: Editions du Cercle de la Librairie.

Bowser, P. Benjamin (ed.). 1995, *Racism and Anti-Racism in World Perspective*, New York: Sage.

Bredin, Frédérique and Charles Jolibois. 1998, "Rapport fait au nom de la Commission Mixte Paritaire chargée de proposer un texte sur les dispositions restant en discussion du projet de loi relatif à la prévention et la répression des infractions sexuelles ainsi qu'à la protection des mineurs," pp. 906 (Assemblée Nationale); 435 (Sénat).

Bréviglieri, Marc. 1998, "L'usage et l'habiter. Contribution à une sociologie de la proximité," doctoral thesis in Sociology, Ecole des Hautes Etudes en Sciences Sociales, Paris.

Brint, Steven. 1994, *In an Age of Experts: The Changing Role of Professionals in Politics and Public Life*, Princeton University Press.

Brown, Richard Harvey. 1987, *Society As Text: Essays on Rhetoric, Reason, and Reality*, University of Chicago Press.

Brownmiller, Susan. 1975, *Against Our Will: Men, Women, and Rape*, New York: Fawcett Columbine.

Brubaker, Rogers. 1992, *Citizenship and Nationhood in France and Germany*, Cambridge, MA: Harvard University Press.

Bryson, Bethany. 1996, "'Anything but Heavy Metal:' Symbolic Exclusion and Musical Dislikes," *American Sociological Review* 61 (5): 884–99.

1999, "Multiculturalism as a Moving Moral Boundary: Literature Professors Redefine Racism," in Michèle Lamont (ed.), *The Cultural Territories of Race: Black and White Boundaries*, University of Chicago Press and New York: Russell Sage Foundation.

Burke, Edmund. 1990 [1757], *A Philosophical Enquiry into the Origin of Our Ideas of the Sublime and Beautiful*, ed. Adam Phillips, Oxford University Press.

Burke, Kenneth. 1969 [1945], *A Grammar of Motives*, Berkeley: University of California Press.

1989, *On Symbols and Society*, ed. Joseph Gusfield, University of Chicago Press.

Calhoun, Craig. 1994, "Social Theory and the Politics of Identity," in Craig Calhoun (ed.), *Social Theory and the Politics of Identity*, Oxford: Blackwell, pp. 9–36.

1998, "The Public Good as a Social and Cultural Project," in Walter Powell and Elisabeth Clemens (eds.), *Private Action and the Public Good*, New Haven: Yale University Press, pp. 20–35.

Callon, Michel. 1986[a], "Eléments pour une sociologie de la traduction. La domestication des coquilles Saint-Jacques et des marins-pêcheurs dans la baie de Saint-Brieux," *L'Année Sociologique*, Paris.

1986[b], "Some Elements of a Sociology of Translation: Domestication of the Scallops and Fishermen of St. Brieuc Bay," in John Law (ed.), *Power, Action and Belief: A New Sociology of Knowledge*, Keele Sociological Review Monograph, pp. 196–229.

Camfield, William A. 1989, *Marcel Duchamp, Fountain*, The Menil Collection: Houston Fine Art Press.

Camus, Agnès. 1991, "Le Rotary-club, une forme de sociabilité américaine dans le bocage normand," *Ethnologie Française* 2: 196–203.

Camus, Agnès, Philippe Corcuff, and Claudette Lafaye. 1993, "Entre le local et le national, des cas d'innovation dans le service public," *Revue des Affaires Sociales* 47 (3): 17–47.

Cardon, Dominique, Jean-Philippe Heurtin, and Cyril Lemieux (eds.). 1995, "Parler en public," *Politix*, 31: 5–19.

Carmilly-Weinberger, Moshe. 1986, *Fear of Art: Censorship and Freedom of Expression in Art*, New York: Bowker Company.

Cerulo, Karen A. 1995, *Identity Designs: The Sights and Sounds of a Nation*, New Brunswick, NJ: Rutgers University Press.

1997, "Identity Construction: New Issues, New Direction," *Annual Review of Sociology* 23: 385–409.

Charles, Jeffrey. 1993, *Service Clubs in American Society: Rotary, Kiwanis, and Lions*, Urbana-Champaign, IL: University of Illinois Press.

Chateaubriand, François-René. 1997 [1850], *Mémoires d'outre-tombe*, ed. Jean-Paul Clément, Paris: Gallimard.

Chateauraynaud, Francis. 1989, "La construction des défaillances sur les lieux de travail. Le cas des affaires de faute professionnelle," in Luc Boltanski and Laurent Thévenot (eds.), *Justesse et justice dans le travail*, Paris: Presses Universitaires de France, pp. 247–80.

1991, *La faute professionnelle*, Paris: Editions Métailié.

Chave, Anna C. 1990, "Minimalism and the Rhetoric of Power," *Arts Magazine* 64: 5.

Clark, Priscilla Parkhurst. 1979, "Literary Culture in France and the United States," *American Journal of Sociology* 84: 1047–76.

1987, *Literary France: The Making of a Culture*, Berkeley: University of California Press.

Clauss, Richard. 1993, "The Clavey River Project: For and Against," *The Modesto Bee*, October 31: A-13.

Clemens, Elisabeth. 1997, *The People's Lobby: Organizational Innovation and the Rise of Interest Group Politics in the United States, 1890–1925*, University of Chicago Press.

Clifford, James and Steven Marcus (eds.). 1986, *Writing Culture: The Poetics and Politics of Ethnography*, Berkeley: University of California Press.

Cockburn, Cynthia. 1991, *In the Way of Women: Men's Resistance to Sex Equality in Organizations*, New York: ILR Press.

Collingwood, R. G. 1960 [1945], *The Idea of Nature*, Oxford University Press.

Collins, Patricia Hill. 1990, *Black Feminist Thought*, New York: Routledge.

Collins, Randall. 1992, "Women and the Production of Status Cultures," in Michèle Lamont and Marcel Fournier (eds.), *Cultivating Differences: Symbolic Boundaries and the Making of Inequality*, University of Chicago Press, pp. 213–32.

Condit, Celeste Michelle and John Louis Lucaites. 1993, *Crafting Inequality. America's Anglo-African Word*, University of Chicago Press.

Confessions of the Guerrilla Girls, 1995, New York: Harper Perennial.

Connolly, William. 1993 [1974], *The Terms of Political Discourse*, third edition, Princeton University Press.

Controversial Public Art (catalogue). 1983, Milwaukee Art Museum.

Cook, Fay Lomax. 1979, *Who Should Be Helped? Public Support for Social Services*, Beverly Hills, CA: Sage.

Corcuff, Philippe. 1991, "Le catégoriel, le professionnel et la classe: usages contemporains de formes historiques," *Genèse* 3: 55–72.

1993, "Traduction et légitimité dans la construction de l'action publique. Les relations entre agents de l'Equipement et élus locaux," in CRESAL (ed.), *Les raisons de l'action publique – Entre expertise et débat*, Paris: L'Harmattan, pp. 217–28.

Corcuff, Philippe and Max Sanier. 1995, "Processus décisionnels et mise en récit rétrospectives. Le cas de la plate-forme multimodale de Lyon-Satolas," CERIEP, IEP Lyon (forthcoming in *Annales Histoire, Sciences Sociales*).

Corse, Sarah. 1997, *Nationalism and Literature: The Politics of Culture in Canada and the United States*, Cambridge University Press.

Coser, Lewis, Charles Kadushin and Walter Powell. 1982, *Books: The Culture of Publishing*, New York: Basic Books.

Costa-Lascoux, Jacqueline. 1994, "French Legislation against Racism and Discrimination," *New Community* 20 (3):371–9.

Crawford, Robert. 1992, *Devolving English Literature*, Oxford: Clarendon Press.

Crawford, Stephen. 1989, *Technical Workers in an Advanced Society: The Work, Careers and Politics of French Engineers*, Cambridge University Press and Paris: Editions de la Maison des Sciences de l'Homme.

Crenshaw, Kimberley. 1989, "Demarginalizing the Intersection of Race and Sex: A Black Feminist Critique of Antidiscrimination Doctrine, Feminist Theory and Antiracist Policies," *University of Chicago Legal Forum*:139.

Cress, Daniel M. and David A. Snow. 1996, "Mobilization at the Margins: Resources, Benefactors, and the Variability of Homeless Social Movement Organizations," *American Sociological Review* 61: 1089–1109.

Cromer, Sylvie. 1990, "France: AVFT," in AVFT (ed.), *De l'abus de pouvoir sexuel: le harcèlement sexuel au travail*, Paris: La Découverte/Le Boréal, pp. 223–8.

1992, "Histoire d'une loi: La pénalisation du harcèlement sexuel dans le nouveau code pénal," *Projets Féministes* 1 (March): 108–17.

1995, *Le harcèlement sexuel en France: La levée d'un tabou 1985–1990*, Paris: La Documentation Française.

Cromer, Sylvie and Marie-Victoire Louis. 1992, "Existe-t-il un harcèlement sexuel 'à la française'?," *French Politics and Society* 10 (3): 37–43.

Cronon, William (ed.). 1995, *Uncommon Ground: Toward Reinventing Nature*, New York: W. W. Norton.

Crowfoot, Joan E. and Julia M. Wondolleck. 1990, *Environmental Disputes: Community Involvement in Conflict Resolution*, Washington, DC: Island Press.

Crozier, Michel. 1964, *The Bureaucratic Phenomenon*, University of Chicago Press.

Culler, Jonathan. 1981, *The Pursuit of Signs: Semiotics, Literature, Deconstruction*, Ithaca: Cornell University Press.

Cummings, Milton and Richard Katz. 1987, *The Patron State*, Oxford University Press.

Dahl, Robert A. 1958, "Critique of the Ruling Elite Model," *American Political Science Review* 12: 463–9.

1967, *Pluralist Democracy in the United States.*, Chicago: Rand-McNally.

1989, *Democracy and its Critics*, New Haven: Yale University Press.

Dalton, Russell J. 1988, *Citizen Politics in Western Democracies: Public Opinion and*

Political Parties in the United States, Great Britain, West Germany and France, Chatham House Publishers.

1994, *The Green Rainbow: Environmental Groups in Western Europe,* New Haven: Yale University Press.

Danto, Arthur C. 1981, *The Transfiguration of the Common Place,* Cambridge, MA: Harvard University Press.

1987, *The State of the Art,* New York: Prentice Hall.

1990, *Encounters and Reflexions: Art in the Historical Present,* New York: Farrar Straus Giroux.

1992, *Beyond the Brillo Box. The Visual Arts in Post-Historical Perspective,* New York: The Nowaday Press.

Darnton, Robert and Daniel Roche. 1989, *Revolution in Print,* Los Angeles: University of California Press.

Darraby, Jessica. 1995, *Art, Artifact and Architecture Law,* Deerfield: Clark Boardman Callaghan.

Day, Samuel. 1994, "Obituary: Erwin Knoll," *The Independent,* November 26.

De Duve, Thierry. 1989, *Résonnances du "ready-made". Duchamp entre avant-garde et tradition,* Nîmes: Jacqueline Chambon.

1990, "Vox ignis, vox populi," *Parachute* 60.

Dekeuwer-Defossez, Françoise. 1993, "Le harcèlement sexuel en droit français: discrimination ou atteinte à la liberté? (A propos de l'article 222–23 du nouveau Code pénal et de la loi n. 92–1179 du 2 novembre 1992 relative à l'abus d'autorité en matière sexuelle)," *La Semaine Juridique* 3662 (13): 137–41.

Delporte, Christian. 1998, *Les journalistes en France (1880–1950),* Paris: Seuil.

Derouet, Jean-Louis. 1992, *Ecole et justice. De l'égalité des chances aux compromis locaux,* Paris: Editions Métailié.

Desrosières, Alain. 1993, *La politique des grands nombres; histoire de la raison statistique,* Paris: La Découverte. (English translation: The Politics of Large Numbers. A History of Statistical Reasoning, trans. Camille Naish, Cambridge, MA: Harvard University Press, 1998.)

Desrosières, Alain and Laurent Thévenot. 1988, *Les catégories socioprofessionnelles,* Paris: La Découverte.

Devall, Bill and George Sessions. 1985, *Deep Ecology,* Salt Lake City: Peregrine Smith.

Dewey, John. 1927, *The Public and its Problems,* New York: Henry Holt.

Diani, Mario. 1996, "Linking Mobilization Frames and Political Opportunities: Insights from Regional Populism in Italy," *American Sociological Review* 61: 1053–69.

DiMaggio, Paul. 1982, "Cultural Entrepreneurship in Nineteenth Century Boston: The Creation of the Organizational Base of High Culture," *Media, Culture, and Society* 4: 33–50.

1987, "Classification in Art," *American Sociological Review* 52 (4): 440–55.

1992, "Cultural Boundaries and Structural Change: The Extension of the High Culture Model to Theater, Opera, and the Dance, 1900–1940, " in Michèle Lamont and Marcel Fournier (eds.), *Cultivating Differences: Symbolic Boundaries and the Making of Inequality,* University of Chicago Press, pp. 21–57.

1994, "Culture and Economy," in Neil Smelser and Richard Swedberg (eds.), *The Handbook of Economic Sociology*, Princeton University Press and Russell Sage Foundation, pp. 27–57.

1997, "Culture and Cognition," *Annual Review of Sociology* 23: 263–87.

Dimen, Muriel. 1993, "Review of *Sexual Personae: Art and Decadence from Nefertiti to Emily Dickinson*," *Psychoanalytic Psychology* 10 (3): 451–62.

Dionne, E. J. 1991, *Why Americans Hate Politics*, New York: Simon and Schuster.

Dobbin, Frank. 1994, *Forging Industrial Policy: France, Britain and the United States in the Railway Age*, Cambridge University Press.

Dobbin, Frank and John Sutton. 1998, "The Strength of a Weak State: The Employment Rights Revolution and the Rise of Human Resources Management Divisions," *American Journal of Sociology* 104: 441–76.

Dobry, Michel. 1986, *Sociologie des crises politiques: la dynamique des mobilisations multisectorielles*, Paris: Presses de la Fondation des Sciences Politiques.

Dobson, Andrew. 1990, *Green Political Thought: An Introduction*, London: Unwin Hyman.

Dodier, Nicolas. 1989, "Le travail d'accommodation des inspecteurs du travail en matière de sécurité," in Luc Boltanski and Laurent Thévenot (eds.), *Justesse et justice dans le travail*, Paris: Presses Universitaires de France.

1991, "Agir dans plusieurs mondes," *Critiques* 529–30: 427–58.

1993a, "Action as a Combination of 'Common Worlds'," *The Sociological Review* 41 (3): 556–71.

1993b, *L'expertise médicale. Essai de sociologie sur l'exercice du jugement*, Paris: Editions Métailié.

1993c, "Les appuis conventionnels de l'action: éléments de pragmatique sociologique," *Réseaux* 62: 63–85.

Dodier, Nicolas and Agnès Camus. 1997, "L'admission des malades, histoire et pragmatique de l'accueil à l'hôpital," *Annales, HSS* 52 (3): 733–63.

Doidy, Eric. 1997, "S'engager en commun. La montée en généralité d'attaches locales à des environnements naturel et urbain," Mémoire de DEA in Sociology, Ecole des Hautes Etudes en Sciences Sociales, Paris.

Dooling, Richard. 1998, "Making Criminals of Us All," *New York Times*, December 30, Op-Ed Section.

Doss, Erika. 1995, *Spirit Poles and Flying Pigs: Public Art and Cultural Democracy in American Communities*, Washington, DC: Smithsonian Institution Press.

Dosse, François. 1995, *L'empire du sens. L'humanisation des sciences sociales*, Paris: La Découverte.

1998, *Empire of Meaning: the Humanization of the Social Sciences*, Minneapolis: University of Minnesota Press.

Douglas, Mary. 1966, *Purity and Danger. An Analysis of the Concepts of Pollution and Taboo*, London: Routledge and Kegan Paul, and New York: Pantheon.

Douglas, Mary and David Hull (eds.). 1992, *How Classification Works*, Edinburgh University Press.

Douglas, Mary and Baron Isherwood. 1979, *The World of Goods*, London, Allen Lane.

Douglas, Mary and Aaron Wildavsky. 1982, *Risk and Culture*, Berkeley: University of California Press.

Dowie, Mark. 1995, *Losing Ground: American Environmentalism at the Close of the Twentieth Century*, Cambridge, MA: MIT Press.

Dryzek, John. 1990, *Discursive Democracy: Politics, Policy, and Political Science*, Cambridge University Press.

D'Souza, Dinesh. 1991, *Illiberal Education: The Politics of Race and Sex on Campus*, New York: The Free Press.

Dubin, Steven C. 1992, *Arresting Images. Impolitic Art and Uncivil Actions*, New York: Routledge, Chapman and Hall.

du Camp, Maxime. 1861, *Le Salon de Paris*, Paris.

Dumont, Louis. 1991, *L'idéologie allemande*, Paris: Gallimard.

Dunlap, Riley and Angela Mertig (eds.). 1992, *American Environmentalism: The U.S. Environmental Movement, 1970–1990*, Washington, DC: Taylor and Francis.

DuPuis, E. Melanie and Peter Vandergeest (eds.). 1996, *Creating the Countryside: The Politics of Rural and Environmental Discourse*, Philadelphia: Temple University Press.

Durkheim, Emile. 1965 [1912], *The Elementary Forms of Religious Life*, New York: Free Press.

Dyson, Kenneth. 1983, "The Cultural, Ideological and Structural Context," in Kenneth Dyson and Stephan Wilks (eds.), *Industrial Crisis: A Comparative Study of the State and Industry*, Oxford University Press

Echeverria, John D. and Raymond Booth Eby (eds.). 1995, *Let the People Judge: Wise Use and the Private Property Rights Movement*, Washington, DC: Island Press.

Echeverria, John D., Pope Barrow, and Richard Roos-Collins. 1989, *Rivers at Risk: The Concerned Citizen's Guide to Hydropower*, Washington, DC: Island Press.

Eckersley, Robyn. 1996, *Environmentalism and Political Theory: Toward an Ecocentric Approach*, Albany: SUNY Press.

Eder, Klaus. 1996, *The Social Construction of Nature: A Sociology of Ecological Enlightenment*, Beverly Hills: Sage.

Ehrenreich, Nancy S. 1990, "Pluralist Myths and Powerless Men: The Ideology of Reasonableness in Sexual Harassment Law," *Yale Law Journal* 99: 1177.

Eisenberg, A. 1995, *Reconstructing Political Pluralism*, Albany: State University of New York Press.

Elias, Norbert. 1956, "Problems of Involvement and Detachment," *British Journal of Sociology* 7: 226–52.

1978, *The History of Manners.*, Vol. 1. *The Civilizing Process*, New York: Pantheon.

1987, *Involvement and Detachment*, New York: Basil Blackwell.

Eliasoph, Nina. 1998, *Avoiding Politics: How Americans Produce Apathy in Everyday Life*, Cambridge University Press.

Ellingson, Stephen. 1995, "Understanding the Dialectic of Discourse and Collective Action: Public Debate and Rioting in Antebellum Cincinnati," *American Journal of Sociology* 101 (1): 100–44.

Elster, Jon. 1995, *Local Justice in America*, New York: Russell Sage Foundation.

Emirbayer, Mustafa. 1997, "Manifesto for a Relational Sociology," *American Journal of Sociology* 103 (2): 281–317.

Emirbayer, Mustafa and Jeff Goodwin. 1996, "Symbols, Positions, Objects: Toward a New Theory of Revolution and Collective Action," *History and Theory* 35: 358–74.

Engelstad, Fredrik. 1997, "Needs and Social Justice. The Criterion of Needs when Exempting Employees from Layoffs," *Social Justice Research* 10: 203–24.

Engelstad, Fredrik and Lars Mjoset. 1997, "Introduction," *Comparative Social Research* 16: xi–xvii.

Epstein, Cynthia Fuchs. 1992, "Thinkerbells and Pinups: The Construction and Reconstruction of Gender Boundaries at Work," in Michèle Lamont and Marcel Fournier (eds.), *Cultivating Differences: Symbolic Boundaries and the Making of Inequality*, University of Chicago Press, pp. 232–56.

Erickson, Bonnie. 1996, "Culture, Class, and Connections," *American Journal of Sociology* 102: 217–51.

Escarpit, Roger. 1965 *The Sociology of Literature*, Lake Erie College Press

Espeland, Wendy Nelson. 1994, "Legally Mediated Identity: The National Environmental Policy Act and the Bureaucratic Construction of Interest," *Law and Society Review* 28 (5): 1149–79

1998, *The Struggle for Water*, University of Chicago Press.

Esping-Anderson, Gosta. 1990, *The Three Worlds of Welfare Capitalism*, Princeton University Press and London: Polity Press.

1992, "Tinkerbells and Pinups," in Michele Lamont and Marcel Fournier (eds.), *Cultivating Differences: Symbolic Boundaries and the Making of Inequality*, University of Chicago Press.

Essed, Philomena. 1991, *Understanding Everyday Racism. An Interdisciplinary Theory*, Beverly Hills, CA: Sage.

Etzioni, Amitai. 1988, *The Moral Dimension: Toward a New Economics*, New York: Free Press.

Evans, Sara M. 1989, *Born for Liberty: A History of Women in America*, New York: Free Press.

Ewald, François. 1986, *L'Etat providence*, Paris: Grasset.

Eymard-Duvernay, François. 1986, "La qualification des produits," in Robert Salais and Laurent Thévenot (eds.), *Le travail. Marché, règles, conventions*, Paris: INSEE-Economica, pp. 239–47.

1989, "Conventions de qualité et pluralité des formes de coordination," *Revue Economique* 2: 329–59.

Ezekiel, Judith. 1995, "Anti-féminisme et anti-américanisme: un mariage politiquement réussi," *Nouvelles Questions Féministes* 17 (1): 59–76.

Fantasia, Rick. 1995, "Fast Food in France," *Theory and Society* 24: 201–43.

Farley, Lynn. 1978, *Sexual Shakedown: The Sexual Harassment of Women on the Job*, New York: McGraw-Hill.

Fassin, Eric. 1991, "Pouvoirs sexuels: le juge Thomas, le Cour Suprême et la société américaine," *Esprit* 177 (December): 102–30.

1993, "Dans les genres différents: le féminisme au miroir transatlantique," *Esprit* 196 (November): 99–112.

1994, "'Political Correctness' en version originale et en version française: un malentendu révélateur," *XX° Siècle* 43.

1997a, "Discours sur l'inégalité des races. *The Bell Curve*: Polémique savante, rhétorique raciale et politique publique," *Hérodote* 85: 34–61.

1997b, "Du multiculturalisme à la discrimination," *Le Débat* 97: 131–6.

Faure, Christine and Tom Bishop (eds.). 1992, *L'Amerique des Français*, Paris: Editions François Bourin.

Feagin, Joe R. and Hernan Vera. 1995, *White Racism. The Basics*, New York: Routledge.

Feher, Michel. 1993, "Erotisme et féminisme aux Etats-Unis: les exercices de la liberté," *Esprit* 196.

Ferenczi, Thomas. 1993, *L'invention du journalisme en France*, Paris: Plon.

Ferguson, M. 1992, "The Mythology About Globalization," *European Journal of Communication* 7.

Ferry, Luc. 1992, *Le nouvel ordre écologique. L'arbre, l'animal et l'homme*, Paris: Grasset.

Fine, Gary Alan. 1997, "Naturework and the Taming of the Wild: The Problem of 'Overpick', in the Culture of Mushroomers", *Social Problems* 44 (1): 68–88.

Fine, Gary Alan and Kent Sandstrom. 1993, "Ideology in Action: A Pragmatic Approach to a Contested Concept," *Sociological Theory* 11 (1): 21–38.

Fiorino, Daniel. 1995, *Making Environmental Policy*, Berkeley: University of California Press.

Fischer, Claude. 1991, "Ambivalent Communities: How Americans Understand their Localities," in Alan Wolfe (ed.), *America at Century's End*, Berkeley: University of California Press, pp. 79–90.

Fischer, Claude S., Michael Hout, Martin Sanchez Jankowski, Samuel R. Lucas, Ann Swidler, and Kim Voss. 1996, *Inequality by Design. Cracking the Bell Curve Myth*, Princeton University Press.

Fischer, Frank, and John Forrester (eds.). 1993, *The Argumentative Turn in Policy Analysis and Planning*, Durham, NC: Duke University Press.

Fligstein, Neil. 1990, *The Transformation of Corporate Control*, Cambridge, MA: Harvard University Press.

Flyvbjerg, Bent. 1998, *Rationality and Power. Democracy in Practice*, University of Chicago Press.

Foucauld, Jean-Baptiste de and Laurent Thévenot. 1995, "Evolution des politiques sociales et transformation de l'action publique," in Bernard Simonin (ed.), *Les politiques publiques d'emploi et leurs acteurs*, Paris: Presses Universitaire de France, pp. 319–49.

Fourcade-Gourinchas, Marion. 1999, "The Internationalization of Economics and the (Re)construction of the Economics Profession," presented at the Culture and Inequality Workshop, Princeton University, March 1.

Fowler, Robert Booth. 1991, *The Dance with Community: The Contemporary Debate in American Political Thought*, Lawrence: Kansas University Press.

Franke, Katherine. 1997, "What's Wrong with Sexual Harassment?" *Stanford Law Review* 49 (4): 691–772.

Frankenberg, Ruth. 1993, *The Social Construction of Whiteness. White Women, Race Matters*, Minneapolis: University of Minnesota Press.

1994, *White Women, Race Matters*, University of Minnesota Press.

Fredrickson, George M. 1971, *The Black Image in the White Mind*, New York: Norton.

Freeman, Gary. 1979, *Immigrant Labor and Racial Conflict in Industrial Societies. The French and British Experience 1945–75*, Princeton University Press.

Frenkel, M., Y. Shenhav, and H. Herzog. 1996, "The Political Embeddeness of Managerial Ideologies in Pre-state Israel: The Case of PPL 1920–1948," *Journal of Management History* 3: 120–44.

Freudenberg, Nicholas and Carol Steinsapir. 1992, "Not in Our Backyards: The Grassroots Environmental Movement," in R. Dunlap and A. Mertig (eds.), *American Environmentalism: The U.S. Environmental Movement, 1970–1990*, Washington, DC: Taylor and Francis, pp. 27–37.

Friedland, Roger and Robert R. Alford. 1991, "Bringing Society Back In: Symbols, Practices, and Institutional Contradictions," in Walter W. Powell and Paul J. DiMaggio (eds.), *The New Institutionalism in Organizational Analysis*, University of Chicago Press, pp. 232–62.

Fuller, Peter. 1980, *Beyond the Crisis in Art*, London: Writers and Readers Publishing Cooperative.

Furet, François. 1988, *Interpreting the French Revolution*, Cambridge University Press.

1997, "L'Amérique de Clinton II," *Le Débat* 94: 3–10.

Gallie, W. B. 1956, "Essentially Contested Concepts," *Proceedings of the Aristotelian Society*, New Series, Vol. 56, London: Harrison and Sons, pp. 167–98.

Gamboni, Dario. 1983, *Un iconoclasme moderne. Théorie et pratique du vandalisme artistique*, Lausanne: Editions d'en-bas.

1997, *The Destruction of Art. Iconoclasm and Vandalism since the French Revolution*, London: Reaktion Books.

Gamson, Joshua. 1997, "Messages of Exclusion: Gender, Movements, and Symbolic Boundaries," *Gender and Society* 11 (2): 178–99.

1998, "Publicity Traps: Television Talk Shows and Lesbian, Gay, Bisexual, and Transgender Visibility," *Sexualities* 1 (1): 11–41.

Gamson, William A. 1992, *Talking Politics*, Cambridge University Press.

Gans, Herbert. 1979, *Deciding What's News*, New York: Random House.

Gariepy, Michel, Olivier Soubeyran, and Gérald Domon. 1986, "Planification environnementale et étude d'impact sur l'environnement au Québec: implantation d'une procédure et apprentissage des acteurs," *Cahiers de Géographie du Québec* 30 (79): 21–40.

Gaxie, Daniel. 1978, *Le cens cache: Inégalités culturelles et ségregation politique*, Paris: Seuil.

Geertz, Clifford. 1973, *The Interpretation of Culture*, New York: Basic Books.

Ginsburg, Gilbert J. and Jean Galloway Koreski. 1977, "Sexual Advances by an Employee's Supervisor: A Sex-Discrimination Violation of Title VII?" *Employee Relations Law Journal* 3: 83.

Giroud, Françoise and Bernard-Henri Lévy. 1993, *Les hommes et les femmes*, Paris: Olivier Orban.

Gitlin, Todd. 1995, *The Twilight of Common Dreams. Why America is Wracked by Culture Wars*, New York: Metropolitan Books, Henry Holt and Co.

Glazer, Nathan. 1996, "Multiculturalism and American Exceptionalism," presented at the Conference on Multiculturalism, Minorities and Citizenship, European University Institute, Florence.

1997, *We are All Multiculturalists Now*, Cambridge, MA: Harvard University Press.

Godard, Olivier. 1990, "Environnement, modes de coordination et systèmes de légitimité: analyse de la catégorie de patrimoine naturel," *Revue Economique* 2: 215–42.

Godfrey, Elizabeth. 1977 [1941], *Yosemite Indians*, revised by James Snyder and Craig Bates, Yosemite Association with National Park Service and American Indian Council of Mariposa County.

Goffman, Erving. 1959, *The Presentation of Self in Everyday Life*, Doubleday: New York.

1963, *Stigma. Notes on the Management of Spoiled Identity*, Englewood Cliffs, NJ: Prentice Hall.

1974, *Frame Analysis. An Essay on the Organization of Experience*, New York: Harper & Row.

Goldberg, David. 1993, *Racist Culture. Philosophy and the Politics of Meaning*, New York: Blackwell.

Goodman, Nelson. 1977, "When is Art," in *The Arts and Cognition*, Baltimore, MD: Johns Hopkins University Press.

Goodwin, Jeff. 1997, "The Libidinal Constitution of a High-Risk Social Movement: Affectual Ties and Solidarity in the Huk Rebellion," *American Sociological Review* 62: 53–69.

Goodwin, Robert E. 1992, Green Political Theory, Cambridge: Polity Press.

Gottlieb, Robert. 1993, *Forcing the Spring: the Transformation of the American Environmental Movement*, Washington, DC: Island Press.

Gould, Kenneth, Allan Schnaiberg, and Adam Weinberg. 1996, Local Environmental Struggles, Cambridge University Press.

Gould, Roger V. 1995, *Insurgent Identities: Class, Community and Protest in Paris from 1848 to the Commune*, University of Chicago Press.

Grabmeier, Jeff. 1992, "Clashing over Political Correctness," *USA Today*, November 12.

Graff, Gerald. 1992, *Beyond the Culture Wars*, New York: W. W. Norton.

Granovetter, Mark. 1985, "Economic Action and Social Structure: The Problem of Embeddedness," *American Journal of Sociology* 91: 481–510.

Greenberg, Clement. 1939, "Avant-Garde and Kitsch," *Partisan Review* 6: 5.

Greffe, Xavier, Sylvie Pfleiger, and François Rouet. 1990, *Socio-économie de la culture: livre, musique*, Paris: Anthropos.

Grémion, Pierre. 1976, *Le pouvoir périphérique*, Paris: Seuil.

Griswold, Wendy. 1981, "American Character and the American Novel," *American Journal of Sociology* 86: 740–65.

1987a, "The Fabrication of Meaning: Literary Interpretation in the United States, Great Britain, and the West Indies," *American Journal of Sociology* 92 (5): 1077–1117.

1987b, "A Methodological Framework for the Sociology of Culture," *Sociological Methodology* 14: 1–35.

1992, "The Writing of the Mud Wall: Nigerian Novels and the Imaginary Village," *American Sociological Review* 57: 709–24.

Guilbaut, Serge. 1983, *How New York Stole the Idea of Modern Art: Abstract Expressionism, Freedom, and the Cold War*, University of Chicago Press.

Guillaumin, Colette. 1972, *L'idéologie raciste. Genèse et langage actuel*, Paris/The Hague: Mouton.

Guillén, Mauro F. 1994, *Models of Management: Work, Authority, and Organization in a Comparative Perspective*, University of Chicago Press.

Forthcoming, *Diversity in Globalization: Organizational Change in Argentina, South Korea, and Spain*, Princeton University Press.

Guillory, John. 1993, *Cultural Capital: The Problem of Literary Canon Formation*, University of Chicago Press.

Gunn, J. A. W. 1989, "Public Interest," in Terence Ball, James Farr, and Russell Hanson (eds.), *Political Innovation and Conceptual Change*, Cambridge University Press, pp. 194–210.

Gupta, Alkil and James Ferguson. 1997, "Culture, Power, Place: Ethnography at the End of an Era," in Alkil Gupta and James Ferguson (eds.),*Culture, Power, Place: Explorations in Critical Anthropology*, Durham, NC: Duke University Press, pp. 1–29.

Gusfield, Joseph R. 1963, *Symbolic Crusade*, Urbana: University of Illinois Press.

1981, *The Culture of Public Problems: Drinking-Driving and the Symbolic Order*, University of Chicago Press.

1992, "Nature's Body and the Metaphors of Food," in Michèle Lamont and Marcel Fournier (eds.), *Cultivating Differences: Symbolic Boundaries and the Making of Inequality*, University of Chicago Press, pp. 75–103.

Habermas, Jurgen. 1975, *Legitimation Crisis*, trans. Thomas McCarthy, Boston: Beacon Press.

1984, *The Theory of Communicative Action*, Vol. 1. *Reason and the Rationalization of Society*, trans. Thomas McCarthy, Boston: Beacon Press.

1990, *Moral Consciousness and Communicative Action*, Cambridge, MA: MIT Press.

1991, *The Structural Transformation of the Public Sphere*, Boston: MIT Press.

Hajer, Maarten. 1993, "Discourse Coalitions and the Institutionalization of Practice: The Case of Acid Rain in Great Britain," in Frank Fischer and John Forrester (eds.), *The Argumentative Turn in Policy Analysis and Planning*, Durham, NC: Duke University Press, pp. 43–76.

1995, *The Politics of Environmental Discourse*, Oxford: Clarendon Press.

Halimi, Serge. 1997, *Les nouveaux chiens de garde*, Paris: Liber éditions.

Hall, John A. 1992, "The Capital(s) of Culture: A Non-Holistic Approach to Gender, Ethnicity, Class, and Status Group," in Michèle Lamont and Marcel Fournier (eds.), *Cultivating Differences: Symbolic Boundaries and the Making of Inequality*, University of Chicago Press, pp. 257–88.

Hall, Peter. 1993, "Policy Paradigms, Social Learning, and the State: The Case of Economic Policy Making in Britain," *Comparative Politics* 25 (3): 275–96.

Halle, David. 1984, *American Working Men*, University of Chicago Press.

1992, "The Audience for Abstract Art: Class, Culture, and Power," in Michèle Lamont and Marcel Fournier (eds.), *Cultivating Differences: Symbolic Boundaries and the Making of Inequality*, University of Chicago Press, pp. 131–52.

1993, *Inside Culture*, University of Chicago Press.

Hamilton, David and Tina Trolier. 1986, "Stereotypes and Stereotyping: An Overview of the Cognitive Approach," in John F. Dovidio and Samuel L. Gaertner (eds.), *Prejudice, Discrimination, and Racism*, New York: Academic Press, pp. 127–64.

Hamilton, Gary and Nicole Woolsey Biggart. 1988, "Market, Culture, and Authority: A Comparative Analysis of Management and Organization in the Far East," *American Journal of Sociology* 94: 252–94.

Hamilton, Richard F. 1967, *Affluence and the French Worker in the Fourth Republic*, Princeton University Press.

1972, *Class and Politics in the United States*, New York: John Wiley and Sons.

Hannigan, John A. 1995, *Environmental Sociology: A Social Constructionist Perspective*, New York: Routledge.

Harris, Paul. 1935, *This Rotarian Age: Rotary International*, Rotary.

Hart, Stephen. 1992, *What Does the Lord Require. How American Christians Think about Economic Justice*, Oxford University Press.

Hayek, Friedrich. 1976, *Law, Legislation and Liberty*, Vol.2. *The Mirage of Social Justice*, London: Routledge and Kegan Paul.

Hein, Jeremy. 1993a, *States and International Migrants. The Incorporation of Indochinese Refugees in the United States and France*, Boulder, CO: Westview.

1993b, "Rights, Resources, and Membership: Civil Rights Models in France and the United States," *Annals, AAPSS* 530: 97–108.

Heinich, Nathalie. 1986, *Ouvrage d'art, oeuvre d'art: le public du Pont-Neuf de Christo ou comment se faire une opinion*, Paris: association Adresse.

1990, "L'art et la manière: pour une 'cadre-analyse' de l'expérience esthétique," in *Le parler frais d'Erving Goffman*, Paris: Minuit.

1991, *La gloire de Van Gogh. Essai d'anthropologie de l'admiration*, Paris: Minuit.

1993a, "Framing the Bullfight: Aesthetics versus Ethics," *The British Journal of Aesthetics* 33 (1): 52–8.

1993b, "Publier, consacrer, subventionner: les fragilités des pouvoirs littéraires," *Terrain* 21: 33–46.

1995a, "Les colonnes de Buren au Palais-Royal: ethnographie d'une affaire," *Ethnologie française* 4.

1995b, "Esthétique, symbolique et sensibilité: de la cruauté considérée comme un des Beaux-Arts," *Agone* 13.

1996, *The Glory of Van Gogh. An Anthropology of Admiration*, Princeton University Press.

1997a, *Le triple jeu de l'art contemporain*, Paris: Minuit.

1997b, "Entre oeuvre et personne: l'amour de l'art en régime de singularité," *Communication* 64.

1998a, *L'art contemporain exposé aux rejets. Etudes de cas*, Nîmes: Jacqueline Chambon.

1998b, "Outside Art and Insider Artists: Gauging Public Reactions to Contemporary Art," in Vera Zolberg and Joni Cherbo (eds.), *Outsider Art: Contesting Boundaries in Contemporary Culture*, Cambridge University Press.

Heinich, Nathalie, Ronald Jepperson, and John Meyer. 1991, "The Public Order and the Construction of Formal Organizations," in Walter W. Powell and Paul DiMaggio (eds.), *The New Institutionalism in Organizational Analysis*, University of Chicago Press.

Heins, Marjorie. 1993, *Sex, Sin, and Blasphemy. A Guide to America's Censorship Wars*, New York: The New Press.

Heinz, John, Edward Laumann, Robert Nelson, and Robert Salisbury. 1993, *The Hollow Core: Private Interests in National Policy Making*, Cambridge, MA: Harvard University Press.

Henry, William A. 1991, "Upside Down in the Groves of Academe," *Time*, April 1.

Herrnstein, Richard J. and Charles Murray. 1994, *The Bell Curve. Intelligence and Class Structure in American Life*, New York: Free Press.

Higonnet, Patrice L. R. 1988, *Sister Republics: The Origins of French and American Republicanism*, Cambridge, MA: Harvard University Press.

Hilgartner, Stephen and Charles Bosk. 1988, "The Rise and Fall of Social Problems: A Public Arenas Model," *American Journal of Sociology* 94: 53–79.

Hirschman, Albert. 1970, *Exit, Voice and Loyalty*, Cambridge, MA: Harvard University Press.

1977, *The Passions and the Interests: Political Arguments for Capitalism Before its Triumph*, Princeton University Press.

1986, "The Concept of Interest: From Euphemism to Tautology," in *Rival Views of Market Society and other Recent Essays*, New York: Viking.

1991, *The Rhetoric of Reaction*, Cambridge, MA: Harvard University Press.

1997, *La morale secrète de l'économiste*, Paris: Les Belles Lettres.

Hochschild, Jennifer L. 1995, *Facing up to the American Dream. Race, Class, and the Soul of the Nation*, Princeton University Press.

Hocquenghem, Guy. 1986, *Lettre ouverte à ceux qui sont passé du col Mao au Rotary-club*, Paris: Albin Michel.

Hodgson, Godfrey. 1976, *America in Our Time*, New York: Random House.

Hoffman, Barabara. 1987, "Tilted Arc: The Legal Angle," in Sherrill Jordan et al. (eds.), *Public Art Controversy: The Tilted Arc on Trial*, New York: ACA Books.

1990, "Law for Art's Sake in the Public Realm," in W. J. T. Mitchell (ed.), *Art and the Public Sphere*, University of Chicago Press.

Hofstadter, Richard. 1943, *Anti-Intellectualism in American Life*, New York: Knopf.

Hollifield, James F. 1994, "Immigration and Republicanism in France: The Hidden Consensus," in Wayne A. Cornelius, Philip l. Martin, and James F. Hollifield (eds.), *Controlling Immigration: A Global Perspective*, Stanford University Press, pp. 143–75.

Horne, Alistair. 1977, *A Savage War of Peace. Algeria 1954–1962*, New York: Viking Press.

Horowitz, Donald L. 1992, "Immigration and Group Relations in France and the United States," in *Immigrants in Two Democracies: French and American Experience*, New York University Press, pp. 3–35.

House, John (ed.). 1995, *Landscapes of France. Impressionism and its Rivals*, London: South Bank Center, and Boston: Museum of Fine Arts (Joanna Skipwitg, coordinator).

Howard, Dick. 1987, *Naissance de la pensée politique américaine, 1763–1783*, Paris: Ramsay.

Hughes, Robert. 1989, "America (book review)," *The New York Review of Books*, June 1.

1993, *Culture of Complaint. The Fraying of America*, Oxford University Press.

Hull, G., P. B. Scott, and B. Smith. 1982, *All the Women are White, All the Blacks are Men, but Some of Us are Brave*, Black Women's Studies, Old Westbury, NY: Feminist Press.

Hundley, Norris. 1992, *The Great Thirst*, Berkeley: University of California Press.

Hunt, Scott A., Robert D. Benford, and David A. Snow. 1994, "Identity Fields: Framing Processes and the Social Construction of Movement Identities," in Enrique Larana, Hank Johnson, and Joseph R. Gusfield (eds.), *New Social Movements: From Ideology to Identity*, Philadelphia: Temple University Press, pp. 185–208.

Hunter, Albert (ed.). 1990, *The Rhetoric of Social Research: Understood and Believed*, New Brunswick: Rutgers University Press.

Hunter, James Davidson. 1991, *Culture Wars: The Struggle to Define America*, New York: Basic Books.

1994, *Before the Shooting Begins: Searching for Democracy in America's Culture War*, New York: Free Press.

Hunter, Mark. 1997, *Le journalisme d'investigation aux Etats-Unis et en France*, Paris: Presses Universitaires de France.

Illouz, Eva. 1997, *Consuming the Romantic Utopia. Love and the Cultural Contradictions of Capitalism*, Berkeley: University of California Press.

Inglehart, Ronald. 1990, *Culture Shift in Advanced Industrial Societies*, Princeton University Press.

Ingram, Helen, David Colnic, and Dean Mann. 1995, "Interest Groups and Environmental Policy," in James Lester (ed.), *Environmental Politics and Policy: Theories and Evidence*, second edition, Durham, NC: Duke University Press, pp. 115–45.

Inkeles, Alex. 1979, "Continuity and Change in the American National Character," in Seymour Martin Lipset (ed.), *Third Century: America as a Post-Industrial Society*, Stanford: Hoover Institute Press, pp. 390–453.

Jack, Andrew. 1997, *Financial Times*, November 24.

Jackson, James, with Daria Kirby, Lisa Barnes, and Linda Shepard. 1992, "Racisme institutionnel et ignorance pluraliste: une comparaison transnationale," in Michel Wievorka (ed.), *Racisme et modernité*, Paris: La Découverte, pp. 244–63.

Jasper, James M. 1990, *Nuclear Politics: Energy and the State in the United States, Sweden, and France*, Princeton University Press.

1992, "The Politics of Abstractions: Instrumental and Moralist Rhetorics in Public Debate," *Social Research* 59 (2): 315–44.

1997, *The Art of Moral Protest: Culture, Biography and Creativity in Social Movements*, University of Chicago Press.

Jasper, James and Dorothy Nelkin. 1992, *The Animal Rights Crusade. The Growth of a Moral Protest*, New York: Free Press.

Jenkins, Richard. 1996, *Social Identity*, London: Routledge.

Jenson, Jane and Mariette Sineau. 1995, *Mitterrand et les Françaises: Un rendez-vous manqué*, Paris: Presses de la Fondation Nationale des Sciences Politiques.

Joas, Hans. 1993, *Pragmatism and Social Theory*, University of Chicago Press.

Jolibois, Charles. 1998, "Rapport: Sénat Session Ordinaire de 1997–1998," February 4, 265: 32–3.

Jordan, Wynthrop D. 1968, *White over Black: American Attitudes toward the Negro, 1550–1812*, New York: W. W. Norton.

Jordan, Sherrill et al. (eds.). 1987, *Public Art Public Controversy: The Tilted Arc on Trial*, New York: ACA Books.

Journal Officiel de la République Française. 1998, 'Sénat débats parlementaires: Compte rendu intégral: Séance du mardi 31 mars 1998," 25: 1369–70.

Kalaora, Bernard and Antoine Savoye. 1985, "La protection des régions de montagne au XIXème siècle: forestiers sociaux contre forestiers étatistes," in A. Cadoret (ed.), *Protection de la nature*, Paris: L'Harmattan, pp. 6–23.

Kalberg, Stephen. 1997, "Tocqueville and Weber on the Sociological Origins of Citizenship: The Political Culture and American Democracy," *Citizenship Studies* 1 (2): 199–222.

Kallen, Horace. 1924, *Culture and Democracy in the United States*, New York: Boni & Liveright.

Kanter, Rosabeth M. 1977, *Men and Women of the Corporation*, New York: Basic Books.

Kastoryano, Riva. 1996, *La France, l'Allemagne et leurs immigrés: négocier l'identité*, Paris: Armand Colin.

Katz, Michael. 1989, *The Undeserving Poor: From the War on Poverty to the War on Welfare*, New York: Pantheon.

Katzenstein, Peter (ed.). 1996, *Culture and National Security*, New York: Columbia University Press.

Key, V. O. Jr. 1958, *Politics, Parties, and Pressure Groups*, New York: Thomas Y. Crowell.

Killingsworth, M. Jimmie and Jacqueline S. Palmer. 1992, *Ecospeak: Rhetoric and Environmental Politics in America*, Carbondale, IL: Southern Illinois University Press.

Kimball, Roger. 1990, *Tenured Radicals: How Politics has Corrupted our Higher Education*, New York: HarperPerennial.

Klaus, Alisa. 1993, *Every Child A Lion: The Origins of Maternal Infant and Health Policy in the United States and France, 1820–1920*, Ithaca: Cornell University Press.

Kluegel, James R. and Lawrence Bobo. 1993, "Dimensions of Whites' Beliefs about the Black–White Socioeconomic Gap," in Paul M. Sniderman, Philip E. Tetlock, and Edward G. Carmines (eds.), *Prejudice, Politics and the American Dilemma*, Stanford University Press, pp. 127–47.

Knorr-Cetina, Karen and Theodore Schatzki (eds.). Forthcoming, *The Practical Turn*, London: Routledge and Kegan Paul.

Kuisel, Richard F. 1993, *Seducing the French: The Dilemma of Americanization*, Berkeley: University of California Press.

Kurtz, Howard. 1996, "Kristol Brings Out the Animal in Dole Aide," *Washington Post*, October 21.

Lacorne, Denis. 1991, *L'invention de la république. Le modèle américain*, Paris: Hachette.

    1997, *La crise de l'identité américaine. Du melting-pot au multiculturalisme*, Paris: Fayard.

Lacorne, Denis, Jacques Rupnik, and Marie-France Toinet. 1990, *The Rise and Fall of Anti-Americanism. A Century of French Perceptions,* trans. Gerald Turner, London: MacMillan.

Ladrière, Paul. 1990, "La sagesse pratique, les implications de la notion aristotélicienne de phronésis pour la théorie de l'action," in Patrick Pharo and Louis Quéré (eds.), *Les formes de l'action,* Paris: Ed. de l'EHESS (Raisons pratiques 1), pp. 15–37.

Lafaye, Claudette. 1989, "Réorganisation industrielle d'une municipalité de gauche," in Luc Boltanski and Laurent Thévenot (eds.), *Justesse et justice dans le travail,* Paris: Presses Universitaires de France, pp. 43–66.

1990, "Situations tendues et sens ordinaires de la justice au sein d'une administration municipale," *Revue Française de Sociologie* 31 (2): 199–223.

1991, "Les communes dans tous leurs états: l'espace local à la croisée d'exigences contradictoires," doctoral thesis in Sociology, Ecole des Hautes Etudes en Sciences Sociales, Paris.

1994, "Aménager un site du littoral: entre politique et pragmatisme," *Etudes Rurales* 133–4: 163–80.

1997, *Sociologies des organisations,* Paris: Nathan.

Lafaye, Claudette and Laurent Thévenot. 1993, "Une justification écologique?: Conflits dans l'aménagement de la nature," *Revue Française de Sociologie* 34 (4): 495–524.

Lamont, Michèle. 1987a, "The Production of Culture in France and the United States since World War II," in Alain Gagnon (ed.), *The Role of Intellectuals in Liberal Democracies,* New York: Praeger, pp. 167–78.

1987b, "How to Become a Dominant French Philosopher: The Case of Jacques Derrida," *American Journal of Sociology* 93 (3): 584–622.

1992, *Money, Morals & Manners. The Culture of the French and American Upper-Middle Class,* Chicago University Press.

1995, "National Identity and National Boundary Patterns in France and the United States," *French Historical Studies* 19 (2): 349–65.

1997, "The Meaning of Class and Race: French and American Workers Discuss Differences," in John Hall (ed.), *Reworking Class,* Ithaca, NY: Cornell University Press, pp. 193–220.

1998, "Community and Exclusion in France and the United States: The Role of Immigration, Race, and Poverty," presented at the 11th International Conference of the Europeanists, Baltimore, MD.

1999, "Above 'People Above': Status and Worth among White and Black Workers," in Michèle Lamont (ed.), *The Cultural Territories of Race: Black and White Boundaries,* University of Chicago Press and New York: Russell Sage Foundation.

2000, *The Dignity of Working Men: Morality and the Boundaries of Race, Class, and Citizenship,* Cambridge, MA: Harvard University Press and New York: Russell Sage Foundation.

Forthcoming, "North-African Immigrants Respond to French Racism: Demonstrating Equivalence through Universalism," in Abdellah Hamoudi (ed.), *Universalizing from Particulars: Islamic Views of the Human and the UN Declaration of Human Rights in Comparative Perspective,* London: Taurus.

Lamont, Michèle and Marcel Fournier. 1992, "Introduction," in Michèle Lamont and Marcel Fournier (eds.), *Cultivating Differences: Symbolic Boundaries and the Making of Inequality*, University of Chicago Press, pp. 1–20.

Lamont, Michèle, Jason Kaufman, and Michael Moody. Forthcoming, "The Best of the Brightest: Definitions of the Ideal Self among Prize-Winning Students," *Sociological Forum*.

Lamont, Michèle and Annette Lareau. 1988, "Cultural Capital: Allusions, Gaps, and Glissandos in Recent Theoretical Developments," *Sociological Theory* 6 (2): 153–68.

Lamont, Michèle and Marsha Witten. 1988, "Surveying the Continental Drift: The Diffusion of French Social and Literary Theory in the United States," *French Politics and Society* 6: 3.

Lamont, Michele and Robert Wuthnow. 1990, "Betwixt and Between: Recent Cultural Sociology in Europe and the United States," in George Ritzer (ed.), *Frontiers of Social Theory: The New Syntheses*, New York: Columbia University Press, pp. 287–315.

Lamoureux, Johanne. 1994, "Felix Holtman contre Jana Sterbak. L'expertise de Monsieur Tout-le-monde," colloque, Lausanne on "Images de l'artiste."

Langlois, Simon, with Theodore Caplow, Henri Mendras, and Wolfgang Glatzer. 1994, *Convergence or Divergence: Comparing Recent Social Trends in Industrial Societies*, Montreal: McGill-Queen's University Press and Frankfurt: Campus Verlag.

La Pena, Frank, Craig D. Bates, and Steven P. Medley (eds.). 1993 [1981], *Legends of the Yosemite Miwok*, Yosemite National Park: California.

Larmore, Charles. 1987, *Patterns of Moral Complexity*, Cambridge University Press.

Larrère, Catherine. 1997, *Les philosophies de l'environnement*, Paris: Presses Universitaires de France.

Larrère, Catherine and Raphaël. 1997, *Du bon usage de la nature – Pour une philosophie de l'environnement*, Paris: Aubier.

Larson, Magali Serfati. 1977, *The Rise of Professionalism: A Sociological Analysis*, Berkeley: University of California Press.

Lascoumes, Pierre. 1994, *L'écopouvoir*, Paris: La Découverte.

Latham, Earl. 1952, *The Group Basis of Politics*, Ithaca: Cornell University Press.

Latour, Bruno. 1983, *Les microbes: guerre et paix suivi de irréductions*, Paris: Editions Métailié.

1987, *Science in Action: How to Follow Scientists and Engineers through Society*, Cambridge, MA: Harvard University Press.

1995, "Moderniser ou écologiser? A la recherche de la 'septième' cité," *Ecologie Politique* 13: 5–27 (for translation, see Latour 1997).

1997, "To Modernize or to Ecologize? That's the Question," in N. Castree and B. Willems-Braun (eds.), *Remaking Reality: Nature at the Millennium*, London: Routledge.

Law, John. 1994, *Organizing Modernity*, Oxford: Blackwell.

Law, John and Annemarie Mol. 2000, *Complexities in Science, Technology and Medicine*, Durham, NC: Duke University Press.

Lebovics, Herman. 1996, "Where and How did the French get the Idea that they were the Trustees of Western Civilization, 1513–1959?," presented at the New York Area French History Seminar.

Le Magueresse, Catherine. 1998, "Sur la nullité des mesures prises à l'encontre d'une salariée victime de harcèlement sexuel," *Droit Social* 5 (May): 437–41.

Lemieux, Cyril. 1992, "Les journalistes: une morale d'exception?" *Politix* 19: 1–30.

1993, "Révélations journalistiques et suicide des hommes politiques: à qui la faute?" *French Politics and Society* 11: 36–46.

2000, *Mauvaise presse. Une sociologie du travail journalistique et de ses critiques*, Paris: Editions Métailié.

Lentricchia, Frank. 1980, *After the New Criticism*, University of Chicago Press.

Lewalski, Barbara K. 1993, "Critical Issues in Literary Studies," *Profession 93*.

Libération. 1992, April 30.

Lichterman, Paul. 1992, "Self-Help Reading as a Thin Culture," *Media, Culture, and Society* 14: 421–47.

1995, "Beyond the Seesaw Model: Public Commitment in a Culture of Self-Fulfillment," *Sociological Theory* 13 (3): 275–300.

1996, *The Search for Political Community: American Activists Reinventing Commitment*, Cambridge University Press.

Forthcoming, "Talking Identity in the Public Sphere: Broad Visions and Small Spaces in Sexual Identity Politics," *Theory and Society*.

Lippard, Lucy. 1989, "Moving Targets/Moving Out," in Arlene Raven (ed.), *Art in the Public Interest*, New York: Da Capo Press.

Lipset, Seymour Martin. 1977, "Why No Socialism in the United States," in A. Bialer and S. Sluzar (eds.), *Sources of Contemporary Radicalism*, Vol. 1, Boulder, CO: Westview Press, pp. 31–149.

1979, *The First New Nation. The United States in Historical and Comparative Perspective* New York: Norton.

Lolive, Jacques. 1997a, "De la contestation du tracé à la reformulation de l'intérêt général; la mobilisation associative contre le TGV Méditerranée," *Techniques, Territoires et Sociétés* 34: 81–99.

1997b, "La montée en généralité pour sortir du NIMBY," *Politix* 39: 109–31.

Louis, Marie-Victoire. 1994, *Le droit de cuissage*, Paris: Les Editions de l'Atelier.

1999, "Harcèlement sexuel et domination masculine," in Christine Bard (ed.), preface by Michelle Perrot, *Un siècle d'anti-féminisme*, Paris: Fayard, pp. 401–17.

Lovelock, J. E. 1979, *Gaia: A New Look at Life on Earth*, Oxford University Press.

Lowi, Theodore. 1969, *The End of Liberalism*, New York: W. W. Norton and Co.

1987, *La deuxième république des Etats-Unis, la fin du libéralisme*, Paris: Presses Universitaires de France.

Lukes, Steven. 1974, *Power: A Radical View*, London: Clarendon.

Lynd, Robert and Helen. 1929, *Middletown: A Study in American Culture*, New York: Harcourt, Brace, and Co.

Lyon-Caen, Gérard and Antoine. 1993, *Droit social international et européen*, Paris: Dalloz.

Lyotard, Jean-François. 1983, *Le différend*, Paris: Minuit.

MacKinnon, Catharine. 1979, *Sexual Harassment of Working Women*, New Haven: Yale University Press.

Maclean, Norman. 1976, *A River Runs Through It*, University of Chicago Press.

Madison, James, Alexander Hamilton and John Say. 1961 [1788], *The Federalist Papers*, ed. Clinton Rossiter, Harmondsworth: Penguin Books.

Madsen, Richard. 1991, "Contentless Consensus: The Political Discourse of a Segmented Society," in Alan Wolfe (ed.), *America at Century's End*, Berkeley: University of California Press, pp. 440–60.

Magazine Littéraire. 1998, "Les nouvelles morales. Ethique et philosophie," 361.

Maksymowicz, Virginia. 1990, "Through the Back Door: Alternative Approaches to Public Art," in W. J. T. Mitchell (ed.), *Art and the Public Sphere*, University of Chicago Press.

Manent, Pierre. 1994, *La cité de l'homme*, Paris: Fayard.

Manin, Bernard. 1989a, "Les deux libéralismes: la règle et la balance," in *La famille, la loi, l'Etat. De la Révolution au Code Civil*, Paris: Centre Georges Pompidou, Imprimerie Nationale, pp. 372–89.

1989b, "Montesquieu," in François Furet and Mona Ozouf (eds.), *Dictionnaire critique de la Révolution française*, Paris: Flammarion, pp. 315–38.

1994a, "Checks, Balances, and Boundaries: The Separation of Powers in the Constitutional Debate of 1787," in Bianca Fontana (ed.), *The Invention of Modern Republic*, Cambridge University Press, pp. 27–62.

1994b, "Frontières, freins et contrepoids; la séparation des pouvoirs dans le débat constitutionnel américain de 1787," *Revue Française de Science Politique* 44 (2): 257–93.

Mansbridge, Jane. 1983, *Beyond Adversary Democracy*, University of Chicago Press.

1990, "The Rise and Fall of Self-Interest in the Explanation of Political Life," in Jane Mansbridge (ed.), *Beyond Self-Interest*, University of Chicago Press, pp. 3–22.

1998, "On the Contested Nature of the Public Good," in Walter Powell and Elisabeth Clemens (eds.), *Private Action and the Public Good*, New Haven: Yale University Press, pp. 3–19.

Marchal, Emmanuelle. 1992, "L'entreprise associative: entre calcul économique et désintéressement," *Revue Française de Sociologie* 33: 365–90.

Martin, Marc. 1997, *Médias et journalistes de la République*, Paris: Odile Jacob.

Maruani, Laurent. 1992, "La valorisation hors prix du livre,"*Cahiers de l'économie du livre* 9.

Mathieu, J. L. 1992, *La défense de l'environnement en France*, Paris: Presses Universitaires de France.

Mathy, Jean-Philippe. 1995, "The Resistance to French Theory in the United States: A Cross-Cultural Inquiry," *French Historical Studies* 19: 331–47.

Mauco, Georges. 1977, *Les étrangers en France et le problème du racisme*, Paris: La Pensée Universelle.

Mazey, Sonia and Jeremy Richardson (eds.). 1993, *Lobbying in the European Community*, Oxford University Press.

Mazmanian, Daniel and David Morell. 1994, "The 'NIMBY' Syndrome: Facility Siting and the Failure of Democratic Discourse," in Norman Vig and Michael Kraft (eds.), *Environmental Policy in the 1990s: Toward a New Agenda*, second edition, Washington, DC: CQ Press. pp. 233–50.

McAdam, Doug. 1988, *Freedom Summer*, New York: Oxford University Press.

McAdam, Doug, John D. McCarthy, and Mayer Zald. 1996, *Comparative Perspectives on Social Movements: Political Opportunities, Mobilizing Structures, and Cultural Framings*, Cambridge University Press.

McCloskey, Donald N. 1985, *The Rhetoric of Economics*, Madison: University of Wisconsin Press.

McConahay, John B. 1986, "Modern Racism, Ambivalence, and the Modern Racism Scale," in S. L. Gaertner and J. Dovidio (eds.), *Prejudice, Discrimination, and Racism*, New York: Academic Press, pp. 91–126.

McGee, Jack J. Jr. 1976, "Note, Sexual Advances by Male Supervisory Personnel as Actionable under Title VII of the Civil Rights Act of 1964: Corne v. Bausch & Lomb, Inc., Williams v. Saxbe," *S. Texas Law Journal* 17: 409.

McMane, Aralynn A. 1992, "Vers un profil du journalisme occidental. Analyse empirique et comparative des gens de presse en France, au Royaume-Uni, en Allemagne et aux Etats-Unis," *Réseaux* 51: 67–74.

McNamara, Kathleen. 1998, "The Political Construction of Globalization," presented at the 11th International Conference of the Europeanists. Baltimore, MD.

McPherson, James M. 1975, *The Abolitionist Legacy: From Reconstruction to the NAACP,* Princeton University Press.

Memmi, Albert. 1965, *The Colonizer and the Colonized*, Boston: Beacon.

Merelman, Richard. 1984, *Making Something of Ourselves: On Culture and Politics in the United States*, Berkeley: University of California Press.

Merryman, John Henry and Albert E. Elsen. 1979, *Law, Ethics and the Visual Arts*, New York: Matthew Bender.

Merton, Robert K. 1987, "Three Fragments from a Sociologist's Notebooks: Establishing the Phenomenon, Specified Ignorance, and Strategic Research Materials," *Annual Review of Sociology* 13:1–28.

Meyer, John W. 1994, "Rationalized Environments," in John W. Meyer and W. Richard Scott (eds.), *Institutional Environments and Organizations: Structural Complexity and Individualism*, Thousand Oaks, CA: Sage.

Meyer, John W., John Boli, George M. Thomas, and Francisco O. Ramirez. 1997, "World Society and the Nation-State," *American Journal of Sociology* 13: 144–81.

Meyer, John W., David Kamens, Aaron Benavot, Yun Kyoung Cha, and Suk-Ying Wong. 1991, "Knowledge for the Masses: World Models and National Curricula, 1920–1986," *American Sociological Review* 56 (February): 85–100.

Meyer, John W. and Brian Rowan. 1977, "Institutionalized Organizations: Formal Structure as Myth and Ceremony," *American Journal of Sociology* 83: 340–63.

Meyers, Peter. 1989, *A Theory of Power: Political, Not Metaphysical*, Ann Arbor: UMI Abstracts Publishers.

Michigan Law Review. 1978, "Note, Sexual Harassment and Title VII: The Foundation for the Elimination of Sexual Cooperation as an Employment Condition," *Michigan Law Review* 76: 1007.

Miles, Robert. 1989, *Racism*, London: Routledge.

Mills, C. Wright. 1940, "Situated Actions and Vocabularies of Motive," *American Sociological Review* 5: 404–13.

Mills, Nicholas. 1974, *The New Journalism*, New York: McGraw-Hill.

Minet, Michel and Francis Saramito. 1997, "Le harcèlement sexuel," *Droit Ouvrier* February: 48–91.

Minkhoff, Debra. 1995, *Organizing for Equality: The Evolution of Women's and Racial-Ethnic Organizations in America, 1955–1985*, New Brunswick, NJ: Rutgers University Press.

Minnesota Law Review. 1979, "Note, Legal Remedies for Employment Related Sexual Harassment," *Minnesota Law Review* 64: 151.

Minow, Martha. 1990, *Making All the Difference*, Ithaca: Cornell University Press. 1997, *Not Only for Myself*, New York: Free Press.

Mitchell, W. J. T. (ed.). 1990, *Art and the Public Sphere*, University of Chicago Press.

Molnar, Virag and Michèle Lamont. Forthcoming, "Social Categorization and Group Identification. How African Americans use Consumption to Change their Collective Identity," in Kenneth Green, Andrew McMeekin, Mark Tomlinson, and Vivien Walsh (eds.), *Interdisciplinary Approaches to Demand and its Role in Innovation*, Manchester: University of Manchester Press.

Moody, Michael. 1999, *Water for Everyone: Interests, Advocacy, and the Possibility of the Public Good in Two Californian Water Disputes*, unpublished PhD dissertation, Princeton University.

Morone, James A. 1998 [1990], *The Democratic Wish: Popular Participation and the Limits of American Government*, revised edition, New Haven: Yale University Press.

Morris, Aldon and Carol McClurg Mueller (eds.). 1992, *Frontiers in Social Movement Theory*, New Haven: Yale University Press.

Moscovici, Serge. 1977, *Essai sur l'histoire humaine de la nature*, Paris: Flammarion.
   1984, "The Phenomenon of Social Representations," in R. M. Farr and S. Moscovici (eds.), *Social Representations*, Cambridge University Press, pp. 3–69.

Mossuz-Lavau, Janine. 1991, *Les lois de l'amour: les politiques de la sexualité en France (1950–1990)*, Paris: Documents Payot.

Muir, John. 1970 [1918], *Steep Trails* William, ed. Frederic Bade, Dunwoody, GA: N. S. Berg.

Naess, Arne and David Rothenberg. 1989, *Ecology, Community, and Lifestyle: Outline of an Ecosophy*, Cambridge University Press.

Nash, Roderick. 1982, *Wilderness and the American Mind*, third edition, New Haven: Yale University Press.

National Center of Education Statistics. 1995, "Bachelor's Degrees Conferred by Institutions of Higher Education, by Discipline, 1970–71 to 1992–93 (Table 243)," *1995 Digest of Education Statistics*, Washington, DC: United States Department of Education.

National Conference. 1994, *Taking America's Pulse: The Full Report of the National Conference Survey on Inter-Group Relations*, prepared by LH Research, New York: National Conference of Christian and Jews.

Navarro, Peter. 1984, *The Policy Game: How Special Interests and Ideologues are Stealing America*, New York: John Wiley and Sons.

Nelson, Daniel. 1984, "Le Taylorisme dans l'industrie américaine, 1900–1930," in C. Montmollin and O. Pastré (eds.), *Le Taylorisme*, Paris: Dunod.

Newsweek. 1990, "Taking Offense. (Political Correctness Movement on Campus; cover story; special section)," Dec. 24.

New York Times. 1983, "Fair Housing Law is Applied in a Sexual Harassment Case," December 11, Section 1: 44.

Nicholl, David Shelley. 1984, *The Golden Wheel: The Story of Rotary, 1905 to Present,* Estover, Plymouth: Macdonald and Evans Publishers.

Nicolet, Claude. 1992, "Le passage à l'universel," in *La République en France. Etat des lieux.* Paris: Le Seuil, pp. 122–68.

Noiriel, Gérard. 1992, *Population, immigration et identité nationale en France XIXième et XXième siècles,* Paris: Hachette.

1996, *The French Melting Pot: Immigration, Citizenship, and National Identity,* trans. Geoffrey de Laforcade, Minneapolis: University of Minnesota Press.

Nora, Pierre (ed.). 1984, 1986, *Lieux de mémoire.* Part 1: *La République.* Part 2: *La Nation,* Paris: Gallimard.

Normand, Romuald. 1999, "La délégation aux objets dans le mobilier scolaire," in J. L. Derouet (ed.), *L'école dans plusieurs mondes,* Paris: De Boeck, pp. 91–109.

North, Michael. 1990, "The Public as Sculpture: From Heavenly City to Mass Ornament," in W. J. T. Mitchell (ed.), *Art and the Public Sphere,* University of Chicago Press.

Novick, Peter. 1988, *That Noble Dream: The "Objectivity Question" and the American Historical Profession,* Cambridge University Press, 1988.

NYU Law Review. 1976, "Comment," *New York University Law Review* 51: 148.

Oelschlaeger, Max. 1991, *The Idea of Wilderness. From Prehistory to the Age of Ecology,* New Haven: Yale University Press.

Offerlé, Michel. 1994, *Sociologie des groupes d'intérêts,* Paris: Montchrestien.

Olivier, Michelle. 1997, "Measuring Symbolic Boundaries among Artists," *Poetics* 24: 299–328.

Olson, Mancur, Jr. 1971 [1965], *The Logic of Collective Action: Public Goods and the Theory of Groups,* New York: Schocken Books.

Omi, Michael and Howard Winant. 1986, *Racial Formation in the United States,* New York: Routledge.

Oppenheimer, David Benjamin. 1995, "Exacerbating the Exasperating: Title VII Liability of Employers for Sexual Harassment Committed by their Supervisors," *Cornell Law Review* 81 (1): 66–153.

Orbuch, Terri. 1997, "People's Accounts Count: The Sociology of Accounts," *Annual Review of Sociology* 23: 455–78.

Ortega y Gasset, José. 1972 [1925], *The Dehumanization of Art and other Essays on Art, Culture, and Literature,* Princeton University Press.

Ostrower, Francis. 1998, "The Arts as Cultural Capital among Elites: Bourdieu's Theory Reconsidered," *Poetics. Journal of Empirical Research on Literature, the Media, and the Arts* 26 (1): 43–54.

Owens, Owen. 1991, *Living Waters: How to Save Your Local Stream.,* New Brunswick, NJ: Rutgers University Press.

Ozouf, Mona. 1995, *Les mots des femmes: Essai sur la singularité française,* Paris: Fayard.

Padioleau, Jean-G. 1985, "Le Monde" *et le* "Washington Post", Paris: Presses Universitaires de France.

Paehlke, Robert. 1990, *Environmentalism and the Future of Progressive Politics*, New Haven: Yale University Press.

Paglia, Camille. 1991, "Ninnies, Pedants, Tyrants and Other Academics," *The New York Times Book Review*, May 5.

1992, *Sexual Personae: Art and Decadence from Nefertiti to Emily Dickinson*, New York: Vintage.

1993, *Sex, Art, and American Culture*, New York: Vintage.

Pally, Marcia. 1994, *Sex and Sensibility. Reflections on Forbidden Mirrors and the Will to Censor*, Manassas, VA: Hopewell.

Palmer, Michael. 1983, *Des petits journaux aux grandes agences. Naissance du journalisme moderne (1863–1914)*, Paris: Aubier.

Parsons, Paul. 1989, *Getting Published: The Acquisition Process at University Presses*, Knoxville: University of Tennessee Press.

Parsons, Talcott.1958 [1922], "Professions and Social Structure," *Essays in Sociological Theory*, Glencoe: Free Press.

Pasquier, Dominique. 1995, *Les scénaristes de télévision*, Paris: Nathan.

Paterson, Alan M. 1989, *Land, Water, and Power: A History of the Turlock Irrigation District 1887–1987*, Spokane, WA: Arthur C. Clark Co.

Pedelty, Mark. 1995, *War Stories: The Culture of Foreign Correspondents*, London: Routledge.

Perelman, C. and L. Olbrechts-Tyteca. 1988, *Traité de l'argumentation. La nouvelle rhétorique*, fifth edition, Brussels: Editions de l'Université de Bruxelles.

Perin, Constance. 1988, *Belonging in America*, Madison: University of Wisconsin Press.

Pertschuck, Michael. 1986, *Giant Killers*, New York: W. W. Norton and Company.

Peterson, Richard A. and Albert Simkus. 1992, "How Musical Tastes Mark Occupational Status Groups," in Michèle Lamont and Marcel Fournier (eds.), *Cultivating Differences: Symbolic Boundaries and the Making of Inequality*, University of Chicago Press, pp. 152–86.

Petracca, Mark (ed.). 1992, *The Politics of Interests: Interest Groups Transformed*, Boulder: Westview Press.

Pharo, Patrick. 1996, *L'injustice et le mal*, Paris: L'Harmattan.

Piller, Charles. 1991, *The Fail-Safe Society: Community Defiance and the End of American Technological Optimism*, New York: Basic Books.

Pippert, Wesley. 1989, *An Ethics of News: A Reporter's Search for Truth*, Washington, DC: Georgetown University Press.

Plenel, Edwy. 1990, "'Words are Weapons' and Le Pen's Army Knows How to Pull the Trigger," *Manchester Guardian Weekly* May 27.

Poggioli, Renato. 1968 [1962], *The Theory of the Avant-Garde*, Cambridge, MA: Harvard University Press.

Popper, Frank. 1975, *Art, Action and Participation*, London and New York.

Powell, Walter. 1985, *Getting into Print: The Decision Process in Scholarly Publishing*, University of Chicago Press.

Powell, Walter and Paul DiMaggio (eds.). 1991, *The New Institutionalism in Organizational Analysis*, University of Chicago Press.

Prendiville, Brendan. 1994, *Environmental Politics in France*, Boulder: Westview Press.

Press, Daniel. 1994, *Democratic Dilemmas in the Age of Ecology: Trees and Toxics in the American West*, Durham, NC: Duke University Press.

Projets Féministes. 1996, "Actualité de la parité," 4–5 (February).

Prost, Antoine. 1968, *L'enseignement en France, 1800–1967*, Paris: Armand Colin.

Pseudo-Longinus. 1965, *Du Sublime*, ed. H. Lebègue, Paris: Les Belles Lettres.

Putnam, Robert D. 1993a, *Making Democracy Work*, Princeton University Press.

1993b, "The Prosperous Community: Social Capital and Public Life," *The American Prospect* 13: 35–43.

Quadagno, Jill and C. Fobes. 1995, "The Welfare State and the Cultural Reproduction of Gender: Making Good Girls and Boys in the Job-Corps," *Social Problems* 42 (2): 171–90.

Ragin, Charles. 1994, *Constructing Social Reserach: The Unity and Diversity of Method*, Newbury Park, CA: Pine Forge Press.

Ramonet, Ignacio. 1999, *La tyrannie de la communication*, Paris: Galilée.

Rangeon, François. 1986, *L'idéologie de l'intérêt général*, Paris: Economica.

Rasmussen, David (ed.). 1990, *Universalism and Communitarianism. Contemporary Debates in Ethics*, Cambridge, MA: MIT Press.

Rauch, Jonathan. 1994, *Demosclerosis: The Silent Killer of American Government*, New York: Times Books.

Raven, Arlene (ed.). 1989, *Art in the Public Interest*, New York: Da Capo Press.

Rawls, John. 1973, *A Theory of Justice*, Oxford University Press.

Reid, Sheila. 1993, *Art without Rejection*, Venice: Rush Editions.

Revue économique. 1989, Special Issue: *L'économie des conventions* 2: 147–97.

Rex, John. 1979, *Race Relations in Sociological Theory*, New York: Routledge.

Ricœur, Paul. 1970, *Freud and Philosophy: An Essay on Interpretation*, New Haven: Yale University Press.

1995, "La place du politique dans une conception pluraliste des principes de justice," in Joëlle Affichard and Jean-Baptiste de Foucauld (eds.), *Pluralisme et équité; penser la justice dans la démocratie*, Paris: Ed. Esprit, pp. 71–84.

Rieder, Jonathan. 1985, *Canarsie: The Jews and Italians of Brooklyn Against Liberalism*, Cambridge, MA: Harvard University Press.

Rieffel, Rémy. 1984, *L'élite des journalistes*, Paris: Presses Universitaires de France.

Ringmar, Erik. 1996, *Identity, Interest, and Action: A Cultural Explanation of Sweden's Intervention in the Thirty Years War*, Cambridge University Press.

Robertson, Roland. 1992, *Globalization: Social Theory and Global Culture*, New York: Sage Publications.

Rodgers, Susan Carol. 1991, *Shaping Modern Times in Rural France: The Transformation and Reproduction of an Aveyronnais Community*, Princeton University Press.

Rorty, Richard. 1980, *Philosophy and the Mirror of Nature*, Princeton University Press.

Ross, Andrew. 1989, *No Respect: Intellectuals and Popular Culture*, New York: Routledge.

Ross, Marc Howard. 1997, "Culture and Identity in Comparative Political Analysis," in Mark Irving Lichbach and Alan S. Zuckerman (eds.), *Comparative Politics: Rationality, Culture, and Structure*, Cambridge University Press, pp. 42–80.

Rossi, P. H. 1961, "The Organizational Structure of an American Community," in Amitai Etzioni (ed.), *Complex Organizations: A Sociological Reader*, New York: Holt, Rinehart, & Winston.

Rousseau, Jean-Jacques. 1959, *La Nouvelle Héloïse*, in *Oeuvres complètes*, Vol. 2, ed. Bernard Gagnebin and Marcel Raymon, Paris: La Pléiade, Gallimard.

1987 [1762], *The Social Contract*, trans. Donald A. Cress, Indianapolis: Hackett.

Rowe, Emery 1994, *Narrative Policy Analysis: Theory and Practice*, Durham, NC: Duke University Press.

Roy-Loustaunau, Claude. 1993, "Le harcèlement sexuel 'à la française': Commentaire de la loi n. 92–1179 du 2 novembre 1992," *La Semaine Juridique* (67) 15: 187–200.

Rubinstein, Michael. 1987, *La dignité des femmes dans le monde du travail: Rapport sur le problème du harcèlement sexuel dans les Etats membres des Communautés européennes*, Brussels.

Rudder, Véronique de. 1995, "La prévention du racisme dans l'entreprise en France," in *Les immigrés face à l'emploi et à la formation. Problèmes spécifiques et droit common: un faux dilemme?* Paris: Groupement de recherches, d'échanges, et de communications, pp. 31–7.

Sabatier, Paul and Hank Jenkins-Smith. 1993, *Policy Change and Learning: An Advocacy Coalition Approach*, Boulder: Westview Press.

Saguy, Abigail Cope. 1998, "Discrimination or Abuse of Authority: Making Sexual Harassment Law in France and the United States," presented at the "JOIE" Workshop, Princeton University, October 12.

1999a, "Sexual Harassment in the Media: France and the U.S. Compared", presented at the Law & Society Association Meeting, May 27–30, Chicago, IL.

1999b, "Sexual Harassment in France and the United States: Rethinking the Meaning of the Workplace," presented at the American Sociological Association, August 6–10, Chicago, IL.

Forthcoming [a], "Puritanism and Promiscuity? Sexual Attitudes in France and the United States," *Comparative Social Research*.

Forthcoming [b], "French and U.S. Lawyers Define Sexual Harassment," in Reva Siegel and Catharine MacKinnon (eds.), *Symposium on Sexual Harassment*, New Haven: Yale University Press.

Sahlins, Peter. 1989, *Boundaries: The Making of France and Spain in the Pyrénées*, Berkeley: University of California Press.

Salais, Robert and Laurent Thévenot (eds.). 1986, *Le travail; marchés, règles, conventions*, Paris: INSEE-Economica.

Sandel, Michael. 1996, *Democracy's Discontent: America's Search for a New Public Philosophy*, Cambridge, MA: Belknap/Harvard University Press.

Schaeffer, Jean-Marie. 1996, *Les célibataires de l'art. Pour une esthétique sans mythes*, Paris: Gallimard.

Schain, Martin. 1987, "The National Front in France and the Construction of Political Legitimacy," *West European Politics* 10: 229–52.

1996, "Minorities and Immigrant Incorporation in France: The State and the Dynamics of Multiculturalism," presented at the Conference on Multiculturalism, Minorities, and Citizenship, European University Institute, Florence.

Schattschneider, Elmer Eric. 1960, *The Semi-Sovereign People. A Realist's View of Democracy in America*, New York: Rinehart and Winston.

Schlesinger, Arthur, Jr. 1992, *The Disuniting of America*, New York: W. W. Norton.

Schmalzbauer, John. 1996, "Living between Athens and Jerusalem: Catholics and Evangelicals in the Culture-Producing Professions," unpublished dissertation, Department of Sociology, Princeton University.

Schnapper, Dominique. 1991, *La France de l'intégration. Sociologie de la nation en 1990*, Paris: Gallimard.

1994, *La communauté des citoyens*, Paris: Gallimard.

Scholzman, Kay Lehman and John Tierney. 1986, *Organized Interests and American Democracy.*, New York: Harper and Row.

Schudson, Michael. 1978, *Discovering the News: A Social History of The American Newspaper*, New York: Basic Books.

1989, "How Culture Works: Perspectives from Media Studies on the Efficacy of Symbols," *Theory and Society* 18: 153–80.

Schultz, Vicki. 1998, "Reconceptualizing Sexual Harassment," *Yale Law Journal* 107 (1683): 1732–805.

Schwartz, Barry. 1981, *Vertical Classification: A Study in Structuralism and the Sociology of Knowledge*, University of Chicago Press.

Sciences Humaines. 1998, "Les valeurs en question," 79.

Scott, Janny. 1996, "Postmodern Gravity Deconstructed, Slyly. (A. Sokal's Parody in *Social Text*), "*The New York Times*, May 18.

Scott, Joan W. 1995, "Vive La Différence!" *Le Débat* 87 (November-December): 134–9.

1996, *Only Paradoxes to Offer*, Cambridge, MA: Harvard University Press.

1997, "'La Querelle Des Femmes' in the Late Twentieth Century," *New Left Review* 226: 3–19.

Scott, Richard. 1987, "The Adolescence of Institutional Theory," *Adminisrtative Science Quarterly* 32: 493–511.

Sears, David O. 1988, "Symbolic Racism," in Phillys A. Katz and Dalmas A. Taylor (eds.), *Eliminating Racism. Profiles in Controversy*, New York and London: Plenum Press, pp. 53–84.

Serra, Richard. 1990, "Art and Censorship," in W. J. T. Mitchell (ed.), *Art and the Public Sphere*, University of Chicago Press.

Serres, Michel. 1990, *Le contrat naturel*, Paris: Flammarion.

Serusclat, Frank M. 1992, "Rapport du Sénat, Seconde Session Ordinaire de 1991–1992," No. 350.

Seymour, William C. 1979, "Sexual Harassment: Finding a Cause for Action Under Title VII," *Labor Law Journal* 30: 139.

Shklar, Judith. 1991, *American Citizenship: The Quest for Inclusion*, Cambridge, MA: Harvard University Press.

Silver, Allan. 1990, "The Curious Importance of Small Groups in American Sociology," in Herbert J. Gans (ed.), *Sociology in America*, Beverly Hills, CA: Sage, pp. 61–75.

Silver, Hilary. 1993, "National Conceptions of the New Urban Poverty: Social Structural Change in Britain, France, and the United States," *International Journal of Urban and Regional Research* 17 (3): 336–54.

Silverman, Maxim. 1991, "Introduction," in Maxim Silverman (ed.), *Race, Discourse and Power in France*, Aldershot: Avebury, pp. 1–4.

1992, *Deconstructing the Nation. Immigration, Racism and Citizenship in Modern France*, New York: Routledge.

Simmel, Georg. 1971, *On Individuality and Social Forms; Selected Writings*, ed. Donald N. Levine, University of Chicago Press.

1981 [1910], "La sociabilité," in *Sociologie et épistémologie*, Paris: Presses Universitaires de France.

Simons, Herbert W. 1990, "The Rhetoric of Inquiry as an Intellectual Movement," in *The Rhetorical Turn. Invention and Persuasion in the Conduct of Inquiry*, University of Chicago Press, pp. 1–34.

Simons, Herbert, E. W. Mechling, and H. Schreier. 1985, "Function of Communication in Mobilizing for Collective Action from the Bottom Up: The Rhetoric of Social Movements," in C. Arnold and J. Bowers (eds.), *Handbook for Rhetorical and Communication Theory*, Boston: Allyn and Bacon, pp. 729–867.

Small, Stephen. 1994, *Racialized Barriers. The Black Experience in the United States and England in the 1980s*, New York: Routledge.

Smith, Rogers M. 1993, "Beyond Tocqueville, Myrdal, and Hartz: The Multiple Traditions in America," *American Political Science Review* 87 (3): 549–66.

Smith, Tom W. 1990, *Ethnic Images*, GSS Topical Report No. 19, National Opinion Research Center, University of Chicago.

Sniderman, Paul M., with Michael Gray Hagen. 1985, *Race and Inequality. A Study in American Values*, Chatham House Publishers.

Snow, David A., E. Burke Rochford, Steven K. Worden, and Robert D. Benford. 1986, "Frame Alignment Processes, Micromobilization, and Movement Participation," *American Sociological Review* 51: 464–81.

Snyder, Gary. 1985, "Afterword: Fear of Bears," in Paul Shepard and Barry Sanders (eds.), *The Sacred Paw: The Bear in Nature, Myth, and Literature*, New York: Viking Penguin.

Society of Professional Journalists. 1987, *Code of Ethics*.

Sokal, Alan. 1996a, "Transgressing the Boundaries: Toward a Transformative Hermeneutics of Quantum Gravity," *Social Text* 45–6 (Spring/Summer).

1996b, "A Physicist Experiments with Cultural Studies," *Lingua Franca* (May/June).

Somers, Margaret R. 1995, "What's Political or Culture about Political Culture and the Public Sphere? Toward a Historical Sociology of Concept Formation," *Sociological Theory* 13 (2): 113–44.

Soulillou, Jacques. 1995, *L'impunité de l'art*, Paris: Le Seuil.

Soysal, Yasemin Nuhoglu. 1993, *Limits of Citizenship. Migrants and Postnational Membership in Europe*, University of Chicago Press.

Spangle, Michael and David Knapp. 1996, "Ways we Talk about the Earth: An Exploration of Persuasive Tactics and Appeals in Environmental Discourse," in Star Muir and Thomas Veenendall (eds.), *Earthtalk: Communication Empowerment for Environmental Action* Westport, CT: Praeger, pp. 3–26.

Spector, Malcolm and John Kitsuse. 1977, *Constructing Social Problems*, Menlo Park, CA: Cummins.

Spender, Dale. 1986, *Mothers of the Novel: 100 Good Women Writers Before Jane Austen*, London: Pandora Press.

Spillman, Lyn. 1997, *Nation and Commemoration. Creating National Identities in the United States and Australia*, Cambridge University Press.

Stanton, Domna C. 1994, "Editor's Column: What is Literature? – 1994," *Publications of the Modern Language Association* 109.

Stark, David. Forthcoming, "Heterarchy: Distributed Intelligence and the Organization of Diversity," in John Clippinger (ed.), *The Self-Organizing Firm*, San Francisco: Jossey-Bass Publishers.

Starr, Paul. 1992, "Social Categories and Claims in the Liberal State," *Social Research* 59 (2) (Summer 1992).

Steinberg, Marc. 1995, "The Roar of the Crowd: Repertoires of Discourse and Collective Action among the Spitalfields Silk Weavers in Nineteenth-Century London," in Mark Traugott (ed.), *Repertoires and Cycles of Collective Action*, Durham, NC: Duke University Press, pp. 43–56.

Steinberg, Stephen. 1981, *The Ethnic Myth: Race, Ethnicity, and Class in America*, Boston: Beacon Press.

Steiner, Wendy. 1995, *The Scandal of Pleasure. Art in an Age of Fundamentalism*, University of Chicago Press.

Stinchcombe, Arthur. 1995, *Sugar Island Slavery in the Age of Enlightenment*, Princeton University Press.

Stoetzel, Jean. 1983, *Les valeurs du temps présent: Une enquête européenne*, Paris: Presses Universitaires de France.

Stone, Christopher. 1974, *Should Trees Have Standing? Toward Legal Rights for Natural Objects*, Los Altos, CA: W. Kaufmann.

Storper, Michael and Robert Salais. 1997, *Worlds of Production. The Action Frameworks of the Economy*, Cambridge, MA: Harvard University Press.

Storr, Robert. 1989, "Tilted Arc: Enemy of the People?" in Arlene Raven (ed.), *Art in the Public Interest*, New York: Da Capo Press.

Strang, David and John Meyer. 1994, "Institutional Conditions for Diffusion," in John W. Meyer and W. Richard Scott (eds.), *Institutional Environments and Organizations: Structural Complexity and Individualism*, Thousand Oaks, CA: Sage, pp. 103–12.

Suleiman, Ezra. 1979, *Les élites en France: Grands Corps et Grandes Ecoles*, Paris: Seuil.

Swidler, Ann. 1986, "Culture in Action: Symbols and Strategies," *American Sociological Review* 51: 273–86.

Forthcoming, *Talk of Love*, University of Chicago Press.

Swidler, Ann and Jorge Arditi. 1994, "The New Sociology of Knowledge," *Annual Review of Sociology* 20: 305–29.

Taguieff, Pierre-André. 1986, "Racisme et anti-racisme: modèles et paradoxes," in André Bejin and Julien Freund (eds.), *Racismes, antiracismes*, Paris: Librairie des Méridiens, pp. 253–302.

1988, *La force du préjugé. Essai sur le racisme et ses doubles*, Paris: La Découverte.

1989, "La métaphysique de Jean-Marie Le Pen," in Nonna Màyer and Pascal Perrineau (eds.), *Le Front National à decouvert*, Paris: La Découverte, pp. 173–94.

1991, "Les métamorphoses idéologiques du racisme et la crise de l'anti-racisme," in Pierre-André Taguieff (ed.), *Face au racisme*, Vol. 2. *Analyses, hypothèses, perspectives*, Paris: La Découverte, pp. 13–63.

Tajfel, Henri and John C. Turner. 1985, "The Social Identity Theory of Intergroup Behavior," in Stephen Worchel and William. G. Austin (eds.), *Psychology of Intergroup Relations*, Chicago: Nelson-Hall, pp. 7–24.

Tarrow, Sidney. 1992, "Mentalities, Political Cultures, and Collective Action Frames," in A. Morris and C. McC. Mueller (eds.), pp. 174–202.

1993, "Collective Action and the Rise of the Social Movement: Why the French Revolution Was Not Enough," *Politics and Society* 22: 69–90.

1994, *Power in Movement: Social Movements, Collective Action, and Politics*, Cambridge University Press.

1995, "Cycles of Collective Action: Between Moments of Madness and the Repertoire of Contention," in Mark Traugott (ed.), *Repertoires and Cycles of Collective Action*, Durham, NC: Duke University Press, pp. 89–115.

Taub, Nadine. 1976, "Keeping Women in their Place: Stereotyping Per Se as a Form of Employment Discrimination," *B.C.L. Review* 21: 148.

Taylor, Charles. 1992, "The Politics of Recognition," in Charles Taylor with Amy Gutmann (commentary, ed.), *Multiculturalism and "the Politics of Recognition,"* Princeton University Press, pp. 25–74.

Taylor, Paul. 1986, *Respect for Nature: A Theory of Environmental Ethics*, Princeton University Press.

Tebbel, John. 1975, *A History of Book Publishing in the United States*, New York: R. R. Bowker Co.

Thévenot, Laurent. 1984, "Rules and Implements: Investment in Forms," *Social Science Information* 23 (1): 1–45.

(ed.) 1986, *Conventions économiques*, Paris: Presses Universitaires de France (Cahiers du Centre d'Etudes de l'Emploi).

1989, "Equilibre et rationalité dans un univers complexe," *Revue économique*, special issue on *L'économie des conventions*, 2 (March): 147–97.

1990a, "La politique des statistiques: les origines sociales des enquêtes de mobilité sociale," *Annales ESC* 6: 1275–1300.

1990b, "L'action qui convient," in Patrick Pharo and Louis Quéré (eds.), *Les formes de l'action*, Paris: Editions de l'EHESS (Raisons pratiques 1), pp. 39–69.

1992a, "Jugements ordinaires et jugement de droit," *Annales ESC* 6: 1279–99.

1992b, "Un pluralisme sans relativisme? Théories et pratiques du sens de la justice," in Joelle Affichard and Jean-Baptiste de Foucauld (eds.), *Justice sociale et inégalités*, Paris: Ed. Esprit, pp. 221–53.

1994, "Le régime de familiarité; des choses en personnes," *Genèses* 17: 72–101.

1995a, "Emotions et évaluations dans les coordinations publiques," in Patricia Paperman and Ruwen Ogien (eds.), *La couleur des pensées: émotions, senti-ments, intentions*, Paris: Editions de l'EHESS (Raisons pratiques 6), pp. 145–74.

1995b, "L'action en plan," *Sociologie du Travail* 37 (3): 411–34.

1995c, "New Trends in French Social Sciences," *Culture* 9 (2): 1–7.

1996a, "Justification et compromis," in Monique Canto-Sperber (ed.), *Dictionnaire d'éthique et de philosophie morale*, Paris: Presses Universitaires de France, pp. 789–94.

1996b, "Mettre en valeur la nature: disputes autour d'aménagements de la nature en France et aux Etats-Unis," *Autres Temps. Cahiers d'éthique sociale et politique* 49: 27–50.

1996c, "Pragmatic Regimes and the Commerce with Things; from Personal Familiarization to Public 'Qualifications'," paper presented at the Conference on "Practice and Social Order," Bielefeld University, January 3–6 (revised version forthcoming in Karin Knorr-Cetina and Theodore Schatzki (eds.), *The Practical Turn*, London: Routledge).

1996d, "Stratégies, intérêts et justifications: à propos d'une comparaison France–Etats-Unis de conflits d'aménagement," *Techniques, territoires et sociétés* 31: 127–49.

1996e, *Le traitement local des conflits en matière d'environnement*, Vol.1. "Une comparaison France–Etats-Unis. Rapport sur les deux enquêtes, en France et aux Etats-Unis," research report for the Ministry of the Environment, Paris: Institut International de Paris – La Défense.

1998, "Pragmatiques de la connaissance," in A. Borzeix, A. Bouvier, and P. Pharo (eds.), *Sociologie et connaissance. Nouvelles approches cognitives*, Paris: Editions du CNRS, pp. 101–39.

1999, "Faire entendre une voix. Régimes d'engagement dans les mouvements sociaux," *Mouvements* 3: 73–82.

2000a, "Actions et acteurs de la procéduralisation," in Philippe Coppens and Jacques Lenoble, *Droit et procéduralisation*, Brussels: Bruylant (Bibliothèque de la Faculté de Droit).

2000b, "Which Road to Follow? The Moral Complexity of an 'Equipped' Humanity," in John Law and Annemarie Mol (eds.), *Complexities in Science, Technology and Medicine*, Durham, NC: Duke University Press.

Forthcoming, *Sociologie pragmatique. Les régimes d'engagement.*

Thévenot, Laurent and Jean-François Germe. 1996, *Le traitement local des conflits en matière d'environnement*, Vol.2. "Jeu éco-logiques. Un jeu pédagogique sur les logiques d'argumentation dans les conflits autour des projets d'aménagement," research report for the Ministry of the Environment, Paris: Institut International de Paris – La Défense.

Thomas, George M., John W. Meyer, Francisco Ramirez, and John Boli (eds.). 1987, *Institutional Structure: Constituting State, Society and the Individual*, Newbury Park: Sage.

Thoreau, Henry David. 1997 [1854], *Walden*, ed. Stephen Fender, Oxford University Press.

Throgmorton, James A. 1996, *Planning as Persuasive Storytelling: The Rhetorical Construction of Chicago's Electric Future*, University of Chicago Press.

Tilly, Charles. 1978, *From Mobilization to Revolution*, Reading, MA: Addison-Wesley.

1986, *The Contentious French: Four Centuries of Popular Struggle*, Cambridge, MA: Harvard University Press.

1993, "Contentious Repertoires in Great Britain, 1758–1834," *Social Science History* 17 (2): 253–79.

1997, *Durable Inequality*, Berkeley: University of California Press.

Tocqueville, Alexis de. 1980 [1835], *Democracy in America*, 2 vols., trans. Henry Reeve, New York: Alfred A. Knopf.

Toinet, Marie-France. 1987, *Le système politique des Etats-Unis*, Paris: Presses Universitaires de France.

Toinet, Marie-France, Hubert Kempf, and Denis Lacorne. 1989, *Le libéralisme à l'américaine: l'Etat et le marché*, Paris: Economica.

Tompkins, Jane. 1985, *Sensational Designs: The Cultural Work of American Fiction 1790–1860*, Oxford University Press.

Touraine, Alain. 1992, *Critique de la modernité*, Paris: Fayard.

Traugott, Mark (ed.). 1995, *Repertoires and Cycles of Collective Action*, Durham, NC: Duke University Press.

Tribalat, Michèle. 1992, *Faire France. Enquête sur les immigrés et leurs enfants*, Paris: La Découverte.

Tricot, Anne. 1996, "La mise à l'épreuve d'un projet par son milieu associé: analyse des controverses du projet autoroutier A8 Bis," *Techniques, Territoires et Sociétés* 31: 175–9.

Trom, Danny. 1997, "La production politique du paysage. Eléments pour une interprétation des pratiques ordinaires de patrimonialisation de la nature en Allemagne et en France," doctoral thesis in Political Science, Institut d'Etudes Politiques, Paris.

Tsay, Angela, Andrew Abbott, and Michèle Lamont. Under review, "Disciplinary Cultures in Transition: Evaluation of Merit in American Higher Education, 1951–1971."

Tuchman, Gaye. 1972, "Objectivity as Strategic Ritual," *American Sociological Review* 77: 660–79.

Turner, Frederick Jackson. 1920, *The Frontier in American History*, New York: Henry Holt.

Turner, John C. 1987, "A Self-Categorization Theory," in John C. Turner, Michael A. Hogg, Penelope J. Oakes, Stephen D. Reicher, and Margaret S. Wetherell (eds.), *Rediscovering the Social Group: A Self-Categorization Theory*, Oxford: Blackwell, pp. 19–41.

Urfalino, Philippe and Catherine Vilkas. 1995, *Les Fonds régionaux d'art contemporain. La délégation du jugement esthétique*, Paris: L'Harmattan.

Van den Berghe, Pierre. 1978, *Race and Racism. A Comparative Perspective*, New York: John Wiley.

Varenne, Hervé. 1977, *Americans Together: Structured Diversity in a Midwestern Town.*, New York: Teachers College Press.

Vermeulen, Joan. 1981, "Employer Liability under Title VII for Sexual Harassment by Supervisory Employees," *Cap. U.L. Review* 10: 499.

Veyne, Paul. 1988, "Conduites sans croyance et oeuvres d'art sans spectateurs," *Diogène* 143.

Wacquant, Loic. 1994, "Urban Outcasts: Color, Class, and Place in Two Advanced Societies," unpublished dissertation, Department of Sociology, University of Chicago.

Wagner, Peter. 1994a, "Action, Coordination, and Institution in Recent French Debates," *Journal of Political Philosophy* 2 (3): 270–89.

1994b, "Dispute, Uncertainty, and Institution in Recent French Debates," *Journal of Political Philosophy* 2 (3): 270–89.

1994c, *A Sociology of Modernity*, New York: Routledge.

1999, "After *Justification*. Repertoires of evaluation and the sociology of modernity," *European Journal of Social Theory* special issue "Contemporary French social Theory", 2 (3): 341–357.

Wagner-Pacifici, Robin and Barry Schwartz. 1991, "The Vietnam Veterans' Memorial: Commemorating a Difficult Past," *American Journal of Sociology* 97 (2): 376–420.

Wallace, Michèle. 1990, *Black Macho and the Myth of the Superwoman*, London: Verso.

Waller, Maureen. 1999, "Meanings and Motives in New Family Stories: The Separation of Reproduction and Marriage among Low-Income Black and White Parents," in Michèle Lamont (ed.), *The Cultural Territories of Race: Black and White Boundaries*, University of Chicago Press and New York: Russell Sage Foundation, pp. 182–218.

Walsh, Edward, Rex Warland, and D. Clayton Smith. 1997, *Don't Burn it Here: Grassroots Challenges to Trash Incinerators*, University Park, PA: Penn State Press.

Walton, John. 1992, *Western Times, Water Wars: State, Culture, and Rebellion in California*, Berkeley: University of California Press.

Walton, Kendall. 1970, "Categories of Art," *The Philosophical Review* 79.

Walzer, Michael. 1983, *Spheres of Justice. A Defence of Pluralism and Equality*, New York: Basic Books and Oxford: Blackwell.

1984, "Liberalism and the Art of Separation," *Political Theory* 12 (3): 315–30.

1988, *In the Company of Critics: Social Criticism and Political Commitment in the Twentieth Century*, New York: Basic Books.

1992, *What it Means to be an American. Essays on the American Experience*, New York: Marsilio.

1994, *Thick and Thin. Moral Argument at Home and Abroad*, University of Notre Dame Press.

1997, *On Toleration*, New Haven: Yale University Press.

Weaver, D. and G. C. Wilhoit. 1991, *The American Journalist*, Indiana University Press.

Weber, Eugen. 1976, *Peasants into Frenchmen: The Modernization of Rural France, 1870–1914*, Stanford University Press.

Weber, Max. 1959, *Le savant et le politique*, Paris: Plon.

1964 [1906], "Les sectes protestantes et l'esprit du capitalisme," in *L'éthique protestante et l'esprit du capitalisme*, Paris: Plon.

1978, *Economy and Society.* 2 vols., Berkeley: University of California Press.

Weil, Patrick. 1991, *La France et ses étrangers. L'aventure d'une politique d'immigration*, Paris: Calmann Lévy.

Weintraub, J. 1997, "Preface," in Jeff Weintraub and Krishan Kumar, *Public and Private in Thought and Practice: Perspectives on a Grand Dichotomy*, University of Chicago Press, pp. 1–42.

Weir, Margaret. 1995, "The Politics of Racial Isolation in Europe and America," in Paul E. Peterson (ed.), *Classifying by Race*, Princeton University Press, pp. 217–42.

Weiss, Philip. 1998, "Don't Even Think About it: The Cupid Cops are

Watching," *The New York Times Magazine*, May 3, Section 6, pp. 42–7, 58–60, 68, 81.

Wellman, David. 1993, *Portraits of White Racism*, second edition, New York: Cambridge University Press.

West, Candace and Don Zimmerman. 1987, "Doing Gender," *Gender and Society* 1:125–51.

Weyergraf-Serra, Clara and Martha Buskirk (eds.). 1988, *Richard Serra's Tilted Arc*, Eindhoven: Van Abbemuseum.

1991, *The Destruction of Tilted Arc: Documents*, Cambridge, MA: MIT Press.

White, Harrison. 1992, *Identity and Control: A Structural Theory of Social Action*, Princeton University Press.

Wievorka, Michel. 1992, *La France raciste*, Paris: Le Seuil.

1996a, "Cultural Differences and Democracy: United States and France," presented at the Conference on Multiculturalism, Minorities, and Citizenship, European University Institute, Florence.

1996b, "Culture, société, et démocratie," in Michel Wievorka (ed.), *Une société fragmentée? Le multiculturalisme en débat*, Paris: La Découverte, pp. 11–60.

Wihtol de Wenden, Catherine. 1991, "North-African Immigration and the French Political Imaginary," in Maxim Silverman (ed.), *Race, Discourse and Power in France*, Aldershot: Avebury. pp. 98–101.

Wiley, Laurence. 1974, *Village in the Vaucluse*, third edition, Cambridge, MA: Harvard University Press.

Wilkinson, John. 1997, "A New Paradigm for Economic Analysis?" *Economy and Society* 26 (3): 305–39.

Williams, Bruce and Albert Matheny. 1995, *Democracy, Dialogue, and Environmental Disputes: The Contested Languages of Social Regulation*, New Haven: Yale University Press.

Williams, Christine. 1995, *Still a Man's World: Men Who Do Women's Work*, University of California Press.

Williams, Rhys. 1995, "Constructing the Public Good Social Movements and Cultural Resources," *Social Problems* 42 (1): 124–44.

Wilson, John. 1990, *Politically Speaking: The Pragmatic Analysis of Political Language*, Oxford: Basil Blackwell.

Wimsatt, W. K. and Monroe C. Beardsley. 1954, "The Intentional Fallacy," in *The Verbal Icon: Studies in the Meaning of Poetry*, Lexington: University Press of Kentucky.

Winant, Howard. 1994, *Racial Conditions: Politics, Theory, Comparisons*, Minneapolis: University of Minnesota Press.

Wissler, André. 1989a, "Prudence bancaire et incertitude," in *Innovation et ressources locales*, Paris: Presses Universitaires de France (Cahiers du Centre d'Etudes de l'Emploi 32), pp. 201–37.

1989b, "Les jugements dans l'octroi de crédit," in L. Boltanski and L. Thévenot (eds.), *Justesse et justice dans le travail*, Paris: Presses Universitaires de France (Cahiers du Centre d'Etudes de l'Emploi 33), pp. 67–119.

Wolf, Naomi. 1992, "Feminist fatale: A Reply to Camille Paglia," *The New Republic* (March): 23–5.

Wolfe, Alan. 1998, *One Nation, After All*, New York: Viking.

1989, *Whose Keeper? Social Science and Moral Imagination*, Berkeley: University of California Press.

Wolfe, Tom. 1976, *The Painted Word*, New York: Bantam Books.

Worster, Donald. 1985, *Rivers of Empire: Water, Aridity, and the Growth of the American West*, Oxford University Press.

Wuthnow, Robert. 1987, *Meaning and Moral Order: Explorations in Cultural Analysis*, Berkeley: University of California Press.

1991, *Acts of Compassion: Caring for Others and Helping Ourselves*, Princeton University Press.

1992, "Introduction: New Directions in the Empirical Study of Cultural Codes," in Robert Wuthnow (ed.), *Vocabularies of Public Life: Empirical Essays in Symbolic Structure*, New York: Routledge, pp. 1–16.

1996, *Poor Richard's Principle. Recovering the American Dream Through the Moral Dimension of Work, Business, and Money*, Princeton University Press.

Zelizer, Viviana. 1994, *The Social Meaning of Money*, New York: Basic Books.

Zerubavel, Eviatar. 1991, *The Fine Line: Boundaries and Distinctions in Everyday Life*, New York: Free Press.

Zolberg, Aristide and Long Litt Woon. 1997, "Why Islam is Like Spanish: Cultural Incorporation in Europe and the United States," unpublished, Department of Political Science, New School for Social Research.

Zolberg, Vera. 1990, *Constructing a Sociology of the Arts*, Cambridge University Press.

1992, "Barrier or Leveler? The Case of the Art Museum," in Michèle Lamont and Marcel Fournier (eds.), *Cultivating Differences: Symbolic Boundaries and the Making of Inequality*, University of Chicago Press, pp. 187–212.

Zucher, Lynne G. 1987, "Institutional Theories of Organiations," *Annual Review of Sociology* 3: 443–64.

Zussman, Robert. 1985, *Mechanics of the Middle Class: Work and Politics among American Engineers*, Berkeley: University of California Press.

Index

Compiled by Judith Lavender